Culture and Aging

This is a volume in the
Arno Press collection

GROWING OLD

Advisory Editor
Leon Stein

See last pages of this volume
for a complete list of titles

Culture and Aging

An Anthropological Study of Older Americans

MARGARET CLARK

and

BARBARA GALLATIN ANDERSON

With the collaboration of

Gerard G. Brissette
Majda T. Thurnher, Ph.D.
Terry Camacho

ARNO PRESS

A New York Times Company
New York • 1980

Editorial Supervision: BRIAN QUINN

―――――

Reprint Edition 1980 by Arno Press Inc.

Copyright © 1967, by Charles C. Thomas
Reprinted by permission of Margaret Clark and Barbara Anderson

GROWING OLD
ISBN for complete set: 0-405-12813-4
See last pages of this volume for titles.

Manufactured in the United States of America

―――――

Library of Congress Cataloging in Publication Data

Clark, Margaret, 1925-
   Culture and aging.

   (Growing old)
   Reprint of the ed. published by Thomas, Springfield,
Ill., in series: The Langley Porter Institute studies of
aging.
   Bibliography: p.
   Includes index.
   1. Aged--United States. I. Anderson, Barbara
Gallantin, joint author. II. Title. III. Series.
IV. Series: California. Langley Porter Neuropsychi-
atric Institute, San Francisco. Langley Porter Institute
studies of aging.
[HQ1064.U5C5 1980]   305.2'6'0973   79-8827
ISBN 0-405-12781-2

Culture and Aging

Culture and Aging

An Anthropological Study of Older Americans

By

MARGARET CLARK, Ph.D.

Senior Research Anthropologist
Langley Porter Neuropsychiatric Institute
Lecturer in Psychiatry
University of California School of Medicine
San Francisco, California

and

BARBARA GALLATIN ANDERSON, Ph.D.

Associate Professor of Anthropology
California State College at Hayward
Hayward, California

With the collaboration of

Gerard G. Brissette

Majda T. Thurnher, Ph.D.

Terry Camacho

CHARLES C THOMAS · PUBLISHER
Springfield · Illinois · U.S.A.

© 1967, by CHARLES C THOMAS • PUBLISHER

With THOMAS BOOKS careful attention is given to all details of manufacturing and design. It is the Publisher's desire to present books that are satisfactory as to their physical qualities and artistic possibilities and appropriate for their particular use. THOMAS BOOKS will be true to those laws of quality that assure a good name and good will.

Printed in the United States of America
N-10

Dedication

To George M. Foster
teacher, colleague, and friend

PREFACE

THE RESEARCH REPORTED in this volume represents a considerable departure from the customary procedures of the field ethnographer. Both of us have been trained as field anthropologists, working with tribal people and in peasant villages. Such research ordinarily includes "moving into" a village, a tribal trading center, or an ethnic enclave, where one lives among the people he is studying, learns their language, and observes them as they go about the affairs of their daily lives. The anthropologist working in the traditional way usually goes to his research site alone, or as a member of a husband-wife team. Most of the ethnic communities or peasant villages we have studied have been small, and a massive research team operation such as that characterizing this research in geriatrics would appear to the inhabitants as something approximating a Mongol invasion.

Because anthropologists have often been the only observers of a society, they have rarely relied upon other specialists in the course of their work. Rather, they have developed a tendency to look at many aspects of life, regarding the whole society as their legitimate concern. An anthropologist's notes may contain information on a wide range of data — styles of dress, details of religious rituals, the implicit contractual understandings underlying trade or monetary credit, and the particular form that the symptoms of hysteria take in the society he is studying. He comes, in time, to see the functional interrelationships among these disparate elements of culture.

Another characteristic of field anthropologists is that they rarely go into a village or ethnic community with questionnaires already prepared. Unless the anthropologist is returning to an area that has already been described ethnographically, he does not know enough about the culture to go in and start taking measurements — "how much of this or how many of that." The anthropologist new to a particular field site will not yet know whether certain questions *can* be asked — he may inadvertently commit a breach of etiquette, break a tabu, or offend a respondent's sense of modesty or decorum.

More and more, however, anthropologists are being asked to apply the concepts they have developed to the study of complex urban societies; furthermore such work is often undertaken by large research teams, usually of a multidisciplinary nature. Such is the character of the research we are reporting here. Research of this kind has both its penalties and its rewards. White (1965) discussed both in a recent presidential address to the American Anthropological Association. With regard to the drawbacks, he said,

> It is not easy to discover the ideals and objectives of . . . anthropology from a perusal of our journals. Our choices seem to be governed rather largely by expediency: get a grant and go out and do field work somewhere. And it is quite possible that some of us would be loath to leave the exotic worlds of the nonliterate and the prehistoric which offer us both an interesting occupation and a placid refuge from the problems, threats, and insecurities of our own culture (p. 636) .

But White also claims that there are great rewards to be gained from those who are willing to approach and "muddle through" some of the complexities of contemporary industrial civilizations:

> Can cultural anthropology undertake, with some hope of success, studies on a larger scale? . . . For the first time in history, culture possesses the ability to destroy itself. We are confronted with an unprecedented situation and with problems of the first magnitude in the face of which "An Unusual Prayer-stick from Acoma Pueblo" seems so trivial as to appear ludicrous. . . . But what do we understand of our own culture? . . . A nation is a sociocultural system just as a band or tribe is, and as such is deserving of study (pp. 631, 634) .

In this work, we have attempted to respond to this challenge by bringing some of the concepts of traditional anthropology to bear upon the problems of the aged in an American city.

It might appear that this report is somewhat encyclopedic, but this has been necessary because we have had at least four kinds of readers in mind in preparing this report: first, anthropologists and other social scientists who are laboring, as we are, to apply the techniques and insights of cultural research to the problems of complex and expanding societies; second, people who are working with or planning for the aged in America — social workers, directors of homes, hospitals, or senior centers, legislators and members of governmental planning agencies, from the local to the federal level; third, clinicians whose practice includes elderly patients. We have hoped to provide for all of these a greater social perspective and cultural context which may enable them to assess more accurately the problems of the elderly individual. Last, we are addressing the aged themselves, who, we believe, may profit from a broader cultural view of the nature of the society in which they live and the tasks it poses for them in their everyday lives.

ACKNOWLEDGMENTS

THIS REPORT IS THE THIRD of four volumes to come out of the first phase of a program of research which has been underway since 1959 — the Langley Porter Institute Studies in Aging. This program has been headed by Dr. Alexander Simon, Principal Investigator, and directed by Marjorie Fiske Lowenthal, Program Director and Principal Co-Investigator. The first volume to come out of this research was authored by Mrs. Lowenthal and entitled *Lives in Distress: The Paths of the Elderly to the Psychiatric Ward,* New York, Basic Books, 1964. The second volume, Lowenthal, Berkman, and Associates, in press at the time of this writing, is entitled *Aging and Mental Disorder in San Francisco,* San Francisco, Jossey-Bass, Inc., 1966. The present report is the third volume in this series. A final volume, now in preparation is a clinically-oriented work, to be edited by Drs. Simon and Epstein and Mrs. Lowenthal and is tentatively entitled *Crisis and Intervention.* The research represented in all four of these volumes has been supported by grants from the National Institute of Mental Health (MH 09145) and the Department of Mental Hygiene of the State of California (R 59-1-4; R 60-1-16.2). We wish to acknowledge this generous support.

A special acknowledgment is due Marjorie Fiske Lowenthal, who, as Program Director, has provided special guidance throughout all phases of the work, and has been instrumental in procuring consultants, readers, and staff assistance for the preparation of this volume. She has also spent long hours trying to help us reconcile the traditional broad and descriptive approaches of cultural anthropology with the necessary methodological rigors of large-sample research.

We owe a special debt to Gerard G. Brissette, the Program editor, whose intensive work on the manuscript has gone far beyond the usual functions of an editor. He has, through his critical appraisals of the work as it progressed, insisted that we sharpen our language, formulate our ideas more clearly, and in this fashion has made a considerable substantive contribution to the content of the volume. He has rewritten portions of the technical material, putting it into a more comprehensible form. He has also aided us in much of the bibliographic research.

Majda Thurnher made a particular contribution to the work in abstracting and coding all the attitudinal data for the intensively-studied sample of seventy-nine subjects. This was tedious and laborious work which occupied nearly twelve months and which involved the reading and classifying of every item of information on the seventy-nine cases which had any bearing on any of the categories of data reported in this volume. During a part of the time, she was aided in this work by David Evans. Dr. Thurnher also completed the content analysis of kinship roles and voluntary associations reported in Chapter VII.

Terry Camacho developed nearly all the statistical materials presented in this report. She was responsible for converting all our quantitative measurements into forms appropriate for electronic data processing, and for providing us with the results of those tabulations. Computer operations were carried out by the Survey Research Center, University of California, Berkeley.

We were also assisted in our data analyses by Robert C. Pierce, Deetje Boler, Alice Westbrook, Clayton Haven, Betsy Robinson, and Isadora Ding. Interviewing of the intensive-study sample was carried out by Elinore Lurie, Peter Chroman, Elizabeth Schorske, Alice Westbrook, Mella Trier, Carolyn Feinberg, Barbara Short, Phyllis Olsen, Majda Thurnher, Deetje Boler, Virginia Dunne, Vivian Strass Jackman, and Terry Camacho.

We wish to thank Santos Flores for compiling and preparing the bibliography. The clerical staff of the Program have seen the manuscript through several revisions and have cheerfully and efficiently aided us in all of them. We would especially like to thank Ruth Prael, Sandra Hobart, Phyllis Olsen, Pauline Burt, Santos Flores, and Milton Fung.

Various of our colleagues on the Geriatrics Research Program were particularly helpful in working with us on preparation of the interviewing guides for the intensive study. In addition to

Mrs. Lowenthal, we should also like to thank Dr. George Burnell and Dr. John Buehler for their help in this undertaking.

We have been fortunate in having the advice and consultation of a number of our colleagues and associates during the course of this work. Those whose suggestions have been particularly helpful include: Dr. John Adair, Dr. Leon Epstein, Dr. William Henry, Dr. Bernice Neugarten, Dr. Richard Williams, Dr. Robert Butler, Dr. Joseph Wheelwright, Dr. Donald Spence. Special thanks are due to Dr. George M. Foster, Dr. Otto von Mering, Dr. Bernice Neugarten and Dr. Robert T. Anderson for their critical reading of the report in its various phases.

We wish to acknowledge the courtesy of Dr. Florida Scott-Maxwell, *The Listener,* and *Harper's Bazaar,* for permission to reprint portions of Dr. Scott-Maxwell's article "We Are the Sum of Our Days."

MARGARET CLARK
BARBARA G. ANDERSON

CONTENTS

Culture and Aging

Chapter I

AN ANTHROPOLOGICAL APPROACH TO AGING

> *Everyone knows the Riddle that the Sphinx asked Oedipus as he traveled along a road alone. 'What is it that walks on four legs, then on two legs, and then on three?' Many men, say the Greeks, lost their lives in not being able to answer it. But all of us know the answer. It is man. As a baby he creeps on all fours; when he learns to walk, he stands erect; and when he is old, he walks with a cane. But the Riddle and its answer are deceptively simple. When studied and thought about, the meaning becomes deeper and deeper. For man is also the mammal whose inner essence lies in his extraordinary ability to love others of his own kind, varyingly with age and circumstance.*
>
> —WESTON LA BARRE,
> *The Human Animal* (1954), p. 208.

INTRODUCTORY REMARKS

AGING IS A CULTURAL as well as a biological process. Also, personal adaptation to it depends upon self-perception, a product of cultural norms and values. This report will show that some views of the self in old age are conducive to relative contentment in old age, while others breed despondency, futility, feelings of worthlessness, and even mental illness. Furthermore, we want to show how self-perceptions of the aged are shaped by social expectations; we will describe, through the eyes of the aged themselves, the means by which American society — intentionally or not — helps in the destruction of some of its members simply because they have grown older. Finally, we want to discuss, insofar as our observations will permit us, the cultural setting in which such a massive waste occurs, for social expectations of the elderly reflect value systems which vary from culture to culture.

One of the immutable characteristics of life is its cyclical nature: conception, gestation, birth, growth, reproductive maturity, senescence, and death are inevitable phases of existence for all animals save the simplest microscopic forms. However, the relative length of these phases, as well as the total lifespan, varies with the species. Thus, while. there is a period of helplessness immediately following birth among all mammals, there seems to be an evolutionary trend towards prolonged immaturity in the order of primates. The young monkey, ape, or human takes years rather than weeks or months to reach maturity and, during this prolonged childhood, he remains quite dependent upon adult members of his own kind — so dependent, in fact, that he cannot exist without them.

It is in the human species that this trend is most marked: the human infant, compared even with those of the great apes, is at birth smaller, more immature, and more helpless; it is dependent on its mother's milk for almost as long a period of time as the lemur, for example, requires to reach full sexual maturity. Nor is this difference due entirely to varying life expectancies, for human longevity is only about twice that of the lower primate forms. *Relatively* more time is required for the human animal to learn to walk, to acquire skill in obtaining its own food supply, and to achieve sexual maturity. Corresponding to this delay in human maturation, there is a longer total lifespan.[1]

While the duration of biological immaturity in man is solely a phenomenon of primate evolution, there are additional factors in his longevity. Physical anthropologists have reported that, by estimating age at the time of death from skeletal remains, only 5 per cent of Neanderthals lived beyond the age of forty, whereas about 11 per cent of later Stone Age men survived to that age (Hooton, 1946). However, there is no evidence that the *potential* lifespan of the human species has increased through the millenia; the differences result from the reduction of threats to life from the environment — that is, the major factors in longevity are cultural rather than biological. In contemporary scientific cultures, greater control of infectious and degenerative diseases continues to lengthen adult life. Thus, just as biological evolution has provided man with a prolonged period of childhood and

---

[1]Additional discussion of trends in human evolution may be found in many general works in the field of physical anthropology, including Howells (1944), Hooton (1946), Washburn and Wolffson (1949), and Eiseley (1957).

youth, so man's greater technological development has provided him with a protracted maturity and senescence.

Returning to LaBarre's statement at the beginning of this chapter, we now have a clearer understanding of the deeper meaning he reads into the Riddle of the Sphinx: it is only in the human species that the helpless crawling infant — "four-legged man" — is so long suckled, warmed, clothed, guarded, guided, loved, and nutured into maturity; and it is only among men that the helpless ancient, hobbling on his cane, may hopefully hold out empty hands to the young hunters. Man alone differs in these ways from the beasts of the jungle, among whom the young must quickly and surely learn the way of survival — and among whom those with toothless jaws or lagging steps quickly perish.

Biology then, determines the potential duration of human life, while technology extends the lifespan toward that potential. We will return later to a consideration of the implications of this technologically-produced longevity. But let us first consider the ways in which culture defines the stages of the life cycle and the transitions from one stage to another.

Perhaps just because extended care of the young and the old is such a uniquely human trait, cultural forms have everywhere been developed which invest both youth and age with special significance. The aged condition in human societies cannot be understood as a simple biological fact or as an accidental by-product of technological development — it must be understood in terms of human culture. With the development of nonmaterial culture — language, ritual, patterned social relationships, and other symbolic understandings among men — the life cycle, in its pristine biological form, began to be embroidered by human invention. Through the agency of culture, members of a particular society come to share certain perceptions of youth, as they do of age. With respect to youth, cultural definitions of its quality and duration are developed, which in time come to be perceived as reality. Most societies have arbitrarily modified the period of time during which the developing individual is considered to be "immature." In simpler cultures, the acquisition of adult status usually coincides more or less with the onset of sexual maturity.

Adult status may be acquired at fourteen or fifteen years of age;
in many parts of the world marriage and social independence
occur shortly after puberty, especially for girls. As cultures become increasingly complex in both technology and symbolism,
the young member of society requires more and more time to
learn all the skills and meanings which he will be expected to
know as an adult participant in social life. Thus, in contemporary
Euroamerican societies, manhood is reached, not according to a
biological calendar, but only with the capacity for economic independence. In some societies, this day may be late indeed in
arriving. For example, among the Western Apache, single persons
are regarded as "youths" or "maidens" regardless of their physiological or chronological age — only marriage can confer adult
status (Opler, 1941). Also, among certain groups of the Irish
peasantry, as recently as thirty years ago, a male might not be
permitted to marry or to function in other ways as an adult until
he was thirty or even forty years old. By custom, he was defined as
a "boy" until he inherited from his father upon the latter's de-
cease or retirement from active farming (Arensberg, 1937).

Just as custom defines the beginning of adult status, so it
decrees the criteria for becoming an elder. In societies where old
age is defined in *functional* terms, it is the onset of biological
deterioration (as this affects mobility, strength, or other abilities
required in adult work) that signals the end of active adult status.
That is, old age is defined by observed changes in physical condition — and its onset corresponds with the individual's need to restrict his activities substantially. However, in human groups
which define old age in *formal* terms, change of status is linked
to other factors — usually to some external event which is
arbitrarily invested with symbolic significance. For example,
among the Maricopa Indians of Arizona, an individual becomes
"old" if he has a grandchild, and the term "old man" or "old
woman" may accordingly be applied to a person in his early
forties (Lowie, 1948).

The definition of old age in contemporary Western civilization — and particularly in American society — is increasingly a
formal rather than a functional one; and, essentially, it is a

temporal definition. The "aged" are more and more designated as those who are known to have lived so many years. Such a definition is understandable, in view of the American elaboration of the concept of time, an elaboration without parallel in the known world. As Hallowell (1955) has pointed out: "It is impossible to assume that man is born with any innate 'temporal sense.' His temporal concepts are always culturally constituted. . . . We moderns are habituated to a uniquely elaborated scheme of temporal norms that impinge upon our lives at every point" (pp. 216-217). It has also been said that, "The American never questions the fact that time should be planned and future events fitted into a schedule. . . . The American thinks it is natural to quantify time. To fail to do so is unthinkable" (Hall, 1959, p. 134).[2]

The American formal definition of old age, then, tends to be a temporal one, based on carefully kept records and calendrical reckonings. It is nearly impossible in American society today to live one's life without having the exact date of one's birth — year, month, and day — made a matter of public record. A child must have been born a certain number of years and months before he can be admitted to a public school, and usually his exact chronological age must be substantiated by a written legal document. A youth must have lived a given number of calendar years before he may, of his own volition, leave school, purchase certain stimulants or intoxicants, or gain legal sanction for operating certain types of transportation devices. The age of consent is judged to be a matter of recorded chronology rather than of physiological maturity. Many places of business require job applicants to

[2]Hallowell, in describing the pervasiveness of temporal reification in American culture and thinking, cites Mumford, who maintains that "the clock, not the steam engine, is the key machine of the modern industrial age. . . . [in the seventeenth century life was reduced] to a careful, uninterrupted routine: so long for business; so long for dinner; so long for pleasure—all carefully measured out, as methodical as the sexual intercourse of Tristam Shandy's father, which coincided, symbolically, with the monthly winding of the clock. Timed payments; timed contracts; timed work; timed meals, from this period on nothing was quite free from the stamp of the calendar or the clock. Waste of time became for Protestant religious preachers, like Richard Baxter, one of the most heinous sins. To spend time in mere sociability, or even in sleep, was reprehensible" (Hallowell, 1955, p. 411).

establish their exact time of birth before they may be employed. In most American commercial and industrial enterprises, a worker is defined as "old" at the age of sixty-five, and at that time he is retired from gainful employment. The Federal Government, through its Social Security Act, has given official sanction to this definition by proclaiming sixty-five to be the age at which old age pension payments shall commence. This ruling, at least, holds for men; women are defined now as "retired" as early as sixty-two — an interesting cultural contradiction of biological findings that females, on the average, have greater longevity than do males. (This was true at the time the study was done; the regulations have since been modified to enable men to retire at the younger age and receive some Social Security benefits.) This social definition of old age, based on chronology, becomes ever more removed from the realities of physical debility. Furthermore, with the intensification of social and economic problems, such as automation, unemployment, and competition for jobs, there are today pressures for setting "retirement age" at an even earlier state in the life cycle — at sixty or even at fifty-five. In our sample, however, a number of people have been informally "retired" as early as sixty; these were people who have been "laid off" or for other external reasons have lost their positions in the few years prior to "official retirement age," and, for reasons of age, have been unable to secure other jobs. Such people are often in desperate economic circumstances: the labor market has defined them as "too old" to work, while the government regards them as "too young" to receive pensions or Social Security payments.

THE CULTURAL CONTRADICTIONS OF OLD AGE

For a moment, let us return to a consideration of extended human longevity. Accompanying the formal-temporal definition of old age we have just described, there have occurred the previously mentioned technological advances in medicine and public health which have begun to provide a longer, healthier later life for more people. Let us examine more closely some of the profound implications of this fact. In essence, our culture is now producing a new life-era—a new phase of considerable duration in the life cycle. With people arbitrarily retired from the responsibilities and economic activities of adult life, sometimes two decades before they experience serious functional impairment, a long hiatus has been created into which we have yet to build new cultural traditions and social institutions. Our culture has delineated the tasks of youth, and we know what they are: to become socialized to both primary and secondary groups; to master the language — both verbal and written; to develop motor skills and dexterity in the use of tools; and to learn the complex cultural patterns required for social and economic self-sufficiency. Similarly, our cultural tradition specifies the tasks appropriate to adulthood: "selecting and learning to live with a mate; rearing children; organizing his or her nuclear family, perhaps within a larger extended family; executing occupational roles in satisfactory fashion; assuming some share of administrative responsibility . . . [and] helping to enforce social pressure" (Honigmann, 1959, pp. 582-583) .[3]

In societies with functional definitions of old age — such as ours had during its preindustrial history — culture also specified the tasks of senescence. The aged were expected to relinquish adult responsibilities and powers in preparation for death, so that cultural continuity might be preserved. Thus, the old man's job was in those times to groom his successors, share his esoteric knowledge, and designate his heirs so that they would be prepared to assume control of his wealth, authority, or power — whether

---

[3]It may seem to the American reader that surely this roster of what we are here calling "culturally-defined tasks" are actually universal human tasks, determined by the biosocial rather than the cultural nature of man. However, such a view is not substantiated in the light of comparative cultural data. Selection of a mate is an individual task in only some cultures—by no means in all. Many peoples have rigid prescriptions for determining marriage partners; some, for example, require that a man marry a particular cross-cousin. Often betrothals are arranged even before the individual's birth. Similarly, culture determines whether or not spouses face the "task" of learning to live together. In our society an adult male is expected to establish a residence for himself, his wife, and their dependent children. In other cultures, however, the family household may not include an adult male at all—in some African tribes, for example, the male head of a polygymous family may have his own quarters, visiting in turn each of his several wives in their separate domiciles within a joint compound. Variations could be elaborated in regard to other tasks as well.

natural or supernatural. This was essential, to assure preservation
within the group of traditions, knowledge, skills, and social institutions. Reports exist in the ethnographic literature of instances
where, in primitive cultures, useful arts have been completely
lost to a people because the requisite knowledge and skills for
practicing them died out with the demise of a few skilled craftsmen. In subsistence societies, such losses of cultural resources may,
for a time, pose a serious threat to survival of the group.[4]

However, in American society today, adult responsibilities are
now relinquished relatively so early that there yet remains for
most older people a long span of years devoid of social meaning.
The roots of many problems of the elderly in our culture lie in
the normlessness of this newly extended life epoch of relatively
healthy old age.

We want to emphasize here the fact that there is a distinction
to be made between healthy longevity and that helpless and near-
moribund stage of life that often just precedes death — that is,
between what we have earlier called formal and functional old
age. Although the American definition of old age, as we have

---

[4]Rivers (1931) points to both social and religious factors in the disappearance of
useful arts in Oceania: "Many of the objects used in the every day life of Oceania
are not made by any member of the community but their manufacture is confined to special groups of craftsmen. Thus, in Tonga and Tikopia canoes are only
made by certain men called *tufunga* who are succeeded in this occupation by their
sons. It is only necessary for such a limited body of men to disappear . . . to account for the disappearance of an art. As we have seen, there is evidence that this
dying out of skilled craftsmen has been the cause of the disappearance of the
canoe in the Torres Island, and . . .the art of making stone adzes in . . . Murua."
Rivers comments that, "from our point of view it would seem most unlikely that
people would stand idly by and allow the disappearance of arts so useful as those
of making pottery and canoes. Nevertheless . . . an art practiced by a special
group of craftsmen is not a mere technical performance but has a definitely religious character and may be regarded as a long series of religious rites. It is not
enough to be able to make a canoe but you must also know the appropriate rites
which will make it safe to use it for profane purposes without danger from
ghostly or other supernatural agencies. To go in a canoe which has not been the
subject of such rites would be to put oneself into the midst of all kinds of hidden
and mysterious dangers" (pp. 531, 533). With the loss of navigation among the
Torres Islanders, large-scale fishing had to be abandoned. Fish could be taken only
with poles from the shore, and there was a consequent serious decline in food
supply.

shown, has changed dramatically, there remain in our society the atavistic attitudes towards all the elderly which were formerly reserved for the *functionally impaired:* the senile, the halt, and all those so frail that it could be reasonably inferred that they were very near dying. So defined, the aged are indeed often very near to death, and many of the primitive fears and anxieties which anthropologists see in nearly all cultures in association with death (as well as with other supposedly magical or supernatural processes) are understandable and predictable. However, with the widespread social acceptance of a formal definition of old age, we have a curious anachronism: a healthy longevity, extended sometimes for a quarter-century after the *rite de passage* of retirement from adult occupations and responsibilities, accompanied by social attitudes appropriate only toward those in the very last days of life.

Discrepancies between functional capacities and cultural mandates, at any stage of life, produce difficulties for the individual. It is said that adolescents in our society have problems because our culture has given the young so much to learn; the elaboration of technology, meanings, and social relationships has become so great that enculturation cannot be completed by the onset of puberty. However, until adolescents learn these cultural complexities, they are defined as classificatory "children" and are expected to behave asexually — despite their physiological maturity. The elderly have problems in our society because it takes them so long to die these days. Society defines them as classificatory "persons-about-to-die," regardless of biological competences, and — as such — they are held to be without significant social value.

The arbitrary designation of certain kinds of individuals as members of a devalued class is certainly not confined to American culture. Nearly all human groups have certain conceptions about what constitutes a "worthless" individual, or a "nonproductive" person — and these conceptions are cultural prescriptions which come to be regarded as reality. For example, in ancient China, and in some tribal societies such as the Toda of India, only one or two daughters in a single family were felt to have any value;

after that, additional female infants were often dispatched at
birth (Rivers, 1906). Among the Kikuyu, an East African tribal
people, offspring are desired and welcomed — unless they are
twins; these are worthless, since they invariably bring bad luck
on the family. One or both such infants, therefore, are killed
(Lowie, 1948). More familiar examples are the Jews of Nazi
Germany and Negroes in nonagricultural areas of the American
Deep South.

Just as the notion that twins invite catastrophe is a cultural
value-judgment, so are the various sentiments societies hold toward the last decades of life in comparison with the first. Such
judgments as are made of the inherent worth of any one segment
of life over another are culturally-determined — that is to say,
these judgments vary from people to people, time to time, and
place to place, *depending upon the ideals of the culture.* It is important to remember that these judgments, furthermore, come
to be canonized as "facts" about variations in human worth, and
provide guides to social behavior.

Perceptions of the value of later life, as we have said, depend
upon the ideals of the culture — and not upon the level of
technological development which characterizes that culture (although the latter influences longevity, as we have shown). Thus,
both in our society and in that of some much simpler peoples,
aging is accompanied by loss of social prestige. Such is the case,
for example, among the Attawapiskat Cree Indians, who live in
northern Canada. These people live by hunting and trapping.

> Community values expect a man or woman to 'always' be
> doing something.... [S]ocial approval depends on strenuous
> masculine activity... among the Cree, [and] the increasing
> debility produced by age may be extremely conflictful....
> [T]here are no activities reserved for the old that would allow
> them to realize social worth. Even an old man's chance to ex-
> press his frustration through sorcery has been largely taken
> away by the growing disbelief in traditional magic that followed
> the arrival of Catholic missionaries. The situation is a painful
> one. Old men tend to remember with retrospective nostalgia
> the games and activities that they undertook in childhood
> (Honigmann, 1954, p. 279).

In many other traditional tribal and peasant societies, however, elders play an indispensable part in social pursuits. The varying circumstances of the aged in primitive societies have been described by Simmons (1945). This writer points out that among many peoples with a subsistence economy, everyone is encouraged to work as long as possible — and since much of the work is not especially taxing of physical energy, some of the tasks can be undertaken equally by children, physically disabled adults, and the elderly. Where there is no written language, the elderly have customarily served as repositories of the people's accumulated usage, lore, and legend. In relatively stable cultures, their store of knowledge forms the keystone of contemporary life. And, in such societies, where famine and disease first strike the very young and the very old, there is no surplus of wise old men and women to guide and advise the young and foolish.

Just as primitive societies differ in the status accorded the aged, so more technologically advanced and literate peoples vary. In contrast to our own society, for example, is the situation of the elderly in Korea, where to reach the age of sixty "puts one practically in the category of the immortals and constitutes one of the greatest possible events in an individual's life" (Osgood, 1951, p. 43).

We conclude that, just as simpler tribal or folk societies do not *always* provide old age with significant functions, the more complex cultures do not invariably *fail* to do so. In order to understand the normless position of the aged in American society, we must look beyond the simple fact of our level of cultural complexity, to certain trends in our culture history.

HISTORICAL INFLUENCES ON THE CONDITION OF THE AGED IN AMERICA

There seem to be four principal historical factors which have influenced the normlessness of the elderly in our contemporary society. The first of these reasons has to do with the weakness of kinship ties. As Simmons (1945) has stated:

> Social relationships have provided the strongest securities
> to the individual, especially in old age. With vitality declin-

ing, the aged person has had to rely more and more upon personal relations with others, and upon the reciprocal rights and obligations involved .... Throughout human history the family has been the safest haven for the aged. Its ties have been the most intimate and longlasting, and on them the aged have relied for greatest security ... [and have found] in family relationships opportunities for effective social participation well into senility (p. 177).

However, the pattern of European settlement and colonization of North America has mitigated against the retention of close kinship ties between the adult generations in the United States.

Up until the present century, America has been a frontier society. As the children of early colonists grew up, married and began to establish their own families, they tended to move away from the parental home and break new ground for themselves in virgin lands. Friedmann (1960) has reported that evidence on household size for early America indicates that the large household of the extended kinship family was probably never the prevailing mode.

Estimates for Colonial America . . . fail to indicate the predominance of the extended kinship household. . . . The enumeration of 'masters' of families for the city of New York in 1703 lists a total of 818 families with an average household size of 4.5 for the white population . . . and further evidence showed that only 4 per cent of all the family units could be considered three-generational. . . . We do not know whether a majority of the aged were ever cared for in this manner in our country's history. Certainly, the amount of mobility which has characterized American life—not just with the onset of industrialization and urbanization but from early in our history with the opportunity for sons to break from the parental household and establish their own households on the frontier—would act to deter the development of a three-generation family system (pp. 130-131).

It is probable, then, that the aged in the United States have always been more often spatially separated from their children and grandchildren than has been the case in many parts of

Europe. Recent studies of rural villages in the Netherlands, for example, show that only now is the traditional three-generational household giving way to the establishment of nuclear family organization. These studies indicate that, even today, "[I]n several towns there are 'extended-family' households on more than 50 per cent of the farms" (Kooy, 1963, p. 45). In the area of family life, then, aged Americans find themselves out of the mainstream. In fact, there is a growing tendency in the United States to segregate the aged into separate communities. This segregation has the effect of further attenuating and impoverishing the familial roles of the elderly.

A second factor which mitigates against the definition of roles for the aged is the rapidity of industrial and technological change. The aged are a "lost generation" in the sense that they are carriers of a dying culture. In the thirty or forty years since they were the actors in the center of social life — the initiating, active, decisive young adult population of their time — the content of our culture has significantly changed. "Progress" has made obsolete the technical skills and knowledge they once painstakingly mastered when they were learning the work and ways of the world. This rapid change was dramatized recently in a television interview with a leading European nuclear physicist, now in his sixties. This scientist remarked that his field of inquiry has now far outstripped him. He has no expectation of contributing further original work to that mushrooming body of knowledge. He lamented that his only hope today is to learn enough so that he will at least understand what his students will be writing within the next ten years. Even a younger person in contemporary society may suddenly realize that his technical knowledge is becoming obsolescent. He may, for instance, discover that he cannot help his own child with his eighth-grade arithmetic homework, because the boy is studying not multiplication tables but set theory and nonparametric measurement.

More and more of our older citizens find themselves excluded from productive work of any kind, and quite often come to accept society's appraisal of them as being of little value in modern western life. To be sure, there are still, even in a rapidly changing culture, social functions for a minority of the elderly. Our society continues to need and employ a sprinkling of elder statesmen, seasoned writers, mature artists, wise theologians, supreme court justices, and emeritus professors. These are the men and women in American society who correspond to the "village elders" of peasant societies. These are the few aged who are still "productive" — and therefore highly esteemed in a work-oriented society. But the bulk of the aged are not so fortunate.

This leads us to a consideration of a third historical factor affecting the status of the aged: there has been a phenomenal increase in the *number* of older persons in our society. In 1830, only one American out of twenty-five was sixty years of age or older; in 1960, one out of eight. This is not a new trend in the United States; the American population has been an aging one during the entire period for which vital statistics have been recorded. At the close of the American Revolution, the median age of white males was about fifteen years. Just before the Civil War, it had increased to nineteen years; by 1900, to twenty-four years; and by 1960, to thirty-one years (Sheldon, 1960, pp. 30-32). The aged in present-day proportions are a cultural anomaly. For the first time in the history of mankind there exist in large numbers men and women already aged by established standards who can anticipate another full decade of life. Industrial society has created a new social group, yet the culture which spawned this increase and brought the group into being has yet to find ways of incorporating it within the ongoing societal system. As we will see later, public concern over the social and economic dependency of the aged has, along with other factors, a profound influence on the personal adaptation of the elderly.

A fourth factor influencing the status of the aged is the dominant emphasis in American culture on the value of productivity, with work assuming an almost sacred character. As Kluckhohn (1949) once put it, "Americans are not merely optimistic believers that 'work counts.' Their creed insists that anyone, anywhere in the social structure, can and should 'make the effort'. . . . The only way to be safe in American life is to be a success. Failure to 'measure up' is felt as deep personal inadequacy" (pp.

233-236). As individuals begin to reach old age, they find it increasingly hard to exemplify this major theme in American culture. Some people in their sixties, and even more in their seventies, experience physical and cognitive changes which impair their speed and, particularly, their endurance in the performance of certain occupations. These commonly observed changes have become codified into a set of social expectations regarding the behavior of individuals when they reach a given age. Thus, as we have previously stated, although many people at the age of sixty-five or seventy are quite intact both physically and mentally, society arbitrarily categorizes them as old and treats them as such. Merton (1957) has commented on this tendency to stereotype individuals, and has related the process to the bureaucratic structure of American society:

> Within the structure of hierarchically arranged authority, the activities of 'trained and salaried experts' are governed by general, abstract, clearly defined rules which preclude the necessity for the issuance of specific instructions for each specific case. The generality of the rules requires the constant use of *categorization,* whereby individual problems and cases are classified on the basis of designated criteria and are treated accordingly. . . . Adherence to the rules, originally conceived as a means, becomes transformed into an end-in-itself; there occurs the familiar process of *displacement of goals* whereby 'an instrumental value becomes a terminal value, (pp. 196-199).

Applying this concept to the occupational situation of the aged, we find that while it is indeed true that some older people become impaired in physical, sensory, or cognitive functions in their sixties and cannot any longer be gainfully employed in their major occupations, many older workers are not so impaired. Bureaucratic rules, however, arbitrarily define such people as "classificatory aged persons," and the result is such uniform social action as compulsory retirement at a given age.

The value placed on work and productivity in our culture, and the implementation of this value through social sanctions, constantly impinge upon the aged individual's self-perception and a struggle for adaptation follows. (Productivity is only one of many values in American culture that we have found to influence the condition of the aged of our society. Others will be discussed throughout the report, particularly in Chapter VI.)

The aged in American life face a dilemma. They are rendered helpless, either by personal default or by social definition, to meet cultural ideals and consequently they are devalued. The principal alternative now provided by society is that of enacting certain secondary cultural values, such as an orientation to play and the emphasis on consumption characteristic of the American leisure class generally. This alternative is available to the affluent aged, but not to the majority.[5] Since the majority of American aged do not have the economic resources for a life built around the process of consumption, many of them feel that they have no recourse but to cling to the productive roles of middle life — often in the face of categorical social denials.

CULTURE AND MENTAL DISORDER OF THE AGED

In the previous discussion we have taken the position that the status of any subgroup within a society is a function of the cultural ideals of that society. We have also discussed some of the events of culture history that have resulted in a devalued condition of the aged in American society today. However, when we turn from the matter of social status to a consideration of mental illness, other questions arise. For example, we find that low social status is sometimes, but not invariably, accompanied by a greater prevalence of mental disorder. If it were, madness would be ubiquitous among socially "inferior" groups everywhere — among Bhangis, Chamars, and other Hindu outcastes; among Negroes in Memphis as well as in Johannesburg; among Jews throughout Central Europe; and among enlisted personnel in the United States armed forces. Clearly, this is not the case: the relationship between culture and mental disorder requires further clarification.

The systematic study of cultural influences in the development of mental disorder is quite a recent enterprise, and we

---

[5]For a recent popular description of a "play-oriented" middle-class retirement community, see Calvin Trillin (1964).

really know very little about it. We know infinitely more about the evolution of the horse, methods for controlling the boll weevil, and the properties of radioactive isotopes. However, we have learned that culture is related to mental illness in at least three ways: First, the signs and symptoms of mental disorders vary from one culture to another; also, definitions of mental illness are not universal, but are established by social consensus, often through the mechanism of specially instituted agencies. Second, many mental disorders are related (by means that are not fully understood at this time) to stress — and cultures vary in the kind, number, and locus of stresses they create for individuals. Third, cultures differ in the resources they provide to people for handling those stresses and thus making themselves more comfortable. Let us examine each of these three points in more detail.

Cultural Definitions of Mental Illness

One of the early contributions of anthropological field workers to the mental sciences was their documentation of the enormous range of psychological behavior which could be readily accommodated within one or another cultural pattern. As Benedict (1948) wrote:

> One of the most striking facts that emerge from a study of widely varying cultures is the ease with which . . . [those who would be defined in our culture as] abnormals function in other cultures. It does not matter what kind of 'abnormality' we choose for illustration, those which indicate extreme instability, or those which are more in the nature of character traits like sadism or delusions of grandeur or of persecution, there are well-described cultures in which these abnormals function at ease and with honor, and apparently without danger or difficulty to the society. . . . It is clear that culture may value and make socially available even highly unstable human types. If it chooses to treat their peculiarities as the most valued variants of human behavior, the individuals in question will rise to the occasion and perform their social roles without reference to our usual ideas of the types who can make social adjustments and those who cannot (pp. 179-180).

In other words, habitual patterns of thought and action which represent severe pathology in the context of one culture may be socially rewarded in a different—though equally viable—culture.[6]

The discovery that "abnormal behavior" is differently defined in different cultures should not be taken to mean that there are whole cultures which are "mentally ill" according to some absolute standard. Rather, it suggests that the conception of the normal is everywhere a function of the definition of the good—that which society approves and rewards. Behavior which is "abnormal"—*i.e.*, antithetical to the attainment of the socially-defined "good"—is sometimes considered to be "symptomatic." Thus, psychiatric symptoms are behavioral patterns which are assumed to be indicative of *generalized incompetence* in the achievement of essential cultural goals.[7]

All "abnormal behavior" is not, however, designated as "mental illness." Some individuals who habitually deviate from "good" behavior are regarded as delinquents, criminals, "antisocial" personalities, or just irresponsible people. In our society, those whose "abnormal behavior" is thought to be intentional controlled, goal-directed (even though the goals to which it is directed are socially deplored), and not accompanied by personal anguish, are likely to be seen as morally rather than mentally deviant—as legal offenders rather than as medical patients. Mental disorder, on the

---

[6]It may be difficult for the reader who has not had personal experience with cultures very different from his own to grasp fully the verity and implications of this finding. He may be aided in this task by reading at least one of the classic ethnographic descriptions of societies where "normative" behavior would, in our own culture, be considered patently psychopathic. See, for example, Czaplicka (1914), Benedict (1934), and Fortune (1932). These early works contain more detailed accounts of behavior than many of the current ethnopsychiatric writings, which tend to be theoretically rather than descriptively oriented.

[7]Wallace (1961) has described the process by which social diagnoses of incompetence may have a "feedback" effect, leading to more and more generalized inadequacy in an individual's performance: "[T]here is no question that any social attitude which interprets a given behavior or experience as symptomatic of a generalized incompetence is a powerful creator of shame, and thus of anxiety, in those who experience or behave in the 'symptomatic' way. . . . This anxiety will further tend to decrease his [the individual's] competence, thus precipitating a reciprocal interaction between 'incompetent' behaviors and anxiety . . . [and] failure . . . will increasingly extend over other behaviors" (pp. 182-183).

other hand, is regarded as somehow beyond the control of the individual, not oriented to any recognized social ends, and accompanied by psychic pain. The extent to which these two types of deviance overlap in social definition may readily be seen in our own culture. For example, police officers, attorneys, and judges are involved in arriving at a judgment of "insanity"— which is a legal as well as a medical status. Furthermore, medical institutions often admit as "patients" alcoholics, drug addicts, and certain types of sexual offenders, although many other people with identical behavior patterns are confined to jails and prisons. A particular behavior pattern within our culture may run the gamut from "normal role behavior" to criminality to psychopathy. For example, habitual gambling may be a respectable profession in Nevada, illegal but not psychopathic if successfully pursued in California, and psychopathic (although not "psychotic") if "compulsively" pursued anywhere.[8]

We conclude, then, that mental illness is that particular type of "abnormal" or deviant behavior, intimately related to cultural factors in its definition, and viewed as requiring strategic control by medical specialists. In other words, mental disorder is a social judgment placed on an individual by various institutions in his society. These may include, in San Francisco, police officers, relatives, landlords, private physicians, hospital admitting officers, ward personnel, diagnosticians, and court officials. We know from other studies that these agencies entertain varying individual interests, and thus may differ in the criteria they use in concluding that a person is a "psychiatric case."[9] Insofar as we can determine, the diagnosis of mental illness in our own as well as in other cultures is defined by a consensus of interested agents. Accordingly, the subjects of this study whom we call "mentally ill" are a group of older people of San Francisco upon whom such judgments were

---

[8]See Aubert and Messinger (1958) for a discussion of changes through time in social definitions of deviance as "illness." Other comments on this subject are found in various chapters of Becker (1964).

[9]See, for example, the detailed analysis of the various agents involved in arriving at decisions to institutionalize members of our hospital sample, in Lowenthal (1964a).

made in 1959. Those whom we will call "mentally well" have had no such social judgments made of them, although in another report on this same sample, mental disorder—as defined by psychiatric ratings—was found among 14 per cent of our community subjects (Lowenthal, Berkman, and Associates, 1966). For the purposes of this volume, we have found it advantageous to utilize the social rather than the clinical definition.

Culture and Stress

Each culture creates a particular configuration of stresses. The cultural environment within which a person must live is an active force in defining the kinds and variety of life situations he must face. Even biological traumata may be culturally influenced: for example, the culture determines whether or not an individual will be frequently exposed to extreme changes in temperature, whether he will experience relatively long periods of hunger each year before the yams ripen or the ice breaks to let the fishing boats through to open water—or whether he will be so chronically overfed with rich foods that his arteries become clogged with fatty deposits and his heart overtaxed in keeping his blood circulating. It is custom that dictates that some individuals shall have their incisor teeth knocked out, substantial quantities of their blood drained off, large areas of their skin incised to produce geometric designs of heavy scar tissue, their sexual organs mutilated in one fashion or another, or their earlobes, nostrils, or lips pierced through with sharp instruments.

Cultures also prescribe certain mental stresses. The anxieties of warfare—whether it be primitive hand-to-hand combat or the vague impersonal threat of the hydrogen bomb preferred by civilized societies—are cultural derivatives. Dread of sorcery, of nightwalking monsters, of eternal damnation in an afterlife, of werewolves, dragons, or spirits of the dead—all these are a part of the individual's cultural heritage. Conflict and anxiety may be generated in more subtle ways, too. Culturally-imposed taboos may prevent the free satisfaction of basic needs; cultural expectations of the individual may be ambiguous, conflicting, or unattainable; drives may be created by the culture, and then individuals, or even whole groups, denied access to the means for their satisfaction.

People may be appointed scapegoats for the evils befalling their fellows; and stigmata may be declared hereditary.

Within a particular culture, certain familial roles may be the locus of especially acute stresses. For example, Barrabee and von Mering (1953) found that the role of adolescent son was particularly stressful in both Jewish and Italian families in Boston. However, the *modes* of stress experienced by those boys varied according to the nature of ethnic values. It was found that severe tensions were generated in Jewish boys by the fact that maternal love and approval was often conditional upon a level of academic achievement that was, for some, unattainable. Among Italian boys, the principal stress resulted from role conflict growing out of acculturation—the majority culture sanctioned prolonged education, while family expectations were that the boy would get a job as soon as possible and begin to contribute to the family finances.[10]

Even within a single culture, one sex may experience more severe stresses than the other, depending upon social expectations of men and women (see Mead, 1949, and Murphy, 1959). Thus, Jaco (1959), in a comparative study of Mexican, Anglo-American, and Negro populations in Texas, provided some evidence for cultural differences in the stresses impinging upon men compared with women. He found that women were under greater psychological pressures than men among the Mexican sample, while the reverse was true among Negroes.

We know from studies of subgroups held to be socially inferior that prevalent attitudes and stereotypes may be extremely stressful for stigmatized individuals. Negative assessments may be internalized by their referents, becoming self-attitudes which erode ego-strength and psychological health. For example, in a study of American Negro personality by Kardiner and Ovesey (1951), it was shown that the Negro, in his relations with whites, receives an unpleasant image of himself that causes him to devaluate himself. Such devaluation in turn, the investigators found, motivates a number of nonadaptive behaviors such as unrealistically high aspirations, self-abnegation, and symptoms of repressed rage.

---

[10]Other literature on the topic of stresses inherent in various role systems has been recently reviewed by Kennedy (1961).

It is one of the tasks of this study to examine the nature and severity of stresses impinging upon the aged in urban American culture. However, as we will show, it is not stress alone that undermines mental health. Still another cultural factor influences the incidence of mental disorder.

Cultural Resources for Tension Reduction

Human groups differ in their provision of resources for tension reduction. Thus, not only does each culture create particular stresses and strains with which the personality must cope; in many cases, these stresses are accompanied by institutionalized techniques for their resolution or management. One such technique in primitive societies is the availability of alternate social roles for persons manifesting certain types of deviant behavioral reactions. A classic example was reported by Kroeber (1952), wherein a Lassik Indian woman, following the death of her baby, experienced recurrent hallucinations, episodes of loss of contact with the sensory world, distress, anxiety and worry, and a feeling of being very ill, equating this state with a calling to become a doctor. In our own culture this report would be diagnosed as a psychotic episode. However, from the point of view of the native cultures of northern California, such an episode is objectively "real," socially useful, and indicative of special ability—considerable prestige attaches to one who has the power to cure or perform other special feats.

Such social roles are available in primitive cultures in many parts of the world. For example, Benedict (1948) quotes an old Zulu of South Africa, who described the pitiable condition of a man who was destined to become a diviner:

> The condition of a man who is about to become a diviner is this: at first he is apparently robust, but in the process of time he begins to be delicate, not having any real disease, but being delicate. . . . He is continually complaining of pains in different parts of his body. And he tells them that he has dreamt that he was carried away by a river. . . . 'On waking one part of my body felt different from other parts; it was no longer alike all over.' At last that man is very ill. . . . At length all the man's property is expended, he still being ill. . . . So the

man may be ill two years without getting better. . . . He has convulsions. . . . He habitually sheds tears, at first slight, then at last he weeps aloud and when the people are asleep he is heard making a noise and wakes the people by his singing. . . . Perhaps he sings till morning, no one having slept. And then he leaps about the house like a frog. . . . At length [in a dream] an ancient ancestral spirit is pointed out to him. This spirit [tells him how to become] a diviner. . . . Then he is quiet a few days, having gone to [a shaman] to have the medicine churned for him; and he comes back quite another man, being now cleansed and a diviner indeed (pp. 179-180).

We have included this rather lengthy description here to indicate the extent of disturbance which may be culturally accommodated through the provision of cultural alternatives which serve to relieve stress and strain and reintegrate the individual within the social fabric.

Some cultures will even induce particular stresses within certain statuses in order to get the individual to perform socially useful functions. For example, among the American Plains Indians, direct contact with the deities was necessary in order for an individual to gain any potential for a good life—to have health, longevity, and well-being, not only for himself but also for his family. This gift of power could only be achieved by individuals who sought and obtained the help of supernatural beings. In order to make direct contact with the guardian spirits, the individual sought to have a "vision" or an acute and highly subjective experience, which provided the basis for all he could hope for during the rest of his life. Every skill, every success, every social or economic gain, hinged upon his establishing actual communication with the spirits and receiving their blessings. The "vision quest" took place at about the time of puberty, when young men were expected to perform certain self-tortures in order to acquire a vision of the spirits. Generally, this consisted of four days of fasting, exposed alone and naked on a hilltop, without food, water, or fire. If a vision did not occur within that time, self-tortures were sometimes inflicted to intensify the suffering. A finger joint might be chopped off, or skewers of wood thrust under pinches of flesh on the breast or back and then attached to ropes, against which the youth would strain and attempt to break the flesh. These extreme measures were taken simply to assure the onset of hallucinatory delirium—a state thought to be essential; for a man's future mental as well as physical health was contingent upon an extraordinary personal psychic experience—only by this means could one encounter the deities and gain a vision of one's life plan.

THE ROLE OF VALUES IN MENTAL HEALTH

To return now to our general discussion, we have seen that mental illness cannot be defined in terms of simple abnormal behavior patterns. In every culture there are aberrant patterns which are institutionalized by means of alternative social roles (as in the status of shaman or diviner), and the behavior then becomes socially sanctioned. Second, we have seen that there is probably no sociocultural system that does not create stresses and strains for its members. In some cases, the stresses are actually cultural imperatives aimed at inducing aberrant mental states thought to serve some higher purpose (as in the vision quest). Third, stresses and strains are not equally distributed among the members of a society—there are certain statuses (familial, hierarchical, sexual, age-linked, or occupational) that are particularly fraught with tension and conflict.

In order to explore more fully the complex interactions of culture, social status, and mental disorder, we have found it useful to consider the concept of cultural values. As the term is generally used in the social sciences, a value is an element of a shared symbolic system which serves as a criterion of the desirable; values influence the selection from available modes, means, and ends of action, and are indispensable to the interpretation of concrete behavior.[11] Values, then, determine what behaviors are desirable in a culture, and how particular behaviors will be interpreted and judged. Every culture, so far as we know, has both dominant and substitute values. Although conformity to the dominant values of a culture determines the hierarchical status of groups of individu-

---

[11]This definition of value is our own paraphrasing of parts of three different definitions of the term—one developed by Clyde Kluckhohn, one by Talcott Parsons (both in Parsons and Shils, 1951), and one by Florence Kluckhohn and F. L. Strodtbeck (1961).

als, cultural alternatives or variant value-orientations exist in all societies. Kluckhohn and Strodtbeck (1961) have stated that neither an individual nor a whole society can exist wholly in terms of a single profile of values:

> To function successfully every society must have within it some persons, either individual persons or groups of persons, who will devote themselves to the differing activities of the several behavior spheres [institutions]. . . . For example, the American man who elects to be a composer of music or the one who chooses to be an academic intellectual is almost always 'variant' in some if not all of his value orientations. . . . [H]istory shows that most of the successful Spanish-American *patrones* were far more individualistic in their behavior than average Spanish-Americans. . . . [T]hey resembled [the American] businessman much more than they resembled the majority of their own people (p. 31).

Thus, we cannot predict conflict or stress for an individual on the basis of conformity to dominant values alone (although we *can* often predict his social status). For we must take into account the variant nature of values available to the individual at each life period. Thus, some social value adheres to low statuses as well as to high ones. For example, although the accumulation of wealth is a dominant value in American culture, this value has its alternates: for some, it is the morality of work; for others, "holy poverty." Furthermore, there are well-established social roles embodying each of these alternate values.

However, we have reason to believe that certain life-positions are not integrated in a functional way into the larger system of cultural values or meanings—either dominant or variant. As we mentioned earlier in this chapter, there are individuals within a society who are faced with conflicting hierarchies of values (as the second-generation Italian-American boys studied in Boston); there are others who are placed in positions where alternative values are not readily available to them—yet they sometimes find conformity to the dominant values impossible (as was found to be true of some Jewish adolescents in the same study). And there may be still other individuals (such as we suspect the aged in America to be) who are faced with the task of making shifts through time in their value-systems, without the guidance of institutionalized alternatives. In such cases as these, the individual is left to respond idiosyncratically to the stresses inherent in his situation.

Such idiosyncratic responses may be culturally defined as psychopathic or as adaptive, depending on their nature. Some responses are more likely to be viewed as psychopathic: if the individual withdraws from social contact in order to defend himself against devaluation; if he interprets all the transactions of society as inimical to his own interests, thereby defending his own self-esteem, but developing "paranoid thinking" in the process; if he so aggrandizes himself in his own mind that he becomes impervious to the influence and judgments of others; or if he succumbs to organic dysfunction in order to claim the exemptions of the "sick role." Many of the older people we will describe in these pages have reacted to the stresses of age in these ways.

However, there are other older people who independently achieve some creative synthesis, satisfactory to others and to themselves, of available but noninstitutionalized alternatives existing within the broader cultural spectrum. We will also describe some of these people, and the processes by which they have accomplished this adaptation.

STRESS AS A PHENOMENOLOGICAL CONCEPT

The available evidence therefore strongly suggests the hypothesis that the incidence of psychopathology within a social group, such as the aged in America today, depends upon: a) the amount and kinds of stress generated within the structure of the life situations faced; b) the availability of techniques for dealing with those stresses; and c) the congruence of adaptive resolutions with the value-structure of the individual and his society. Acting on this hypothesis, our understanding of the stresses impinging upon the aged individual requires that we try to see the world through his eyes. We cannot content ourselves with an "objective" assessment of how untoward or stressful his circumstances are, basing such assessments on external criteria. We must reconstruct as faithfully as possible the perceptions the aged individual has of himself in relation to the world about him. In other words, we must try to describe and study the *personal system* of the aged individual. In this undertaking, we will not concern ourselves with questions of personality dynamics as such. Our level of discussion will be that which Hallowell (1955) has called "phenomenological"; that is, "a frame of reference by means of which it may be possible to view the individual . . . in terms of the psychological perspective which his culture constitutes for him and which is the integral focus of his activities, rather than . . . the perspective of an outside observer . . . . [T]he actual data that can be described on a phenomenological level [are] *e.g.,* self-awareness, self-perception, self-reference by means of language, [and] self-conception" (pp. 79-80). Our phenomenological data will also include certain social perceptions of the aged—the outlook of the self as it perceives the structure and properties of its behavioral environment. That is, our data are in large part derived from what older people have told us they perceive, think, feel, and believe to be true about themselves and the world in which they live as it impinges upon them.

As social scientists, however, we are also interested in certain more "objective" measurements of the place of elderly people in society. Thus, we will also discuss the *social system,* describing it by means of certain measures of the degree and nature of the articulation of the aged person with his social world. We will attempt in this book to describe the range of interactions which occur between the personal and the social systems during the process of aging, and to differentiate those interactions which distinguish the mentally well from the mentally ill. And, as we have stated, our definition of mental illness in this volume will be the social consensus of "abnormal" behavior leading to assignment of strategic control to medical specialists (in this case mental hospitalization).

ORGANIZATION OF THE VOLUME

The plan of this book will be as follows: in Chapter II, we will first describe the setting of the study and some of the subjects. Then, in the second part of the chapter, we will present information on what we are calling the "phenomenological field"—that is, the perceptions that elderly people in our sample share concerning the characteristics of old age and the problems it presents. Chapter III describes the nature of our study sample—a group of 435 elderly people in San Francisco, some of whom are living as residents of the community, have not received treatment for mental disorders, and are thus, according to our definition, mentally healthy; and others of whom have undergone hospitalization for psychiatric or emotional reasons during the later years of life. We will present information on the social, economic, and physical characteristics of this sample, and will describe it in terms of our measures of physical and mental health.

Chapter IV will be devoted to a discussion of two quantitative measures of personal function: self-image and morale. We will show how these attitudinal dimensions relate to a number of background characteristics (such as income and sex), and how they relate to each other as well as to mental and physical health. Chapter V will also deal with quantitative data, in this case with measures of social function. We will discuss the relationship of various social roles and interactions to mental and physical health. We will also describe in that chapter how subgroups within American society vary in the kinds and number of social relationships available to the aged. In Chapter VI, "normal" and "pathological" dynamics of the personal system of older people will be presented and compared. In Chapter VII, we will discuss social perceptions of the aged, and, in Chapter VIII, we will describe the relation between social involvement and personal adaptation. In the final chapter we will discuss the adaptive tasks of aging in American culture, the various barriers that individuals face in accomplishing those tasks, and the relationship of aging adaptation to American cultural values.

Chapter II

THE SUBJECTS OF THE STUDY IN THEIR SETTING

INTRODUCTION

ALTHOUGH AGING IS AN inevitable biological event, it is nevertheless influenced by the cultural setting in which it occurs. There is probably no life process built into the human organism that is not shaped in some way—intimately or remotely—by society and its cultural norms. This shaping force penetrates into even the deepest functions, mistakenly dubbed autonomic. Patterns of sleep, of hunger, of motor behavior, of ingestion, egestion, copulation, growth, and pain perception—all are profoundly affected by cultural learning. All human beings feel hunger, but it is our culture that teaches us, if we are Americans, to be hungry *three* times a day: upon arising in the morning, then at noon, and then shortly before evening. However, if we were members of a different society, say that of the Bemba of Africa, we would feel hungry only *twice* a day: midmorning and again late in the afternoon—except from November to March, when we would be hungry only *once* a day, at about sundown.[1]

Similarly are we taught through early training that egestion is not a simple or automatic function of our physiology but a cultural event, closely hedged about with rules and proprieties. Elimination must be accomplished only at designated places where sphincter release is permitted—and, among certain peoples, only at appropriate times. It is in this sense that we say cultural patterns are quite literally "built" into the human organism. Even our physiologies must adjust their most primitive functions to the codes of the culture. From the earliest days of infancy, our be-

---

[1] Herskovits (1948) pointed out that in many primitive societies, the number of meals eaten a day is inversely correlated with food requirements. That is, the time of greatest energy output—the agricultural growing season, when everyone works very hard—is the time when least food is eaten. Among the Bemba, it is during the leisure months of the dry season that two meals a day are eaten. Thus, he concludes, custom rather than physiological need determines hunger patterns (pp. 280-281).

havior is molded into patterns of prescribed conduct for culturally defined situations (Frank, 1948). If, therefore, even such basic functions as hunger and excretion are structured by society's norms, we have good reason to believe that human reactions to aging are also shaped by the sociocultural environment.

The focus of our study is on the process of aging as it has been structured by American society today, but ours is not a simple, homogeneous culture. It is characterized by tremendous richness and variety, even within the boundaries of a single city. In San Francisco, the locale of this study, the elderly are sometimes very rich, often very poor. Many were born here and have not ventured more than a hundred miles or so from their homes in a lifetime; others are living the last years of their lives half-way around the earth from their native soil. Some are illiterate; others learned. Some are surrounded by relatives and friends; others completely alone. Some are healthy and energetic; others, frail and bedridden.

This complex heterogeneity creates two problems for any investigation of cultural influences on aging. First, to what extent are problems in aging adaptation simply a function of these social variations within our culture? Put otherwise, are there major subgroup determinants of mental illness in later life? Does contentment with one's old age always follow upon being physically healthy, financially secure, and well educated? The second problem is one facing any anthropologist working in a complex civilization: how does one define and describe the common cultural matrix shared by widely differing individuals and subgroups? What are the shared symbolic understandings—the beliefs, values, goals, and even perceptions of reality—that bind us together into one vast society with uncountable interdependencies?

With respect to the first question of subgroup influences on aging adaptation, we will follow two different procedures in this volume. In the following three chapters we will describe the *statistical* distribution of various social characteristics in our sample and examine the influence of these characteristics on aging individuals.[2] In the present chapter (as in Chapters VI and VII),

---

[2]It should be remembered, however, that the study of social factors in the mental disability of the aged is not the primary aim of this report. As was pointed out in the Preface, that topic is being explored and reported in another study within our larger program of research in aging (see Lowenthal, Berkman, and Associates, 1966).

we shall be following a second method by introducing a set of brief case descriptions in order to mark out the *qualitative* differences in life circumstances among a few of the elderly people of our sample. In this way we hope to show something of the range of social and environmental settings within which the aged of San Francisco live.

Turning now to the second problem, that of defining *common* cultural factors influencing the aging process, we have been aided by the fact that all the subjects of this study, in spite of their differences, have two things in common: all are growing old, and all are faced with the task of adapting to that process within the cultural framework of American urban society. We have postulated, therefore, that most subjects will share certain views of later life, its character, and its problems in our society. Accordingly, in the second portion of this chapter, we will present information on the perceptions of old age held in common by our subjects, regardless of their respective stations in life or differences in their private worlds.

SOME NEIGHBORHOODS WHERE OLDER PEOPLE LIVE

The men and women whose lives we studied are San Franciscans. While few were born in the city, the majority have lived a third or more of their lives within this urban environment. They occupy a wide range of subcultures within a city famous for its heterogeneity—a cosmopolitan area of Latins and Orientals, Polynesians and Slavs, Negroes and Caucasians. The aged are everywhere in San Francisco. They constitute 18 per cent of the city's population—a proportion found in few other places in the country, despite the growing numbers of old people in the nation generally.[3]

---

[3]The sparsest statistics dramatize the phenomenal increase in longevity that is taking place in this country. The "senior citizens," as they are often referred to by our legislators and social workers, constitute the second fastest growing age group in our nation, exceeded only by children aged five to fourteen. Today, people sixty-five and over number more than 17 million. Each day their numbers experience a net increase of 1,000. By 1970, they will total 20 million. Today the "very old" age group—those eighty-five and over—exceed 900,000, an increase of 920 per cent since 1920 (United States Senate, 1963; p. ix).

San Francisco is not an unattractive place in which to grow old. This is, at least, the consensus of our informants, both men and women. Perhaps this is why so many elderly people live here. They like the year-round mildness of the climate, the parks and museums and libraries with places to sit and take the sun, the big downtown shopping area that attracts the browsers, the profusion of movie houses and restaurants, the relative compactness of a city flanked on three sides by water. They like the panorama of the ships in the bay and the rows of white houses clinging to the many hills. They like to identify with a city of legends and character, and many old-time residents are eager to recreate their personal involvement with the "old San Francisco" of the days before the 1906 earthquake and fire leveled it to the ground. They embroider their recollections with vaudeville headliners of the old Barbary Coast; robber barons transformed into society greats by their mansions on Nob Hill; the romantic history of old Chinatown and North Beach. These were the days when the gaslighter made his rounds at dusk and one could ride the cablecars for a nickel.

But the old have mixed feelings about the city today. Most of them would not live anywhere else, but they do deplore the present high cost of living in San Francisco, the steep hills they can no longer climb, the congestion, the speed of urban life, the inadequate transportation system, and the disappearance of old landmarks which—like their dwindling inventories of friends and relatives—year by year impoverishes their present world. Also, many are saddened by the denigration of the old ways of doing things, the old skills, the old beliefs. Somehow, the old virtues were nobler, and the old sins more understandable.

Our study of elderly San Franciscans brought us into still greater intimacy with a city we already knew very well. (One author was born in the city; the other has been a resident of the area for seventeen years.) In many ways, however, this was a new intimacy with neighborhoods through which we had previously moved but with which we had never so deeply identified before. Through our informants, we entered hitherto unexplored little worlds within the city; the South-of-Market district where, for old men, home is a seedy hotel, barely a step removed from the squalor and depression of a flophouse; the Telegraph Hill district —the "Little Italy" of San Francisco—where many aging Italian men gather in the sunny parks and sit for hours on the benches, idle in their retirement and wistful of their lost virility; the Mission district, where sons and daughters, siblings and friends, *compadres* and *comadres* close ranks and sustain the closing lives of Latin-Americans; the Sunset district, where familiar flats with long halls and empty bedrooms remind many old San Franciscans of their scattered children and vanished roles. And there are other areas, perhaps initially less defined in our thinking but later familiar, where the narrow base of living for the aged becomes painfully clear: the upper Geary Street hotels where life is a ten-by-twelve-foot room and a cut-rate cafeteria; or a makeshift studio, once a basement, on Ocean Avenue, where sometimes the sunlight reaches through sidewalk-level windows, where the two-block walk to "the Greek's" grocery store stretches ever longer, and where the dampness of winter is never dispelled from old house or old bones. There are also neighborhoods at the other end of the economic scale: a Pacific Heights mansion, where a retired stock broker cultivates his charities, or where an aging widow fills her days with continual, scrupulous grooming and afternoons of bridge.

A minority of the men and women we studied are still a part of the business world of San Francisco. In a Market Street building, not too far from the Tenderloin district, an ancient janitor goes home at noon to prepare lunch for his bedridden wife. Chic and vital at seventy, an indomitable Austrian refugee aids her son in his gift shop. In a Montgomery Street employment office, Miss Potter lies with moderate success about her seventy years and finds temporary stenographic employment in an insurance office. A few individuals—for the most part, men and women in their early sixties—continue their work as shopkeepers, teachers, nurses, clerks, and technicians. Among our subjects is a bank guard, a tailor, and even a longshoreman who puts in a good day's work— when he can get it. Some have part-time jobs now, often different from and more modest than their major life occupations. They are servants, handy-men, baby-sitters, messengers, and dishwashers. The majority live on retirement income, savings, Social Security, charity or a combination of these. Some live with or are supported by their children—a situation regarded as categorically undesirable by the vast majority of our subjects.

For the most part, they deplore dependency and value self-reliance and autonomy. To achieve these precious goals, they create for themselves manageable worlds within which they can perpetuate for a little while longer their meaningful patterns of life. But their degree of participation in social life often comes to depend upon proximity to stores, churches, or friends. One's own San Francisco then shrinks to the boundaries of an immediate world—one's room or apartment, one's two-or-three-block neighborhood.

SOME AGED SAN FRANCISCANS

Such is the natural setting in which the subjects of this sample find themselves, but only a small part of one's environment is topography. A much more profound influence is exerted upon our lives by our highly developed technology: for instance, it determines that Widow Jones will not raise cabbages or chickens or keep a cow in San Francisco, but that rather she will need money to purchase all her food from public markets; it also determines, to some extent, where these markets shall be located in relation to her dwelling as well as the distribution, transportation, and communication networks which make it possible for both Mrs. Jones and the foodstuffs to get to market. Then there is a social environment which will regulate her behavior: her social position will determine how much money she will have to spend at the market, whether or not she will have others to assist her with certain tasks, what her living arrangements will be, and the quality of housing, clothing, food, medical care, ceremonial life, and recreation she will have access to.

But even these considerations fall short of circumscribing the total setting of human life. Symbolic meanings, derived from the total culture, are also a part of the environment. From the point of view of the individual, each person lives in his private world of meanings and feelings—a world, in part, fashioned by the agencies of culture available to him and, in part, constructed out of his own selection of those available resources. Put in the fullest terms, the regulation of individual behavior is a joint function of (1) environmental limitations; (2) the position of the individual within a network of social relationships; (3) culturally prescribed patterns of meanings and sentiments, and (4) the idiomatic interpretations of and responses to those patterns which grow out of specific events in the individual's unique history. It may be useful to think of this tetrad as the individual's "life space" — the behavioral environment that represents his "reality" and provides the stage for his actions.

Applying this model to our hypothetical widow, let us undertake the following exercise: if Widow Jones has no food in the house and the market is four blocks away, her behavior in resolving this problem of getting groceries will depend upon the following conditions: (1) her environmental limitations, such as whether she will have to climb a hill, whether the weather is fair or stormy, and whether transportation other than walking is available to and from the market; (2) her social relationships, such as whether she is wealthy enough to have a servant get her the food, whether she lives with others who can assume the responsibility of seeing to it that she is fed, whether she has a neighbor with whom she can exchange such services, whether she has friends or kin living in the area upon whom she can call for help; (3) her own culturally prescribed meanings and sentiments, such as whether she places her major trust in individual rather than group responsibility, what significance she attributes to physical discomfort, what contractual obligations she would be willing to incur (either in money or services) in exchange for assistance, what culturally defined exemptions from individual responsibility she will permit herself to assume (e.g., accepting the "sick role" or old-age status) ; and finally, (4) such individual factors as the state of her health, her stamina, her capacity for aggressiveness, her sensitivity to social sanctions, her anxieties concerning dependency, her convictions of her own personal worth, the felt legitimacy of her claims, and her personal skills in establishing and maintaining binding relationships with others.

Within one behavioral environment, Widow Jones *A* would simply walk down the street, buy her meat and bread, come home and eat with neither pain nor stress. Within another behavioral environment, Widow Jones *B* might be emotionally tortured for hours, caught between the twin evils of personal peril and shameful admission of incompetence. Within still a third behavioral environment, Widow Jones *C* would not even be aware of the fact that food must be purchased—this task would be someone else's responsibility; she would simply eat when food was placed before her.

With these principles in mind, we are now ready to turn a closer look into the behavioral worlds of eight subjects selected from the sample. The first four subjects have never been defined as mentally ill, but they have been so selected as to represent a continuum of socioeconomic status, from very poor to very wealthy. The fifth case is a man who, too, is mentally healthy, but he differs from those in the first group in that he is caught in a particularly stressful situation; he is dying of cancer. The last three people have been socially defined as mentally ill. They have been selected to represent three kinds of mental disorders: the first, organic brain disease (i.e., chronic and progressive senility) ; the second has functional symptoms, specifically, a severe episodic depression whose origin seems clearly related to aging problems; and finally, a man with a lifelong history of deviant behavior which first came to social attention only during his later life.

Growing Old on Skid Row

Gregory Makrinos[4] lives at the Paramount Hotel south of Market Street. It is a hotel for men only—dark, airless, and very run-down. His second-floor room is small, occupied largely by an old iron bed, a bureau, a washstand, and two straight chairs. On the wall has been thumbtacked a full-page newspaper photograph of John F. Kennedy. Under it, Mr. Makrinos had crisscrossed a tiny American flag and a plastic rose. Above the bedstead are four calendars, one with a picture of a nude and the others showing nature scenes. Under one of these, in bold black type, is MARTIN'S MEATS with the yellowed legend, 1943—OUR TENTH YEAR IN YOUR SERVICE. Beneath this, the curling pages of the

---

[4]Names of all individuals and of many specific places—hotels, clubs, business establishments—have been camouflaged in this report in order to protect the identity of members of the sample.

obsolete calendar remain apparently intact. On the single bureau is a mound of old newspapers, a glass with a spoon in it, and a small collection of medicine bottles. Tucked into the mirror-frame are several holy cards, new pennies taped on two of them. There is also a photograph of a young man with slicked black hair and a tight black suit. "That's me," Mr. Makrinos says, "when I come to this country fifty-one years ago."

Mr. Makrinos was born in Greece, but has been in the United States since he was fourteen. Though he completed high school in Greece, he was, upon his arrival in this country, put to work almost immediately as a dishwasher by his older brother, an earlier immigrant. Mr. Makrinos spent his first few years in the United States living and working in Greek colonies, first in New York, and later in North Dakota, where he was a water boy for the Great Northern Railroad. He has never learned to speak English well. In 1918, when his brother joined the Army and went to France, Mr. Makrinos came to San Francisco. "America's a great country," he says. "The best in the world. But North Dakota—that was too cold. San Francisco, I like it because I like to stay in one place. I like the climate—all the time. I'm forty-three years here; I can find the places here."

Mr. Makrinos is a slight man, greatly underweight. His clothes are very old and patched and far from clean. Somehow, however, his frailty and poise lift him above the makeshift quality of his clothing and surroundings. His face is very lined for his sixty-eight years, and his complexion yellowish, though his eyes are very fine and bright.

He has lived in the Paramount Hotel for almost fifteen years. "When I went to the hospital with a busted spleen, I guess they [the hotel management] thought I'm gonna die. Well, they give this guy my room. They was sure surprised when they see me walking back in. I got my room back. I'm a good tenant. Always ready with the money." That was seven years ago. "From that time on, I've never been real well. Always sick." Nevertheless, Mr. Makrinos continued to work with some regularity as a dishwasher until two years ago, when he was again hospitalized briefly and released. Asked if he misses work, he replies, "What to do? I'm not strong to work. But I was twenty-seven years in the union as a dishwasher. Pension's okay—I don't drink or spend money foolish."

His already limited world has now shrunk to an area that encompasses the Kentucky Bar and Grill, his usual eating place, the Greek Orthodox Church a few blocks away, and a neighboring hotel where Biff, his closest friend, lives. He makes maximum utilization of meager financial and social resources, retaining a strong sense of pride in his continuing autonomy. "I pay a fella [Biff] one dollar a day to take me up and down to the restaurant. Can't make it alone no more. The restaurant is the only place I go. No, that's not right. I'm still Greek Orthodox. I go to church— with Biff—pretty close to every Sunday."

Mr. Makrinos has friends within the hotel and "guys I know in the restaurant or on the block. They come up to see me and ask me if I want money. I say no." There is a local self-help cul- ture in this part of town. "You see a lot of boozers. Well, I'm telling you, there's lots of guys like me. I no spend one penny on booze. I have lots of appetite to eat. Everything is high. It costs me at least $2.50 a day to eat. This other guy, he lives just this side of the restaurant. He has a little kitchen. Well, if he sees something cheap at the grocery—'Come on and eat,' he says. Some- times stew. He cooks pretty good. Well, I always give him some- thing. He tells me what it costs."

How else does he spend his time? "Well, I sleep in the lobby. I talk and look at TV." The hotel man later said that Mr. Makri- nos does not usually sleep in his bed. He curls up in a corner of the lobby on an overstuffed chair at night. "But sometimes I can't sleep," he explains. "I only slept two hours last night. I ask myself, 'What you gonna do up there alone anyhow? And who's gonna know if you get sick or something...?'"

He has few complaints. "I feel stronger, better. I like to be with friends and with everybody. I say to that doctor, 'Listen, Doctor, if I stay in this hospital, I die. Already I feel dead inside.' If I'd'a stayed two more weeks, it would have been the end . . . I'm not afraid. I wasn't afraid when I came here. I'm never afraid. What was in my mind when I came to San Francisco was to work a couple of years, save money, and go back to Greece. But then I decided no. America's a great country and San Francisco is a pretty good place to live. I'm glad I stayed. I don't bother nobody. I laugh. A good life, lots of friends. Not so bad off for an old guy."

Like the majority of the old people with whom we spoke, Mr. Makrinos begins and ends his days a man alone. He never married at all, resembling in this regard one out of every five of our subjects. The situation, however, is not the same for Mr. Schwann, although—like Mr. Makrinos—his route to San Francisco was a circuitous one. Mr. Schwann was born not in the United States but in Switzerland. He is part of the minority of our sample (28 per cent) whose spouses are still alive. Actually, Mr. Schwann is a relative newly-wed, having married late in life. His home environment—his San Francisco—is a different world from the one in which Mr. Makrinos lives.

The Farmer Takes a Wife — at Sixty

Mr. Axel Schwann and his wife live in an apartment off Van Ness Avenue, one of San Francisco's main arterials, in a district of similar apartment houses between Russian Hill and the Marina district. His manner is simple and courteous and he is the soul of cleanliness and good grooming. He looks his seventy-five years but seems healthy and almost cherubic, with a slightly rotund body and round pink face.

Mrs. Schwann keeps the apartment sparkling. The furniture shines and smells faintly of furniture polish. There are wax flowers, many small pictures of Swiss scenes, and a collection of potted plants in the wide window. The curtains are white, bouffant with starch, and their chintz tie-backs match the cushions on the maple dining chairs.

Mr. Schwann takes pride in his wife's housekeeping and is delighted to be married after living as a bachelor for sixty years. Describing his earlier life, he says, "I was almost forty when I came to San Francisco. Before I had worked on a ranch in Arkansas. I like it all right. I came to this country from Switzerland when my parents died—I was fourteen. I worked hard on that ranch, but we had a pretty good life. I never thought about much of anything but farming, but I didn't like the winters there. It's very cold and windy and it snows there. I decided to come West."

Through another Swiss immigrant, Mr. Schwann found his first work in the city as a janitor. In the beginning, he did not like the city: "I was lonesome for being in the open and homesick for the country, but I thought: 'Well, I'm in it now and I'll stick to it.' I didn't get much time off in those days; there were oil burners to tend, early and late."

He met his future wife at a friend's house and, after a long and intermittent courtship, they were wed. That was fifteen years ago. Mr. Schwann is still a janitor, but gets little money for his work beyond the rent of the apartment which represents the principal part of his earnings. However, with a small income to add to their savings, the Schwanns live in moderate comfort. Mr. Schwann is pleased to be working at his age: "I do a little work around two apartment buildings, take care of their furnaces. I clean, I repair—there's always things you have to do, but that's all right. It gives me a feeling of . . . of . . . well, of taking the sameness out of the days, of having a time to work and a time when you don't."

For the Schwanns, life revolves around the immediate neighborhood: "We very seldom go out at night. Once in a while I go downtown and tend to business. We go to church on Sunday— Saint Bridget's. We know the priest. And each year we try to make a little trip of a week or so. We went with some friends who have a car to Washington and Oregon. Once to San Diego and Palm Springs. Two years ago, we went to Wyoming on the train."

Mr. Schwann spends much of his leisure-time reading and watching television programs: "We have some programs we like to watch, and we plan our days so we can catch them. And I play cards every day a couple of hours with my wife—a Swiss game. I always like to be home at nighttime. You come out of the heat and there are the bridges wrapped up in cool fog and it's a welcoming sight. There's no place like home, and especially when you get old." Mr. Schwann then laughs, then sighs: "I got a good cook, a good housekeeper. I don't know what else to say—except that I'd like to live to be a hundred. Who knows? Maybe we both will!"

An Aging Lady of the Lamp

The world of the very old is overwhelmingly one of single people, and longlived men and women like Mrs. Sarah Bennington have to leave, with the passage of years, their shorter-lived roles behind them. Mrs. Bennington is a retired nurse and widow and her step-children live in another city. At eighty-three, she leads a very different life from the one she knew as a middle-aged matron. But her days are filled with absorbing and purposeful activities. Upon the skills, assets, and friends of the past, she has built an impressive and rewarding old age.

Mrs. Bennington is a short, rather frail-looking woman; her curly gray hair is always covered with a hair-net. Neat and feminine in appearance, she dresses attractively. "I never liked skirts and blouses even when I was young. I think a woman is prettiest in a nice dress, don't you?" She uses lipstick, rouge, and nail polish—although in a shade a little darker than is now in vogue—and rose cologne.

Her two-room apartment is light and sunny and neatly kept. It is located on the seventh floor of a charming old building on Jones Street. "I could never live here without the elevator, of course. And I do like it. I knew a number of the people who lived here before I moved in. As a matter of fact, it was two of the people on this very floor who got me in. Why, moving in was like coming home!" Her apartment has many old pictures in it, including her high school graduation picture and pictures of her parents and other relatives.

She moves about very easily but is slightly stooped. She looks to be more in her seventies than eighty-three. Her hearing is perfect, her memory seems excellent, and she wears glasses for reading but not otherwise.

Mrs. Bennington is extremely cordial. She is always eager to show off her home, dotting the conversation with references to "my roof" and "my elevator" and "my garden." Thus, she loves to go up to "her roof," taking her time to hang out her clothes and enjoy the view over the rooftops of San Francisco. She also spends some time in the little garden of the building, with its birdbath, orange geraniums, and a new pathway of white pebbles.

"I like it here," she says. "But then, you know *that,* I'm sure. So far, I'm getting along very well by being careful and not extravagant and not buying clothes every day. Beyond that, I'm simply not a worrier. I think I have a lot to be thankful for, having good health and being able to just go along and afford what I can now. I have a comfortable apartment. Plenty of heat and there's plenty of sunshine. It's not a dark apartment, and when you get along to my years, that's very important. Of course, some people, they want the moon and other things. They're never happy."

Mrs. Bennington has been in the city since she graduated from high school. "I wanted to be a nurse, so I came here to train. I liked private practice, and I stayed in it until the First World War. I enlisted as a nurse and I married a soldier I'd met overseas. I was widowed just five years later. A car accident. You never know. When World War II came along, I was retired, but I took a refresher course and got work here at the General Hospital. They were happy to have me and I enjoyed working again. I worked long enough to get Social Security.

"I guess you'd say nursing is still a big part of my life. A good part of my time goes to the nurses' association I belong to. I'm an officer. Have been for thirteen years. My duties before and after meetings are prayer, and then some of the nurses, when they become ill, I visit them or send them cheer-up cards and let them know they're not forgotten."

Mrs. Bennington has a keen sense of humor and laughs readily. She gives the impression of having an astonishing breadth and variety of social relationships which she actively keeps up. In addition to visiting many people within the building, she has two close friends on her floor. Also, "I spend one afternoon a week with a retired nurse who's lost her eyesight. I read her correspondence and answer some of her letters. She was in the service with me."

Finally, Mrs. Bennington rounds out her social life by attending public lectures at least once a month, keeping up with the children of her husband, seeing cousins, celebrating birthdays with a group of old high school classmates, visiting her fellow nurses, and generally conducting a social life that would be remarkable at almost any age. "Of course, I am careful to have enough time to take proper care of my little house here."

Mrs. Bennington is looking forward to going to an "old nurses' home" in Northern California, a home for nurses who have been in the service and for which she is eligible. When asked about the probable restriction of activities that would be involved, she concedes that she would not be able to see her friends as much, but that security is all-important at her age and "after all, you have to adjust yourself," a response she was to repeat often in our many interviews with her.

"Besides," she says, "it's a lovely place, and I'm in line for it. I'm on the waiting list, is what I mean. There are quite a few nurses there that I know . . . and I'll make new friends. It's security. If you become ill, they take care of you there. Otherwise, if you become ill now—well, I have no immediate relations. I have cousins, but you can't expect them to look after you if you become ill, so here's hoping that I will get there in time. Because it's a lovely place and it's lovely country up there too . . . . Of course, I'll make new friends. Wherever you are—you just can't sit around waiting for something to happen. Give it a little push. Doesn't do any harm."

A Benevolent Autocrat

Few of our subjects are as affluent as Mr. Phillip Knight. Wealth has shaped the character of his world just as distinctively as poverty has molded the pattern of Mr. Makrinos' life. The majority of our subjects lie somewhere in between these extremes. Certainly, we must share in Mr. Knight's assessment of his own position as "scarcely representative of the bulk of San Francisco's old people."

Mr. Knight's residence is in an upper-class neighborhood. It is a very pleasant home of brick, beautifully landscaped with a front and rear garden and the whole encircled with an ivy-covered stone wall. The house itself sits on the crest of a knoll which slopes away to a spectacular view of the bay and the Golden Gate Bridge. Mr. Knight's first-floor study is at the back of the house and is designed with floor-length windows to take advantage of this view.

"There were leaded windows and window-seats when I bought the place," Mr. Knight explains. "With the ivy and all—effectively British, I suppose, but cluttered—and you couldn't see a thing but the glossy reflection of the panes. Had it redone, first thing."

The study itself is quite cluttered, especially the desk, but perfectly pleasant, with a number of books and expensive furnishings. On two walls are several brightly matted and framed watercolors. The room looks well used.

Mr. Knight feels that his home is in one of the most expensive neighborhoods, if not *the* most expensive, in San Francisco. As he puts it: "To be fair, I think I can truthfully say I live on the fringe of the most expensive few blocks in the city—if not in the entire country."

When he speaks of himself and his way of life, Mr. Knight chooses his words with precision and pride, giving his speech a somewhat stilted quality. "People ask why I stay here alone. My doctor particularly would like me to move into the club or into an apartment. He sent me one of those advertisements for those new condominiums going up at Aquatic Park. Well, I tell them I have lived this way for a very long while and I like it and I do not see the logic of their arguments. My wife is gone, yes, but I made that adjustment fifteen years ago. And, of course, I am not exactly alone. My younger boy is in graduate work at Stanford and he gets home about two weekends a month, and we spend most of the summers together. And I have Martha and her husband [the servants]—it was she who let you in." How long has he maintained these domestics? "Well, they have been with me for years, and they know my ways and take care of things with little need for me to become much involved, although I keep my hand in. You know, you can't let a home—or a business, for that matter—run itself. They'll go to pieces eventually, even with the best staff. And that's what I've always tried to do, at home or work: get the best and guide them with a loose rein."

Mr. Knight dresses elegantly. During this visit, he is wearing a gray suit and vest and a slender, dark-red tie with a tiny pearl stick-pin. His moustache and hair are white, copious, and artfully but conservatively trimmed. Under the desk, his feet are placed precisely, heel by heel, toe by toe. His small-looking black shoes shine.

"When I have a good bit of work piled up, I like to put on a smoking jacket and spend most of the day right here," he explains. "Martha brings a tray for lunch. I used to have my desk facing the windows, but I found myself watching the ships and the gulls too much, so I turned the blamed thing around. Now, when I get all fatigued, I just swing around and look at the view and, in ten minutes, it's as though I'd just had a nap."

In discussing his present life, Mr. Knight responds somewhat impatiently to a question asking if there were anything he would like to do but could not: "What *can* you do when you are seventy-five, except keep in good health? I'm active mentally. I continue to contribute what I can to the shipping firm with which I've long been associated. But largely that's a matter of a few meetings a month and a lot of telephoning between. I don't go in to the office any more. Haven't for ten years."

But what about those activities outside of work? "I find it hard to separate fun and work actually, I guess. I do charitable work and enjoy it, but I work rather seriously at it when the situation calls for it. It's my way . . . . I have dinner parties. I go to them and I give them in return. I take people out to dinner. I go to the theater and the opera."

Any involvement at all in the neighborhood? "I know everyone in the neighborhood. Of course, our family is one of the 'Old Guard' hereabouts. They're not the same people I used to know. Some died. Some moved away—though I never knew any who were glad to . . . . Now there is a fine crowd of younger people. They give many neighborhood parties here." Mr. Knight then proceeds to render quite a scrupulous inventory of the people in his neighborhood, citing length of residence and profession or occupation for each.

Mr. Knight describes himself as "the average run," but feels that with age he has become "wiser, more tolerant and patient, more easy-going." However, Mr. Knight will elaborate no further on this theme of change because he categorically denies all notions of development, stages, or change. He considers his stubbornness to be his greatest weakness: "I am stubborn toward radical change, physical change, change of any kind." This resistance is equally evident in his flat refusal to discuss anything relating to personal, intimate relationships. In his austere isolation from any warm contact with others, he disclaims ever having had a friend: "I have no friends—just associates. I like people but I don't expect anything of them, nor should they expect anything of me. I only maintain a friendship when it's convenient all around." In fact, his relationship with his gardener "is about as close as [he] will ever get to anybody." He can hardly see what good a man of his station in life could do in responding to questionnaires on old age. Consequently, Mr. Knight advises us to interview people less successful than he, for their problems will have greater relevance to the world. As he succinctly puts it: "My problems are scarcely theirs, and vice versa."

A Dying Philosopher

Mr. Samuel Wheeler manages on an income of less than $2000 yearly; however, he is resourceful and largely content with his way of life. One cannot help but highly respect his sense of humor, for—like so many old people—Mr. Wheeler lives intimately with disease. He will die of cancer very soon, and he knows it. Yet he seldom refers to his sickness when he discusses his present way of life.

"I'm not one of the big pushers that's making the world go round," he says. "I did some bumming around in the Thirties: rode the rails, saw the country, got by like a lot of people were doing in those days. But when I got to San Francisco, it didn't take long before I knew it was the place for me. I knew then I had found the spot where I wanted to spend the rest of my days, and it seems as though I will."

Mr. Wheeler considers work the high point of his life: "I talk about bumming, but I never made a career of it. I was a newspaper man and I enjoyed my work and lived it and it filled my life for more than twenty years. Oh, I married—a girl I had known since we were kids, but it only lasted two years. No, I've enjoyed my life. I've been very fortunate. Never been sick and never had a physical until last August when they found I had cancer."

Mr. Wheeler is seventy-nine, but he looks older. He walks with a shuffle and is quite emaciated. His hands shake and he has difficulty with his hearing. He usually dresses in an old blue suit, the trousers of which need mending. Occasionally, he tends to ramble off from the topic in philosophic speculation—a tendency he is aware of.

His basement apartment in the Mission district can be reached only by going through the basement of the apartment to the rear. It is somewhat dirty and the paint is peeling off the walls. When the heat goes on, there is a thunderous clanking and a kind of shudder goes through the apartment. Mr. Wheeler takes no notice of this, perhaps because of his hearing defect. In spite of these disadvantages, the apartment has enormous windows which look out on a lovely garden in back. Mr. Wheeler works in the garden and keeps it up, speaking of it as "my garden." He also has plants inside the apartment.

The furnishings are old: a leather couch, once brown, now rubbed nearly white along the seat cushion and in the center of the back; two kitchen chairs painted turquoise to match the hand-painted door and the paneling around the kitchen table. Across from the couch is a built-in unit of shelves which contains many tools of different kinds, primarily hammers. Wedged in between the door and a desk is a narrow iron bed. On the desk are sharpened pencils neatly lined up and quite a number of books, including many world almanacs. There are three working clocks in the room.

One of Mr. Wheeler's hobbies is repairing clocks: "Sometimes I buy an old alarm clock for a quarter, one that isn't supposed to be repairable, and I have a go at making it work. I put these shelves in the room. Actually, I've learned to do quite a few things for myself; part of it is a matter of economy, part of it is having something to do and the pleasure of accomplishment. That's not always easy to come by, when you've left your life's work and feel out of things. I do my own shoe repairing. I put soles, heels, and patches on. I do my own barber work—cut my own hair. Sometimes when the toilet gets broken, I fix that. I connected the stove in my little kitchen and built a small counter alongside the little sink that was in it, so I've got a good little drainboard now."

Mr. Wheeler's closest friend is Mr. Davis, the manager of the apartment building in which he lives: "I met him at the Senior Citizens' Center at Aquatic Park. I got to be well acquainted with Henry and his wife. They lived down on Polk Street and we used to visit quite a bit. I used to be very busy. Enjoyed it." Since his illness Mr. Wheeler has restricted some of his activities: "I dropped out of the Senior Citizens' Center. After my check-up, I dropped quite a few activities. I dropped the Crystal Dancing Club. I used to drop down there once or twice a month to see my friends. When you're sentenced to cross the 'Great Divide,' you better leave such things alone. Actually, I guess I would go to the Crystal Club about six times a month. I looked forward to it."

He speaks little of his physical condition: "What difference does it make—a man my age? I have the days that are left, in the health I have left."

Mr. Wheeler has a number of friends, mostly men of his own age: "We don't do much real entertaining. It's difficult for one reason or another for everyone to be at the same place at the same time, and it costs—even for the simplest things. You associate with others whose thoughts run along the same line you do. Sometimes we talk of the past, but, for the most part, it's the chance for an exchange of views about life, the world, ourselves as much as anything, I suppose.

"I used to go out around and visit the poor devils who couldn't get out a lot. A friend of mine came to see me this morning—a visitor. He wanted me to go out and sit in the sun with him—go out to rest. I visit with him about once a week. I have two friends who live nearby, very close. They come up and sit in my place every night after nine o'clock, when the newspaper comes out. One is a linotyper, the other a retired newspaperman too.

"Once in a while, not very often, I used to go to the park. Like I said, I'm not much of a hand for big crowds. But you can find anything you want down in the park—watch the birds, the people coming and going, think, relax, sleep sometimes, and there is always someone to strike up a conversation. Sometimes you keep it going, sometimes not. I used to get a kick out of watching the others. The benches get their little cliques and people protect their special spots—in the sun or in the shade, good spots out of the wind. You see the same old-timers, although I wasn't there often enough myself, but the faces become quickly familiar."

His day is minimally routinized: "For the past six or eight months particularly, I have pretty much let the spirit move me. I get up at ten o'clock, have breakfast, and then don't eat again until five o'clock in the evening. That's a pretty big meal usually. I think when you reach an age like me, the best thing is to take things as they come and not worry. I eat well and I sleep well. My recreation is reading—history, biography, and travel. No novels. Especially history."

Mr. Wheeler finds San Francisco an expensive place to live, now that he is old and his income reduced: "I like it, but it's not a poor man's town, and, lately, its character seems to be changing . . . . Oh well, I won't worry about it. I'll just enjoy it while it lasts."

There is trial and sickness in Mr. Wheeler's life, but it is not an unhappy one; he is occupied with the business of living, not of dying. Above all, pride in his own ability to cope with his destiny— however dire—gives purpose to his daily life as well as to his dwindling tomorrows.

* * *

In the following pages are descriptions of three people who have been hospitalized for mental illness in old age: Miss Christianson who now lives in a public home for the aged; Mrs. Powers who was discharged from the hospital into the care of her husband; and, finally, the exceptional and eccentric Mr. Spenser who was released to resume his own precarious but not unrewarding existence in the open community.

Citizen of the Past

Miriam Christianson's own words provide a window into her world at the county home for the aged. A rather thin, slightly bent woman who looks her mid-seventies, Miss Christianson is one of the 1062 men and women who live in the county-maintained home for San Francisco's aged. During this visit with her, she is wearing a long cotton dress and a straw hat, because she is just returning from chapel. Her gait is slow and shuffling, and her face is ridged with several prominent arches of deep wrinkles, giving it a permanently startled look. The very dark red areas around her eyes are due to her frequent weeping whenever the thought of her mother or sisters crosses her mind. On the other hand, Miss Christianson is very friendly to others. She waves to everyone who goes down the hall, often receiving no response, but this does not seem to bother her. Her facial expression is exceedingly mobile, alternating between very pleasant and very sad—pleasant toward others, sad whenever she speaks of herself. When disabled men pass by, she turns to the interviewer and whispers: "War victim!" She is generally responsive to the questions put to her, although vague and somewhat discrepant in her replies. She has great difficulty recalling details. For instance, Miss Christianson retired *fifteen* years ago, not a few months as she sometimes thinks. She has been in the home now for *six* years, but, in her words, this period has been "a very short time." All the years of this woman's old age have been collapsed into one brief moment. Her distant past, though, is full and real.

"My life was an ordinary life . . . a very delightful life. My mother . . . she passed away several years ago. Oh, but she was a lovely person." Miss Christianson must again wipe her eyes with the large wrinkled handkerchief she keeps permanently wadded up in her hand.

But your *present* life, what about things *now*? "It's an ordinary life . . . a very delightful life . . . . Oh yes, I remember now. I was going to tell you something interesting—that I worked on three continents. Secretarial work, you know. I was competent. Spent two years in Cairo, one summer in Paris, and a long, long time in Italy." Further questioning reveals that after Miss Christianson left Italy (really only a two-months' stay) and until her retirement, she had worked for the federal government in Washington, D.C. and then for twenty years in San Francisco.

"I retired two years ago because my sister needed me at home. Later she died, and then I was quite alone. I wasn't enthusiastic at all about retiring. No, indeed! I enjoyed working, being around, seeing people. You know, those Parisians learn English, so I wasn't embarrassed at all."

Asked about her life in San Francisco, Miss Christianson replies, "We all came out to California. My mother and my two sisters. That was a lifetime ago. Then she died—my mother. All my sisters died too, so I'm all alone now." Tears begin to well up anew in her eyes.

But what about your current interests? "Oh, I have interests. I'm interested in many things, but no means to carry them on. I do a great deal of reading. I've read all of Dickens, Thackery, G. B. Shaw. My mother was a great reader too. She'd sit up half the night reading. I don't read much at night; don't put undue strain on my eyes, and I don't even wear spectacles anymore. And I don't care for the color of these walls."

Of her friends she says, "Not here; my friends are in various places, moved elsewhere. I've only been here a short time, so I haven't gotten acquainted, except very casually."

Asked to describe herself, she says, "A very mediocre person. I've enjoyed my travels and various and many things I've seen in the world." Plans? "No, I have no plans—quite futile at my age. Nothing to look forward to. All alone in the world now."

Someone down the halls asks another person where Ward L is. "Ward L? Ward L?" Miss Christianson asks. "Do you know who he is? I know the name so well."

Asked again about herself, she replies, "I'm sorry I wasn't successful in planning more advantageously, but I don't criticize myself. My financial status was too uncertain to plan much. My, I admire your blouse.

"Oh, yes, I had a brother." This is the first time Miss Christianson has mentioned this brother. "My brother was in the Middle West. He went to Canada and was lost. We never heard of him again. Someone probably killed him in the woods where wicked and unscrupulous men go to kill someone. Yellow paint is inappropriate in a large building," she says again, scowling at the walls. "That's what I'd call mustard yellow, and I don't care for mustard yellow."

But she continues on: "Father died when I was very young.

He didn't enter into our conversation very much. I wonder what inspired them to use that yellow paint. This is an interesting building. I'd like to know how many hundreds live here. I think it could carry upwards of a thousand people. So many interesting people here. I hope they'll soon get tired of that mustard yellow paint. I don't care to talk anymore about myself. Other people are more interesting." Then quite suddenly, again to the interviewer: "I think that is a pretty blouse. And they gave me this!" Dolefully, she points to the purple dress she is wearing. "I'm a back number. My mother and sisters are all dead now, and I had such a happy home. I'm all alone." She daubs at her eyes again. "I'm just enduring here until I can find something else. I don't like a public building. That mustard yellow really gets me."

A nurse now walks by, exchanging a friendly greeting with Miss Christianson. Miss Christianson gaily waves back. "It must be interesting to be a reporter. I never thought I had the mind for it. What paper did you say you work for?"

Finally, another nurse comes by to escort Miss Christianson back to her ward. Walking along, she becomes quite unsteady on her feet. She lunges out to catch something to hold on to, landing on the nurse's arm. The nurse asks if she is feeling dizzy. "No," she says, "my leg gave out. I broke it a few months ago, you know." The nurse smiles tolerantly—Miss Christianson had broken her foot *ten* years ago. They finally reached the locked ward. Miss Christianson turns, waves, and then says to the nurse, "That's it. Close the door. It's quieter, and I think I'll just rest until dinner time."

A Case of Failing Gentility

Mrs. Ellen Powers lives with her husband in a modest but trim five-room house in the Sunset district of the city. Her home is spotless and orderly, although filled with highly personalized antiques, mementoes, and souvenirs: a favorite rocker which had been brought around the Horn, a Delft blue pitcher salvaged from the earthquake and fire, and over the mantel a daguerrotype in a gold and velvet case of a Negro girl who had been raised by Mrs. Powers' mother. Every item is rich with personal association for Mrs. Powers, reminding her constantly of the status she admires, of the family from which she is descended, of the places she has visited, of the way of life she cherishes.

Mrs. Powers gives the impression of being tall, angular, and fragile, but her erect posture and dignified bearing remind one of a grand, old, Edwardian matron. Her narrow, pale, and finely wrinkled face reveals fully her seventy-seven years. She sits now in her treasured rocking chair and discusses her chief current problem in life: "There is only one thing I would like to have—my sight. I wouldn't have so many troubles. When you have been a reader—a reader of good books—and you have been active and used your hands, it is very difficult. My husband has to be my eyes. I carry a white cane. Getting on and off a bus—why, I don't think I've done it more than three times in the last three years." Because of this encroaching blindness, Mrs. Powers can no longer enjoy the many things which have given her life meaning and purpose: going to restaurants, to theaters, sewing in her workroom, reading new books, working for organizations, participating in political activities. There is a melancholy tone in her voice as she speaks, but also a grim determination.

Four years before this interview, Mrs. Powers had had to be admitted to the county hospital because an increasing agitation and "nervousness" had caused her to start "shaking" and to lose control over her hands. For several years, she had been receiving treatments for nausea and an "atrophic stomach." On the admitting ward, she was diagnosed as having a "psychotic depressive reaction." Ever since then, Mrs. Powers has suffered numerous other "nervous spells," physical complaints, and accidents: "I liked my doctor at Weldon but didn't like to go back because he gave me too much medicine. Gave me diarrhea and gastric upsets. About five to six months ago, they picked me up in an ambulance and rushed me to the hospital again. Probably, I was there eighteen days. I imagine I had been there a week or so when I had a terrific vomiting spell, so I was very, very sick and it weakened me so and I haven't gained since. Do you want this information? No shock treatments. What probably brought all this on is shingles. I still have them. In April, I fell on the kitchen floor and broke my nose. I had surgery in July—returned the third of July. After I was at home for about three weeks, I fell down the back steps. I cracked the bone in my foot, and then I went into a nervous collapse."

In searching for the event which might have precipitated the depression resulting in her county hospital experience, Mrs. Powers recalls a shocking recent event: "I had had poor vision in the right eye for six to seven years. Didn't know what was causing it. But, you know, you are just as well off with one eye as with two. Didn't bother me. Then, the sixteenth of August—I was in a beauty parlor. I had a kind of flashing in my eye. I went to the doctor and on the nineteenth it fully developed. It took about four months before the right eye really became poor. I have ruptured veins in the retina. Try to imagine one day in your life not to be able to do what you wanted to. I can sweep the kitchen floor, but I can't get the dirt together. All I can do now is run around with a dust cloth, get flowers out of the yard. I can cook but I haven't learned anything in three years because I can't read."

With such difficulties as these it seems incredible that Mrs. Powers is able to sustain a very active social and organizational life, but she does. She recalls her many years of service as an organizer for a local church, as president of the auxiliary of her husband's professional association, as a leading officer of the sodality connected with her husband's lodge. "I belong to the Senior Citizens now. It is a nice group, not large. When they had their first convention, I was fortunate to be one of the delegates, and my husband too. It was really very interesting and I met a lot of nice people . . . . We also belong to a social club—meets every Thursday. We've belonged for fifteen years. We have entertainment, we play cards and, at special times of the year, we have parties. It's rather a select group too. You can't get in there without an invitation."

One senses a frenetic quality to much of this behavior. Mrs. Powers seems determined to cling to life to the very end, exposing herself to as many new experiences and old pleasures as she can. She will almost never forego a trip or social gathering: "Even if I don't feel good sometimes, I go. I'm just as well going as sitting here and watching TV."

Mrs. Powers hates to be left alone in her house and whenever her husband is away for any length of time, a friend is asked to come and stay with her. There is little doubt that visitors are a frequent occurrence in the Powers household, for during each of the many interviews we have had with her, mention was made of friends who had dropped in during the week or were about to do so: a lady from Piedmont who appears unexpectedly whenever she pleases; a gentleman Mrs. Powers has known since she was five years old; a homosexual who drops in whenever his ship is in port; the sister-in-law who spends Sundays with the family. Then there was a cousin from Idaho who spent a week at the house and with her Mrs. Powers went on shopping expeditions and tours around the city. The following week, she had as house guests an ex-neighbor and her friend and together they took trips to Sonoma and Mendocino counties. Mrs. Powers admits that these visits exhaust her, but nevertheless feels it would be nice to have a larger house and be able to put up more people. She finds it extremely painful when a friend begins to drift away, and she is proud of the effort she exerts to maintain the relationship. She loves to talk about her many friends and relatives, but after one bewildering recital of the countless offspring of her relatives, she was led to reflect: "Oh, but I do feel awfully lonesome sometimes."

It is not certain how long Mrs. Powers can continue on with this merry chase of friends and experiences, but it is clear that she fully intends to try.

An Aging Eccentric

In the previous vignette, we have seen that institutionalization is, by no means, a road of no return for all men and women who suffer breakdowns in old age. In our study sample, two years after hospitalization, as many had been released to resume their lives in the community as remained in homes or hospitals. Among these is Mr. Gerald Spenser, a lifelong eccentric whose six months on the psychiatric ward prompted within him some significant concessions to the social system in terms of his style of life but not in his heroic criteria for self-evaluation.

"Today I do not feel my age, and I'm full of vim and vigor," he tells us. "I am a man of many skills and great creativity. I have been a miner, a baker, a farmer, a plumber's helper. I can do as good work today as any plumber in the city. A carpenter, a bricklayer. I'm an expert furniture refinisher—any kind of finish—original, too. I am a barber, a modeler of clay, a maker of artificial flowers from various materials—tin, wood, paper. I'm a designer of planters. I'm a sculptor, an inventor. I have new and novel ideas, using what would be debris to most people. I use these materials to create works of art. I'm a creative person. Does that sound all right?"

Despite these impressive assets, Mr. Spenser has, since his institutionalization, abandoned his various bids for public recognition to lead the life of a recluse. He is reluctant to risk the attention of an unsympathetic and unappreciative audience. He has withdrawn, however, not to the sombre quiet of a study but to a three-storied pandemonium.

An encounter with Mr. Spenser in his own quarters is an experience not likely to be forgotten. His home is an old, dilapidated, three-story affair where he resides alone. Every floor is a storehouse for his thousand and one personal creations and inventions. The bathroom serves as a workshop, his workbench consisting of a slab door placed over the bathtub. Mr. Spenser lives in the kitchen which is crammed with boxes and assorted debris. Perched and climbing over all this chaotic medley are a cat, a rabbit, a large white guinea pig, and two pigeons. In startling contrast to this is a backyard with its well-tended plants and its border of shelf upon shelf of potted cacti.

In the house next door lives Mrs. Spenser—an arrangement the Spensers have worked out for many years now because Mrs. Spenser could not stand the filth in the original home. It was she who notified the Health Department and medical authorities in 1959, an action resulting in Mr. Spenser's six-month commitment in a state mental hospital. Under these circumstances, Mr. Spenser's resentment of his wife is understandable. "I've been married for fifteen years to a woman I hadn't known very long. I didn't know that she didn't like cats when I married her. When she moved in, she started complaining about the place. I had trouble with her over the building. She complained that it was a fire hazard and that she didn't like the rats running around." The psychiatric diagnosis given to Mr. Spenser upon his admission to the hospital was cerebral arteriosclerosis and senile brain disease.

Since his release from the hospital, Mr. Spenser has tried to comply somewhat with the demands made upon him by his wife and the Health Department. He has closed his barber shop where he had entertained with his "cat circus" what few customers could tolerate the squalor. He has repaired somewhat the foundations and porch of his ramshackle home. But he still trains kittens to walk a tightrope and is still struggling with the problems of his great experiment in conditioning cats and rats to live peaceably together. And, of course, he is still working on his many inventions. "Older people are sick in their minds," he says. "They need a hobby. Every night I lie in bed and think of something new. Right now I have several inventions that I want to get patented. One of them is a little instrument. I call it a choreaphone. It's just a little wire that I bend and I get all kinds of music. I can't show it to you. I'm going to get it patented."

However, with each successive visit, Mr. Spenser has become progressively grimier and shabbier. His clothing, skin, and hair seem more and more disheveled. Living alone as he does, it is obvious that he misses meals and neglects personal hygiene. Nevertheless, he retains the comportment of a courteous British gentleman, and his enthusiasm for work is disarming. He has a fine sense of humor for everything except his projects. He is very proud of his release from the hospital, interpreting it as his personal victory over foolish psychiatrists and a vindictive wife. He has compelled society once more to validate his worth.

He regards himself as an outstanding man on the threshold of his greatest accomplishments, "really ready for any new brainstorm. Well, we have a Grandmother Moses; can't we have a Grandfather Spenser?" He points out that it was not until he was seventy that he realized his greatest ambition, namely, to be a sculptor, and that "by the time I reach eighty, I will still be in possession of my thinking capacity. It's getting better and better every day." He regards his new interests as he does his advancing age: "a new, I might say, enriched phase of my life." Although he recognizes no changes in his intellectual functioning, Mr. Spenser will admit to physical changes. Asked what he sees when he looks at himself in a mirror, he replies, "I'm seventy-five. My skin is not as plump as it used to be. Slightly neglected. Of course, this really comes from age. But this condition could be improved. In fact, a good grooming from head to foot would do wonders. A few lines in my face today. I'm just old."

PHENOMENOLOGICAL DESCRIPTIONS OF AGING PROBLEMS

The preceding vignettes have shown that the experience of growing old is by no means the same for everyone, that within a single American city aging happens with a myriad of adaptations to many particular environments. Indeed, Mr. Knight is correct. His problems are different from those of Mr. Wheeler or Mr. Spenser. Yet, we have been led to ask, are there not some problems that are commonly shared by the subjects of our sample? Since the purpose of our research has been to explain the patterns of adaptation to the experience of aging, what are those stresses or problems which aging people think they have to adapt to?

Accordingly, we asked our subjects to generalize their feelings and observations about old age in response to such questions as "What would you say are the main problems people have as they get older?" By means of a qualitative content-analysis of responses, we have been able to delineate the major problem areas of old age, as these are perceived by our subjects. Seven themes appear consistently in their attempts to characterize these difficulties:

1. A change in physical appearance
2. Partial or total retirement from active duties
3. Lower energy level
4. Greater possibility of ill health
5. Greater possibility of need for help
6. Changes in cognitive and intellectual functioning
7. Greater uncertainty about the duration of life

The order of this listing does not necessarily represent any ranking of frequency of mention, and it should be noted that, as perceptions of problems, they do not necessarily represent perceptions of one's *own* difficulties. The questions were phrased in such a way as to stimulate the generalizing faculties of the subjects. For example, when asked these questions, Mr. Spenser was eager to make a distinction between himself and old people in general ("I may be considered old, but some of my ideas are young."), but, nevertheless, he considered cognitive and intellectual change to be the major problem of old age ("It isn't age that counts, and one should not consider himself old as long as your faculties and way of thinking are reasonable."). This may be a problem for others, but not for Mr. Spenser! (In later chapters we will see how the factor of mental health or illness has conditioned these perceptions.)

These seven items, therefore, are seven areas our subjects see for potential stress. They are the major changes occurring in the aging process which offer the greatest threats to one's equilibrium. In a culture such as ours, where youthfulness and sexual attractiveness are prized, often to ridiculous extremes, those who lack these qualities will be forced to decide: accept the devalued, second-class status of the un-youthful or compensate in one way or another—as best as one can—for the missing youthful attractiveness. In much the same way, forced retirement is a problem within a culture that is primarily oriented to work and productiveness. In short, behind each of these areas of potential stress lies its antithesis, the major value of the dominant majority, the goals of those who are young, productive, energetic, healthy, independent, alert, and rich in a future.

In general, how well are older people coping with these stresses and compensating for their failure to exemplify the primary values? Quite obviously, Mr. Knight—who can well afford it—grooms himself fastidiously and dresses in elegant attire. We have also seen the other end of the spectrum in Mr. Spenser's slovenliness and almost total unconcern for such amenities as bathing. Mr. Knight still cherishes physical attractiveness as a value in life for himself and, denying stages or change as he does, regards himself as a continuing exemplar of this ideal. Mr. Spenser, on the other hand, dismisses this value as worthless in the first place, taking refuge in his "genius-in-a-garret" role. Others of our subjects can realistically admit that physical changes have taken place, but they vary in what they will conclude from this admission. Mrs. Rena Trocopian, for instance, has chosen to fight these changes with all that is in her: "I hate to look in the mirror. I see changes, and I'm not happy about it. I try to stay as I am. Nine

times out of ten I'm not pleased with myself. I'd like to stay as
young as I am . . . . I'm not like I was five years ago. Five years
ago I was like forty. Now I don't have the desire for clothing."
Others seem to acquiesce supinely to the devalued state, such as
Mrs. Amelia Harris seems to be doing: "I look like a fat old slob.
I'm just gradually getting worse. I've lost a good deal of interest
in keeping up my appearance . . . . I don't wash my face at night—
don't take my makeup off. I let it rub off on the sheets. Only one
tub a week." Still others, like Miss Mildred Barton, accept the
change and their metamorphosed selves: "No, I wouldn't want to
change anything about my appearance. I look as I am supposed
to look." Mrs. Gertrude Miller considers the change a challenge to
take extra pains to look, if not exactly youthful, at least humanly
attractive: "I think it's more important to keep up your appearance as you get older." Finally, one subject, Miss Louise Potter,
has taken such elaborate (and expensive) pains through cosmetics
to undo the workings of her seventy years that her appearance
might well be called a masquerade.

Retirement—and especially that new trend, forced retirement—
poses a problem for those who still want to (and can) work. Mr.
Edward Hopland is particularly indignant at being thrust into a
nonworker status: "We're not getting the same rights that we did
when we were younger. We don't have an equal chance with the
middle-age man to get a job or to do things. It used to be more
equal. They'd hire elderly men; now they won't. Age shouldn't
interfere with a job. Older people should be hired." Mr. Alberto
Alioto is more passive and hopeless: "When I see all those younger
men at the employment department, I can tell that an old man
like me doesn't have much of a chance." Some, as in the case of
Mr. Wheeler, recognize that their illness or disability quite naturally diminishes their effectiveness in playing out a worker role.
Such subjects as these generally settle down to less exhausting
pursuits, such as puttering in the garden, reading the books one
never had time enough for or tinkering with old clocks. Others
may turn to philanthropic activities, such as Miss Bennington and
Mr. Knight are doing. Others, like Mr. Harold Lewisohn, philosophically accept the culturally-defined category of "obsolete
man." Mr. Lewisohn prizes a robust economy and is glad to be

part of one, even if only as an observer: "Yes, the younger man takes it over. But it is a change for the better. They have different, younger views. The older person might be too conservative. I'm well satisfied with the present situation." Finally, for others, retirement is not a bane but a blessing. Mrs. Mary Kramer is an eloquent exponent of this attitude: "Getting older is getting out of pressures—you sit back. When you were working, you couldn't read, see parades. Now is the time to do all the things you wanted to do all your life. It is a luxury to get up in the morning and have a leisurely breakfast, not to have to dress or catch a street car to work. You can enjoy it. You can make plans for the day with no pressures." There is considerable evidence from the sample that retirement can be a welcomed change in one's life and that here as last is the chance to do "all the things you wanted to do all your life," but we have already seen in the case of Mr. Spenser that one can over-compensate in a veritable frenzy of projects. In this instance, we find unrealistic appraisals of one's resources, such as sheer physical strength.

Almost all the subjects recognize that old age is accompanied by a decline in energy, but, again, some will deplore this or fight it or surrender to it or wisely reorder their lives to accommodate for it. A few, like Miss Mona Bachstein, flatly deny it: "I don't act like any older people I know. I've always had lots of pep. No, I never thought about it [older people having less energy]. If we get older, we don't know about it." However, those who are willing to admit to the change take comfort in what they might perceive as the compensatory advantages of old age, such as Miss Bennington does: "You just don't think about it. As you grow older, if you have comfort, you are satisfied. You just have to accept what life is at the present time." Despite this loss in energy, Mr. Lemuel Bauer feels needed: "Some of the things I used to do I figure I'm not capable of doing now—like painting the apartment and waxing the floor, and walking long distances. I tire easier, but there are still many things I can do; I never feel that I am not needed."

The greater possibility of poor health poses a threat to older citizens of a society that honors the independent, autonomously-productive man. The advent of Medicare for older people in the

United States promises some alleviation not only to the illnesses themselves but to the many worries the old entertain over the *possibility* of suffering a chronic illness without the financial means to take care of it. Mr. Lawrence Southern articulates such worries when he states: "Upon reaching sixty-five, everyone probably worries some about becoming ill, having to go to the hospital, keeping up their savings. I have a problem trying to find medical insurance for past sixty-five. This really is a problem." Many subjects realize that old age is a time when one must take extra good care of one's body. One can fight illness by living sensibly and taking preventive measures. Mrs. Gertrude Miller stresses good eating habits: "I think all older people should be prepared. And I think you can help yourself as far as illness is concerned. There's a subject that fascinates me very much and that's nutrition. I've been studying it for eleven years. Getting proper food and preparing it well is very important. And good exercise, too; older people get too stiff and inactive." Mrs. Miller's resolution of this problem—self-help—also appears to be a way to resolve the next problem.

In a culture such as ours which glorifies the do-it-yourselfer, the lone cowboy, the maverick, and the hero-against-the-world, it is difficult to admit to realistic dependency needs without condemning oneself. Americans have some very unkind names for dependent people—moocher, sponge, leech, bum. We have been struck in our study of older people by the enormity of this problem in their lives. We shall explore it in greater detail in succeeding chapters, but we need to notice here how highly cherished the value of independence is for them. Mrs. Sarah Bennington, we have seen, has carefully planned for her eventual move to a nurses' convalescent home. "I don't feel my relatives should be responsible for me," she insists. "I want to be independent—just don't want to have to depend on anyone else." In much of the social isolation and avoidance of others which we see among the elderly, there is also the suggestion of the need to be self-reliant, of not engaging too much in public or social activities lest others foist help upon them while they still want to try "going it alone." Mrs. Ada Bevin hints at this when she says, "[The main problems people have as they get older] are—oh, they get—they think people are bothered with them, don't care to help them, so they keep to themselves. They don't go out as much as they used to." Many will do anything to avoid "going on welfare." Others support social welfare programs for the aged where the help does not smack too much of charity and where one has had a hand oneself in the assistance being offered. "Social Security is a godsend to all people," says Mrs. Gladys Dillon. "If a person works, he is entitled to something back—financially is what I mean," says Mr. Boris Mersky. Mr. Lemuel Bauer would "advise the doctors to lay off [of Medicare]. They're opposed to old people getting hospitalization. It would be a good thing." Many in our sample face their old age a little more confidently, knowing that help—if ever really needed—is more available to them today. "The position of older people has changed for the better," says Mrs. Lois Willoughby. "Older people are better taken care of than they used to be. They used to put them on the poor farms and forget about them. Today we have Social Security and welfare. Although the welfare payments are too low, we can exist where we couldn't before. The government and state are doing what they can."

Changes in cognitive and intellectual functions create problems for old people attempting to survive in a highly urbanized environment. Split-second decisions are often necessary in high-tempo traffic. Busses and trains must be caught on time. One must carry about in one's head an enormous amount of vital information: directions, names, places, numbers (zip code, telephone, Social Security, etc.), and times (due bills, appointments, hours of business, etc.). Our awareness must be sharp and our memory keen, if we are to get through the day successfully. As in the case of Miss Christianson, a significant loss in this area of function demands that society take over the responsibility for the total functioning of the individual. We have also seen how Mr. Spenser's relatively good management in this area gained him a release from society's custodial care. Often the issue of hospitalization is hinged upon this one factor alone: do enough of the mental faculties remain intact for this person to survive in a fast, complex society? Minimal loss can be compensated for; it can be reinterpreted: "But older people can do things better because they're mature thinkers," according to Mr. Elwin Ebenhauser.

Accept the change, some of these subjects seem to say, and capitalize on what remains: "If you're old, you shouldn't act like a kid . . . . I know what life is about now, what suffering is, and struggle," according to Mrs. Marta Valente. Mrs. Trocopian counsels exertion and exercise of the capabilities which have not changed: "They have to be thoughtful and use their minds. If they do not think, they get dull and their memory gets poor."

Finally, the problem of greater uncertainty about the duration of one's life forces older people to grapple with the encroaching enigma of death. Mr. Wheeler is urgently confronted with this problem, and we have seen how calmly and philosophically he is trying to come to terms with it. Mr. Spenser, so enthusiastic about the bewildering ingenuity of his own mind, is hopefully reaching out for many more years yet: "I wish I could live another twenty-five years! I could *really* do something then! My grandfather lived to be a hundred and seven." Both he and Mrs. Powers are cramming the days full, not only to live as fully as they can while yet some time remains, but somehow to make oneself more *worthy* of an extended reprieve on life. In their long inventories of projects and friendships, one cannot help but hear the whispered hope: surely Death will not take one so sincere, so hard-working, so honest, so true to the ideals of friendliness and industry. Some, like Mr. Apostolos Phidrios, can be frank about their perplexity: "I'm afraid of it because—how do I know what it's going to be?" Mr. Ronald Forest tries to avert his eyes from any long, hard look at this Gorgon's head, lest it be too paralyzing and turn him into stone, as the old stories relate: "Strange feeling that I fear death. I've just got to hang on to the idea I'll live forever [laughed]." So troublesome is the problem that it seems only a tender humor can properly appraise it: "The older people grow and the closer they get to dying, the more likely they are to take up religion. [Grinned] They get too old to sin, so they take up religion," as Mrs. Amelia Harris put it. For a small group—those who have been forced to endure prolonged physical and emotional stress—one's own death can be viewed as a welcomed release. Mr. Horace Kepler feels that the only advantage of being old "is that this life is getting close to the end." This subject even admitted to having considered suicide and said, "I'm hoping that something will happen that isn't my fault. If I weren't sure there was a God, I'd end it all."

With the approach of death, one must subdue worry and muster up one's courage to live. "I can't help but think about it sometimes," says Mrs. Edna Langtry. "But I certainly don't worry about it. I'm not much of a worrier. What good does it do? I go bake a cake instead." Mrs. Doris Tillford, a woman who successfully worked her way back from a state hospitalization, expresses much the same feeling in the way she now criticizes the friends and relatives of older people: "Don't sit them down in a corner and say, 'That's the end of it.' I think they live longer if you bring them something pretty — something you make or flowers." Mr. Harry Hokusai finds it relatively easy to muster this courage, perhaps because he values an Oriental poise and wisdom in these matters: "I'll feel sorry to be dead and lose my enjoyment and activities in this world, but I'm not afraid." Almost all who were willing to discuss this difficult question with us felt it necessary to render some formula for coping with it. Usually, this advice was phrased in a "you-must," "you-ought" fashion, almost as though these subjects were admonishing, comforting, and counselling themselves. Miss Mildred Barton, for instance, says, "Don't be too critical of the changes in life and do your share of taking part in living." Mrs. Bennington does much the same thing when she says, "It's just as well not to think about it, I think. You feel better if you just kind of forget what you did in the past and just kind of accept what is happening at the present time."

CONCLUSION

Showing the rich and wide variety of adaptations to aging has been the major purpose of this chapter. It remains for us to account for this variety and to seek out those modes or patterns of behavior which seem to provide the most successful means for coping with the major stresses of aging in contemporary American life. We have already seen how certain individuals are aided in coping adequately because of one personal advantage or another. For example, it is clear that Mrs. Bennington's lifelong nursing of others has taught her how to make practical arrangements for the time when she will no longer be able to nurse and care for herself. So, too, Mr. Knight has a definite advantage over the great majority of aging people in an affluence that permits him to maintain a staff of domestics who help him take care of himself and his property. We have also seen how certain lifelong patterns of adjustment have proven to be maladaptive in the later years. For example, Miss Christianson's long dependency upon her mother and sisters has contributed, in the end, to her undoing. Mrs. Powers' drive to be a leader and manager of others pushed her beyond the point where she can now adequately cope with the physical and mental demands of such a strenuous role.

But there are other factors which determine how well or poorly an individual will confront the central problems of aging. Certain cross-cultural expectations, transplanted into American urban life, have proven to be inappropriate and stress-provoking for some of the foreign-born people in our sample. In this regard, one thinks immediately of Mr. Spenser who, born in Sussex, England, now finds his English eccentricity poorly tolerated in an American milieu. The reader will meet others, such as Mrs. Trocopian who has long nurtured in her heart a dream for her old age, which she has carried with her from Armenia, but which now proves to be the major burden of her life. A study of the personal and social factors most relevant to a good or poor adaptation in old age is the major work of this volume, but before this can be undertaken, there yet remains one final introductory task— an analytic description of the study sample.

Chapter III

HISTORY AND CHARACTERISTICS OF THE SAMPLE

INTRODUCTION

AMONG THE MANY KINDS OF readers of a scientific work, there are always those who do not particularly care to know how an author went about collecting his data or what the demographic description of his sample might be. Such readers approach a scientific work with the primary purpose of learning whatever useful or interesting ideas the author might have or whatever facts, previously unknown to them, he might have uncovered. Such readers, with clear conscience, may bypass this chapter and proceed directly to the findings we report in the rest of this book. Other readers—especially our professional colleagues—may be interested in knowing how this study was designed in order that they might better evaluate our conclusions. This chapter, therefore, has been written for them.

The subjects we have already introduced and those with whom we shall be concerned throughout this volume are the survivors of a group of 1,134 old people, selected by the Langley Porter Institute Studies of Aging in 1959 for extensive longitudinal study. The original sample contained mentally ill as well as "normal" old people. Briefly, the original "normal" group—or, as we shall call it the "baseline community sample"—was a probability sample from eighteen census tracts in San Francisco. We selected 600 people sixty years of age and over, whom we stratified by age, sex, and social living arrangements, because these three characteristics have been shown to have considerable bearing on the prevalence and type of mental illnesses found among the aged.[1] The original "baseline mentally-ill sample" consists of persons, sixty years of age and over, who were admitted to San Francisco General Hos-

---

[1] For a more detailed description of the community sample, see Lowenthal, Berkman, and Associates (1966). For a further discussion of the stratifying variables used in selecting our community subjects, the reader is referred to Lowenthal (1963). See also Simon and Neal (1963).

pital's psychiatric screening wards during the calendar year, 1959. This method of sampling provided a pool of 774 elderly persons, a number which was reduced by further screening criteria. First, in order to maximize *age-linked* problems rather than lifelong ones, all persons who had had a psychiatric admission or a history of arrests prior to age sixty were excluded. Patients who had not been residents of the county for at least one year were also excluded on the grounds that they might be discharged to institutions in another county or state and therefore be difficult to follow up. After these exclusions, there remained 534 men and women in this mentally-ill sample.[2]

Most of the perceptual and attitudinal data that form the basis for this book were collected at the end of the second year of the study. By this time, there had been two rounds of interviewing (one at the inception of the project—the baseline—and the first follow-up of a year later). There remained 435 members of the two larger or parent samples (the community and hospital baseline samples) who were still alive, could be located for interviewing and were willing and able to give coherent replies to questions about themselves, their past and present lives, and their attitudes towards aging. These 435 people have become the *study sample* of the present research.

THE STUDY SAMPLE

Within this study sample are 264 nonhospitalized, community subjects. The remainder are the surviving members of the originally hospitalized group. By the time of the second follow-up, eighty-one were still in state psychiatric hospitals, and ninety had been discharged back to the community or to nonpsychiatric institutions.

The study sample includes 206 men and 229 women. While they range in age from sixty-two to ninety-four, nearly half of them (48 per cent) are under seventy. Another one-third are between seventy and seventy-nine; and the remaining 18 per cent are eighty or older.

---

[2] A volume describing the hospital-sample subjects and their mental and physical illnesses (Simon, Lowenthal, and Epstein, publication pending) is in preparation and publication is planned for the forthcoming year (working title: *Crisis and Intervention*).

About a third of these subjects were born outside the United States, predominantly in Europe. Another third, although native-born, are of foreign parentage. The educational level[3] for half of the sample is eighth grade or lower; about one-third of the subjects have had some high school education, and about one in six have had one or more years of college training. White-collar and blue-collar workers are represented equally—about 35 per cent of the sample falls into each of these categories. The remainder are housewives with no other major long-term occupation. It should be noted that this group of housewives represents only half of the women in the sample; 50 per cent of the women had spent the greater part of their adult lives employed outside the home.

In general, these aged people are poor;[4] half of them have a per capita income of less than $2,000 a year, and one-fifth of these receive less than $1,000 annually. Only 13 per cent of the sample report an income of $2,000-$3,000 a year, and another 13 per cent report incomes of $3,000-$5,000. However, there is a significant "wealthy" minority (20 per cent) whose yearly income is over $5,000. Only a fifth of the sample are homeowners; most are renters. Since so many within the sample have so little money,

---

[3]The educational and occupational statuses of the study sample were evaluated as of their middle-adult years, as measured by the Index of Social Position—a two-factor index developed by Hollingshead (1957). This index is composed of a seven-point education scale and a seven-point main-gainful-occupation scale. The education score is given a factor-weight of 4, and the occupation score may combine in various ways to produce a high or a low Index of Social Position (ISP) score. For instance, a high ISP score will usually mean high school or college education and an executive, managerial, or professional type of occupation; a low ISP score will usually mean less than a high school education and a skilled or un-skilled manual-type of occupation. A managerial occupation, however, may off-set a grade-school education to produce a relatively high score. Hollingshead and Redlich (1958) describe a similar three-factor index in the appendix to their book, *Social Class and Mental Illness*.

[4]An index designed to measure socioeconomic status at the time of interview has been described in Lowenthal (1964a, p. 5). Briefly, the components of this index are rent paid per month, total annual income, and the Tryon Index (Tryon, 1955) which yields a score assigned to the census tract in which the individual resides. An individual's socioeconomic status score depends on his position with respect to the sample median on each of the three variables. Scores range from zero (low) to three (high).

they tend to live in cheaper quarters in poor neighborhoods. Over a half pay less than $75 a month in rent, and more than a fourth pay less than $40 a month.

Most frequently, the subjects in this sample are widowed (36 per cent), although nearly as many are presently married (28 per cent). Of those who have been married at some time, almost half now have children living in the San Francisco Bay Area.

MENTAL HEALTH AND ILLNESS IN THE STUDY SAMPLE

Since the major goal of our study is to explore patterns of reaction to the stresses of old age, we must here specify the composition of the sample in terms of mental health and illness. As has been stated, our criterion of mental status is a straightforward one: the presence or absence of a history of admission to a psychiatric hospital for the first time after the age of sixty.[5] However, since our study sample is a group selected two years after the initial sample selection, we have been serendipitously provided with an intermediate group—those who were fortunate enough to be discharged from psychiatric institutions within this two-year period. Within the interim, these men and women were released to their homes or sent to private institutional care. This group provides us with an unusual opportunity to study patterns of adaptation in a continuum.

In short, the study sample is divided into three major groups differing in mental status:

(1) 264 *community* subjects with no history of a psychiatric hospitalization after the age of sixty;[6]

---

[5]This social definition of mental health *versus* mental illness has not been used in other reports from the Langley Porter Studies in Aging. In Lowenthal, Berkman, and Associates (1966), for example, it is reported that when psychiatric judgments were used to evaluate the mental condition of community subjects, 14 per cent were rated as psychiatrically impaired and in need of professional care.

[6]Among the members of the original baseline community sample, there were a few individuals who had a history of psychiatric hospitalization in later life, but, at the time of baseline, they were living in the community. In addition, one community subject had had to be psychiatrically hospitalized shortly after the community locating survey and before the baseline interview. Five such community subjects who survived to the time of the second-year follow-up were excluded from this study sample in order to maximize the group's mental-health status.

(2) An intermediate group of ninety *discharged hospital* subjects with a history of psychiatric hospitalization after, but not before, the age of sixty, and now residing in the community; and

(3) A mentally-ill group of eighty-one *inpatients* who show no history of a psychiatric hospitalization prior to age sixty, but who were confined to a psychiatric facility at the time of the attitudinal interview.

On the basis of these subgroups, the attitudes, morale, and life-views of *community* subjects are regarded as representative of older, mentally-well residents of urban San Francisco and the *inpatients* of psychiatric institutions as representative of the mentally-disturbed older people of the city. Also, we expect the *discharged* patients to reflect attitudes and values intermediate between those of the mentally-well community group and those of the mentally-ill inpatient subgroup. For some analytical purposes—particularly where we want to apply fullest weight to our dichotomy of mental health as against mental illness within the two-year period—we present tables combining subgroups (2) and (3). Appendix A describes these three major groups in further detail.

In addition to these major divisions of the study sample, we have dichotomized each of the three into those with good and those with impaired physical health, yielding six subgroups which will be used in our analyses wherever the issue of physical health is relevant. The characteristics of all the physically unimpaired and physically impaired, and the procedures used in establishing all six of the subgroups are also described in Appendix A.

As the tables in this volume will clearly indicate, community and hospitalized subjects are analyzed as discrete subgroups for the purposes of comparison and contrast. In the qualitative analysis of the case materials, both kinds of subjects are often quoted within the one context, but, wherever this occurs either the context or an (HS) or (CS) after the subject's name will clearly distinguish for the reader the members of the hospital or community samples. Nowhere do we intend to deal with these two samples as a single homogeneous group.

THE STUDY AND PARENT SAMPLES COMPARED

Since we are dealing here with a 'survivor sample," it can be legitimately asked: Has not attrition of subjects during the two years selected out the healthiest and most fortunate in such numbers as to skew whatever differences are found to exist between the mentally healthy and the mentally disturbed? Will not intervening deaths, refusals, and moves from the area inordinately maximize (or minimize) the differences that existed most clearly at the time of the initial sampling? In order to answer this, we have intensively examined how representative the 435 men and women of the study sample are of the original 1,134 men and women drawn into our purview in 1959. In brief, the old, community-resident San Franciscans with whom we spoke regarding their attitudes towards age are quite representative of the larger baseline community sample from which they were drawn. In the area of psychological function—one of the major dimensions of comparison in this volume—community survivors are as well off as the baseline sample. In other ways, too, the survivors differ but slightly from the total group. They are a little healthier physically; they are a little better off financially, and a few more of them are married. None of these differences, however, is statistically significant. We conclude that the study sample living in the *community* is at least as healthy mentally as the larger parent sample.

Our comparison group of elderly men and women with a history of psychiatric illness linked with old age differs in two respects from the hospital baseline sample to which they belonged at the time of their institutionalization in San Francisco. Those who survived are younger and healthier than the total parent sample. In terms of all other characteristics we have examined, however, they are quite representative of the original hospital sample. Our conclusion, then, is that the *hospital study group* is no worse off than the hospital baseline sample (and, in fact, is better off in these two mentioned areas) .

To return to the question we asked at the beginning of this topic: Has attrition of subjects during the two years since the original sample was selected served to magnify the differences that existed at that time between the mentally healthy and the mentally ill? We can now state with reasonable certainty that no such exaggeration exists. Differences in attitudes found between the community and hospital study samples, therefore, can be taken as *minimal* differences between the perspectives of the mentally-well aged as compared with the mentally-ill aged. Had we been able to collect these data from the two original baseline samples, we would no doubt have encountered even greater discrepancies. In other words, we have found no intervening factors related to survival in either sample which would tend to exaggerate differences over those prevailing in the total baseline sample and which would be distortive of the mentally-well/mentally-ill dichotomy we will be examining in terms of aging adaptation.

METHODOLOGY

Three major bodies of data have supplied the materials of this report. Two of these are *quantitative* in nature and were developed from the baseline and follow-up interviews. In the first place, we have utilized background information on each subject in the form of coded responses to questionnaire items. These have provided us with information on age, income, family structure, employment status, living arrangements, education, place of birth, and other such factual matters. A second group of quantitative variables are scales, indices, ratings, and scores derived from the examiner's observations of the subject, the subject's performance on certain tests and measurements, or his responses to a set of questions designed to measure some aspect of his cognitive, perceptual, or emotional life. These data have provided us with such measures as level of self-evaluation, the nature of time orientation, physical and psychological disability ratings, and morale cluster scores. These first two bodies of data are available for the total study sample of 435 older persons and provide the basis for most of the tabulations presented in this report.[7] For some of these

---

[7]Except for the development of the attitudinal measures, we ourselves did very little of the work involved in deriving quantitative measures of such characteristics as socioeconomic status, role index, or social interaction score. Our sociologist colleagues on the program, with the aid of a very able staff of research assistants, provided us with these measures. We have attempted to acknowledge this contribution by referring to other project publications in which the measures are more fully described.

measures we have relied on a technique known as *quantified content analysis*. The data on self-image and perceptions of stress, in particular, have been analyzed by the authors in this way. A full description of this procedure is presented by Lowenthal (1964a, pp. 15-21).

The third type of information we have used is that provided by what we call *the intensive study*. About three years after the baseline interviewing, a subsample of both community and hospital subjects was selected to provide us with more detailed attitudinal and life-history information than was available for the larger sample. This subsample includes forty people from the original community sample and thirty-nine from the hospital group—a total of seventy-nine intensively-interviewed subjects. (Copies of this interview guide are available upon request.) In studying these materials, we have employed yet another technique known as *qualitative content analysis*. This technique can be briefly described as follows.

Qualitative content analysis attempts to develop a taxonomy which will comprehensively and systematically describe—at a somewhat higher order of conceptualization than is possible with quantified content analysis—a large and diverse body of narrative or descriptive data. Verbatim transcriptions of subjects' responses are read through and examined for major themes which recur with some frequency. Usually notes are made as the analysis proceeds, indicating the range of elements being placed under a single category and their relative frequency of mention in the sample. When preliminary categorization has been completed for the sample, there will almost invariably remain a body of unclassified residual data. Some of this may be discarded at this stage as being irrelevant to the topic under investigation. Other statements may be placed in a miscellaneous category of minor themes occurring too infrequently to warrant inclusion in the taxonomy. After having prepared a list of preliminary categories, these data are next examined for possible integrating concepts which would permit a secondary grouping into a smaller number of somewhat broader categories. The various residual items in the "miscellaneous" category are usually examined at that time to determine if these more broadly defined categories will now permit inclusion of some of the previously unclassified data. Eventually, one has developed a taxonomic system which lends itself to several types of analyses. If similar kinds of data are available for a larger sample, for instance, one may want to use the taxonomy as a set of codes for a study of the distribution of these patterns and their relationship to other variables. (This application is exactly that made in the case of the *quantified* content analysis, as mentioned above.) In other cases, the investigator may be interested in the kinds of emphases given to a particular category or set of categories by certain people in the sample and not by others. In this work, we have often used content analysis in this way—specifically to differentiate patterns characteristic of mentally-ill subjects from those more characteristic of mentally-healthy ones. In some cases, the observed differences will be simply matters of frequency; in other cases, the differences will be in qualities rather than quantities of the elements falling in a particular category.

Within Chapter VI of this report, an example of *quantified* content analysis is found in the section on time-orientation; an example of a study of comparative frequencies of a common set of content categories among differing groups of subjects is found in the analysis of sources of high and low morale; and a presentation of *qualitative* differences within each category of a set is presented in the discussion of values underlying self-esteem in the aged. Direct quotes from the interviews have been used freely throughout the book to provide illustrative, anecdotal material.

As can be inferred from the foregoing explanations, this approach to the collection of data is somewhat different from that ordinarily employed by anthropologists. For instance, no participant observation was included in our methodology, and there was little information obtained from people other than the subjects employed in this study. Since this is a study of the perceptual world of the aged, we have, in short, largely confined our investigations here to reports given by the aged subjects themselves. Our data, therefore, are *their* perceptions, beliefs, attitudes, and feelings, as *they* expressed them to us, in *their* own words.

Chapter IV

THE PERSONAL SYSTEM: SOME MEASURES OF PERSONAL FUNCTION AMONG THE AGED

Although any particular individual is rarely of great importance to the survival and functioning of the society to which he belongs or the culture in which he participates, the individual, his needs and potentialities, lies at the foundation of all social and cultural phenomena. Societies are organized groups of individuals, and cultures are, in the last analysis, nothing more than the organized repetitive responses of a society's members.
—RALPH LINTON,
The Cultural Background of Personality (1945), p. 5

INTRODUCTION

No DOUBT, one of the reasons for the many differing kinds of aging experience we observe in our culture is the advent of uniquely *personal* thoughts and feelings which flood into consciousness at this time. In this respect, life-after-sixty shares with adolescence an intensification of the intimate and self-reflexive. At both times of life, the question, Who am I? assumes poignant relevance. Both are times of mental and physical metamorphosis, as both adolescent and elder become absorbed in the workings of their own bodies and minds, watching these internal changes with a mingling of wonder and dismay. Then, too, a kind of loneliness or increasing sense of privacy grows as a natural consequence from this self-absorption. Both growing and aging individuals seem to experience these two very important phases of the maturation process with a more profound than usual sense of personal distinctiveness, one's unique difference from others. As one of our subjects has wisely described this process, incorporating into his remark both trends of increasing self-absorption and sharper self-articulation: "The older I get, the more I grow into myself."

Old age in our society is a life-period when an inner equilibrium or sense of well-being is often very difficult to maintain. For example, fluctuations in physical functioning, often quite sud-

den or rapid at this time, can produce alarm or discouragement.
Older people also run a great risk in unexpectedly losing a spouse,
a friend, or a sustaining relative. We shall see in Chapter VII how
difficult it very often is to replace these losses and regain equilibrium.

In this chapter we shall look into the personal system[1] of our
aging subjects and assess, if we can, the nature of the life lived in
that privacy. But there is a superabundance of inner states of
being—moods, lifelong strivings, intellectual capacities—that can
be profitably explored in relation to aging. One recent study of
personality in later life (Reichard *et al.*, 1962) has measured 115
different personality characteristics thought to be related in some
way to the aging process. As anthropologists, however, we have
chosen not to study personality organization in any comprehensive sense, but rather to examine individual adaptation (equilibrium) and the factors most crucial to its maintenance. In consequence, our view here of the individual is somewhat less elaborate than one might find in a study of personality psychology.

In short, our focus here will be on global *perceptions* of the
self and whatever generalized *feelings* our subjects entertain about
themselves and the world at large. To what degree do our subjects
sense their individual worth at this time of change and potential
threat to the ego? Is there evidence that growing old, in itself,
erodes the concept of one's intrinsic value or one's ability to remain buoyant in life circumstances? We have derived both of
these measures of personal function from the set of attitudes our
subjects have expressed about themselves. In regard to self-evaluation, we ask whether the elderly person judges himself in positive
or negative terms. Our second measure, morale, deals with the
affective dimension of experience and is somewhat independent

---

[1]It should be noted that, although we did not begin this research on the phenomenology of aging with any particular theoretical stance in mind, the model which
we did develop during the analysis is somewhat suggestive of the theory of action
formulated by Parsons and his associates (Parsons and Shils, 1952). Note, however,
that our use of the term "personal system" differs from the usual psychological
formulation of "personality system" in that we are dealing primarily with expressed attitudes rather than with such inferred psychodynamic formulations as
basic needs, instinctual strivings, subconscious symbolism, or individual defense
mechanisms.

of judgments regarding one's own intrinsic worth. In simpler terms, self-evaluation tells us whether the subject thinks he is good or bad, valuable or worthless; morale tells us whether or not he is happy with his way of life. Behind both of these measures is the theoretical conception of mental health as essentially pivoted upon self-esteem (Becker, 1962).[2]

SELF-EVALUATION

The major hypothesis underlying the succeeding discussion is that a positive self-appraisal is essential to good adaptation to aging, and that, during the process of aging, the criteria for evaluating oneself as a worthy individual must, of necessity, be modified in keeping with one's changing interests, roles, and capabilities. In this section we will describe how a sample of aged persons view themselves, and whether or not mental and physical problems are related to a weakened self-image in the later years of life. We will also describe the influence of sex, advancing age, and other personal characteristics upon their self-perceptions.

Information on self-image was obtained from the 435 members of the study sample during the course of a general social interview. Each person was asked two questions about his self-image. First: "How would you describe yourself—that is, as a person? What sort of person would you say you are?" And second: "How would you describe yourself when you were about fifty—

---

[2]Becker (1962) states that "[t]he basic predicate for human action is a qualitative feeling of self-value . . . . This whole learning process [in human development] is a training in switching modes of maintaining self-esteem . . . . [T]he individual learns to constitute himself, symbolically, an object of primary value in a meaningful world. There is a further crucial fact, attendant upon this discovery, which it would be impossible to overstress; namely, that the vital sentiment of self-value is derived from symbols. The self-system is a locus composed of internalized social rules of behavior . . . . [One must accent] the purely social creation of the symbolic self, rather than the social frustration of a biological self" (pp. 162-163). Becker relates cultural considerations to self-esteem when he states: "[T]he function of culture is to make continued self-esteem possible. The main task of culture, in other words, is to provide the individual with the conviction that he is an object of primary value in a world of meaningful action . . . . [W]hen culture falls down on its job . . . life grinds to a halt . . . . [T]he depressed patient, too, threatens us by his loss of interest in life. The possibility of loss of zestful commitment to the cultural goals makes us defensively self-righteous about our fragile fiction. With pride we electroshock the depressed back into our world" (pp. 81-83).

the kind of person you were then?" Only general probes such as: "Can you think of anything else?" were used during this portion of the interview. Each subject was allowed to structure his answers as he saw fit, and his responses were recorded verbatim. The responses were rated on the positive-negative dimension of self-image, which we here call *self-evaluation*.

In addition to the survey questionnaire material described above, much more detailed self-image data were obtained from the intensively-studied subsample of seventy-nine subjects. In these intensive interviews, the subjects were asked during the life-review to tell us what they were like when they were children, teenagers, young adults, and middle-aged people, as well as what they are like at the present time. In recounting each period of his life, the subject was asked: "How would you describe yourself at that period? How do you think other people would have described you? What did they think about you? Why was that, do you suppose?" In the second phase of the intensive interview in which the subject was asked to focus on changes, discontinuities, and continuities throughout his life span, the respondent was again asked to describe himself in terms of his strong points and his weaknesses at various stages of his life.

Furthermore, the hospitalized and discharged patients in the intensive interview sample were asked to participate in a mirror experiment. Each subject was asked what he saw when he looked into an 8 x 10 inch mirror held before him by the interviewer. His spontaneous reactions, comments, and free associations about himself were recorded, together with responses to a series of questions about his appearance and how it had changed over the years.

In addition to these specific questions on the subject's view of himself, information on self-image was volunteered throughout the intensive interview. A part of this reservoir of information on the self derived from the subject's description of his philosophy of life. In this portion of the interview, the subject was asked to evaluate his present life and compare it with his past, discussing his over-all happiness, his reminiscences, and what he regarded as the important things in his life. He was asked about goals for his children in terms of achievement, experience, and personality, and to compare these with his own. He was asked about the place

of old people in general and of himself, in particular, in contemporary society. In these and related topics, the subject gave us
a picture of his view of himself as an aging individual. Finally,
broader dimensions of self-image were often discernible and could
be defined and explored from this entire complex of intensive
interview materials.[3] The intensive-interview data relevant to self-
evaluation will be incorporated in the following discussion as
illustrative examples of the major findings.

In studying the circumstances under which our subjects viewed
themselves positively or negatively, our main questions were:

1. Is old age itself invariably accompanied by a decline in self-
   esteem and does this decline become more pronounced with
   ever-advancing years?
2. If so, is the more negative view of the self due to age alone,
   or is it the result of changes frequently accompanying old
   age—widowhood, deteriorating intellectual capacities, loss
   of health and vigor, loss of occupation, or reduction of
   income?

To aid us in answering these questions, we developed a measure of self-evaluation, a rating of each self-image response on a
five-point scale, from strongly negative to strongly positive.[4] The
following examples illustrate the range of self-evaluations given by
our subjects in response to the survey question. A strongly negative self-evaluation was reported by Mrs. Newman (HS), an
eighty-six-year-old former school teacher, who was found to be in
poor physical and mental condition at the time of the interview.
She described herself as "a broken-down old fool. No, it doesn't
matter about me. I'm of no consequence." Further questioning
was useless; she would say no more. By contrast, Mrs. Bruzinsky
(CS), an elderly semi-retired widow of seventy-nine described
herself as:

---

[3]Several other characteristics of the self-image responses were coded, including time-
orientation. This will be treated in Chapter VI of this report; others will be discussed in separate papers.

[4]These ratings were shown to be highly reliable, with a rho *ab* of 1.0 based on a
35 per cent reliability subsample.

Quite normal. I like music. I like to play bridge. I like to
see people. I don't like to be by myself. I like to read. I am an
easy person and I don't like to quarrel. I'm not a hypocrite; I
try to be honest. I'm straight; I say what I feel and I don't say
things I don't mean . . . I am happy in a way. I used to be
much gayer, but I'm happier now than most people my age.

This description was rated as strongly positive.

For preparation of preliminary tables, the five-point scale of
self-evaluation was collapsed to a three-point scale: subjects with
strongly positive and positive responses were combined into a
single group, as were those with negative and strongly negative
responses. The three new catgeories were called simply "positive,"
"neutral," and "negative."

Our measure of self-evaluation showed that only one out of
ten people in the sample rated themselves as negative. Nearly
two-thirds were positive, and the remainder were neutral about
themselves. Among these old people, self-esteem, on the average,
appears to be quite high.

Since so few people in the study sample expressed frankly
negative views of themselves, it therefore seemed desirable, from
a statistical point of view, to divide the sample nearer the median.
In part for this reason, we set up most of our tables as simple
dichotomies—comparing those subjects with a positive self-evaluation with the group *failing* to express positive self-views—i.e., we
combined the "neutral" and "negative" responses into a single
"not positive" group. This procedure did not interfere with the
examination of our hypothesis that a *positive* self-appraisal is
crucial to aging adjustment. Thus, both statistically and conceptually, the simplification of the data seemed justified.

Age

Since most subjects described themselves in positive terms, is
it perhaps the most aged who most disparage themselves? Several
other studies comparing self-esteem in youth and age suggest that
this is a reasonable explanation. A decline in self-esteem at about
age fifty has been demonstrated in studies which include subjects
of all ages. For example, Bloom (1961), studying eighty-three

white males, ages twenty to seventy, found a drop in positive self-
attitudes in the sixth decade of life, that is, between fifty and
fifty-nine years. All subjects over the age of sixty, however, were
combined into one group, and changes with increasing age beyond
sixty were not examined (pp. 534-538). Mason (1954) studied
two groups of old people, one institutionalized and the other not
institutionalized, as well as a group of young adults, in order to
study the relationship of environment to self-concept. She found
that old people—whether in institutions or not—felt less personal
worth than did young adults. She concluded, therefore, that old
age itself—apart from environmental factors—is related to some
negative feelings of self-worth (pp. 324-337).

Although these studies show that the old have lower self-
esteem than the young, studies of age differences *within a geriatric
group* show no inexorable loss in feelings of self-worth due to
advancing age. When our sample is divided into five-year age
groups, the proportions with positive self-evaluations are nearly
identical.[5]

Our finding no relationship between age and self-evaluation
within a geriatric population is not surprising, in the light of
other research done on this problem. In the Kansas City Study of
Adult Life, Havighurst, Neugarten, and Tobin (1963) found no
correlation between their measure of self-concept and advancing
age in a sample fifty years of age and over (p. 302).

Mental and Physical Status

Although self-evaluation is not necessarily age-linked, it is
definitely related to mental and physical status. The mentally well
are much more likely to speak positively of themselves than either

---

[5]The tables in this chapter showing the various dimensions of self-image stratified
by demographic characteristics, such as age, sex, socioeconomic status, and religion, show a larger total N (714) than the tables showing stratification by disability groups (N=435). The reason for this discrepancy is that self-image data
were available for a larger sample than the one selected for this volume, but not
all attitudinal data were collected for the larger sample. It was decided to retain
the largest possible group for examining the influence of background characteristics on self-image, to provide maximum utilization of available information. This
procedure was considered feasible since marginal distributions of levels of self-
evaluation were nearly identical for the two samples.

TABLE I
INFLUENCE OF SELECTED CHARACTERISTICS ON
SELF-EVALUATION FOR TWO MENTAL STATUS GROUPS

| | Proportion Reporting Positive Self-evaluation | | |
	Community Sample (N=519) %	Hospital Sample (N=195) %	Total Sample (N=714)[a] %
Physical Status[b]			
Well	69	61	67
Sick	76	51	58
Age			
60-69	63	57	62
70+	70	48	62
Sex			
Male	58	51	56
Female	74	52	67
Socioeconomic Status			
High	71	74	71
Low	60	45	54
Ethnicity			
Native-born	66	60	65
Foreign-born	67	40	59
Education			
Some college	68	(75)[c]	68
9-12 grades	69	50	65
0-8 grades	63	58	61
Main Gainful Occupation			
White collar	67	57	65
Blue collar	59	49	56
Housewife	76	47	68

[a] This is the N of the total self-image subsample. It includes 519 community subjects, drawn from the community Baseline Sample, and 195 hospital subjects drawn from the Hospital Follow-up I Sample. Small variations in these N's may occur, depending on the number of subjects for whom data on the independent variable being used is unavailable.

[b] Figures on self-evaluation by physical disability are based on a sample of about 380 subjects, including about 250 community subjects and about 130 hospital subjects. This is due to the fact that these two disability measures are based on data available only for the Follow-up II samples, which were considerably smaller than the Baseline and Follow-up I samples.

[c] Percentages in parentheses are based on N's of less than 20.

the inpatient or the discharged mentally ill. Seventy-one per cent of the community sample, compared with 55 per cent of the discharged and less than half (46 per cent) of the inpatients, gave positive self-reports.

An examination of the intensive case data on these three mental status groups suggests a possible explanation of these findings. A community subject is likely to compare himself to others of the same age when asked to describe himself. He does not focus on losses in function or unachieved goals, but rather looks at himself in comparison with others living under much the same .circumstances. This yields a picture of himself which is positive, particularly if he has preserved his physical health. For example, Sarah Bennington (CS), an eighty-four-year-old widow, was discussing her physical appearance. She said, "I think I look older than my age but not as old as some people. My friends think I don't look so old. I guess that's because they're the same age I am and the looks are just about the same." Another community subject, Marta Valente, described herself as "about average for my age—I've seen younger people and they don't do what I do—they just sit around and wait for somebody to give 'em money which I certainly don't." Mrs. Clara Bruzinsky (CS) was able to accept her memory loss without self-condemnation, if she thought of her situation in comparison with other people her age. At the age of eighty she stated, "Sometimes I forget the name of a store or sometimes the name of a movie, but it does not happen too often. Compared to many other people, I know I am much better off than them."

By contrast, more members of the hospital sample, particularly those discharged and living in the community, describe themselves in comparison with how they *used to be.* They speak of opportunities lost, of goals unachieved, of what they might have been or done. The basic comparison is between the aged self and some idealized adult image.[6] Such a comparison is nearly always invidious. For example, Mrs. Doris Tillford (HS) commented on her physical appearance: "You're so ashamed to have someone see you, sometimes you grit your teeth. I look like I came out of an old bucket." Miss Louise Potter (HS) said that she didn't live as an old person, her friends were all younger, and she did not think of herself as old. She stated,

> Oh, how I hate to talk about myself! I never liked old people in my life, and now that I'm old, I hate myself! I'm such a stupid jackass, saying such silly things. To me, I look old as

---

[6]For similar findings in a study of a non-aged sample, see Achenbach and Zigler, 1963, pp. 197-205. These investigators found that a measure of social competence correlated highly with discrepancies between perceptions of the real and the ideal self as well as with psychiatric disability.

Methuselah. I don't like me, but I can't get away from myself.
You can get away from everything else but not yourself. I'd
like to change, but I can't change enough to like myself.

Among the hospital sample, even when the subject compares
himself with others his own age, he sometimes selects an outstanding elderly person and finds himself mediocre by comparison. Mr.
Horace Kepler (HS) described himself as "elderly—more than I
should be by my years. Look at that guy Adenauer—he's a big shot
in Germany." This man thought of himself as "uninteresting.
I'm aging before my time, and I'm not doing it very gracefully."

Others in the mentally-ill sample seem to find a defense against
aging in the belief that they have extraordinary talents and abilities which are simply not understood or appreciated by society.[7]
We have already met Mr. Spenser who exemplifies this trait, but
another example is Rena Trocopian, a hospital dischargee, who
stated, "I am just as normal as anyone; maybe I am above normal,
I am so alert. My mind is very active. I'm a capable person. I'm
artistic and intelligent." There are times, however, when Mrs.
Trocopian's defenses break down and she realizes that she has
unfulfilled potential:

> I wish I had about four hours a day to consult people, give
> them suggestions when they are in trouble, because I have so
> many experiences. The truth is, I could have been somebody!
> I could have been lots of good to myself and could have helped
> others, too. My son-in-law said, 'Your mother is not an ordinary
> Armenian woman. Lots gone to waste.'

Another hospital-discharged subject, Gilbert Caruthers, saw
himself as a most unusual and talented man, although his life
history belied this characterization:

> I'm not interested in having any more interviews unless I can
> see the results of the work I'm doing. My time is very valuable.

---

[7]The tendency to perceive the self in grandiose terms is, of course, related to a
psychiatric diagnosis of paranoid reaction. In this volume, however, we are concerned primarily with the perceptual patterns of the aged and their relation to
social adjustment. For this reason, diagnostic entities are not being discussed here
in any detail. For a fuller discussion of the psychodynamics of such reactions
among the elderly, see Simon, Lowenthal, and Epstein (publication pending).

They need me to work at the university every day, sometimes
at night. . . . I'm a writer and composer of music, somewhat of
an artist and inventor — I don't generally tell people; let them
guess; that's what they have to find out. I have eight well-
developed talents and let them find out for themselves.

In these cases the grandiose self-perception differs so much
from the views that others hold of the subject that it is sometimes
impossible for him to avoid social conflicts and problems which
may result in his hospitalization.

The hospital-inpatient group is perhaps best characterized by
denial. Many of them find innumerable ways to refute aging, illness, or change. Their self-descriptions are meager in content.
They often say little beyond, "I'm normal—I'm not sick—let me
out of here." For example, eighty-three-year-old Mrs. Alida Trumble (HS) described herself as:

Forty-five years old. The only way I have changed is, I changed
in my work. I enjoyed my work in the post office. I'm lovable
and truthful. I don't like lies . . . I still live in my home
[patient was hospitalized] and I'm happy in my home. We go
to church twice a day.

Another state hospital patient, Miss Karen Jernigan was asked
if she thought she looked older or younger than her age. Her
reply was, "I don't know. I don't know my age." Miss Jernigan
attributed any change in her appearance to institutionalization.
She said, "I used to have red hair; every week I fixed my curls.
Just impossible here to keep up my appearance . . . . If I get an
apartment, it may change."

In spite of these denials of aging and changes in health and
appearance, the real horror which the mentally-ill feel in self-
confrontation is sometimes revealed when they are asked to look
at themselves in a mirror. Molly Gifford refused to look at her
reflection: "Take it away!" she cried. "I don't want to see! I'm not
interested in my appearance . . . I am ready to go now." Many
subjects were surprised at how old the mirror image appeared.
Charles Cambry said, "I don't look so well. I didn't think I was

that old." Another hospital subject, Mr. Avery Jackson, simply refused to believe that it was truly himself reflected in the glass:

> Gee, don't I look like hell? I'm looking at an old man. How old I look! Does this make you look older than you are? I think it's a trick mirror: you can't fool me. What a poor, damn fool I am! This is a trick mirror!

Although we found that age is not related to self-evaluation in our total study sample, when subjects are divided into the mentally well and the mentally ill, there is some relationship between advancing age and self-evaluation. Within the mentally-ill sample (this group combines both the inpatient and the discharged), fewer very old patients have a positive view of themselves than do the younger subjects in the group. The differences in proportion are small but regular. Among the mentally well, on the other hand, self-approval actually *increases* with age. This reversal in trend is somewhat difficult to explain. It may be that, in the absence of mental illness, simple survival to extreme old age through effective self-maintenance is a source of personal pride. Whereas many people in their sixties still base their self-judgments on the goals and values of middle life, which become increasingly difficult for them to attain, the very old may be able to accept change in themselves with more resignation and better grace. In the presence of mental illness, however, increasing age with its accompanying decrepitude may inflict assaults upon the ego which some individuals find impossible to accept.

Physical disability has an influence on self-esteem, but, for the sample as a whole, this influence is not great; about 10 per cent more of the physically well gave positive self-descriptions than did the physically sick. If we examine the combined effects of mental and physical disorder, we find that physical disability has a negative influence on self-esteem *only* among the discharged patient group and not among either the community or the inpatient samples. Among discharged patients, only 43 per cent of the physically sick, compared with 68 per cent of the physically well, have maintained a positive self-image. It would seem that physical illness has dealt a more crushing blow to the discharged mentally ill than to the rest of the subjects.[8] It may be that when an elderly person is trying to maintain himself in the community and provide for his own needs, the combined misfortunes of failing health and emotional disturbance are an impossible burden. Physical illness alone is not disabling to nearly such an extent, and emotional problems can sometimes be managed reasonably well if one keeps one's strength and stamina.

The influence of physical illness on self-esteem was directly verbalized by Mr. Makrinos. When he was asked to describe himself, he replied, "If I feel good, I say I am okay. If I feel sick, I say I am not so good." Many community subjects gave self-descriptions which seem to belie the burden of physical illness under which they labor. For example, Mr. Angus Pillsbury (CS) was partially paralyzed as the result of a series of strokes. He had lost bowel and bladder control, and congestive heart disease seldom left him free of pain and labored breathing. However, Mr. Pillsbury described himself as young for his age. "Lots of guys around here, lots older [than I am], they die—nothing particularly wrong with them." At seventy-four and in poor physical condition Mr. Pillsbury still felt attractive to women: "I do [think I'm attractive]. I think I must be . . . . Years ago they'd say, 'Oh, that's an old country boy.' Now you take these older women—not as choosy as they used to be." He described himself as "not too bad a guy . . . I've always been a good worker. Physically, it's not too bad, a lot of people I see are worse than I am." This man was not denying the fact of physical illness. He spoke freely of his disabilities and progressive deterioration, but somehow preserved an image of himself as an attractive and worthwhile man.

Mrs. Viet (CS) had similar health problems. She discussed her

---

[8]In a special project study of the discharged patients of our hospital sample, Lowenthal and Trier (publication pending) have found that, by the time of first follow-up one year after admission, those discharged directly from the screening wards—many of whom are in our present discharged group—"were worse off psychiatrically and even more so physically, than those who had been committed [and subsequently released from state hospitals]." This subgroup was also more socially isolated than state hospital dischargees. Also, we know from this study that the physically-ill inpatients and, by and large, physically-ill old people in the community sample receive regular medical care. The physical ills of the discharged mental patient, on the other hand, are often neglected.

heart ailment with its accompanying shortness of breath. She complained of a recent stroke which had partially paralyzed her limbs, greatly restricting all her physical activity. Her vision was impaired by glaucoma. Yet her primary complaint about herself was that she was gaining weight. "Everything I buy is fattening." However, she went on to say, "I think I am something. I am clean. I am good. I look good and I try to be nice to everybody." Mrs. Viet was even able to see some advantages in advancing years: "Maybe you take more interest in yourself; you're smarter or wiser."

The hospital discharged group, on the other hand, contains many people who seem unable to perceive themselves apart from their physical incapacities. For example, Mr. Leveritt (HS) confined his self-description to the results of his illness: "I do very little now because of my leg and my foot—I used to be on the go all the time, but now the most important thing to me is my bed . . . . I don't have any idea how other people would describe me." Mr. Alioto (HS) described himself in these terms: "I can't do anything, that's all. I like to listen to television programs— baseball, Art Linkletter. I'm just living like an old man now. I wish I could walk around more." Mr. Edward Hopland (HS) described himself in terms of a disabling accident which forced his retirement from work, and which just preceded his psychiatric illness (a severe agitated depression followed by a suicide attempt) : "It all came back to me that I was such an able man, and here I was—all busted up. Made me kind of want to die."

There is some indication that physical illness poses a greater threat to the hospital discharged subjects than to the community subjects, in part because the mentally-ill group have been more dependent on productive employment to give them a feeling of worth. Proportionately, nearly five times as many hospital subjects as community subjects mentioned loss of employment in connection with their self-descriptions. Secondarily, economic deprivation resulting from physical inability to work may be a source of self-condemnation. Thus, Mr. Hopland complained bitterly about loss of income following his disablement; he felt that others blamed him for his improvidence. He said, "My son and grandson, for example—they think we should be dead because we're not rich."

In some cases, however, discharged subjects maintain a positive image of themselves even in the presence of physical disability. Sickness can serve as a reinforcement of one's sense of personal worth. For example, Mr. Hopland revealed some of the dynamics through which he was able to adjust to his disability:

> I still believe I have the ability to do things. I want to think
> I still have the strength to do a lot of things I'm not doing. . . .
> Always had an idea in mind I'm a little better than other men
> . . . I still say I'm as good as the next man. . . . Don't feel no
> different today than forty to fifty years ago — that is, my mind.

He considers himself "naturally healthy, but not old—I'll tell you that." This man is secure in the knowledge of his worth, even of his superior worth. Sickness is the fact that has stepped between what his life might have been and what it actually is. He sees himself as a capable, worthwhile human being cut off from a promising destiny by the invasion of sickness or disability. "As far as I know, I'm the same. The only change is physical [an accident]. Feel just as young as I did thirty to forty years ago."

When some of the ailing discharged subjects are face-to-face with the intrusive reminders of aging in its many guises, they apparently find it easier to reflect that they are more sick than old. The incapacity of sickness can be dreadful, but it is a circumstance which can often free one from reflections about what kind of job one has done with the business of growing old. In essence, this de-emphasis of aging amounts to almost an inability to consider aging apart from the context of sickness. While it is understandable that serious ill health can have a pervasive negative effect on a subject's view of himself, it needs to be emphasized that it can as readily contribute to a positive image of the self. There are basically two kinds of "messages" about sickness and the self which can be inferred from the self-views of the discharged group: either, "I am an outstanding person, apart from the question of aging, but this sickness masks from the world my good qualities and potential;" or, "I am not much of a person—witness my sorry physical state of incapacity and nothingness." It is of interest that both views of the self lie in a dimension where age is not a reference.

As we have seen above, self-evaluation levels among the institutionalized sample do not vary with physical disability. Inpatients who are in good physical health (although there are very few in this group) are conscious of the value of good health for the aged individual. When Mr. Ronald Forest (HS) was asked how much happiness he found in his life these days, he replied, "A good deal because I've enjoyed fairly good health . . . old in years, young in spirits. I don't even feel old." Similarly, Mr. Henry Worth (HS) evaluated himself in terms of a sense of well-being and vigor. At the age of seventy-seven he said:

> I would say my appearance is fairly good for my age. I can't say that I changed any. I still have the same mind and I have the same feeling. I'm young for my age. I hop around here like a rooster.

This emphasis on good physical health, of course, provides an excellent pivot for the diversion of one's own and others' concern with problems of mental health and the evidence of mental illness. For some of these institutionalized subjects, it is simply a rationale for the denial of mental sickness; they say, "Look at me—I am healthy." These institutionalized people grope desperately for a source of pride, a legitimate asset. For them, good health provides that source.

Among the inpatients, there are a few for whom physical illness seems to have a positive ego function, providing them with a more acceptable rationale than mental illness for their confinement to an institution. For example, Mr. Charles Cambry (HS) became quite concerned about remaining in the hospital as soon as his cardiac disease was controlled and his medications reduced: "They don't give me any medicine. If a person's sick, they give medicine to make them well . . . I don't think there is nothing wrong with my brain. I can read, write, talk. I can do everything. Why did they put me here in a place like this?"

Judging from the intensive interviews, most of the physically-sick inpatients, however, tend to deny or minimize physical disability, just as they do psychiatric illness. For example, Mrs. Alida Trumble (HS) was so critically ill during 1962 that she was given the last rites of her church. Yet, when she was asked a few months later how her health had been during the previous year, she said it had been "very wonderful, doctor. I haven't been sick! I've been feeling very well. My health is good . . . I've always had good health—never had bad health." Another inpatient, Miss Susan Roth, who had become almost blind and had developed a crippling lymphedema of her right leg insisted that there had been no changes in her general health—that it was better than it ever was. "I'm the same old whistle," she said.

It may be that patients who give such unrealistic descriptions of their health status are quite aware of their disabilities, but choose to minimize them for some reason—possibly because they hope for release from the hospital. Another explanation, which seems just as reasonable, is that many aged people in state hospitals have severe memory loss, particularly for recent events. It may be that intermittent pain and suffering is quickly forgotten, and the recollection of recent ills fades shortly after the symptoms abate. In any event, it is neither the mentally healthy nor the institutionalized for whom physical disability results in loss of self-esteem. Quantitatively, this trend is confined to the discharged mentally ill who are struggling to maintain themselves and meet the expectations of "normalcy" demanded by their society. Failing health surely compounds the arduousness of this struggle.

Other Personal Characteristics Influencing Self-evaluation

We have shown in the preceding pages that self-evaluation is positively related to both mental health and physical well-being. Since our primary concern in this section is to explore the influence of mental illness on attitudes towards the self, we should examine more closely the positive relationship we have described between these two variables.

Within our sample, levels of self-evaluation decline with mental disability. Our three mental status groups, however, differ from each other in a number of ways other than in their mental condition. Those in the community group (as we discussed in Chapter III) are younger, better educated, have higher standards of living, and are more often still employed than the mentally-ill groups. The two hospital groups, on the other hand, have disproportionately large numbers of women and fewer in these groups are married or have children living in the Bay Area. Since we are studying such dissimilar groups, the question arises as to whether the differences in self-evaluation among them are indeed related to mental health status alone or whether they are rather due to some other set of personal characteristics which differentiate the mental-status groups.

Although community subjects are younger on the average than the mentally-ill groups, we have already shown that there is no regular relationship between age and self-evaluation. Age differences, therefore, do not account for lower levels of self-esteem among the mentally ill.

Sex Differences. There are proportionately more women among the mentally ill than there are in the community. However, when we examine the relationship between sex and self-evaluation, we find that, in the total sample, women are 11 per cent more likely to describe themselves in positive terms than are men. The reverse would have to be the case if sex differences contributed to the disparity in self-evaluation levels among the disability groups.

It is of some interest that sex differences in self-evaluation in the total sample are the sole result of differences in the community group. In the hospital sample—both discharged and inpatients—males and females are equally likely to describe themselves in positive terms. Among community subjects, on the other hand, females show 16 per cent more positive reports than do males. The reasons for this difference are not completely clear. An examination of case data, however, suggests four contributing factors:

(1) Loss of physical strength and the assaults of illness and disability seem to inflict greater damage to the self-perception of men than they do to women. For example, when one community resident was asked to describe himself as a person, he replied: "I'm not a whole person. I've only one leg . . . . At fifty, I was a hard-working commander of a merchant vessel. I was always small, but I knew what I was doing. I didn't go to Annapolis or Brooklyn, but I went to the top of my profession. But what can you be with only one leg? I was fifty-six when I lost my leg."

(2) Loss of occupation affects the self-appraisal of older men more than it does that of older women. Of course, this is partly due to the fact that the majority of the females in the sample have been housewives most of their lives, a role which is not affected by a compulsory retirement age. While many of the male community subjects have adjusted well to retirement, a number of them feel that they are less worthy than when they were fully employed, and their numbers bring down the male average self-evaluation level. For example, one retired man said: "Well, I really have a problem, you see; I am not unhappy but I don't like this way of life. My sisters see that I am well supplied . . . but I need to be doing something where the good old hard cash comes in every week. I am not a member of my own society . . . I am very happy, except I should be working." Even among the elderly men who had not yet permanently retired, the problem of inability to find work, or to find it only sporadically, was sometimes reflected in self-image responses. A community male subject who had been trying unsuccessfully to find work for a number of months described himself as follows: "Well, I don't know what I am. One way I'm not very much because, you know, I had no education. I guess I can work . . . . Nothing else to say about me."

(3) The men in the community sample seemed to be more modest in describing themselves than the women. They seemed to take a certain pride in reticence, leaving unspoken the implication that they are really exceptional fellows. The following are examples of such responses: "Just look at me and say what you want. You toot my horn—I don't toot it. Only silly asses brag about themselves. I wouldn't know. I don't have the ability to answer that. No, modesty forbids me, my dear!" The women in the sample, on the other hand, sometimes made a gesture in the direction of modesty, but reluctantly allowed themselves to be drawn out anyway. For example, one community woman said, "I don't know. I can't tell on myself. I wouldn't say that I am pretty or intelligent. Of course, you know it yourself, but you don't say so to other people."

(4) Perhaps the most significant factor affecting sex differences in self-esteem has to do with culturally defined sex roles and role-expectations. The self-descriptions of aged men and women

in our community sample indicate that self-esteem for an individual is very often based on the conviction that his way of life fits well with the values and goals of his society, and that he is thus assured of approval from that society. In describing themselves as they were at age fifty, subjects with a positive self-evaluation tend to speak in terms of their social roles, basing their self-esteem on a demonstrated ability to meet the societal standards for these roles. For a man, it is important to have been a good husband, father, provider, worker, and perhaps civic leader, as well as to have demonstrated the ambition, strength, and general competence associated with the male role. Thus, Mr. Cutler begins his age-fifty self-description, "Then I was working, and I was married . . . I made much money and had a good house." Similarly, Mr. Robart said, "I was active then. I organized the culinary association . . . I was well-informed . . . I was ambitious . . . ." For the women, success as wife, mother, homemaker, and hostess, and skill in the more general female role of "helper," "giver," "friend" are most significant. Typical of the woman's age-fifty descriptions is that of Mrs. Feliz who says, "I was a very gay person, a very happy person when I had a home. I loved company and I loved parties and to entertain and I was a very good cook," or that of Mrs. Donato, "I considered myself a good mother and wife . . . very busy and active with my family . . . ," or Mrs. Granville, "I played bridge, had parties, danced, helped with the poor. I always belonged to organizations that helped with the underprivileged." For both sexes, effectiveness in these major roles supplied the individual with an adequate basis for a positive view of himself as a person.

For a small number of our elderly subjects, activity in one or more of these roles still serves as the basis of the self-image and of self-regard. Mr. Werner, an eighty-year-old man, says of himself today, "I am a good American citizen. I have a good wife and I am a good provider." Similarly, Mrs. Wilcox, at the age of eighty, describes herself in this way: "Well, I like to do for other people. I like to wait on my husband. I like to do all my housework. I like to go out with my friend. I'm a good cook." For the majority, however, the active life of the middle years is no longer possible. Most of the men are retired; many subjects are widowed, and usually live far from their grown and independent children; and, in nearly all cases, the physical and social changes accompanying old age have forced these people to slow their pace of life to the point where they can no longer take part in much of the productive activity of their communities. For some, this loss of clearly defined functions and the gradual decrease of activity brings with it a decline in self-esteem. Thus, Mr. Merrill says of himself today, "I don't know what kind of man I am. I'm nobody . . . . If I was working, then I would be somebody." Similarly, Mrs. Yarborough says, "I don't see anybody anymore to know who I am."

However, loss of self-esteem in this way is the pattern for only a minority of these elderly people. Over half of them maintain a generally positive view of themselves. Moreover, for the majority, self-esteem continues to be directly related to the individual's claim to social approval. The change is to be found in the kinds of behavior and the personal qualities on which that claim is based; i.e., it appears that those elderly men and women who maintain their self-esteem in the face of major role losses do so in part by focusing on new sources of social approval.

The change in focus is less dramatic for the women than for the men. For the woman, current self-image differs from the prime-of-life image primarily in the amount of activity described. With age, the focus shifts to the passive attributes, those personal qualities and attitudes which had been the underpinning of the expressive activities of younger years; the areas of concern—chiefly interpersonal relations—do not change. Looking back on their middle years, the women remember that they had an active social life, went to parties and dances, did a lot of entertaining, were good wives and mothers, and had a lot of friends. Now they describe themselves as "friendly towards people," "loving," "sympathetic," "pleasant to be with." For example, Mrs. Deutsch, an eighty-three-year-old woman describes herself today as ". . . kind and sympathetic . . . I really like people. I am the kind who gives a lot . . . I have the nature that makes people lean on me"; but, at age fifty, she was "energetic—the days weren't long enough when I was younger . . . . People came to me for help . . . I gave plenty of advice when I was an office nurse." Although she is no longer in a position to use her sympathetic understanding qualities in actively helping others, the knowledge that these things are in her "nature" enables her to maintain a sense of her own worth.

For the men, personal qualities and attitudes usually cannot take the place of productive activity as a basis for self-esteem. If an elderly man still thinks and talks about himself with reference to his role as worker, provider, or head of a family, it is apt to be in a negative manner, with emphasis on the things he no longer can be or do. For example, Mr. Mallory says of himself today, "I'm getting old, I can tell . . . I am occupied with my writing of course, but I don't write the same as I once did. The fire is not there now." Nor do past achievements often continue to be a source of personal esteem; specific successes and accomplishments of earlier years are not frequently mentioned. By far, the most common basis of self-esteem for our aged men is the *absence* in their lives of any disruptive, socially condemned behavior. Their self-descriptions consist largely of statements about what they do *not* do: they do not drink heavily; they do not fight; they "stay out of trouble," "mind their own business," and avoid immoderation of almost any sort. With age, the ability to live peacefully within the rules of the community and to avoid conflicts with others becomes the new claim to social approval and self-esteem. Although these accounts of moderation and sobriety must be considered generally positive self-appraisals—and, indeed, are occasionally concluded with direct statements such as "I think I'm a good person"—they lack the enthusiasm and the sense of real self-esteem that is found among the responses of the women. Compare, for example, a self-description such as that of Mr. Marsh, who says, "I'm five feet, six inches tall, weigh 145 pounds. White—grey hair—brown eyes. A quiet person, do not gamble, do not smoke, do not drink. Was never arrested . . ." with that of Miss Vittori: "Cheerful, I have a smile for everyone. I love people. Easygoing. I love to do photography. I lean towards art. I love animals. I'm cheerful and humorous. At times, I'm melancholy, but I come up with a smile. I'm kindhearted to the extreme. I have always tried to be helpful to others." The women name the ways in which they are worthy of praise, the things that are positively good about them; the men often tell us only that they are acceptable, and name the ways in which they are not to be condemned.

Although both men and women have been forced to modify their self-views somewhat as age has brought changes in their abilities and activities, there is a greater continuity with past self-image and earlier roles for women than for men. This ability to transpose the substance of past self-image into the context of old age appears to account, in part, for the fact that our aged women are generally happier about themselves than are the men. The adult female role in America is largely based on personal attitudes or qualities rather than on achievements in various activities. Consequently, traits such as "friendliness," "warmth," or "generosity" are important in the role of the younger woman, but need not disappear as she becomes old and less active. Furthermore, much of the American female role centers around interpersonal relations, an area from which the elderly woman is not likely to be cut off completely.[9] Although many of the primary relationships of earlier years may be gone, contacts with friends, storekeepers, nurses, and neighbors may provide opportunities for her to remain somewhat active as helper or friend, and to continue using some of the social skills which were important earlier as wife, mother, and hostess.

In contrast, the major male roles of worker, provider, and community leader focus on competitive activity which cannot be translated as easily into the more passive form of personal qualities and attitudes. Nor can men often continue to function in these roles on a smaller scale; there is little opportunity for working, earning money, or directing the affairs of the community at a pace which is comfortable or even possible for the elderly man. With forced retirement and the physical decline of old age, the roles which supplied the basis for self-image and self-esteem in earlier years are often eliminated completely.

Among the mentally ill, however, these factors differentiating

---

[9]Zena Blau (1961) has found significant class differences in the patterns of friendship among aged widows. Specifically, "widowhood for the working class woman, more often than for the middle class woman, imposes severe economic deprivations which operate to drastically limit her social activities" (p. 439). Our statement in the text, therefore, needs to be qualified with this contingency.

the sexes in the community sample were overshadowed by the more pressing issue of personal disorganization, hospitalization for mental illness, and the associated assaults on self-esteem.[10]

Socioeconomic Status. Returning to the major theme of this section—those factors other than mental status which account for differences in the self-views of our three subgroups—we note that those who are mentally ill are much poorer on the average than the mentally healthy. And poverty, like mental illness, is reflected in self-evaluation; 17 per cent more subjects of high socioeconomic status gave positive self-reports than did those of low status.[11]

Financial condition and standard of living are clearly reflected in many self-descriptions. For example, a retired contractor in the community sample was pleased with himself for having made adequate plans for his old age: "I am a thinking man. I'm a little different, you see. You ask all these questions about problems, but they're not for me, because I don't have to work. I have saved my money and I am healthy, so I will soon live on the farm I am buying." People without financial resources were often quite critical of themselves. For example, a hospital patient said, "I'm a no good bum—one place to the other. All that I know is all I've had since I was young. I worked in the fields in corn, digging potatoes, and so forth." Another man of lower socioeconomic status in the hospital sample described himself as "out—done—no comeback as far as I can see." Even when he was fifty, he was "just a monkey. Camping, earning a few dollars, I've never been anything in this country."

Is the low level of self-evaluation we see among the mentally ill simply the result of their lower standard of living? To some extent, this is true. If socioeconomic status is high, mental illness does not greatly affect self-esteem; in both the community and the hospital samples, over 70 per cent of the people with a relatively

---

10One artifact of the research may have influenced sex differences in self-reporting by the community and hospital samples. Wylie (1961) has discussed the "contaminating" effect on self-disclosure of the sex of the interviewer in relation to that of the subject (pp. 31-32). In our study of self-image, as many hospital subjects were interviewed by men (49 per cent) as by women whereas community interviewers were mainly women, with whom our male subjects sometimes tended to be a little coy.

11For definitions of high and low socioeconomic status, refer to Chapter III.

high standard of living described themselves in positive terms. Among the poorer subjects, however, mental illness did make a difference in level of self-esteem. Among the poor aged, 60 per cent of those in the community sample gave positive self-reports, whereas only 45 per cent of those in the hospital sample did so.

Looking at these facts in a slightly different way, we find that while poverty lowers self-esteem slightly (11 per cent) among the mentally well, it had three times the impact on self-image among the mentally ill (29 per cent lower). Thus, poverty and mental illness combine to produce a situation in which comparatively few old people can speak well of themselves.[12]

The relationship between poverty and attitudes of the aged towards themselves and others should be studied in more depth than we are able to do with our data. Some questions that we are unable to answer definitively, for example, are: (1) Is there more anxiety and self-condemnation about having uncertain and unreliable funds than about having a low income as such? (2) Is there a lower level of self-esteem among the aged who have always had a low standard of living—who have grown old in poverty—than among those who have been self-sufficient workers during adult life, but, with loss of employment, find themselves dependent on family members or public assistance? In other words, is sliding down to the bottom of the economic scale in old age worse than never having been able to rise above it?

We cannot answer such questions definitively because we lack

---

[12]It should be noted that, for hospital sample subjects, a low SES score generally represents a lower level of income, lower rent per month, and a lower census tract rating than it does for community sample subjects. Similarly, a high SES score for community subjects indicates a somewhat higher rent, income, and census tract rating than does the same score for hospital sample subjects. This is due to the fact that while a particular SES score represents the same *range* of income, rent, and census tract ratings for both samples, the distributions of subjects over that range differs between the two samples. The distributions of our hospital sample subjects with an SES score of "0" are skewed towards the lower end of the income, rent, and census tract ranges included in that score, while the distributions of the community sample subjects with a score of "0" are skewed towards the higher end of that range. The distribution of hospital subjects with a high SES score are also skewed—in this case, toward the median. For a more detailed analysis of the relationship of socioeconomic status to mental disability and self-evaluation among community subjects, see Chapters I and II in Lowenthal, Berkman and Associates (1966).

The Personal System 103

information about income levels of all our subjects during the
earlier stages of their lives. For a subsample (270) of our subjects,
however, we do have information on change in standard of living
since age fifty. These subjects were asked if their current standard
of living was better, worse, or the same as it had been earlier. This
information (see Table II) provides some clues about the combined effects of past and present socioeconomic status on self-
esteem in old age. While observed percentage differences are
small, they do indicate some interesting trends.

TABLE II
PROPORTIONS OF TWO SOCIOECONOMIC STATUS GROUPS
REPORTING POSITIVE SELF-EVALUATION BY CHANGE
IN STANDARD OF LIVING SINCE AGE 50

| | Proportion Reporting Positive Self-evaluation | | |
	Low SES (0-1) (N=145) %	High SES (2-3) (N=125) %	Total (N=270) %
Change in Standard of Living			
Worse	47	73	53
Same	54	72	66
Better	(78)	83	81
Total	52	74	63

Looking first at the poorer half of our sample—those with low
current socioeconomic status—we see that people whose present
poverty represents a decline from earlier years are less apt to have
a positive self-image than are those who were no better off financially at age fifty. For subjects currently at a higher socioeconomic
level, however, a decline in standard of living from the earlier
years does not have this same negative influence. This suggests
that economic "sliding" in old age is detrimental to self-esteem
only if it seriously impoverishes the individual. When the subjects
of low socioeconomic status are further subdivided into the poor
(those with a score of 1) and the very poor (those with a score of 0),
we find that financial decline is damaging to self-esteem only when
it represents a fall to the *very lowest* of our four levels of socioeconomic status: an annual income of less than $2,500, a monthly
rent of less than $60, and residence in a quite substandard neigh-
borhood (one having a rating of 4 or lower on a scale of 10).[13]

13For a further explanation of this scale, see footnote 4, Chapter III, and Tryon
(1955).

An improvement in current socioeconomic status, on the other hand, has a positive effect on self-image at all levels. While a comfortable present standard of living is conducive to a positive view of the self in old age, it has an even greater significance if it represents an improvement over earlier years. Interestingly enough, a rise in standard of living since age fifty seems to be even more important to self-esteem when current status is on the lower half of the scale. That is, subjects who are poor now, but used to be poorer, report positive self-evaluations just as frequently as do subjects with a currently high status (about 75 per cent positive), and half again as often as do all other poor subjects. Even though this finding is based on a small number of subjects it suggests that even a slight economic gain in old age may partially offset poverty's corrosive effect on self-esteem.

Intensive case studies provide further information about the impact of poverty on the self-image. For example, Mr. Janisch (CS) made several comments relevant to question (1) above: he emphasized the worries he formerly had about uncertain income. He describes himself as "a pretty good guy . . . understanding . . . patient . . . I'm quite satisfied now . . . I can get along with everyone . . . something I could not do when I was young." This semi-retired clothing salesman attributes his happy old age to economic security. Actually, his income is about the same now—allowing for inflation—as it was when he was fifty, twenty-five years ago. However, he reports that things are getting better for him in his old age "because of the retirement plan and having a source of income that I don't have to worry about." In describing himself at age fifty, he says:

> My life was a strain then. At that age, it was during the depression. I was never sure of my job; I just never felt safe. I was so insecure. I worried all the time about my family. My old age has been much happier for me. I feel safer than I did when I was young. It is because of the pensions and the Social Security and hospital plans we have now. . . . Of course I don't have a family now to take care of, which means less worries. . . . I look forward with pleasant expectations to vacation — all those things I didn't have when I was young.

Mr. Janisch claims that his old age has been the most satisfying time of his life "because of the economic security I feel I have today that I never had before."

The relative impact on self-esteem of life-long poverty and age-linked poverty can be seen in comparing the stated attitudes of Mr. Hopland (HS) and Mrs. Martinez (HS). Mr. Hopland is a "slider"; during his middle years he had an income of about $500 a month from his earnings as a self-employed moving-van operator. The work consisted of heavy physical labor, however, and a disabling accident forced his retirement. Because he had been self-employed, he received no retirement pension, and his small Social Security and disability income proved inadequate to support him and his wife. Mr. Hopland complained of having no money to buy shoes or other necessary clothing, of having no money for transportation to visit friends out of the neighborhood, of having to tell his son not to come for meals because "he was taking the food out of our mouths." Mr. Hopland admitted that he has a more dependable income now than before, "if you call that anything . . . . The mailman brings the money right to the door." But he added that he didn't like his current way of life: "It's not very easy what we're going through . . . . There's nothing to look forward to, absolutely nothing." As an afterthought, he mentioned that in about one year his wife would be eligible for Social Security benefits of $14 a month, and that they were eagerly looking forward to this, since the slight increase of income would allow them to purchase necessities they must now do without. Mr. Hopland's formula for successful aging reveals his preoccupation with his current poverty: "Save everything you can—not just money; try to save your health and ability to do things; get some insurance—health and accident." Yet, in spite of the financial deprivations that Mr. Hopland is now suffering, he managed to describe himself as a person in quite positive terms: "I still think I'm okay; still proud of myself—very proud of myself."

Mrs. Martinez (HS), on the other hand, has grown old as a lifelong pauper. She was born to poverty, one of eight children of an itinerant Puerto Rican farm laborer. As a child, she worked in the fields with her parents, doing well to obtain a few years of elementary education. When she was fourteen, her father died of malnutrition and tuberculosis, leaving his family to support themselves as best they could. Nor did Mrs. Martinez escape from the specter of want in her married life. She made several unstable alliances with men of a similar socioeconomic level to her own, but these all ended in separation or divorce.

When Mrs. Martinez was hospitalized for a "neurotic depression" in 1959, she had no regular income at all. She was living as a housekeeper, receiving only board and room but no money, from one of her ex-husbands, who had since remarried. She weighed only eighty-five pounds at the time of admission, and attributed her difficulties to "worrying too much." She said that she had no money and was worrying about that. Her attitudes towards her past life were particularly revealing. When she was asked to name the happiest period of her life she said, "I can't remember. I don't think I had any happy days." The least satisfying period was, "Ah, since I was born. I've been unhappy all my life." She said things have been better since she is older—sometimes people cook something and bring it in for her to eat. In describing herself, Mrs. Martinez could find little to say: "I don't know. I'm like you—everybody's' got faults. I don't want to live long—so much sickness . . . . Nothing is important to me . . . . Young or old is the same to me. There's no difference."

Mrs. Martinez was extremely reluctant to leave the county hospital; she cried when she was told she would have to go home, and commented that she would have liked to stay there for the rest of her life. At least, there she had a clean bed, good food to eat, no worries about being cold or hungry, and everyone—doctors, nurses, and even other patients were "wonderful" to her. A stay in a psychiatric receiving ward at a county hospital was, for this woman, one of the rare luxuries in a life of misery and deprivation.

Comparing these few cases, it seems that life-long poverty is more damaging to self-esteem than is a deteriorating standard of living in old age. Some of these differences in *types* of poverty among the aged and their influence on attitudes and adjustment will be explored in more detail in a later study.

Education and Occupation. In this sample, the mentally-well and mentally-ill groups differ in average educational level and type of occupation. The hospital sample is composed of people who are less well educated and are less likely to have earned a living in white collar jobs than the community sample. These differences, however, had very little influence on self-judgments. The slight differences observed seem to be simply a reflection of variations in current standard of living. Self-esteem among these elderly people is related less to educational or occupational achievement than to currently available social and economic resources. Mrs. Lois Willoughby (CS), for example, complained about her poor education, but it was clear that the deficiency she felt was her inability to earn money rather than lack of schooling as such. Her husband had died in 1958, leaving her completely dependent on Social Security payments.

> The third of every month I get my Social Security check so I wait till I get my . . . bills, then figure out how much I have to live on. . . . I'm sick, thoroughly disgusted and depressed at times, and very dissatisfied, because I don't think I've accomplished a great deal — and to me that means a lot. . . . I could have gone to work and made something of myself if my husband could have allowed me to finish my high school. Well, it costs money. I had my housework to do. I just give up — I wasn't going to have a 'knockdown-dragout' with him. . . . I could see all this coming, the financial end of it. It could have been altogether different if my husband had allowed me to finish my high school. Now I may have to go on welfare. I've always feared being a charity.

Others of our subjects expressed some pride in having been able to get and hold responsible positions in spite of educational limitations. Mr. Hopland admitted wishing that he had more education, but in spite of this lack, he looked upon himself as a man who had excelled in his work:

> Foremen always liked me better than the other men. . . . I had to keep books for the government; I didn't have the education for the job but I did it. I always liked that.[14]

---

[14]It is of some interest that our subjects on the average tended to report that they had received less formal education than their children reported for them. We suspect that educational achievement is a greater value for the filial generation than for the parental one—our elderly subjects seemed quite content, on the whole, to view themselves as self-made men and women.

Subjects in the sample who were well-educated rarely mentioned the fact in connection with their self-evaluations, except insofar as educational achievement has had practical value in terms of financial security. One community subject, Mr. Knight, with a graduate degree in engineering, described himself as "the average run . . . not a brilliant engineer, but I could cut the buck enough to fool the boss. I plan all the time to see that my capital is intact." In some cases, subjects with high educational levels denigrate themselves for not making more of their opportunities. Mr. Edwin Butler (CS), for instance, is a public school teacher nearing retirement age. He has a good income, and can look forward to a comfortable pension when he retires. In spite of this, he said:

> I am a person who missed the boat. I think I really could have done something worthwhile, if I had followed through, cut out the liquor, and not done some of the things I did. I blame myself for this. I can't just shove my mistakes aside any more.

In the case of Mr. Butler, the educational achievement and professional status which might have served as a source of pride and feeling of accomplishment was offset by the fact that he set goals for himself which were beyond the reach of most professional men—he not only wanted to be a successful educator and make a comfortable living for his family; he wanted to be rich. He bemoaned the fact that he had "lost a potential half million dollars" on an ill-fated business venture.

We were struck in our study of intensive interviews with the absence of an emphasis on white-collar occupation as a source of self-esteem, apart from monetary considerations. The notion that some occupations might be more "respectable" than others seemed a foreign concept to this sample of subjects. Craftsmen, tradesmen, and people who had occupied semi-skilled or service positions were just as likely to think well of themselves in old age as were those who had been brokers, teachers, or newspapermen. For example, Mrs. Valente (CS) had worked as a farm laborer and domestic servant most of her life; yet she thinks well of herself and takes pride in the work she has done:

I'm an easy-going person. Stand up for myself and pay my way
... about average for my age. I don't feel old, especially when
I'm working. I'm pretty satisfied the way I am. I have been
well-liked for my work, if no other reason. I'm not lazy; I can
cook a roast, put on the potatoes, take over the house, I know
how to get around. I think I enjoy life as much as young people.

For Mrs. Valente, as for most of the elderly people we have
studied, it is not the kind of work one has done that contributes
to self-esteem—it is the fact that one has worked hard, done a
good job, remained self-reliant, and earned a living. Value is
placed not on occupational class status but on industry, usefulness, and financial security.[15]

Ethnicity: In this analysis, ethnicity is defined simply in terms
of two groups: those born in the United States as compared with
those born in some other country. Although we found that self-
evaluation is unrelated to native *versus* foreign birth in the community sample, foreign birth does strongly influence self-esteem
among the mentally ill.

In this connection, two areas of difference related to ethnicity
are significant. The first is a difference found *within* the foreign-
born group. Birth abroad appears to have a significantly different
effect on the self-evaluations of community subjects compared
with hospital patients. The two groups differ by 27 per cent. This
leads to the question of why foreign provenience has such a
strongly negative effect upon the mentally ill. In comparison with
the native-born in the hospital sample, the mere fact of immigrancy appears to be related to the corrosive effect of mental illness on
self-perception. One naturally wonders at this point if other factors, such as a greater poverty or a poorer physical condition, are
serving to compound the difficulties of these foreign-born patients.
In exploring this possibility, however, we found that poverty and
physical disability exert strikingly parallel effects upon the foreign-

---

[15]We suspect that the aged in a more class-stratified society than that of San
Francisco might place a greater emphasis on white collar occupation and professional status as a source of personal pride. Occupational status might have a
different meaning, for example, in rural New England or in the Deep South than
it does in urban California.

and native-born. In both groups of patients, self-evaluation is most highly influenced by socioeconomic status—a finding that is consistent with the importance we have already seen this factor to possess in the shaping of one's self-evaluation. The lesson to be learned at this juncture, however, is that a lack of poverty is a circumstance for the foreign-born still not strong enough to sweeten their lot. Thus, high socioeconomic status, which is found to have the highest correlation with positive self-evaluation in both groups and which increases the proportion of positive self-evaluation among the native-born to 75 per cent, raises positive self-evaluation among the foreign-born to only 56 per cent. The same is true of physical health. There is a dramatic persistence of low self-evaluation among the foreign-born patients even in the face of conditions that tend to enhance self-esteem among the native-born.

The conclusion that may be derived from this analysis is that low self-evaluation among immigrants is not related to any allied physical or economic condition, but that the fact of foreign birth in itself—of being an immigrant to a new country—is the telling issue.

Mental illness and institutionalization evoke greater repercussions on the self-esteem of the foreign-born and appear to arouse a more intense sense of failure and uprootedness. Immigrants to America generally place high value on a successful adjustment to their new community and are also hopeful of achieving a higher standard of living than would have been possible for them in their country of origin. One ex-patient, Mrs. Trocopian, reminisced during one of the interviews and recalled her early struggles to adjust to a new country:

[Did being an immigrant make any difference?] Humph. For twenty years I had inferiority. The first six to seven years I was too young. I was only twenty or twenty-one. The first years we were struggling. Then we bought a new bungalow in a tract. Then I noticed the difference. . . . Myself, I was a first-class citizen all around. But for twenty years, they didn't greet us. They made me have an inferiority complex, but that didn't make a great impression on me.

This same person, later in the interview, took special care to emphasize the success of her final adjustment: "I got changed. I'm more American. I'm 99 per cent American. If not, I am 90 per cent." The vehemence of her declaration implies for us that assimilation is rarely so complete for the foreign-born as to erase from their awareness the fact that they are still distinguishable from the native-born. This is often the case when immigration occurs after the years of childhood and when an accent tends to persist even after a mastery of the English language has been completed. This respondent took particular pride in the difficulty others had in guessing her nationality: "I don't feel Armenian. I feel American and just another human being, decent human being," and yet, in spite of this, all the friendships reported by this subject were limited to people of Armenian extraction.

It is not improbable, therefore, that institutionalization—the removal from an environment they had voluntarily sought out and from a society they had attempted to align themselves with—calls forth or reactivates a sense of isolation, alienation, and failure. In addition, while social interaction in the community has not always been limited to members of their own ethnic group, a sense of solidarity persists and the strongest ties and most meaningful friendships tend to be formed with individuals who share their common cultural heritage. When another ex-patient, Mr. Louis Czernich, was asked at what time in his life he had enjoyed being a friend the most, he replied:

> Well, a couple of friends, we were singing, was in choral of church of old country [Yugoslavia] for four years. When I came here [United States, aged twenty] there were couple of friends and we would sing songs. I was the leader. Slovenian songs, German songs, and American too. Had book of songs. [Respondent sang a Slovenian song for the interviewer.]

The loss of these relationships with compatriots can be especially poignant when, as was the case with this man, a lifelong bachelor, the attrition of time removes the old, familiar faces. Recalling his closest friendship, he mused:

> Joe Zabarach. A great singer. Wherever we went was pretty lively — I can tell you that! Lost track of him. Don't know if

he is still alive. . . . Well, many of them [old friends] die off. Ha! And new friends? I don't want too many. You like your friends, then you don't see them for awhile. If you go to see them, then maybe others in family don't like you. And their children are different.

Mr. Janssen (CS), a Dane and also unmarried, told his interviewer when he most enjoyed being a friend: "When them old Danes was alive, about ten years ago. In the old days I had a lot of close friends. We always came together, drink, and eat together. All dead now, and some of them went back home to Denmark."

Hospitalization may, consequently, be experienced more acutely by the foreign-born than by those who are native Americans. They are more dependent on contacts with the outside community and, if hospitalized, suffer a deeper sense of separation from the members of their own ethnic groups. Also, this potentiality for a sharper sense of alienation may partially account for the fact that unmarried status has a considerably more negative effect upon the foreign-born than upon native Americans: contacts with the outside community increase significantly if one has a spouse and children.

Returning for the moment to the mentally-healthy group, we ought now, because of the foregoing discussion, to be doubly impressed with the fact that, in the *community*, the incidence of positive self-evaluation among the foreign-born is the same as that in the native-born group. Can this finding be a contradiction of what we found to be true for the foreign-born mentally ill? Analyzing our community sample further, we find that the apparent uniformity among community subjects, native- and foreign-born, is deceptive; for, in dividing the foreign-born into ethnic subgroups, it becomes evident that this correspondence has resulted from the fact that the high level of self-esteem attained by one group has cancelled out the low level attained by another.

Because immigrants from Europe are fairly numerous in the community sample, it has been possible for us to compare sizeable groups of subjects originating from four general European culture areas: Northern Europe, Central Europe, Southern Europe, and Slavic Europe.[16] This analysis shows us that Northern European and Slavic subjects reported proportions of positive self-evaluations closely similar to that of the native-born population. Central and South European subjects, on the other hand, were found to differ significantly from these two groups. The self-descriptions of the Central Europeans were considerably more favorable than any of the others and, in contrast, those of the Southern Europeans were much more negative.

Since the self-evaluation of both the community and hospital samples has already been shown to be related to socioeconomic status, it was decided to find out if this correlation obtained for the four ethnic groups in each of the two socioeconomic categories of high and low. Since the number of subjects falling within each category was too small to ensure reliability, we examined further the general distribution of wealth within each ethnic group. Considering these two distributions in one global view, it appears that the foreign-born in the community do not deviate from the native-born with respect to the influence of socioeconomic status on self-evaluation. However, while not conclusive, the data suggest that economic conditions have a much stronger bearing on the self-esteem of Northern Europeans and Slavs than they appear to do for the native-born. However, the positive self-evaluations of Central and Southern Europeans tend to be unrelated to socioeconomic status. A low socioeconomic status does not decrease the proportions of positive self-evaluations among Central Europeans[17] and high socioeconomic status does not raise the percentage of positive self-evaluations among the Southern Europeans. These differences between Central and Southern Europeans are given additional support when one examines the general socioeconomic levels attained by the individual ethnic groups. The Southern European sample, with its low frequency of positive self-evaluation, is shown to have as many affluent members (59 percent) as the Slavs (60 per cent) and the native-born (62 per cent). Central Europeans, whose self-descriptions were extremely positive, are found to have fewer affluent representatives (48 per

16Representatives from other continental areas were so scattered in this sample that further analyses of them would be unwarranted at this time.

17"Central Europe" includes Austria, Germany, and Switzerland.

cent) than the other ethnic groups, excepting the Northern Europeans (44 per cent) .[18]

The question arises now to what extent it is valid to regard these differences in the effect of socioeconomic status on self-esteem as artifacts of the culture of the subjects' provenience. The fact that the self-evaluations of the Southern European sample appear to be unaffected by the presence or absence of wealth may be viewed as a manifestation of the value-system of their original background. In describing the attitude of Spaniards towards wealth, Pitt-Rivers (1955) has written: "Wealth itself is not, as in much of European society, an intrinsic merit. Conversely, poverty implies no inferiority in other spheres than the economic . . ." (p. 60). The tendency to regard the more prosperous members of a community as morally inferior and potentially evil appears to be rather widespread among the peasantry of Southern Europe.

It is more difficult to explain the relationship between socioeconomic status and self-evaluations shown in the Central European sample. In his study of German and Austrian social structures, Lowie (1954) has described the importance given in these societies to social stratification, "the pedantic insistence on minute gradings within a class" as well as the presence of an "unequivocal materialism of peasant ideology." His analysis of these cultures would lead one to expect the self-esteem of Central European subjects to be more related to material status than was shown to be the case in our community sample. It may well be that the Central Europeans selected for inclusion in our San Francisco study are representative of a pattern of immigration and acculturation different from that operative with the Southern Europeans. Our research program has projected a future study wherein these finer subcultural differences in our sample will be more intensively explored than is possible here.

Summary of Factors Related to Self-evaluation

Among our subjects a relationship exists between self-evaluation, one component of the personal system, and mental health.

---

[18]It may be that gradations of prejudice within the majority society are inducing these patterns, but we have no way of testing these differences with our present data.

An analysis of other characteristics shows that this relationship is not a spurious one, but that other factors, especially physical disability and poverty, add to the likelihood of a more negative self-image among the mentally-ill aged. We have found age alone—within a geriatric sample—to be unrelated to self-evaluation. Among hospital subjects, the fact of foreign birth has a negative influence on self-esteem. Among community subjects, there are appreciable differences in self-perception among subcultural groups, with Southern Europeans more frequently reporting negative self-attitudes than the remainder of the foreign-born, as well as native Americans. In the community sample, women report positive self-views more frequently than do men; but among the hospital sample, these sex differences are overshadowed by the greater assaults of emotional disturbance and institutionalization.

MORALE

Preliminary Remarks

There is a large amount of literature in the behavioral sciences dealing with the subject of morale. Students of human groups have considered it to be a crucial factor in how much factory workers will produce, how hard soldiers will fight to win, how great a turnover there will be in an office staff, and how fervently critically-ill patients will struggle to live. Anthropologists have found that, under particularly traumatic conditions of intercultural contact, whole societies may be demoralized, and some to the point where their members even show a serious disinterest in the continuity of the group.[19]

Etymologically the term has the same Latin root as the word, *moral* (as in "a moral man" or "a moral life"). Both words derive from *moris* (plural, *mores,* as in the exclamation, *O tempora, O mores!*) *Morale* was first used in English as borrowing from French, where it connotes "morality," that is, right and good behavior. With time, however, a slight shift in meaning has occurred until finally it has come to refer to some mental state shared by

---

[19]Cf. Ralph Linton's study of Marquesan Islanders, as reported in Kardiner (1939).

members of a group, such as an army. More recently, it has taken on the additional meaning of zeal, spirit, confidence, or hope.

With the development of the field of social gerontology, the term has found wide application as a highly relevant factor in the study of mental states of the aged (Kutner *et al.*, 1956; Cumming and Henry, 1961; Wilensky, 1961). Although we will not here attempt a formal definition of this term, we have developed a measure from a particular set of interrelated attitudes which we believe is a measure of morale and which is conceptually distinct from self-evaluation (see Appendix B). Thus we regard morale as an additional component of the personal system of aging individuals. It differs from self-evaluation in two basic respects: first, morale, as we will use the term, refers to the level of satisfaction with one's own *lot,* whereas self-evaluation relates to the level of satisfaction with one's personal characteristics. Second, morale is an *affective* dimension of individual awareness, while self-evaluation is more a *perceptual* and judgmental function. Certainly, the two dimensions are not completely independent of each other; in fact, the indices we have developed for measuring each of the two proved to be correlated at a fairly high level (*Phi* = .32). However, cross-tabulations show that the two dimensions are far from identical.[20]

Morale and Mental Status

For the total study sample, morale (as measured by scores on a depression/satisfaction scale described in Appendix B) is distributed as follows: 35 per cent of the subjects reported very high morale, 27 per cent moderately high, 22 per cent moderately low, and 16 per cent very low. For purposes of economy, we have

---

[20]The problem of dividing the personal system conceptually into component dimensions is one that many behavioral scientists are coping with. Cumming and Henry (1961), for example, took two components of the personal system which had been defined by other investigators as separate dimensions (Kutner's measurement of morale and Srole's scale of anomia) and combined items from both into a single scale with Guttman properties, which they called a scale of "positive thinking." In the same Kansas City study, another team of investigators (Neugarten, Havighurst, and Tobin, 1961) developed what they called a measure of "life satisfaction." This was composed of a set of ratings, including a dimension they dubbed "self-concept" (similar to our "self-evaluation"), and also two other dimensions of "zest" and "mood tone." We have not differentiated these last two dimensions in our morale measure.

dichotomized the sample into two groups: those with high morale (62 per cent) and those with low morale (38 per cent of the total study sample).

The three mental status groups in the study sample differ in morale levels: community subjects have quite high morale in 74 per cent of the cases.[21] Among the ex-patients, only 38 per cent reported high morale, and only 30 per cent of those who were still inpatients did so. There is not much difference, then, between the two mentally-ill subgroups. About two-thirds of each group have low morale, compared with only one-fourth of the community sample.

However, there are those who have high self-esteem, but low morale. Thus, Mrs. Trocopian, a dischargee, who described herself in glowing terms ("accomplished, talented, alert") readily admitted to a low level of life satisfaction: "My spirit is not high. I suffered too much. Things bother me. I worry . . . . There are dissatisfactions in my life. I am not happy." Mr. Apostolos Phidrios, another discharged patient, was quite neutral in his self-description ("Just average"), but was unequivocal in admitting to low morale: "What happiness can I have in life today? How much would *you* have? I'm not in good spirits—that's all . . . . This is the hardest time I've ever had to face. No pleasure in anything—I got nobody to enjoy. I worry—more than I used to."

Cases such as these show that while there is a greater correspondence between levels of satisfaction with the self and with the circumstances of life among mentally-well subjects, the disparity increases with mental illness. The focus of dissatisfaction is projected onto circumstances and events outside the self, or beyond the control of the individual. Differences in the perceived sources of high and low morale among intensively interviewed community and hospital subjects are discussed in the following pages.

Morale and Physical Status

Without making reference to the level of mental health, the presence of disabling physical illness has a dramatic influence on level of morale. In Table III, we see that subjects without physical

---

21 I.e., scores below a cutting-point of 47. For our method of determining cutting-points for "high" and "low" scores, see Clark, Pierce, and Camacho (publication pending).

disability reported high morale in 73 per cent of the cases, while only 43 per cent of the physically sick did so. This is not quite as large a difference as that seen in the various mental-status groups, but it is certainly a marked one. This difference of 30 percentage points is much greater than the differences related to ill health in self-evaluation (a difference of only nine percentage points).

TABLE III

INFLUENCE OF SELECTED CHARACTERISTICS ON MORALE FOR
TWO MENTAL STATUS GROUPS

	Proportion Reporting High Morale		
	Community Sample (N=255) %	Hospital Sample (N=110) %	Total Sample (N=365)ᵃ %
Physical Disability			
Well	82	28	73
Impaired	51	37	43
Age			
60-69	79	43	70
70+	69	27	54
Sex			
Male	75	42	66
Female	74	27	59
Socioeconomic Status			
High	82	40	76
Low	61	33	48
Ethnicity			
Native-born	77	37	67
Foreign-born	69	32	57
Education			
Some college	72 ⎫ 78	(0) ⎫ 22	68
9-12 grades	81 ⎬	24 ⎬	70
0-8 grades	68 ⎭	40 ⎭	58
Main Gainful Occupation			
White collar	75	39	69
Blue collar	70	29	54
Housewife	77	38	64

ᵃ This is the number of subjects for whom morale scores (based on Follow-up II data) are available. It includes 255 community subjects, and 110 hospital subjects. These N's remain constant in all tables, subject only to minor variations, according to the number of subjects for whom data on the independent variable is not available.

If we examine morale levels for the mental-status groups, dividing each into the physically well and the physically ill, even more striking differences emerge. These data show that physical illness has the greatest influence on morale among the community sample. While 82 per cent of the physically healthy among community subjects reported high morale, a bare majority (51 per cent) of the sick managed to report more happiness than unhappiness in life.

Among the physically-healthy community subjects, good health is not taken for granted, but is rather regarded as a blessing. They are particularly reminded of their good fortune when they see the consequences of poor health among their peers. Mr. Mark Janisch (CS), for example, recalled his more robust earlier status with a certain wistfulness, but he maintained a realistic and good-natured perspective of negative change: "Now I am more tired, listless, and my memory may not be as good. I know my hearing is not as good." However, these are conditions he feels he can cope with: "I note that in a warm sunny climate I feel much better—very beneficial to me." Furthermore, despite these limitations, he could say, "I'm about average for my age. Not as vigorous as when I was sixty, but I have had no serious diseases." This man is relaxed, and his morale is good: "Old age is a nice time of your life, as long as you have your health."

This seems to be the consensus of healthy community subjects. They see themselves as free from disease, but operating at a lower threshold of good health than was the case, generally, when they were middle-aged. This development is without great alarm, for they view it as part of the natural order of things. "You are living at a lower ebb," said Mr. Janisch, and Mrs. Myrtle Manx (CS) said, "At sixty-five, I feel most fortunate in being as well as I am."

The possibility of serious disease strikes a frightening note in this otherwise relatively stoical group. The interviewer asked Mrs. Lois Willoughby (CS), "Is there anything you're very much afraid of today?" and she replied: "It's just my fear about my health sometimes. I'm not too often afraid because I know I can't do anything about it. No, I'm not exactly afraid of it. Just something I detest." The relationship between good health and the value of independence is a familiar theme among community subjects. As Mrs. Clara Bruzinsky (CS) said, "I am still healthy and am not a burden on anyone." One's ability to perform in familiar roles with the dignity of autonomy sets the boundaries of good health. These aged community people do not expect vigor or robustness. They ask only not to be incapacitated—to be able to keep going without an undue ordeal of weakness, suffering, or pain. They regard it as absurd and unrealistic to ask for too much—to yearn for the impossible health norms of middle-age or young adulthood. Thus, Mr. Albert Jay (CS) could say, "I'm slowing down a little. Some days I'm full of pep and some days not so full. Well, I guess nature is taking its own course . . . . There's nothing I can do about it. I guess I just have to take it as it comes."

Mrs. Gertrude Miller sums up the perspective of healthy community subjects in this way: "I don't think anything about my life has changed. The main thing has been to be independent and not dependent on my children. And I have a perfect horror of lying in a hospital bed."

Among the physically-ill community subjects, self-evaluation remains quite high (76 per cent reported positive self-views), but morale declines (51 per cent have high morale). Thus although about half of this group is demoralized, most do not regard this as a personal failing—sickness is merely an interloper that puts them at a tremendous disadvantage. They see themselves as strong personalities but bemoan the effects of sickness. They are frustrated with the limitations it imposes on them. As Mrs. Rita Viet (CS) said, "I want to do things—but I can't do everything I have it in my mind to do."

Mrs. Selma Reinhart (CS) has quite a positive self-image, but very low morale, directly linked with her physical incapacities. She is confined to a wheelchair and has increasing paralysis of all her limbs. She described her morale this way:

> My spirits are all right, but I get depressed at times over my inactivity. . . . Absolutely miserable, as far as comfort is concerned — not out of the house for the last four months. . . . How uncomfortable I am! I've been in this wheelchair since 1946. It's very frustrating and annoying. I can't do anything about it. The only thing I want to do — and I had everything planned — was to do away with myself, so I wouldn't be a burden to the family. Now I am so incapacitated that I can't be sure that I would be *able* to commit suicide . . . I feel useless.

I can't hold a book or turn the pages easily. I have to look at TV no matter how stupid it is because it is the easiest thing to do. I can't play records. I have to be shifted from one position to another, and I'm always uncomfortable.

Generally, then, physical illness proves to be quite detrimental to the morale of the community subjects. Curiously, however, neither the discharged nor the inpatients are adversely affected in terms of morale by physical disability; in both instances, those among the mentally ill who were *also* physically ill were more likely to report high morale levels than were those who were mentally ill *only*. In fact, out of all six physical status groups, the two most demoralized were the physically-*well* hospital subjects, either in or out of institutions.

In some ways, this is a very different picture from what we saw in the case of self-evaluation. Previously, we saw that physical illness made no significant difference in levels of self-evaluation among either the community or the inpatient groups, but that it had a clearly erosive effect on self-esteem among the discharged. We speculated that perhaps physical illness is a greater burden to the discharged patient than to the inpatient because he must maintain himself in the community and provide for his own needs, while the physically-sick inpatient at least has food, clothing, shelter, as well as medical and nursing care provided to him by the institution. Individual case studies suggest that there are some people among the inpatients for whom physical illness has a positive ego function, providing them with a more socially acceptable rationale for their hospitalization than mental disorder. Perhaps this same rationalization is also reflected in higher morale levels among the physically-ill inpatients. The data for the hospital discharged, however, seem contradictory.

SELF-EVALUATION AND MORALE LEVELS BY
PHYSICAL DISABILITY, HOSPITAL DISCHARGED SAMPLE

	Physically Well	Physically Sick	Total Discharged
Per cent with positive self-evaluation	68	43	55
Per cent with high morale	32	42	38

Since we know that self-evaluation and morale are positively correlated, a difference of this sort can seemingly be explained only by some intervening factors. Possibly it is due to some of the differences in background characteristics we describe for the discharged in Appendix A. In order to investigate this possibility, it is necessary for us to examine the relationships between morale and a number of characteristics which we have seen differentiate the various health-status groups.

Other Personal Characteristics Influencing Morale

All three major background characteristics which were related to self-evaluation (sex, socioeconomic status, and ethnicity) influence level of morale to an even greater extent, although, as we shall see, sometimes in a different direction. In addition to these factors, three other variables—age, education, and main gainful occupation—which are unrelated to self-esteem, are significantly correlated with morale scores. We will first describe the relationship of each independent variable to morale in the total sample, and then discuss any differences in the influence of the factor among the various health-status groups, both mental and physical.

Age. Age is unrelated to self-evaluation, as we have shown. Morale, however, shows lower levels with increasing age. Among those between sixty and sixty-nine years of age, 70 per cent report high morale, while 54 per cent of those seventy and over do so. Since we find a significant age difference, we can ask this question: at what particular age does the decline in morale begin, or does it show a consistent drop from the youngest to the oldest age group? If we stratify our sample by five-year-age-groups beginning with 60-64, we see this pattern:

	60-64	*65-69*	*70-74*	*75-79*	*80+*
Per cent with high morale	70	70	52	60	51

We see then that, in our total sample, morale scores do not begin to decline at age sixty and thereafter continue downward in a regular curve, but rather that the scores remain at a fairly high level throughout the sixties. In the age group from seventy to seventy-four, there is a rather sharp drop, with 18 per cent fewer reporting high morale than those in the younger groups. The next older group, those between seventy-five and seventy-nine, shows a tendency to regain higher levels of morale, with 60 per cent giving positive reports. In the oldest group, those eighty and older, the level again drops, with only 51 per cent claiming high morale. Other studies of the aged in our society have reported a similar "trough," occurring in the 70-74 period, in mood, life satisfaction, or other measures of morale.[22]

Since, as we noted in Chapter III, our hospital sample has an older average age than the community sample, the question arises as to whether the differences in morale levels seemingly related to mental illness are not, in fact, partially the result of this difference in age. While age is related to morale among both community and hospital samples, the fact of mental illness has a much more pronounced influence. Thus, if we control for mental illness, we see that the community sample, 79 per cent of the younger subjects (those under seventy) and 69 per cent of the older ones reported high morale—a difference of 10 percentage points. The age difference is somewhat greater in the hospital sample: 43 per cent high morale in the younger group and only 27 per cent high in the older patients—a difference of 16 percentage points. However, even the *younger* group in the mentally-ill sample have 26 per cent fewer reports of high morale than does the *older* group in the community sample. Controlling for age, among those in their sixties, 36 per cent more of the mentally well than the mentally ill show high morale. And among subjects seventy and older, the difference is even greater—42 per cent more community than hospital subjects have high scores. Two conclusions can be drawn from these findings: first, mental illness is far more demoralizing than increasing age; and second, mental illness is considerably more demoralizing among people over seventy years of age than it is when it first occurs during the sixties.

One explanation of this latter finding is that younger geriatric patients with psychiatric difficulties tend to show patterns of illness different from those in later stages of life; younger age groups within the hospital sample show a higher incidence of the functional disorders, which are generally assumed to be of a reversible nature, i.e., under optimal circumstances one can anticipate re-

22See Cumming and Henry (1961), but also Kutner *et al.* (1956; pp. 51-52) wherein this "trough" is found only among men and at an earlier period. Havighurst (1955) has also observed this phenomenon.

covery or, at least, some improvement. Older psychiatric patients, on the other hand, are more likely to be suffering from organic deterioration of the central nervous system stemming from senile changes or cerebral arteriosclerosis.[23] These conditions are generally thought to be progressive and unamenable to any but palliative treatment. The patient may know of these medical theories, or he may infer something of the kind from the nature of the innumerable nonverbal cues which he might pick up from hospital personnel or, equally important, from his own relatives and friends. These may influence his morale as much as his actual condition.

A second factor in the greater demoralization of the older compared to the younger mentally-ill patient may lie in the realm of social supports. The older patient is more likely to be widowed, to have lost his old friends, and is less likely to have an adequate income or funds for drugs, private medical care, or access to outpatient facilities. His social world is smaller and those who care about him fewer. Under these circumstances, the onset of serious mental or emotional disturbance can indeed be a frightening prospect.

Sex. Sex differences in morale for the total sample are quite small—66 per cent of the men and 59 per cent of the women in the sample report high levels. However, when we examine each of the samples, community and hospital, independently, we see that all of this difference is due to the mentally-ill group; there are no sex differences in morale among the mentally-healthy sample. Among the mentally ill, a significant difference is seen: 42 per cent of the men and only 27 per cent of the women in the hospital sample claim to be more satisfied than dissatisfied with life. An examination of the personal characteristics of men compared with women in the hospital sample, however, indicates that this morale difference is simply the additive result of three other intervening variables, and probably not related to sex difference *per se* at all. The women in the hospital sample are older than the men, as we reported in Chapter III. They are also more apt to be physically

---

[23]For a diagnostic profile of the hospital sample, see Simon, Lowenthal, and Epstein (publication pending).

ill; among hospital subjects for whom we have morale scores, 52 per cent of the men compared with 74 per cent of the women are physically disabled. Men are also more likely to be discharged than are women in the hospital sample: in the mentally-ill group, only 37 per cent of the men compared with 55 per cent of the women were still confined to psychiatric facilities at the time the morale scores were obtained. We have already seen that these three factors, older age, poor physical health, and inpatient status, make for low morale. Since the women are more likely than the men to have all these characteristics, the correlation with sex in this sample is probably a spurious one.

Socioeconomic Status. Poverty has a potent influence on morale among all age groups, including the elderly.[24] In fact, mental illness itself is the only other factor of all those we examined which is more strongly related to morale level. In the total sample, 76 per cent of the more economically comfortable people had high levels of satisfaction, while only 48 per cent of the poorer segment did so.

When Mr. Edwin Butler, one of the more prosperous community subjects, was asked to name the main satisfactions in his life, he replied, "I have security for retirement. We have a good income for the rest of our lives. It couldn't be easier; there is nothing I actually need that I can't afford." By contrast, Mr. Lawrence Southern (CS), who is trying to support himself and care for his seriously disabled wife on an income of just over $100 a month, reported:

> The one thing I fear most is my physical and financial set-up. Blue Cross really cuts you off when you are sixty-five, just when you need it. Most old folks worry about security. Health goes and takes all your money. Doctors and hospitals really take you. They charge 60 cents for aspirin; they charge 75 cents for three-cent pills — the ones I buy at home for my wife . . . seems

---

24Harrington (1963) has written quite eloquently on the many evils of the "New Poverty" in this country, not the least of which is low morale. Epidemiological studies of mental illnesses in communities have also uncovered ample evidence of this correlation. Readers are referred to two outstanding recent studies of poverty and mental illness: Leighton *et al.* (1963) and Langner and Michael (1963).

like everybody's cheating . . . I worry; everybody gets in the
dumps sometime — I'm no different. I'd say that was quite
normal.

Again, since we know that the hospital sample has, on the
average, a considerably lower economic level than the community sample, we need to investigate the relative influences of poverty
and mental illness on morale. For the total sample, 28 per cent
fewer of the poor than of the more affluent subjects reported high
morale. Comparing community and hospital samples, we see that
the impact of poverty is much greater upon community subjects
than it is upon those in the hospital group. In the community
sample, 21 per cent more of the high socioeconomic group than
the low reported high morale; among the mentally ill, the difference is only 7 per cent. However, these figures also demonstrate
that poverty is less corrosive to life satisfaction than is mental
illness. Thus, if we control for socioeconomic status, looking first
at those in the wealthier portion of the sample, 82 per cent of
the wealthier in the community sample reported high morale,
compared with only 40 per cent of the wealthier in the hospital
sample—a difference of 42 per cent. A similar difference (28 percentage points) is seen among the poor in the two samples. In fact,
even the poor in the mentally-healthy group have significantly
higher morale scores than the wealthier group in the hospital sample (a difference of 21 percentage points). To summarize these
findings, wealth and mental health are both conducive to high
levels of satisfaction, and seem to be additive in their influence
on morale levels; but emotional illness is considerably more damaging than poverty. In fact, as we see in comparing the two mental
status groups, mental illness has a leveling effect on morale differences related to financial status: the majority of both socioeconomic groups in the hospital sample have low morale, while
among the mentally healthy, the majority of even those elderly
people with serious financial worries are able to find more happiness than unhappiness in life.

Ethnicity. Place of birth is a fourth background characteristic
that we examined in relation to morale. In the total sample,
morale differences between the native born and the foreign born

are not great, but they do reach the level of statistical significance. Ten per cent more of the native-born aged than those born abroad had high morale scores. This difference, we suspect, is in part the result of greater intergenerational conflict between immigrants and their children, as we will discuss in Chapter VII, and in part the simple fact of growing old in a different culture from that in which one was reared.[25] American society provides less well-defined role models for the aged than do many other cultures, particularly those of a peasant type. Even in cases where the aging immigrant is from another industrial society and understands what is expected of him in American culture, the internalized standards of his parent culture may continue to impinge upon him, causing him to behave in ways which are devalued here, and leaving him with a sense of disappointment, unrest, and frustration.

Gerald Spenser (HS), for example, was born and reared in a rural village in Sussex, England. His father had been very much the same sort of man in his later years that Mr. Spenser is now. Mr. Spenser's father, though, lived out his life on his native soil, where his behavior—somewhat eccentric, to be sure—was not only accepted but even rather highly sanctioned, as adding color and interest to the local scene. Mr. Spenser is striving for the same kind of social approval in his later years, doing many of the same things with the same goals in mind that his father did. In a village in Sussex, fifty years before, Mr. Spenser's father was regarded as an eccentric, but nevertheless a man of character and an asset to the community. In San Francisco in the 1960's, Mr. Spenser is regarded as "a character," and his behavior as bordering on the bizarre. His neglect of some of the basic values of American life (primarily, conformity to our standards of sanitation) resulted in serious conflicts with his American-born wife and children—and, finally, even the wisdom of allowing him to remain at large was called into question. His family had him picked up and held for psychiatric observation. We have met Mr. Spenser in earlier pages of this report; he is mentioned here again to illustrate a type of man who has learned only one way in which to grow old grace-

---

[25]These ethnic differences do *not* result from differences in socioeconomic status, as was demonstrated in the first part of this chapter.

fully in his native culture but finds this pattern quite unacceptable in his adopted land. His optimism is becoming more frantic
and more forced and signs of indignation and despair are beginning to appear.

Another subject who has suffered a decline in morale because
of ethnic differences is Mrs. Rena Trocopian (HS). Mrs. Trocopian was born and reared in Armenia and brought to the United
States as a young bride for Mr. Trocopian who had preceded her
and had made the arrangements to wed her through a native marriage broker. As a small child, Mrs. Trocopian had witnessed the
slaughter of her parents in the religious wars that raged in Armenia at this time. In consequence, Mrs. Trocopian was reared
by her grandmother, an elderly woman of strong character, who
was respected in the peasant village of the homeland as a folk-
curer of considerable gifts and esoteric knowledge. This old woman was the repository for all the traditional herbal remedies
and was held in an awe bordering on fear by the ordinary villagers
who attributed such medical skills less to intellect and learning
than to a possible indulgence in the black arts. As Mr. Spenser
modeled his old age upon his father's, so Mrs. Trocopian, after a
lifetime of service to a demanding, vituperative husband, strug-
gled to attain the privileged and respected status of a great healer.
"I am very talented," she said, "creative. I have a strong mind to
overcome the weak. I could have been a physician. I am strong in
my mind, both a scientist and a poet. I can create energy. I have
the power to heal." But, unfortunately for Mrs. Trocopian, there
was no place in her new world for her to reincarnate her old
grandmother. Her husband, twenty years older than she, entertained a culturally-conditioned view of women as a lesser breed.
This, coupled with his impatience with her youth, the discrimination she suffered at the hands of her Protestant, English-speaking
Anglo-Saxon neighbors, and her children's condescending distaste
for her "old country" ways and ideas, all conspired to bring her
to the threshold of old age with deep anxieties concerning her
own worth and ill-concealed anger for a lifetime of humiliation.

Mrs. Trocopian yearned for the respect and influence her
grandmother had been able to muster. She began to speak to her
friends and neighbors about her special healing powers which she

had inherited from this woman, referring to her as "a doctor." She tried to convince people of her sincere interest in the suffering of others ("Whenever somebody gets sick, first thing I think of— what can I do to help them?") and of her natural gifts to heal. In 1959, her feelings of resentment against her neighbors and her unappreciative family burst into open suspicion and hostility, resulting in her admission to the psychiatric wards of the county hospital. Now discharged, she has come at last to face the realities of living in an urban, technologically-sophisticated society where medicine is practiced exclusively by highly trained specialists with university degrees and where healing is regarded as a scientific technique—not a mystical power of the mind, no matter how poetic. Mrs. Trocopian is still convinced of her gifts, but knows that the seeds of her creativity lie in sterile ground. "Lots gone to waste," she laments. Without the prestigeful and exciting role that she had envisioned would be hers in her declining years, her morale sinks lower and lower. She sees no other possible use for her remaining years. She describes herself as deeply unhappy: "For the last four years, I don't even feel like talking. I just have to do it, go on like this, to the end of my days. Only when I go to church does my spirit go up. Many times I'd rather die. There is nothing more to look forward to."[26]

These two abbreviated case reviews show some of the typical problems faced by immigrant aged, but the quantified data point to one additional finding that merits attention here. In Table III, we note that mental illness has an equally great impact on the

---

[26]This case presents many striking parallels with the development of *brujas*, the "witches" of Spain. The Spanish historian, Caro Baroja (1964), comments about these social deviates in a way that could well be a gloss on Mrs. Trocopian's life: "The witch of country areas is usually an old woman, an outsider, who is both feared and despised, and who has some knowledge of quackery . . . . It is a pity that modern psychologists have not had a chance to examine some of the women in question. They would almost certainly have found them to be rather insignificant people in their normal environment, who wanted to be far superior to, and very different from, what they really were. Ultimately they came to believe they had the status they desired . . . [that they] could do the most remarkable things. They usually started their activities when they were middle-aged or old . . . . [A] woman usually becomes a witch after the initial failure of her life as a woman; after [her circumstances] have left her with a sense of impotence or disgrace . . . . In old age, perhaps her only satisfaction is [her practice of magic] . . . ."

morale levels of both native and foreign-born subjects—a slightly different situation from what we saw to be the case with self-evaluation. In that analysis, we found that mental illness had a more negative influence on self-esteem among the foreign-born than among native Americans. We speculated that immigrants might have a greater sense of alienation and failure once they are institutionalized, since institutional life provides them with no reference group of compatriots, such as they might have enjoyed in community life. Apparently, such an interpretation does not apply equally to morale—although one might reasonably expect alienation to be reflected in both dimensions of the personal system we treat here, self-esteem *and* morale. Both native and immigrant Americans find mental illness and institutionalization greatly demoralizing. Evidently, both groups are depressed with their plight, but more of the foreign born are adding self-blame to their already heavy burden.

Education: Educational level also offers some interesting contrasts with findings for the same variable in regard to self-evaluation. There, we found that educational level was unrelated to the self-view, but, in contrast, we find some relationship to morale, although it is an irregular one in the total sample. In this larger sample for whom we have computed self-evaluation and morale scores, we find 10 per cent of the most highly educated group (those with some college background) reporting higher morale than do those of the lowest educational level (no more than eighth grade). However, the intermediate group (some years of high school) show an equally high morale: 70 per cent are in good spirits, compared with 68 per cent of the college-educated and 58 per cent of the elementary school group. When we look at community and hospital subjects separately, however, we see a picture that is quite in contrast with this. The mentally well from the community show much the same pattern we saw in the total figures: the elementary-school group reports the lowest morale scores (only 68 per cent so reporting) and the high school group reports a larger proportion in comparison (81 per cent), but community subjects who have attended college lie in between these two: only 72 per cent of them report high morale.

We suspect that two factors are operating here. First, the trend toward a higher morale among those with more education is very likely a reflection of differences in socioeconomic status—a factor we have already seen to be highly correlated with morale. Second, the slightly lower morale level among those with some education beyond secondary school may be a reflection of differences in class values. We suspect that people who were born before the turn of the century—as most members of this sample were—and who succeeded in attaining quite high educational achievements for that period in American life, may have had very different levels of aspiration from those who did not go beyond high school. There is also the possibility that higher education induces a greater facility to articulate grievances as well as a keener dissatisfaction with life, when it fails to measure up to optimal expectations—as is likely to happen in old age.

However, when we look at the morale figures for different educational levels in the *hospital* sample, we see quite a different picture. Among the elementary group, 40 per cent report high morale; only 24 per cent of those with high-school training do so; and not a single person with a college background who was also mentally ill claimed to be free of depression.[27] Clearly, the higher the educational level of the subject, the more he finds mental illness incompatible with any feeling other than that of despair. This is one instance in which higher educational level is no asset; the most poorly educated seem best able to tolerate cognitive and emotional disturbances in later life. Although education and socioeconomic status are positively correlated among hospital subjects as well as those in the community, the fact of greater financial security does not begin to compensate for the loss of mental health among those who, perhaps, had expected a great deal more in their declining years as a result of the educational "advantages." This becomes even clearer if we look again at the educational-level data in Table III. These figures show that men-

---

[27]Note, however, that there are only a handful of people in the hospital sample who attended college. A more reliable procedure would be to combine all those with education beyond the elementary level into a single group, and—if this is done, 22 per cent prove to have high morale, compared with 40 per cent of the elementary group, as shown in Table III.

tal illness has exactly twice the impact on morale among all those who went beyond elementary school as among those who did not (a difference of 56 percentage points in the better educated group, and only 28 per cent in the poorer).

Occupation: The last of the factors we examined in relation to morale is that of main gainful occupation. The total sample was divided into three groups: those whose major life work was in a white collar job, those with principally blue collar employment, and those who had spent most of their adult lives as housewives. Looking at the total sample, we see that 15 per cent more white collar than blue collar workers reported high levels of morale, with housewives at an intermediate level of morale. These differences need not be explored any further, however, since they result entirely from the intervening effect of socioeconomic status. As blue collar workers get old, they have greater financial problems than people in white collar jobs, in almost exactly the same degree as they have lower levels of morale. There are no significant differences in these relationships when we control for psychiatric disability. Occupation, then, seems to exert no independent influence on morale in this sample.

To summarize the foregoing analysis, we have found five variable characteristics in this sample of elderly people which have significant independent influences on the amount of depression or satisfaction they report having in their lives. These are, in descending order of importance, the advantages of:

(1) Mental health
(2) Physical health
(3) Adequate standard of living
(4) Relatively younger age
(5) Native birth

However, these relationships are imperfect ones. There are older people in our sample who remain content with their lives despite illness, poverty, or advanced age. This suggests that there may be qualitative differences in the underlying sources of satisfaction or depression among different groups of older people. To this end, we have undertaken a content analysis of intensive interviews, in the hope that we may be able to trace different patterns of needs and need-satisfactions among the mentally well and the mentally sick. A knowledge of such differences may add to our understanding of adaptive and maladaptive patterns in the personal system of the aged.

CONCLUSION

In this chapter, we have been able to identify and measure two dimensions of personality and show how these dimensions function within two major groups of elderly people, the mentally healthy and the mentally ill. This kind of quantitative analysis provides some preliminary insights into the personal worlds of our subjects. There will be further explored in the wealth of narrative material from the intensive interviews. However, we know that each personal system is embedded deep within a social matrix. Indeed, separating the personal from the social, which we have done for analytic purposes, is an over-simplification of life experience: no selfhood can develop without the verification and expectations of others; no buoyant sense of the self can be maintained for long outside of a viable reference to fellow beings in our milieux. Nonetheless, we must measure the basic components of this interaction of our subjects with the world around them. Chapter V does so for two of these components, social activity levels and social roles. In Chapters VI and VII, we will combine our two methodological approaches and attempt to be more faithful to the living, dynamic experience of this interaction between the self and the others.

Chapter V

THE SOCIAL SYSTEM:
SOME MEASURES OF SOCIAL FUNCTION
AMONG THE AGED

INTRODUCTORY REMARKS

In this chapter and what follows, the social world of the aged will be assessed. In so doing, we turn away momentarily from the phenomenological approach and observe our subjects from the point of view of the social analyst. From the self-reports of our subjects, statements from collaterals, and interviewer observations, we have developed two measures of social functioning: a social-status index and a scale for levels of social interaction. These measures afford us a somewhat objective over-view of the social behavior of these people.

THE SOCIAL-STATUS INDEX[1]

Old age, for most of our subjects, is a time of dramatic change in one's social (and, of course, personal) significance. Whole sets

---

[1]In this discussion, the definitions of *status* and *role* are those formulated by Linton (1945) and further developed by Merton (1957). Linton defined status as a *position* occupied by designated individuals in a social system; he defined role as a *behavior* resulting from the patterned expectations attributed to that position. Linton writes: "Every status is linked with a particular role, but the two things are by no means the same from the point of view of the individual. His statuses are ascribed to him on the basis of his age and sex, his birth or marriage into a particular family unit, and so forth. His roles are learned on the basis of his statuses, either current or anticipated. Insofar as it represents overt behavior, a role is the dynamic aspect of a status: what the individual has to do in order to validate his occupation of the status" (p. 77). Merton expanded this notion by pointing out that a particular social status involves not a single associated role but an array of associated roles. He calls this group a *role-set,* defining it as "that complement of role relationships which persons have by virtue of occupying a particular social status" (p. 369). Merton further designates a second term, *status-set,* as the complement of various statuses in which individuals find themselves, for example, the varied statuses which one woman might occupy conjointly, such as a teacher who is also a wife, also a mother, a Catholic, a Republican, and so on. In terms of the plan of this book, this chapter will be primarily concerned with *statuses.* Chapter VI will treat the perceptions of *roles.*

of statuses may be lost or, to all intents and purposes, become non-functional within the short space of a few years. Children grow up, marry, and leave home. Forced retirement may ease a man out of his worker status. The chances of widowhood increase. And our culture provides almost no statuses to replace these. Modern social conditions have chipped away at whatever meaning the status of grandparent had in American life to the point that— for many in our sample, at least—it is simply a nominal one. Lacking the social prerogatives for a wide participation in social life, it is no wonder that we observe the phenomenon of social withdrawal among many of the elderly. And, in contrast with other findings, our data lead us to believe that most of the old people we interviewed were not at all happy to rest content with this "inescapable fact" of growing old.

In order to assess the relative levels of social function in our sample, we developed a measure we have called a social-status index. By means of direct questions and corroborated evidence, we determined the occupancy of the following eight social statuses for all subjects:

Spouse
Parent
Grandparent
Sibling
Friend
Employed person
Organization member
Religious person

This list by no means exhausts the possible statuses that might be occupied by older people; it simply represents those we have considered to be the most significant. Another feature of this list needs mention at this point but will be developed later: i.e., the first four statuses refer to kinship (ascribed) relationships, the last four to nonkin (achieved) statuses.

Before proceeding further, we must point out that occupancy of only a few of these statuses does not necessarily imply social isolation or a low level of social involvement *in all cases*. Exceptions abound enough for us to take cognizance of them, as the following case will illustrate.

Mr. Grant VanDamm's life pattern illustrates how some individuals occupying only a few of the statutes on the index are not necessarily socially isolated. At sixty-one, Mr. VanDamm was still employed when we first encountered him, but his principal motive for remaining in the work force was not financial (he was receiving an adequate pension since his retirement from the Marine Corps nine years before) but social. A lifelong bachelor, he became bored with his life after his retirement. "I loafed for about a year . . . but after this period of loafing, I soon realized that I could not exist like this. My nature was to be active, more active than just loafing around." Consequently, he took a job with a bank. Within three years he had worked himself up to a position of supervisor, directing a small group of men who, in cars, drop off and pick up securities and cash for the bank. With this team of men, Mr. VanDamm reconstructed his social life much along the lines he had known in the Marine Corps. "The six of us who are close — we meet one or two times a month and go to dinner." Mr. VanDamm lives in a one-room apartment with no cooking facilities or private bath, but he keeps his living quarters military-neat and continues to make his bed in the tight military style. He finds it "a cinch to be tidy. There are two ways of doing things — the right way and the wrong way." However, his bachelorhood sometimes distresses him ("I've gotten used to being around people") and he freely admits that "the worst times are when the weather is bad and I can't leave my apartment. I just sit around the room and look at the four walls or read or watch TV. It's the worst time for being tense or nervous." But when such moments arrive, "usually I call my girl friend to go out on a date or to a show or dinner. At those times, I like to talk to her and be around people." To all appearances, his relationship with "Babe" is settled and mature: "I don't think there's any plan of ours to get married — been a bachelor too long — but we enjoy each other's company and we can talk about many things without being embarrassed or feel foolish or anything like that." His only "real worry" is his ninety-year-old mother who was quite ill in a nursing home in a nearby city. Thus, although Mr. VanDamm occupies only two of the statuses included in the index (friend and employed person), he nevertheless functions within these limitations to his fullest capacity.

Subjects have been rated on this index simply by the number of these statuses occupied at the time of the *baseline* study. We chose to take a tabulation of statuses at that point in time in order to eliminate from our consideration the problems of enforced role attrition resulting from the institutionalization of our hospitalized subjects and their subsequent removal from their customary arenas of social activity. When information on status-occupancy was collected from hospital subjects, they (or their collaterals) were asked to report on *usual* role performance in the period just prior to the onset of any recent disabling symptoms which had led to the hospitalization. For instance, if a subject had been regularly employed prior to an episode of congestive heart failure which had led to an acute brain syndrome resulting in his hospitalization, that person was counted as an "employed person" at the time of the baseline study. The same is true for such statuses as organization member or religious person. Also, to be counted as occupying the kinship statuses of parent, grandparent, or sibling, a subject need not have been active recently in these positions. He might not have seen any of his children for a year or more, but if he reported living children, he was counted as a parent.

Mental health in old age is positively correlated with continuous and active social involvement in the post-sixty years: 85 per cent of the community subjects were occupying five to eight of the selected statuses at the time we first met them. As far as the hospital subjects are concerned, only 30 per cent of those who were later to be discharged functioned at such a high level of social involvement and only 12 per cent of those who were still in the hospital two years later and had been so involved at the time of their admission. Thus, even before confinement to a psychiatric institution, the mentally ill were much less involved, in a formal sense, with society.

Before these differences can be attributed entirely to mental health or illness, however, we must look at another important influence previously noted: the mentally-healthy aged are also more likely to be physically healthy and are thus in a better position to occupy certain statuses, such as that of employed person or organizational member. In our total sample, many more (76 per cent) of the physically well occupy five or more social statuses than do those who are physically disabled (49 per cent). In sum, it seems that both physical and mental illness are related to a paucity of social statuses, but mental illness has by far the more potent influence.

TABLE IV

INFLUENCE OF SELECTED VARIABLES ON SOCIAL
FUNCTION MEASURES FOR TWO MENTAL STATUS GROUPS

| | Baseline Social Status Index[a] (Per Cent Occupying Five or more Statuses) | | Baseline Social Interaction Level[a] (Per Cent Engaged in Social Activity Outside Dwelling Unit) | |
	Community %	Hospital %	Community %	Hospital %
Physical Status				
Physically well	89	22	90	25
Physically impaired	75	21	70	12
Age				
60-69	86	26	89	19
70+	84	19	78	13
Sex				
Male	80	24	79	13
Female	90	20	88	17
Socioeconomic Status				
High	92	25	89	15
Low	73	22	76	15
Education				
Some college	90	(0)	90	21
9-12 grades	89	12	88	16
0-8 grades	78	32	73	17

[a] The sample for whom baseline status index scores were available is 332. The sample for baseline social interaction level, however, includes all baseline subjects for whom the scores could be obtained. The larger sample was utilized in this case to permit multi-variate analysis while maintaining single cell n's of sufficient size to obtain reliable distributions. The total n in this case is 823.

The influence of physical illness on the status index for community subjects as compared with hospital subjects, however, shows a curious pattern (Table IV). Physical disability is related to a low status index *only* among community subjects. Of these,

89 per cent of the physically healthy score five or more on the status index; but among the physically ill, fewer (75 per cent) occupy a comparable number of statuses. By comparison, among the mentally-ill subjects (whether they were later discharged or remained as inpatients), the proportion occupying five or more social statuses prior to admission was the same for both the physically sick (21 per cent) and the physically well (22 per cent)

These findings are further dramatized by examining mean status index scores for six groups of subjects in the study sample, as follows:

Community Physically Well	Community Physically Impaired	Discharged Physically Well	Discharged Physically Impaired	Inpatients Physically Well	Inpatients Physically Impaired
6.2	5.7	3.6	3.9	3.1	2.9

It is clear from these figures that as disability increases, there is an accompanying decline in the social statuses occupied by older people. There is, however, one irregularity in this trend: discharged hospital subjects who are also physically well show lower scores on the status index than do the discharged who are physically impaired. This is a pattern similar to that we found in our study of disability and morale scores. In Chapter IV, we suggested that physical illness among the hospital discharged seems to serve a compensatory function for the mentally ill, perhaps providing them with a more acceptable rationale than "insanity" for their period of hospitalization, and thus permitting them to maintain higher levels of morale. This possibility, however, is inadequate to explain why the physically-healthy members of the discharged hospital sample also have fewer social statuses than those who are disabled. One probable explanation lies in differences in the characteristics of the two groups. In the hospital sample (as we have shown in Appendix A), the physically healthy are more likely to be younger males, a group which, among those who were discharged by the time of the second follow-up interview, contained many alcoholics, and most of these men had come to the county screening wards from the Skid Row district of the city. Bogue (1963) offers a poignantly dramatic description of the anomic, roleless existence of these men. Another probable factor in this finding is related to state hospital policy governing the discharge of elderly patients. If a patient is physically ill or disabled and thus in need of care and assistance, he must have social supports—someone to provide that care—before the hospital will release him (see Lowenthal and Trier [in press] and Lowenthal, Berkman and Associates [1966], Chapter 13).

But the main point in these figures is that mental illness alone, even without the compounding influence of physical disability, is associated with markedly lower levels of status occupancy in our sample. However, the differences in age levels, sex distributions, and socioeconomic conditions between the community and hospital samples need to be examined as independent influences on the status index.

Age and Status Index

In the total sample, people under seventy years of age occupy more statuses on the average than do those seventy and over. Thus 73 per cent of the younger group and only 60 per cent of the older group occupy five or more statuses. However, since the mentally-healthy sample is proportionately younger than the mentally-ill group, some of this difference might be a reflection of mental status rather than age *per se*. In order to explore this possibility, we examined the influence of age while controlling for mental illness. Most of the age variation in the total sample disappears when each mental status group is examined separately. Thus, among community subjects, there is virtually no difference in the proportions of younger and older subjects scoring high on the status index: 86 per cent of the younger subjects and 84 per cent of the older ones have scores of five or more. And, among hospital patients, status index scores are uniformly low, regardless of relative age. Twenty-six per cent of those under seventy and 19 per cent of those seventy and older were occupying five or more statuses prior to hospital admission. The apparent age differences in the total sample, then, are simply artifacts of different age distributions in the two mental status groups. In the sample, if we control for mental illness, there is no significant reduction with age of formal social statuses below the level of five on the index. (To be sure, there is *some* status attrition with age—more of the older group than the younger are retired or widowed, in both samples. The principal finding in these data, however, is that, in terms of proportions having scores above and below the midpoint on our scale of statuses, there are no differences between age groups.) In other words, there is nothing in the fact of increasing age alone, apart from mental or physical disability, that necessarily or drastically diminishes the individual's score of *formal* positions as a member of his society.

Sex and Status Index

Although there are no sex differences in the total study sample in proportions scoring high on the status index, some differences do emerge when we control the data for mental status. There are no sex differences in status index in the hospital sample; community women, however, appear to have more social statuses on the average than do community men. Ninety per cent of the mentally-healthy females occupy five or more statuses, compared with 80 per cent of the males. This seems a little strange, since we would expect more of the men in the community sample to be employed and fewer of them to be widowed—other things being equal—and therefore to have more opportunity for earning higher scores. However, the women prove to be more socially involved than the men. Before attributing this difference entirely to variations between the sexes in social attitudes or life styles, we examined our data for the possible intervening influence of poverty. In other words, we wondered if it might be that the men were on the average poorer than the women in our community sample. We therefore examined in more detail the relationships among three factors: social involvement, sex, and socioeconomic status.

Socioeconomic Status and the Status Index

In our total study sample, which includes both community and hospital subjects, we find that the occupancy of a relatively

large number of social statuses is a characteristic of the wealthier members, but not of the poorer ones. A large majority (84
per cent) of the more affluent subjects occupy five or more social
statuses, while less than half (49 per cent) of the poor are involved to that extent in the social structure. At first glance, it
would seem that financial and social riches go hand in hand.
The mentally ill in this sample, however, are poorer on the average than the mentally healthy. How much of this dearth of social
relationships, then, is the companion of poverty, and how much
of it is related to the presence of mental illness?

The figures on socioeconomic status and the status index
taken for the two samples individually (Table IV) show that
hospital subjects, regardless of economic condition, have few
formal statuses. Only 22 per cent of the hospital poor and 25 per
cent of the hospital "rich" have as many as five social statuses.
(Precious few are actually "rich" by ordinary standards; here we
are referring to those who score above the median on our index
of Socioeconomic Status.) Again, as in the figures on physical disability, we see evidence of the "flattening" effect of mental illness with respect to the functional level of the individual; that
is, in the presence of mental illness, neither good health nor relative wealth serves to allay social poverty. Or, looking at these facts
in a slightly different way: *if an aged individual is bereft of social
alliances, neither an adequate standard of living nor good physical health diminishes his risk of mental breakdown in later life.*

Among community subjects, however, there is a clear relationship between social involvement and financial condition.
Nearly all (92 per cent) of the wealthier community subjects
have high scores on the status index. Fewer (73 per cent) of the
poorer subjects show that degree of social involvement. Let us
emphasize, though, that even the poorest group of elderly people
in the community are far more socially affiliated than even the
affluent among the mentally ill.

Let us return now to our discussion of sex differences in the
degree of formal social involvement among community subjects.
The following percentages show the relative influence of poverty
on the status index for men compared with women:

STATUS INDEX BY SOCIOECONOMIC STATUS AND SEX, COMMUNITY SAMPLE

Socioeconomic Status	Men (per cent occupying 5 or more statuses)	Women (per cent occupying 5 or more statuses)
High	91	92
Low	57	87
Total	80	90
	(N=104)	(N=118)

These figures show that poverty has an entirely different influence on the number of social statuses held for men and for women in the community sample. There is a strong and positive relationship between financial condition and social statuses among the men—91 per cent of the wealthier men score high on the status index. This is almost the same proportion as seen among the wealthier women (92 per cent). Similarly, the poorer women as well hold many social offices (in 87 per cent of the cases). It is only among men of low socioeconomic status that we see a marked drop in the proportion occupying five or more positions (only 57 per cent). In other words, the relationship between economic and social poverty (as defined by the status index) is a characteristic confined to the men in our community sample. Among women, the relationship disappears entirely.

These findings provide further understanding of the relationship we have already described between sex and number of social statuses. It seems apparent that poverty has a significant social meaning for elderly men—a meaning which fails to affect women in the same way. Why should this be so?

We have already seen, in Chapter IV, that self-esteem among men in our sample is strongly linked with the work role, and that success in that role (as measured by financial achievement) is more critical for men than for women. Thus, within the *personal* system, high levels of function among elderly men and women have different foundations. Furthermore, our data on the status index suggest that the same differences in sex-linked values and goals may also relate to *social* function. This complex set of relationships among several factors—sex-roles, poverty, self-esteem, and social supports—is a difficult one to unravel. We will have more to say about these dynamics in Chapter VII, where perhaps we may gain more insights from looking at social life patterns characteristic of some of our intensively-studied male and female subjects—especially those in the poorer segment of the community sample. By way of preview, one thing is suggested by those case studies: men are quite dependent upon work contacts and upon their wives for populating their social worlds. But relationships with fellow-workers are seldom sustained long past retirement age, and if a man has no wife (or woman) to play the role of hostess and social arbiter for him, his contacts with others may undergo serious attrition in old age. The following case illustrates this.

Mr. Lemuel Bauer (CS) exemplifies quite well this frequent pattern of male dependency upon females for participation in the social world. At seventy, Mr. Bauer lives with his daughter which he has done for twenty years following a divorce from his wife. He quite frankly admits that his daughter is "the man of the house." While she works as a minor executive for a five-and-dime chain, Mr. Bauer stays home and does all the housework, shopping, and cooking. He is especially proud of his cookies which he frequently offered to interviewers during our sessions with him. To all accounts, he is an excellent cook and housekeeper; as one interviewer phrased it: "The apartment is neat as a pin from one end to the other." Mr. Bauer appears to be in no way conflicted about his role in this unusual relationship with his daughter. He is cheerful, and freely asserts that he wants "to see the good side of everything." Aside from the friends his daughter brings home to entertain, Mr. Bauer has only minimal contacts with others — shopkeepers, for the most part. Outside the home, he limits himself to solitary walks in the neighborhood. Since living with his daughter, he has dropped all former associations: "It takes quite a bit of money to belong to them organizations, you know." When asked about friends, he could respond only in terms of the few fellow workers he had been friendly with prior to his retirement at fifty-six, none of whom he had seen since then. [No friends at all currently?] "Well, my daughter has her friends and they come over. I chew the fat with them. We have people over to dinner." [But would you consider remarriage?] "No, in the first place, if I got married I'd be excommunicated from the church. . . . But another thing, I can go when I want now, go downtown, go out at night. I don't have to say, 'Can I go out at night?' You can't do that when you're married." In short, Mr. Bauer is well content with his present mode of life and sees no need for any change.

On the other hand, older women seem more often to sustain former social relationships into old age—perhaps, in part, because fewer of them are linked to joint employment. But the older women in our sample also seem more adept at establishing new relationships—making new friends, getting acquainted with new neighbors, and creating for themselves new networks of social involvement to replace the often lost relationships to home, husband, and children. The traditional female role thus provides some lasting benefits for even the poor aged women in our society (*cf.* Blau, 1961).

Education and the Status Index

Among members of the total study sample, education is clearly linked to the number of formal social statuses occupied. The relationship is not as marked as it is for socioeconomic status, but it is in the same direction. Of those in the total sample with some college education, 86 per cent score five or more on the status index, as do 72 per cent of those who attended high school. However, among subjects with only an elementary education or less, only 61 per cent score five or higher on the index.

These figures, however, in part simply reflect differences in average educational levels of the mentally-healthy and mentally-ill groups. When we control these data for mental illness, we see the same pattern among community subjects that prevails for the study sample as a whole: the higher the educational level, the greater the number of social statuses. Among hospital subjects, however, the relationship is reversed. In the presence of mental illness, social involvement *decreases* with educational level. Thus, while 32 per cent of hospital subjects at the lowest educational level have five or more social statuses, only 12 per cent of those who reached high school score as high, and not a single one of those who attended college occupy as many as five social statuses.

Two interpretations of this finding are possible. First, it may be that individuals with a high educational level have higher aspirations and expectations of themselves than do those with rudimentary schooling. If so, the onset of psychiatric symptoms may result in greater self-recrimination than among those with more modest expectations of themselves and their abilities. Self-blame, in turn, may stimulate withdrawal from some of the voluntary social alliances (friendship, organization membership, and religious participation, specifically) that we have examined (*cf.* Lowenthal, 1964b).

These same findings, however, can be interpreted in a second way. Lack of education may create for the individual certain stresses (economic problems, a menial job, less stable employment, or other factors) which maximize the threat of emotional disturbance in old age—a threat which is only partially offset by social involvement. In the presumably less stressful life situation of the more highly educated person, mental breakdown would, in many instances, be less likely—unless there were an accompanying social alienation. In other words, perhaps the implicit process by which our hospital sample was instituted has selected out a singularly isolated group of former college students. Actually, this second explanation is more likely the correct one. As we will discuss in following pages, our second measure of social function —level of social interaction (which measures social *volition* to a greater extent than does the status index)—shows no increase in voluntary social withdrawal among the more highly educated group in the hospital sample. It is more probable, therefore, that the higher the educational level of the individual, the more dramatic a social deprivation he must suffer in order to succumb to mental breakdown in old age. And (returning to the data on the total sample) people with more education are likely to have the advantage of more numerous social relationships.

We do not know exactly what it is about having completed more years of formal schooling that promotes a proliferation of social statuses. More than likely it is a reflection of differences in social class behavior, described in other studies as having an influence on social participation (Dotson, 1951; Axelrod, 1956).

Summary of Factors Influencing Status Index

To review the previous findings, our data indicate that mental illness is accompanied by a dramatic decrease in the number of formal social positions held by an aged individual. Physical disability also lessens his involvement, but mental illness has by far the greater influence. In fact, it is only in the *absence* of mental disorder that physical impairment is a potent factor in social deprivation; in the *presence* of mental disorder, the addition of physical disability has no independent effect.

In our sample, the status index is correlated with four demographic characteristics: age, sex, socioeconomic status, and educational level all influence the number of statuses occupied. (Ethnicity and religion proved to be unrelated.) However, the observed age differences in the total sample were almost entirely due to the intervening influence of mental illness. In other words, the mentally ill were older on the average than the mentally-healthy subjects in our sample; and, when we controlled for mental status, age differences in social involvement disappeared entirely. Sex, socioeconomic status, and education, however, exerted independent influences on the index. The last two of these are closely interrelated, since in our sample (as is generally the case in Western cultures) there is a fairly high correlation between education and economic condition. There are, then, four major independent influences on the number of formal social positions held by the elderly: mental status, social class factors, and (in the absence of mental disorder) physical disability, and sex roles. The dynamics of these relationships are discussed in further detail with case analyses in Chapter VII.

Ascribed and Achieved Statuses and Mental Health

One further question about the social statuses of the aged arises from the foregoing analysis: With the development of mental illness, do *achieved* statuses, such as those of employed person or organization member, tend to be dropped, and *ascribed* or kinship statuses persist? To explore this question, each of three mental status groups was examined for the proportion who occupied

each one of eight social statuses at the time of the baseline
interview. No such difference was found between ascribed and
achieved statuses; rather, for every social status examined, regardless of its kind, a larger proportion of community subjects
occupied the position than did hospital subjects. Similarly, within
the hospital sample, those who were later to be discharged were
more likely to occupy the status than were those who were so
impaired as to remain inpatients. For each of the statuses, then,
there is a regular progression from higher percentage occupancy
among mentally-well subjects to lower levels among the more
severely impaired.

TABLE V
PROPORTIONS OF THREE MENTAL STATUS GROUPS OCCUPYING
EACH OF EIGHT SOCIAL STATUSES AT BASELINE

| Social Statuses | Per Cent Occupying Status | | |
	Community %	Hospital Discharged[a] %	Hospital Inpatient[a] %
Spouse	34	22	10
Parent	73	50	42
Grandparent	57	38	24
Sibling	94	84	67
Friend	88	72	54
Employed Person	49	19	6
Organization Member	52	22	17
Religious Person	76	34	28
(N=100%)	(264)	(90)	(81)

[a] Although status occupancy was measured at baseline, the sample used in this
table is the Study Sample described in Chapter III, the 435 subjects for whom
attitudinal data were collected at second-year follow up. "Discharged" and
"inpatient" refer to location at the latter time.

However, there is a trend toward greater differences between
community and hospital subjects in the *achieved* statuses. If we
rank-order the percentage-point differences between the mentally-
healthy and mentally-ill samples, they are as follows:

	Percentage Difference	
Religious person	45	⎫
Employed person	36	⎬ Achieved Statuses
Friend	32	
Organization member	32	⎭

Parent	31	
Grandparent	25	Ascribed Statuses
Sibling	19	
Spouse	18	

Although these percentage differences are certainly not great, there seems to be a slight trend toward the greater persistence of ascribed than achieved statuses among the mentally ill. The main point to be emphasized, however, is that it is not merely the occupancy of achieved statuses that differentiates the two groups: regardless of the measure of social relatedness we select, *the mentally ill are invariably less socially involved, and that in direct proportion to the severity of the mental illness they suffer* (as measured by subsequent disposition).

SOCIAL INTERACTION LEVEL

The social status index alone does not give us a very complete picture (even in broad quantitative terms) of the social function of our sample. It tells us something about the potential for social contact available to the elderly individual; it does not indicate whether he actually avails himself of those resources in his daily life. The case of Mr. VanDamm shows that it is possible for a person with relatively few social statuses to lead a life of intense and satisfying social communication with the few others that he does have some relationship with. On the other hand, there are those whose greater potential for contact with others is wasted—they may be alienated from even close kinsmen, allow friendships of long standing to lie fallow, and retain only nominal memberships in churches or other associations. For these reasons, a second measure of social function is useful as a supplement to that of the status index. This is the measure called *social interaction level*. It has nothing to do with any particular social roles, but rather attempts to estimate the individual's overall degree of social participation, without reference to the identity of the particular people with whom he interacts. It asks this question: To what extent does the subject extend himself into the social world

around him? This measure distinguishes five degrees of social
extension, as follows:

1. Takes active part in business, cultural, charitable, religious,
   or political affairs;
2. Attends social functions or visits friends and/or relatives
   outside his own household;
3. Is visited by friends and/or relatives living outside his own
   household;
4. Social activity with other household members;
5. Less than the above, or no social contact.

These levels may be thought of as forming an orthogonal
scale; i.e., each subject was coded at the level which represents
his greatest degree of social extension. For example, if an individual is scored at level 2, it may be assumed that he does *not*
engage in the social interactions described for the higher level of
1, but may engage in those described for any or all of the lower
levels—three through five.[2] For most purposes in this report, it
has been desirable (because of the small numbers of subjects in
some categories in cross-tabulations) to divide the scale between
levels 2 and 3. This procedure divides the sample into, first, subjects who regularly and of their own volition seek social contacts
outside their own homes, and second, those whose only social
contacts occur within their own places of residence. These groups
might be thought of as: (1) a socially active group, and (2) a
socially passive group. Such designations are, however, only approximate; there may be housebound or even bedridden elderly
persons who actively initiate social contacts—perhaps by telephone—arranging for people to call on them in their own homes,
as the following case will illustrate.

Mrs. Selma Reinhart, at sixty-two, was suffering from multiple sclerosis which, at the time of intensive interviewing, had
advanced to such a point that she could manage only the smallest voluntary gestures. Committed to a wheelchair, she is forced

---

2A detailed description of this scale, examples of kinds of activities represented by
each level, and the original more elaborate form of the scale, may be found in
Clayton Haven, "Social Interaction," Geriatrics Research Program Staff Memorandum No. 3B.37, November 26, 1963 (copies available upon request).

to sit for hours either looking at television or gazing out the window of her magnificent apartment in the Nob Hill-Pacific Heights district of the city. Mr. Reinhart, a retired professor of economics, is always nearby for companionship, but for most of the day he is occupied with the writing of a book — the *magnum opus* of his long and illustrious career — in his study at the other end of the apartment. However, the Reinharts maintain a small domestic staff, including round-the-clock practical nurses for Mrs. Reinhart, so, for much of the day, she is not entirely unattended. In consequence of this enforced mode of living, Mrs. Reinhart can achieve only a "socially passive" score on the measure of social interaction. In her case, though, this low score implies no social deprivation. Despite her crippling disability, Mrs. Reinhart has miraculously maintained her wit and aristocratic charm, and, because of this, has managed to maintain a wide circle of friends. Hardly a day goes by without several of them dropping in for chats or a few rubbers of bridge. Her three children still live in the area and pay her calls at least once a week. Then, too, "my doctor sees me once or twice a week and says I'm in perfect health — at least my heart and lungs." After a long, full life, lived as a patrician, filled with extensive world cruises, leadership in exclusive organizations, and an important role in her echelon of San Francisco society, Mrs. Reinhart continues to function in her social milieu, despite the deep incursions of a debilitating disease.

Mrs. Reinhart is not typical of the housebound aged, however. For the most part, people who do not leave their own premises in order to see others rarely take the initiative in getting others to call on them.

It should be noted that no effort was made to differentiate any of these levels on the basis of the duration, content, or frequency of the social interactions. For example, if an individual receives only brief though regular visits from a relative who drops by simply to leave groceries or deliver messages, he receives as high a score as does one who is the object of long and frequent friendly calls from numerous friends and relatives. Obviously, these are two quite different degrees of social participation; but, for the purposes of this gross measure, they are combined.

During the course of our program of studies in geriatric mental illness, social interaction level was ascertained for each subject on three different occasions—at the time of the baseline interview, and at first-year and second-year follow-up interviews. Our baseline measure of social interaction for hospital subjects referred to the period of time just *preceding* hospital admission (as was also the case in our scoring of the status index) in order that the measure be unaffected by institutionalization *per se*. It is this baseline measure, then, that we will utilize in the following discussion.[3] However, we will also refer from time to time to the social interaction level as measured at the time of the second-year follow-up interview—the time at which measures of personal function (such as the morale items) were made. In other words, the discussion of the relation of social function to mental illness utilizes the baseline measure, to avoid the problem of external restrictions on free movement, such as occurred in later rounds of interviewing, when some subjects were confined to psychiatric hospitals. But, whenever we discuss the relationship of social interaction level to personal function (such as morale), we will utilize scores determined at the same point in time—the second-year follow-up study—when we also made our measurements of morale.

Before discussing our findings, we should set forth the particular questions underlying this analysis:

1. Is social withdrawal one of the inevitable consequences of advanced age—some aspect of the developmental process in later life, in *all* societies?

2. Does social interaction depend primarily upon physical health—having the strength, mobility, and freedom from

---

3Our coding instructions for the baseline social interaction level called for the interviewer to ascertain, for the hospital sample, the level of function during the day that the decision was made to seek hospitalization, with some qualifications. The instructions read as follows: "If an item implies a time-span longer than the day of decision [to seek admission to the psychiatric screening ward], the principle of consistency is applied . . . . That is, if the patient did not perform such an item on the day of decision for circumstantial reasons, or because it was not his usual custom to so perform on that day, but had been regularly performing over a one-to-two week period prior to day of decision, he is given credit for that item." Much the same convention was used for the community sample coding.

pain and discomfort which would sufficiently enable the elderly individual to seek out and enjoy the company of others?

3. Is the frequently-observed social isolation of old people largely a product of prevailing cultural patterns, with a high frequency in our youth-oriented, rapidly-paced, and individualistic Western society, but rare in contrasting cultures?

4. Regardless of the factors underlying social alienation, is it one of the causative or contributory factors in the development of mental illness among the elderly?

5. Or is the social isolation of many of the aged merely a symptom of a psychiatric disorder, a consequence of the illness, and without other significant antecedents?

The problem of mental illness and social isolation is our primary concern in this analysis. Although our sample shows a clear and dramatic relationship between these two characteristics, we lack information which would enable us to distinguish cause from effect. However, the case histories presented in Chapter VII suggest some formulation of the dynamic interrelationships between these two factors. The following quantified data suggest only the direction that future inquiries might take.

Social Interaction and Mental Status

At the time of the baseline interview, we collected information on social interaction levels from 1077 subjects; 591 of these were community residents and 486 were members of the hospital sample. (Incomplete information was obtained for fifty-seven of the total of 1134 subjects comprising the full baseline samples.) For this group of over a thousand elderly people, social interaction levels were as follows:

Social Interaction Levels	Per Cent
1 (Takes active part in business, cultural, charitable, religious, or political affairs)	6
2 (Attends social functions or visits friends and/or relatives)	44
3 (Is visited by friends and/or relatives living outside household)	22

4	(Social activity with other household members)	9
5	(Less than the above, or no social contact)	19

100

(N=1077)

As these figures show, by no means all, nor even the majority, of elderly subjects in our sample are socially isolated. Exactly half of them have high levels of social interaction, i.e., regularly engage in social activities outside their own households. The remainder have low levels of social interaction, but many of these (22 per cent of the total sample), are visited regularly in their own homes by friends and relatives who live outside the household. However, 28 per cent of the sample are socially secluded—they either have no regular social contacts (19 per cent), or interact only with other members of the household (9 per cent). To what extent is this social withdrawal a function of mental disorder?

The distribution of community compared with hospital subjects on this scale shows a contrasting picture:

Social Interaction Levels	Community Sample (per cent)	Hospital Sample (per cent)
1 (High)	10	1
2	72	11
3	9	37
4	3	18
5 (Low)	6	33
	(N=591)	(N=486)

The most obvious difference between the two samples is that the bulk of community subjects are in the high range of the scale, while most of the hospital patients are in the low range. There are other, more subtle, differences between the two groups, however, that merit comment.

Among the socially active subjects (scores of 1 or 2 on the scale), relatively few in either sample are at the *highest* level. That is, even among the mentally-healthy aged, there are not many who are "prime movers"—who take active part in the planning and organization of community life. (It should be noted that the simple fact of employment or church or club attendance does not qualify a subject for inclusion in this category—he must do more than simply go to work or to church regularly. He would only be included in this highest level if, for example, he helped to organize or administer an employees' association, served on committees, assisted in fund-raising drives, or did precinct work for some political cause or candidate.) Thus, although most community elderly people engage in social activities outside their own homes, few of them assume *responsibility* in such activities. We have no information on younger age groups in San Francisco and the degree to which they play responsible social roles in community life. We can only guess that the proportions of younger people so engaged would be higher. If this were so, then the decline in social activity with age among the mentally healthy would not be in the nature of withdrawal from social activities altogether, but rather a shift from social responsibility to simple participation. Many comments made by our subjects in the intensive interviews would seem to suggest this.

Mrs. Edna Langtry (CS) was born "in the Southland" into a very religious Baptist family. Her father, although a layman, commanded wide respect and influence as the editor of a denominational magazine. "Father was revered all over the South for his integrity. He was a very wise man," Mrs. Langtry reports. Throughout her life, she followed in her father's footsteps in this regard, immersing herself in church work whenever and wherever she could. In all our interviews with her, Mrs. Langtry frequently alluded to the many tasks the church had put upon her. Speaking of her youth, she recalls, "I was very active then with church activities." Recalling another period of her life, she muses, "I enjoyed the Mission Society." After a move to Nevada, she recalls, "I went to church there and the deacons gave me work to do, and I got very busy again there with my church work, so I wasn't lonely." Now in her mid-seventies and remarried after a distressing period of widowhood, she no longer participates in church activities and has even begun to notice a decline in church attendance: "But Mr. Langtry and I, we don't take part in church activities. You know there is a lot of jealousy in any organization like that and we feel that we've done our share."

Similarly, Mr. Hokusai (CS) has retired from the board of an organization he had helped form after World War II, but his reasons were somewhat different from Mrs. Langtry's. Mr Hokusai felt that it was "time to give the younger men on the board a chance to bring in new ideas." Both of these physically- and mentally-healthy subjects appear to be suggesting what much of the intensive data has led us to suspect: that subtle cultural pressures have much more to do with this apparent social withdrawal among the aged than any "natural" decline in physiological strength or interest. Where Mrs. Langtry has felt "jealousy" in those arenas of life long familiar to her, Mr. Hokusai senses cultural change in the form of "new ideas." Both subjects have thus come to feel no longer useful or in demand within the spheres of their usual social contributions, and so have graciously and obligingly "stepped aside."

Comparing the socially active members of the community and hospital samples, however, it appears that proportionately more of the community subjects are in the highest group—that involving initiation of activities or responsibility for their maintenance —than are hospital subjects. Looking *only* at the people who are engaged in outside social activities, one-out-of-eight community subjects but only one-out-of-fourteen hospital subjects play active roles in community life.

At the lower end of the scale, too, some differences appear between the two samples. Among people who are socially inactive (i.e., do not leave their own households for social interaction), proportionately more of the community subjects receive visits from friends and relatives. Half of the housebound community subjects receive regular visitors, much as we saw in the case of Mrs. Reinhart, while slightly fewer (two-fifths) of the housebound hospital subjects do so. In simpler terms, community subjects who *are* active are *more* active, and hospital subjects who are inactive are *more* inactive than their counterparts in the other group.

When the two samples are separated between levels 2 and 3 on the social interaction scale, even more dramatic differences are seen. At the time of the baseline study social activity levels of community subjects were much higher, compared with two groups of mentally-ill subjects—those who were eventually discharged back to the community, and those who remained confined to an inpatient psychiatric facility at the time of the second-year follow-up interview. A very large proportion of the community sample (88 per cent) were socially active at that time, compared with only 16 per cent of the hospital subjects later discharged, and 24 per cent of those who continued to be hospital inpatients. Over four times as many, proportionately, of the mentally well were socially active as were the mentally ill.

Does this mean that mental illness in later life is almost invariably accompanied by seclusion? These figures would tend to support such an inference, but there are other factors that must be examined before we draw it. From other data, not previously presented in this volume, we know that over half of the original hospital sample were suffering from an acute brain syndrome at the time of their admission to the psychiatric receiving ward.[4] As a rule, we have chosen not to deal in this report with the relationships of attitudes and behavior to various diagnostic labels—they seem so highly interrelated that to explain one on the basis of the other would be somewhat tautological. (What is to be gained, for example, by noting that most patients with a diagnosis of depressive reaction reported low morale?) However, this is one case in which we must consider the *nature* of the mental illness in order to understand the observed behavior we are studying.

Consider the following information: Hospital patients who were later discharged were considerably higher on the *status index* than those who remained as inpatients. The discharged had fewer statuses than community subjects, but more than those who stayed in the hospital. That is, in terms of formal social supports, patients who were later discharged (and, therefore, presumably less psychiatrically impaired according to our criterion) showed a higher level of social function than did those who never recovered enough to get out of the mental hospital. But, in the case of *social interaction level*, the subsequently discharged patients were no

[4]Simon and Neal (1963, p. 466) reported: "Of the study group [our baseline hospital sample of 534], 287 patients (55 per cent) had the primary diagnosis of acute brain disorder."

more socially active than the people who remained as inpatients. At least, this was so at the time when the baseline measure was taken—i.e., in the week or two just preceding admission to the receiving ward.

This seems to be a contradiction, but it is not. The explanation is that the group who were later discharged were more frequently diagnosed at baseline as suffering from an acute brain disorder. Such conditions ordinarily cause greater disturbances in consciousness, orientation, and other mental functions than do the *chronic* brain disorders—although the latter more often lead to a lifetime of hospital confinement. In other words, patients who were later discharged had more social *supports* than the inpatients; however, just prior to admission, more of them were socially *inactive* because of severe though temporary organic problems which rendered them delirious, confused, violent, or even comatose (Simon and Neal, 1963, pp. 458-459). Such temporary mental states would, of course, drastically curtail the usual pattern of social interaction.

These findings raise the whole issue of cause and effect in the relationship between mental illness and social isolation. Returning to the questions posed earlier in this discussion, what can we now say about this one: Is the social isolation of many of the aged merely a symptom of a psychiatric disorder, a consequence of the illness, and without other significant antecedents? We cannot yet say anything about "other significant antecedents," but we can state that, in our baseline sample of elderly mentally-ill patients, many were rendered *incapable* of social interaction by the symptoms of an underlying organic pathology. In other words, if one's brain isn't working very well, he is not likely to be terribly sociable. An *involuntary* social withdrawal, secondary to an acute malfunction of the brain, can be thought of as a consequence of the illness in 55 per cent of our hospital sample. However, we have seen that more than 55 per cent of the sample were socially inactive: 82 per cent of them were. What accounts for the social seclusion of these others?

Does *volition* have anything to do with social interaction, or is the variation in our samples solely the result of differing *abili-*

ties to engage in activities? In order to study this question, we examined the social interaction data for our community and hospital samples in terms of whether or not subjects were able to get around. (This measure of locomotor activity was also made at the time of the baseline study.) The findings are presented in Table VI. These figures enable us to look first at only the segments of each group, community and hospital, who were *capable* of leaving their own households (and who had, in fact, done so during the time referred to in our measurement of social interaction). These two groups—both capable of moving about—can then be compared for social interaction levels. We asked this question: given two groups of elderly people, both capable of moving about without difficulty beyond their own immediate environs— one mentally healthy and the other suffering from a mental disorder—what relative proportions seek the company of other human beings? The data show that, of those in the community sample whose locomotor activity is high, 86 per cent also have a high level of social interaction. However, among the mentally ill, only a third (32 per cent) of those capable of social interaction outside the home are actually so engaged. Looking at these facts in a slightly different way, *voluntary* seclusion is over *four times* as common among the mentally-ill as among the mentally-well elderly.

TABLE VI

SOCIAL INTERACTION LEVEL AND LOCOMOTOR ACTIVITY
FOR TWO MENTAL STATUS GROUPS[a]

	Locomotor Activity at Baseline			
	Community Sample		Hospital Sample	
Baseline Social	High[b]	Low[b]	High[b]	Low[b]
Interaction Level	%	%	%	%
High[c]	86	37	32	3
Low[c]	14	63	68	97
Total	100	100	100	100
N	(548)	(43)	(148)	(289)

[a] Note that this table utilizes data from all baseline subjects for whom the two measures were obtained (591 community subjects and 437 hospital subjects).

[b] High locomotor activity is that level which permits the subject to go about the neighborhood, one city block or further. Low locomotor activity is defined as that level which permits the subjects to go *less* than one city block from his own premises.

[c] High social interaction level indicates that the subject regularly engages in social activities outside his own household. Low interaction defines his social activity as confined to his own dwelling unit.

The other figures in this table are also provocative. Looking just at the subjects with limited mobility—those incapable of going as much as one city block from their own homes—some additional differences based on mental status are seen. The figures for the hospital sample are not surprising; they show that 97 per cent of the housebound group sought no social activity outside their own homes, and this we would anticipate. However, the figures for the immobilized community subjects are somewhat surprising. Of these subjects, 37 per cent managed to engage in regular social activities outside their own households. Thus, over a third of the mentally-well aged who can walk no more than a few yards without assistance contrive to get out regularly to see other people. Such a subject might only chat a bit with a neighbor across the back fence, or walk down the hall of his apartment building to have coffee with fellow-tenants; he might have to be moved by wheelchair—but he succeeds somehow in maintaining active extensions into the world of people around him.

In fact, as many of the *immobilized* community subjects (37 per cent) as of the hospital subjects *capable* of moving about (32 per cent) maintain high levels of social interaction. It is fairly clear from these findings that, while a good deal of the social isolation of the mentally ill is a consequence of locomotor impairment, much of it is not. There may be other characteristics of the mentally ill, however, which would explain the social isolation of the group whose locomotor functions are intact. For example, it might be that, even though they *can* get around if they must, their state of physical health is such that pain, weakness, or such embarrassments as urinary incontinence would prevent their engaging in much social activity. Let us look next, then, at the influence of physical impairment on social activity.

Physical Status and Social Interaction

In the total study sample, many more of the physically well than of the physically impaired are socially active (84 per cent of the well and only 50 per cent of the impaired). Since there is more physical illness among hospital than among community subjects, the influence of physical status was examined separately for the two samples. Physical impairment proved to have an independent influence on social activity in each sample. Among community subjects, 90 per cent of the physically well, compared with 70 per cent of the physically disabled, are socially active. In the hospital sample, 25 per cent of the physically well but only 12 per cent of the physically ill are active.

There are several significant points about these findings. First, regardless of physical disability, mental illness is highly correlated with social withdrawal. Thus, even the most physically fit people in the hospital sample have dramatically lower levels of social interaction than even the most disabled in the community. Seventy per cent of the latter and only 25 per cent of the former are socially active. Social activity, then, is *not* simply a matter of physical health—of having the physical energy and freedom from pain and discomfort to permit the individual to engage in contacts with other people. Mental illness is far more socially isolating to the elderly than is physical impairment.

Second, physical illness does have some influence in and of itself on social isolation. It is an added deterrent to social interaction among the mentally ill, and it has a potent single influence among the mentally healthy.

Third, physical impairment has different relationships to social interaction and to the status index. As reported, it was only among community subjects that physical illness was related to a dearth of social statuses. Among the mentally ill, it had no independent influence on the status index. That is not the case with social interaction, however. Physical illness further erodes social activity even among the mentally ill. It seems likely that the status index is more sensitive to mental illness alone than is the social interaction level. An elderly individual suffering from a mental disorder—although his physical health is good—may give up any or all of his nonkin social positions. He may drop his church or club memberships, withdraw from his friends, or resign from his job. In such cases, physical illness would not further deplete the number of his social affiliations, but it might well decrease the amount of his social activity (coffee with a neighbor, an outing with a relative, a visit to a neighborhood bar, or a chat with the local storekeeper). Such activities are not common among even physically-healthy mental patients, but they are rare indeed among the physically disabled.

Age and Social Interaction

One of the most widely discussed questions concerning the aged in America today (at least, among social scientists) is whether or not it is natural and desirable for the elderly to withdraw from social involvement. A much fuller discussion of this topic of "disengagement" is presented in Chapter VIII; in the present context, only the following questions are raised: Do older people in this sample have lower levels of social interaction than younger ones? If so, are there particular characteristics of the very old, such as poor health or poverty, that encourage social withdrawal— or do the healthy aged also show a pattern of social seclusion as they reach advanced years?

In the total sample, age is associated with a lower level of social activity: Three-fourths of the younger subjects (those under seventy) are socially active, but only half of the older group (those seventy and over) attend social gatherings or visit people outside their own homes. However, these figures are largely a reflection of age differences between the community and hospital samples. Controlling for mental status, the figures show a perceptible age difference in social activity among community subjects, but the difference between older and younger hospital patients is negligible. Because there is a high correlation between advanced age and physical illness, we have examined the combined influences of age and physical impairment on social interaction (Table VII). Among community subjects, increasing age has no appreciable influence on social interaction, as long as the individual is in reasonably good physical health. Among the physically well, 91 per cent of the younger subjects and 88 per cent of the older ones are socially active. Physical illness, however, lowers social activity levels among both the younger and older subjects—but the influence is greater among the older group. Of those who are physically impaired, 81 per cent of the younger group and only 63 per cent of the older group are active. In other words, physical impairment and age together make for greater

TABLE VII

SOCIAL INTERACTION LEVELS FOR TWO MENTAL STATUS GROUPS
BY PHYSICAL STATUS AND OTHER SELECTED CHARACTERISTICS
(BASELINE DATA)

| | Social Interaction Levels (Per Cent Engaged in Social Activity Outside the Dwelling Unit) | | | | | |
| | Community Sample Physical Status | | | Hospital Sample Physical Status | | |
	Well %	Impaired %	Total %	Well %	Impaired %	Total %
Age						
60-69	91	81	89	20	18	19
70+	88	63	78	28	10	13
Sex						
Male	87	65	79	(22)	11	13
Female	93	76	88	26	13	17
Socioeconomic Status						
High	95	73	89	(24)	12	15
Low	82	67	76	26	13	15
Education						
College	95	79	90	(23)	20	21
9-12 grades	92	75	88	27	12	16
0-8 grades	79	63	73	(31)	13	17
Total	90	70	84	25	12	15
(N=100%)			(575)[a]			(248)[b]

[a] Of the total 600 community baseline subjects, data on social interaction were not obtained for 25.

[b] This number represents only half the baseline hospital sample—those seen during the last half of the calendar year of 1959—for whom physical status ratings were made.

social seclusion—but age alone does not. It is likely that the *degree* of impairment of the older subjects among the sick is greater than among younger subjects. In other words, if the subject is sick and *old,* he is sicker than if he is sick and relatively *young.* Our interpretation of these findings is that, not age, but degree of physical impairment is related to social isolation among community elderly.

In the figures for the hospital sample, we see much the same pattern: the only notable differences in social interaction levels are due to physical illness rather than age *per se.* In fact, it is among the older patients (those seventy and over) that we see the greatest variation in social interaction levels: 28 per cent of the physically well but only 10 per cent of the physically impaired were socially active at the time of their psychiatric ward admission.

Sex and Social Interaction

In the total sample, there are no differences between the proportions of men and women who engage in social activities outside their own homes. This is also true of the mentally ill as a
subgroup; that is, mental illness is equally restrictive of social
activity among both sexes. However, there is a slight trend among
the mentally healthy for the women to get out more than do the
men. Although the difference is not great, it does suggest that
members of the two sexes are responding differently to some factor that promotes or inhibits their social interactions.

Since physical health is the most potent of these factors, its
relative influence on men and women was examined. Physical
impairment does indeed have a greater effect upon social activity
among men. If men are physically healthy, almost as many have
high levels of social interaction as do the healthy women. Among
the disabled, however, men are less socially active. Thus, men are
not only more isolated than are women by poverty (as we have
seen) ; they are also more isolated by physical illness. We have
described, in the case of Mr. Bauer, how retirement from the
active male roles associated with work often produces a social
passivity and dependence upon women; we find this passivity
even more exaggerated if the man becomes physically disabled.

Socioeconomic Status, Education, and Social Interaction

In Table IV are presented data on the relationship between
the two social class factors and levels of social interaction. There
is nothing new in these findings that has not already been discussed above. Again we find that mental illness has a levelling
effect on social activity—neither poverty nor lack of education has
any additional influence in the hospital sample. Among community subjects, however, both factors are related to social activity.
The poor and the uneducated are more socially isolated than
other elderly people.

Because poverty and low educational level are so often associated with physical disability, however, we have examined the
relative impact of these factors on social isolation among the community aged. These several disadvantages prove to be cumulative

in their tendency to produce greater social isolation. For example, there are quite large differences in the proportions of people who are socially active, if we add the factors of poverty and physical impairment. Ninety-five per cent of those who are free from both disabilities are active; by contrast, only 67 per cent of those who are both poor and disabled have any outside contacts.

One of the most interesting things about all these findings on the community sample is that no single personal disadvantage—or combination of disadvantages—produces the degree of social isolation which characterizes even the most fortunate of the hospital patients. Mental illness alone, regardless of any other factors, is marked by a dramatic withdrawal from human society, at least in the acute phase of the illness.

Social Interaction Following Psychiatric Hospitalization

In all of the foregoing discussion, we have been describing the social life of the elderly, comparing community subjects with the hospital patients, as these were during the *acute* phase of the mental illness that led them to become hospitalized. In many ways, this comparison is somewhat misleading, although it is a dramatic one. As we noted, the majority of our hospital sample were acutely ill and grossly disturbed at the time the baseline measure was made. Yet it is clear from a reading of individual case studies of hospital subjects that social function varies enormously from one stage of the illness to another.

Mrs. Nella Sandusky provides an excellent example of the changes in levels of social interaction through the various phases of illness and recovery. This sixty-four-year-old woman and her husband were brought to the hospital by their younger son because the landlord of their apartment had phoned the son (who lived in a nearby city), threatening to evict the Sanduskys if something were not "done immediately." Both parents were alcoholics, each consuming a pint of whiskey a day. Mrs. Sandusky had lost sixty pounds in the preceding two years and had fallen into a state of pitiful neglect. She and her husband did little else during the day but drink and watch television. According to the son's account, the apartment looked "a horrible mess" — empty whiskey bottles strewn about

the floor and many charred places in the furniture and rugs
where Mr. Sandusky had set minor fires from carelessly dropped
cigarettes. At this time, their highest level of social interaction
was limited to monthly visits to their younger son's home and,
of course, regular trips to a local liquor store. This pattern
of drinking had developed only within the preceding three
years. Before this, both of them had been employed — he as a
repair man with an electrical company and she as a clerk in a
large department store. Mrs. Sandusky attributed the increased drinking and social isolation to their retirement and
the fact that their younger son was seeing action at that time
in the Korean War. Nine days after their admission to the hospital together, Mr. Sandusky died from a perforated ulcer,
Mrs. Sandusky was sent to a state hospital where, fortunately,
she showed remarkable progress. She began to extend herself
again socially, interacting with other patients and even assisting
the nurses in their duties on the ward. Since her discharge from
the hospital, Mrs. Sandusky has lived with her younger son
and his wife. Her present major satisfactions in life revolve
around the home and a small circle of "dear, dear friends,"
but she frequently expresses a desire to return to work. It is
unlikely that at her age she will be successful in this pursuit,
but she nevertheless yearns for the wider social opportunities
which employment might afford.

Thus we see in this case considerable change in levels of social
interaction through the years we have been in contact with this
subject. To be noted especially is the shift from an almost complete social isolation in near *folie à deux* circumstances to a re-
engagement of the social self within a circle of family and friends,
as she regained her mental health.

It would be informative if we could document for a large
sample of mentally-ill subjects the kinds of social disturbances
which characterize various phases of psychiatric disorder. Ideally,
we would like to have been able to study the mentally-ill group
before the acute phase of the illness, to see if there were any
early signs of social withdrawal, and, if so, whether these signs
preceded or followed the onset of psychiatric symptoms. We do
not have such data, however. To some extent, we were able to

get some notion of social impairment among the aged *not acutely ill* by looking at a subsample of the hospital group whose loco-motor functions were relatively unimpaired. There we saw that, of all subjects capable of moving about the neighborhood, almost three times the proportion of community as of hospital subjects were socially active.[5]

A second sort of comparison can be made by looking at men-tally-ill subjects *after* they have passed through the acute phase of the illness and have been restored to their homes and families in the community. Table VIII shows a comparison of mentally-healthy and mentally-ill subjects at two times: first, just prior to institutionalization of the hospital subjects; and second, two years later, when many of the mentally ill had recovered from the acute phase of the illness and had been discharged to the community. The study sample was divided into the three mental status groups (community, discharged, and inpatients), and each of these into the physically well and the physically impaired. Pro-

TABLE VIII
SOCIAL INTERACTION LEVELS FOR SIX DISABILITY GROUPS
AT TWO POINTS IN TIME

	Goes out of Dwelling Unit	
	Baseline Interview %	Second Year Follow-up Interview %
Community		
Physically well	93	92
Physically impaired	75	62
Total	88	84
(N=100%)	(262)	(260)
Hospital Discharged		
Physically well	(20)	63
Physically impaired	13	61
Total	16	62
(N=100%)	(38)[a]	(68)
Hospital inpatient		
Physically well	(25)	(11)
Physically impaired	24	2
Total	24	4
(N=100%)	(45)[a]	(79)

[a] Physical disability ratings were given only to the last half of the Hospital Sample in the baseline study.

---

[5] Such a reconstruction of historical data (although with a somewhat different focus) was reported by Lowenthal (1965).

portions with high levels of social interaction in each of the six groups so formed were compared. In the total community sample, there is little change in level of social interaction at baseline and two years later: at baseline 88 per cent of the community subjects were active, and at second-year follow-up interview, 84 per cent. Both groups of hospital patients, however, show dramatic changes in social activity within the two-year period. At baseline, as we have already noted, both groups had few socially active members. Two years later, however, both groups had changed considerably. The inpatients were even less active—only four per cent (compared to 24 per cent at baseline) now engaged in social activities away from the hospital. These were the few who were permitted to leave the institution fairly regularly for visits to friends or relatives on the outside. The discharged patients, however, had much higher levels of social interaction than they had reported just prior to hospital admission. Before admission, only 16 per cent had been active; after discharge, 62 per cent were regularly engaged in outside activities.

Physical disability showed some interesting effects on social interaction over the two-year period. At baseline, 93 per cent of the physically-healthy community sample were active. These people showed no decline in social involvement with the passage of time; two years later, the same large proportion (92 per cent) were active. The physically disabled, however, showed some decline in social function after two years: at baseline, 75 per cent had been active, but a high level of interaction was sustained by only 62 per cent two years later. It appears that physical illness among the community aged may become more debilitating with the passage of time, and thus more socially restrictive.

Physical impairment does not have the same social ramifications, however, among the hospital discharged. At neither of these two points in time—baseline or second year follow-up study—were there appreciable differences in social interaction levels related to physical health. Both the physically healthy and the impaired achieved fairly high levels of activity following discharge from the hospital, and, it should be noted, this was precisely the same proportion of socially active people found in the physically disabled *community* sample.

CONCLUSION

Now let us summarize these findings:

1. Among the mentally- and physically-healthy aged, we find no evidence of decline in social activity with age over a two-year interval.
2. Among the physically-healthy discharged patients, over a third remain socially secluded.
3. Among physically disabled but noninstitutionalized older people, regardless of their state of mental health, the same proportion—a little over a third—are socially inactive.
4. Among aged psychiatric inpatients, only one out of twenty-five is permitted to make regular visits outside the institution, if they have been hospitalized for as long as two years.

The findings relative to physical impairment and institutionalization are easy to understand: it is more difficult for severely disabled people—whether the illness is primarily physical or largely psychological—to get out of their own quarters than it is for healthy ones. However, we still must explain why 37 per cent of the physically healthy discharged patients, who are no longer in any acute phase of the mental disorder which once led them to the psychiatric receiving ward, habitually remain closeted in their own quarters—although they are quite capable of getting about. The case of Mr. Charles Leveritt gives us some insight into this question. For this patient, now discharged and living alone in San Francisco, social isolation functions as a screen, protecting him from further hospitalization for mental illness.

At seventy-eight and a retired train engineer, Mr. Leveritt now spends almost all of his time in a $17-a-month room in the Tenderloin district of the city. He has no friends, no contact with relatives or neighbors, and leaves his room only to make essential purchases. He is totally absorbed in his preoccupation with "this bunch of electronic brain-wave machines turned on me. The Communists and the AMA have got transmitters and receivers in the floors and the sides of the room. [But what about your neighbors — do you see much of them?] Don't do any visiting because there's too many of them in this [conspiracy]. Who's to trust?"

In 1959, Mr. Leveritt had to be hospitalized for an attempt to jump from his window three stories up from the street — an act climaxing a solid two months of heavy drinking. He was discharged twelve days later and has no recollection of this hospitalization. From that time to the present, he has had to cope with a full-fledged delusional system and auditory hallucinations. To keep out the voices, he has taken to wearing ear plugs. To protect himself from the infernal machine he claims is in his room, he has devised an elaborate meshwork of wires about the floors and walls and ceiling, but, laughingly, he will admit that his system does no good in fending "them" off: "Now they've got the machine tuned in on me. Can't you hear it? [No.] Haven't found anyone who could, except someone they were bugging."

Mr. Leveritt even claims that "they have bugged" his canary, causing it to lose its tail feathers; and, indeed, the unfortunate bird does give an unkempt, woe-begone appearance — much as does Mr. Leveritt himself — as it huddles, tailless, in one corner of the cage. Despite the squalor of the room and the omnipotent presence of "the machine," Mr. Leveritt appears to function with good spirits. He is an avid reader of newspapers and magazines, clipping out articles which interest him. He has even written a television script entitled "Second Childhood" — a poignant tale written with simplicity and skill wherein he portrays the affinity existing between the very old and the very young. In fact, he is proud of having retained his childlike qualities which others have often criticized as "odd" or "crazy." His greatest wish, he says, is to be rid of the voices so that he can resume his creative writing and get some of his works published. He has stopped drinking and spends all of his time in these elaborate, solitary activities behind the bolted door of his rented room. As long as he continues in this way, it seems less likely that Mr. Leveritt will be led to commit the kind of public act which had triggered his previous hospitalization. As one of our interviewers has put it: "Although his delusional system continues to be a source of chronic apprehension, his self-image appears to have suffered but little. He seems very much alive and involved, and it is probable that he derives much satisfaction from his 'reasoning' and philosophizing."

Another publication emanating from our research program (Lowenthal, Berkman, and Associates, 1966) treats this phenomenon of "social invisibility" in greater detail. We only wish to note here that the modern metropolis affords many old people with borderline mental and physical disabilities what we might call "pockets of anonymity" where one can be literally secreted away from official or even unofficial notice. Our research on the mentally-ill and community-resident aged indicates that many of these "invisible" older people can survive for years in this fashion, and that it is only when some dramatic, public gesture of distress is committed that they are led away into institutions. Fortunately, as psychiatry moves more and more into the community to institute agencies of preventive therapy, these people can be identified sooner and ameliorative treatment offered to them before the dramatic, disruptive gesture forces policing agencies to intervene.

Chapter VI

DYNAMICS OF THE PERSONAL SYSTEM: VALUES AND PERCEIVED NEEDS

The "I" signals nothing less than the beginning of the birth of values into a world of powerful caprice.
ERNEST BECKER, *The Birth and Death of Meaning* (1962) , p. 30.

INTRODUCTION

ONE OF THE CHARACTERISTICS of the personal system is its basis in perception. Quite literally, the personal system—the self—has no properties, no meaning, no existence, except in relation to something else beyond itself. We cannot understand why an old man believes himself to be a good man, or a bad man, or a mad man—or no man at all—without reference to standards his culture offers him for evaluating his own behavior. We cannot understand why an old woman claims to be contented or discontented, happy or sad, satisfied or dissatisfied with her lot, unless we can determine what she thinks her lot *ought* to be—what she believes is required in the pursuit of a reasonably pleasant life. These values and needs are the center of our investigation in this chapter. Our first concern will be with the goals and values upon which self-judgments among the old are based; our second, the conditions which influence their morale.

In a previous chapter on the measurement of personal function, we reported on the ways in which a sample of older people answered the implicit question: Are you a good person? In that analysis, we found that the ability to sustain a positive self-view in the later years of life indicates something about the mental health of the respondent. But the simple dimension of yes-or-no tells us nothing of the *reasons* for the answers. We would like now to know why older people answered as they did, and if those reasons tell us anything more about mental disorders among the elderly and the culture in which these disorders occurred. Accordingly, we examined the self-reports from our sample of older people from the point of view of their actual content.

172

ANALYSIS OF SURVEY RESPONSES
(PRELIMINARY ANALYSIS)

From the total sample of about 700 subjects who had given us descriptions of themselves (see footnote 5, Chapter IV), we selected a random fifty cases, examining this time the content of the responses, and found that we could classify each topic in each response in one of a set of twenty-four fairly specific categories (such as appearance, health, affect, motivation, relationship to family members, quality of social interaction, vocation, avocation, and the like). In turn, these twenty-four specific categories, we found, could be grouped into five more general areas of life—physical characteristics, mental or psychological characteristics, interactional characteristics, social relationships, and activities or interests.

We expected that mentally-ill subjects would be more likely to emphasize the physical, interactional, and psychological areas; in contrast, we expected that community subjects would be more likely to describe themselves in terms of activities and interests and their past or present involvement in particular social roles (work, marriage, family relationships, or membership in organizations). We proceeded to test for these differences by means of a quantified content analysis of the data from the total sample. There were four principal findings from this analysis: (1) community subjects described themselves at greater length and in more variety than did psychiatric patients; (2) regardless of the topic being discussed, the mentally ill were more likely than the mentally well to speak of it as a deficiency in personal worth; (3) general probes (such as "What else?" or "Can you tell me a little more?") were not very productive; usually both hospital and community subjects would simply embellish their previous statements a bit or would say that they couldn't think of anything else; and (4) even among groups of subjects that differed grossly, the distributions of major content categories were almost identical. We found strikingly similar patterns in the content of responses to the general self-image question when we compared the mentally-well and ill groups and the physically-well and ill groups.

Even when the elements in each of the five major areas are

further broken down into the twenty-four subareas, their distributions among the hospital and community samples are still very similar. Although the overall pattern varies little in the two samples, there are a few differences that appear in the distribution of subareas mentioned. We will summarize these briefly.

Failing health is a greater concern in self-descriptions for the hospital than for the community sample, a preoccupation which is consistent with a higher actual prevalence of physical illness among the mentally-ill sample. Hospital subjects are more likely than community ones to compare themselves to others (i.e., to make normative judgments of themselves) than are mentally-healthy respondents—but in both samples, such comparisons tend to be invidious (we have previously discussed this fact, in Chapter IV). There is a greater emphasis among the mentally healthy on conformity to social expectations (being "law-abiding" or "respectable") than is true for hospital subjects. Friendship provides a basis for self-esteem among the mentally healthy; but among the mentally ill, the social contacts described in connection with self-image are of a very casual or transitory nature. Nearly half of the social relationships mentioned by hospital subjects are contacts too casual, infrequent, and passing to come under the heading of friendship. These are the random conversations with a stranger on the park bench, in a coffee shop or bar, or the exchange of greetings with other hotel or apartment-house residents, none of which have ever developed into continuing relationships. Avocational interests are important to mentally-healthy subjects—mentioned even more often than work; the reverse is the case with the mentally ill. When physical aging is mentioned in either sample, the comments usually refer to negative attributes, but when the psychological aspects of aging are mentioned, the community subjects are overwhelmingly positive about it, the hospital sample quite negative.

These findings are tantalizing, but their underlying dynamics could not be explored with our available survey data—we asked no questions about values and their importance in life, or about the functional meaning of substitute activities for productive labor (although we have a great deal of *descriptive* data on how many hours were spent in reading, watching television, and listening to the radio) . For these reasons, our quantitative data do not reveal any major *dynamic* differences in the personal systems of healthy aged individuals as opposed to sick ones. To be sure, there are some significant differences in response among groups within the sample, but these differences lie in some of the most covert characteristics of the replies—for example, in the dimension of self-evaluation already discussed—and not in the particular components of identity selected by the subjects for discussion.[1]

QUALITATIVE CONTENT ANALYSIS

Fortunately, our research plans provided for intensive interviewing of subsamples of both mentally-well and mentally-ill subjects, and we were in the process of developing plans for this interviewing at about the time that we completed the quantified content analysis of self-image materials from the larger sample. So, at least for a subsample of aged people, we had an opportunity to develop and pretest a series of more detailed and evocative inquiries into self-perception.[2] All available information on self-

---

[1]We made a second attempt to identify particular attitudes toward the self which might distinguish the mentally-well from the mentally-ill aged in our sample. An adjective check-list of forty-eight items was administered to matched subsamples of about eighty community and about eighty hospital subjects. Again, we found a tendency to describe the self in stereotypic terms. Traits highly valued in American culture, such as independence, sociability, and industriousness, were attributed to the self by almost everyone, whatever their condition or state of health. Most subjects admitted to being reasonable, responsible, truthful, and modest, but few agreed that they were alcoholic, dull, or sloppy. On only one item did we find a statistically significant difference between the mentally-well and the mentally-ill groups: the mentally ill more often described themselves as lonely.

[2]We found the positive-negative dimension of the self-image responses of the larger sample to be reliable and useful and so based the analysis reported in Chapter IV on this dimension. This was likewise true for several other dimensions, one of which—time-orientation—will be reported on in this chapter. However, we did not find this to be true of the *content* of the replies. We have already hinted at the probable reason for this: the single self-image question asked of the larger sample was of such a general nature that the bulk of the responses tended to be stereotypic; personal characteristics which had some dynamic relationship to problems of

————Footnote continued to next page

perception for each subject in the intensive subsample was abstracted, given an assigned code number, and filed according to mental and physical status. These data were then subjected to qualitative content analysis (see conclusion of Chapter III for methodology). This analysis yielded a set of general areas that constitute the bases of self-esteem as outlined in this chapter.

We were able to identify six new major clusters of traits which the aged called upon in describing themselves. These six clusters differed qualitatively from the five original categories developed in the quantified content analysis of responses to the single self-image question. For example, in the survey responses, only four per cent of the community and five per cent of the hospital samples mentioned either health or financial resources, although we knew from other analyses that sickness and poverty were serious problems for many older people; yet, in the intensive interviewing, when subjects were encouraged to talk at length about their circumstances of life, both of these factors were emphasized by nearly every subject again and again, and it became apparent that having adequate personal resources for meeting one's physical needs was one of the principal criteria of self-judgment among members of the sample.

We were further able to conceptualize these six major clusters as a system of personal goals—a set of standards against which the

---

adaptation or basic issues in the aging process were glossed over, diluted with relatively meaningless but innocuous phraseology, or ignored altogether. Wylie (1961) criticizes many self-image studies for their failure to take into account the tendencies of the replies to become stereotypic. In her own study of 1957, she found that open-ended essays of subjects' self-image tended to be cliché-ridden (Wylie, 1957). In the intensive interviews, however, we were able to profit from our earlier experiences, and the subjects were asked about themselves in a variety of ways, in many contexts, and with focused probing to elicit detailed and dynamic descriptions of how they perceived themselves, and what factors underlay those perceptions. In many cases, the collection of current self-image material supplied by a single subject ran to six or seven double-spaced pages of verbatim transcript, with as much or more information on personal characteristics of the self in earlier life. The volunteered and unprobed responses to the survey question on self-image, on the other hand, rarely exceed three or four sentences. In many cases, only a single phrase or two or three adjectives comprised the total response which could be obtained. This led to a paucity of material which could hardly be examined dynamically.

aged seem to judge themselves. These six dimensions are as follows:

PRINCIPAL GOALS UNDERLYING SELF-ESTEEM IN THE INTENSIVE SAMPLE

1. Independence
2. Social acceptability
3. Adequacy of personal resources
4. Ability to cope with external threats or losses
5. Ability to cope with changes in the self
6. Having significant goals or meaning in later life

We next examined the nature of these goals as they were described by the mentally-healthy intensive sample, drawing comparisons with the mentally-ill group on each of the dimensions. In the following pages, each goal will be discussed, as it relates to self-esteem. Value-orientations relative to each of these goals will be identified in terms of whether they are adaptive or maladaptive for the aged individual.

Independence

The ability to provide for one's own needs is an important aim for the majority of all the elderly people in our intensive sample, regardless of their state of health. Community subjects made statements like the following:

> "I hope to always be able to take care of myself and continue in good health."

> "I'll tell you one thing — I'm not going to live in any of those rest homes and I'm not going to live with my daughters. I have a small income."

> "I wouldn't want to get on welfare. I just wouldn't go to see them. I wouldn't want to do that."

> "The most important things my parents did for me was that they gave me love and self-confidence; they taught me how to be independent and self-reliant."

Members of the hospital sample also emphasized independence:

> "The important thing in my life today is I don't want to

get sick again. I want to be well, take care of myself. I don't
want to be dependent on my children."

"Well, my parents taught me to stand on my own two feet.
I'm not living up to it since I'm on an old age pension. I
wouldn't be doing it if I were not so weak."

"The best way of getting along in life is minding your own
business and taking care of your own finances."

This theme of independence is recited over and over again in
the intensive interviews, but if one looks into the stated reasons
for wishing to be independent, an important dynamic difference
between the mentally-well and mentally-ill subjects becomes apparent. The healthy aged want to be independent as a point of
pride and to avoid inconveniencing others. Miss Mildred Barton
(CS) for example, says, "I never faltered from the idea that I'd
never be dependent on anybody. I tried not to bother other people with my troubles, much more so since I got older. I think my
liking for people has stayed the same. By independence I mean
that, financially, I could take care of myself. I want to keep going
as well as I can, take care of myself, to bring at least pleasantness
to the lives I contact. It's very important that I do not become
a burden on somebody." Mr. Angus Pillsbury (CS) reports that
the most important thing in his life is ". . . security, so that I can
take care of myself and won't have to impose on anybody. I'll
make it; I'm a pretty fair horse player." Mrs. Clara Bruzinsky (CS)
is quite explicit in linking her own independence with her concern for her children's welfare: "I hope to stay healthy, care for
myself, and hope my children are happy and healthy. To be independent, that is what I want to keep. If you can be happy and
enjoy life all the time, others around you will do the same. People are what makes life so wonderful and exciting. Without love,
life is really not worth too much."

Mentally-well subjects are sometimes quite explicit about the
fact that one should call on people for help if it is really needed;
they simply hope that they themselves will never require such
help. Mr. Sebastian Keller (CS) puts it this way: "I was very lucky
all the way. I never asked for money . . . but I always knew I could.
I think that's very important. A good friend would lend it to

you." Another community subject, Mr. Ed Hart, when asked if he had any relatives who would take him in if he needed a home, replies: "Yes, indeed—my daughter; she would. Both my daughter and step-daughter have offered me a home. My daughter and her husband both had begged me to stay with them, but I won't go until I have to; I wouldn't want them to take care of me when I have security here. I can see a time may come when they will have to step in and tell me what to do and I'll have to do it, but I hope that time doesn't come. I don't want to disrupt their lives just to take care of me." For the healthy aged, then, the desire for independence is a relatively benign one; they want to retain the respect of others and their own pride as well as to avoid bringing a strain into the lives of people they care for.

Hospital subjects also emphasize independence, but there is a somewhat different climate in the nature of their comments on this theme. For example, Mrs. Mildred Tully, a patient discharged from a state hospital and living alone in San Francisco, discusses her future as follows: "I don't know how my life will change. I don't want to live with my family. I couldn't do any work for them. My relatives would like to put me in a rest home." Mrs. Sandusky, also a discharged patient but living with her son and his family, gives this opinion: "I think that the basic fundamental of older people having happiness is to have their own feeling of independence and security. If people do have the opportunity to build something around themselves, so that *when they're kicked out* [emphasis ours] they have some independence." Mr. Arnold Ritter, a discharged patient, also sees the world as not very supportive of those with needs: "I've come to the realization that the world doesn't give you anything. You get out of things just what you put into them—pull the saw and don't ride it. And it's been my observation and experience that if you do that, you'll get along in the world. When all is said and done, it's still a rat race." Mr. Louis Czernich, who had also been a state-hospital patient for a time, reports, "In my sickness [his hospitalization for mental illness], I learned something. I always trusted too much. If you trust people too much, they will take advantage of you. But now I don't need friends. What's the use to chat? That don't improve me." Mr. Alberto Alioto (HS) is even more explicit:

"I don't go to anybody with my problems; I just work it out. I never care about what the other fellow does, and he don't care about me."

Among the mentally ill, then, there is an air of fear and mistrust of others that makes the goal of independence seem like a driving defense against the potential malevolence or neglect of others. They seem to be striving not so much for the positive value of autonomy as against the dangers of dependency. However, as we will see later in this chapter, even the seemingly desirable goal of autonomy can prove, under some circumstances, to pose serious problems as people grow older.

Social Acceptability

Social acceptability is the second primary aim for the aged in our intensive sample. They approve of those qualities in themselves which they believe will earn for them the good will of others. Although both the mentally-well and the mentally-ill aged agree upon this goal in life, an examination of their comments indicates that they differ to some extent in their views of the appropriate means for achieving it. The mentally well are more likely to esteem themselves for being congenial, pleasant, easy to get along with, and for not being querulous or making trouble for others. Mr. Lawrence Southern (CS), asked how he would like his son to be like himself, in reply emphasizes these characteristics: "My son had a good disposition, a nice personality, meets people well, and is well liked. The best way of getting along in life is to take a little and leave a little. I like people better now than I used to. I don't want too much out of life; I have no ambition to be a millionaire." Mr. Phillip Knight (CS), a quite wealthy and successful business man, does not describe himself in terms of his financial achievements (although he discussed them in other contexts) ; rather, he describes himself as ". . . genial. I get along with people. I think I am pleasant; everybody says the same thing, so it must be so. I always found something in anyone to like, and I got along with everybody." Even when speaking of his financial success, he explains its importance to him in these terms: "It's important to me because, if my money is intact, my children can be happy and have the opportunity to share or help others with the extra dough. After all, you are your brother's keeper, to some degree." Mrs. Bennington (CS) says, "I try to be as congenial as I can. I tend to my own business and am not quarrelsome. I try to get along with people and be as tolerant and congenial as I can be. I like people, and it's up to the individual to make himself interesting to them."

Community men make mention of avoidance of fights, staying out of jail, and not getting drunk and disorderly, as previously noted in this chapter. Subjects of both sexes, however, cherish friendship, and pride themselves on their abilities to make and sustain their friendships.

"I have a few friends, but I've had those friends all through the years."

"I enjoy meeting new friends — more stable friends. I think this is the first time in my life that I have really had a core of friends who see every day and can talk to for some time — really have enough time to stick by them. I'm enjoying life now more than ever before. Not as active, but I have good friends."

Many of the mentally-healthy subjects claim to have developed a more accepting attitude toward others; they present themselves as less critical and demanding than when they were younger. They seem to expect less of others—and more of themselves. For example, Mrs. Bennington says, "Well, I think as we grow older, we become a little bit more alert as to other people's personalities, what kind of characters they have. I guess we become more tolerant of people, overlooking their faults, understanding them and their circumstances and so forth—not so critical. Some people may think *I* have faults. I think when I was younger I was not so tolerant." Mrs. Mary Kramer (CS) speaks of liking ". . . to give a lift to people. I like to praise people. I find we don't do enough of it. I'm schooling myself to do more." The notion implicit in all these statements is that people are attracted to optimism and supportiveness in others.

The mentally-ill subjects in the intensive sample were just as likely as the aged in the community to emphasize the importance of social acceptability to self-esteem. However, the mentally ill characteristically perceive social approval as deriving from entirely different sources. As a group, they are skeptical of the idea that others will accept them simply for being pleasant, congenial, or agreeable—in fact, they often mention these traits as a sign of weakness. Mrs. Amelia Harris (HS) , for example, when asked how she thought her personality had improved as she got older, said: "I've gotten a little hard-boiled, not quite as gentle. I weaken if someone asks me for something, but perhaps not all the way— that's the hard knocks I've gotten through life. Got to get some warts on your hide." Another mentally-ill subject, Mrs. Frieda Caldwell, expresses the thought this way: "I've always been too friendly; I was always so willing."[3]

Preservation of self-esteem among the mentally-ill, rather, is contingent upon the individual's belief that he must be superior to others in some way in order to gain or preserve social acceptance. In some cases, the subject spoke of being of noble descent, or a member of an old and respected family: "My father was a nobleman in Austria, and my mother was a descendant of the Castro family. My grandfather was given a land grant in California by the King of Spain." This patient, Miss Mona Bachstein, several times expressed a desire to move back to the site of her ancestral home in order "to be near our family burial plot." Mrs. Powers (HS) describes herself as a descendant of an "old American" family. "The genealogy of our family dates back to pre-Revolutionary days on both sides. I'm sitting in a chair that is over a hundred years old; it's my pet. And that sofa came around Cape Horn—it's not really very comfortable." Furthermore, Mrs. Powers expresses chagrin about the fact that her neighborhood has changed so much during the forty years she has lived there. Formerly, she regarded most of her neighbors as her social equals:

---

[3]As we noted earlier in this book, we are not including a discussion of particular psychiatric diagnostic groups in this analysis. However, it should be mentioned that the set of personal attitudes and values we are describing here as characteristic of the mentally-ill group were by no means confined to patients with so-called psychogenic diagnoses (those including patients with paranoid reactions, for example) but were also distributed among those whose only psychiatric diagnosis was some type of organic brain disease. Thus, for the two subjects quoted in these last examples, one had a psychogenic diagnosis and the other was given the single psychiatric diagnosis of senile brain disease.

"Some I have known as many years as I have lived here, but we are all on a social status." Now, however, a "poorer class" of peo- have moved in: "How can you help a neighbor like that—wrong people in the wrong place in the wrong neighborhood?"

Mr. Ritter (HS) expresses the belief that the most admirable person is ". . . one that is up and moving, contributing something to society, accomplishing something on his own—one who would make good and not make excuses. I know this because I've been engaged in supervisory work for years with men and women and you learn a lot of things. It's only the incompetent, stupid, unedu-cated people you have trouble with. Anyone who is educated and ambitious is easy to get along with, but the incompetent and un-educated cause all the trouble in the world." For many of the mentally-ill subjects, competence is defined in terms of outstand-ing talent, ability, or creativity. The following are a few examples of this idea: Mr. Czernich (HS): "I would like to put some of my inventions on the market—I would like to do it now, but it will take time. That is my biggest ambition—I hope that I will be able to put something over. I'm working on it now. You see, you have some kind of mind set up for something. I've got all kinds of inventions. We have to keep trying. I also think I could be a good physical educator. I may do that, too. I would like to tell people how to get rid of rheumatism and so forth." Miss Potter (HS): "I want to settle down and do something I've always wanted to do—write a story. A friend just wrote that she'd sold one of her paintings and sold a story. We both lived at the 'Y' and she used to paint pictures. She was so artistic. I've always been awful-ly nervous—nervous and restless. I'd like to think of some way I could do some good in the world before I pass out of it."

We do not mean to imply here that mentally-healthy elderly people have no interest in hobbies, creative endeavors, or new enterprises—they certainly do. However, such activities among the mentally-healthy aged are pursued for personal enjoyment; among the mentally-ill, they take on the character of compulsive strivings for self-vindication and social approval. The activity it-self is not important—it is the recognition by others of one's super-ior worth. As Mrs. Caldwell (HS) says, "I try to do things, but . . . if I only had someone who could praise me."

In sum, while the mentally healthy see social acceptability as deriving primarily from congeniality, supportiveness, and consideration of others, the mentally ill characteristically perceive the key to social approval as having status, power, or recognition for some talent, special ability, or other outstanding trait. They do not seem to agree with the theory that people respond with love and care to those who try to give happiness and pleasure to others; rather, they feel that the only path to social respect is to command it from a position of strength.

Adequacy of Personal Resources

George Bernard Shaw, during his own highly productive senescent years, once said, "Economy is the art of making the most of life." This is a philosophy that many of our mentally-healthy aged subjects find understandable and congenial. They tend to perceive as one of the tasks of old age the *conservation* of self and resources. They seem to feel that the anabolic phase of life is past, so to speak, and that it is unlikely that their store of health or wealth will be replenished. For this reason, they emphasize an economy or husbandry of the resources that remain. Mrs. Kramer (CS), for instance, says, "I would love to go to that parade downtown, but I don't feel I should attend as it is too hard on me. My family is practically all gone, so I feel I should take care of myself. You have to keep going with the tide, taking care of your health." When we asked Mrs. Gladys Dillon (CS) what her major current plans were, she said, "I think mainly just keeping in good health so that I don't have big hospital bills and doctor's bills. My other plan is to visit my family." Mrs. Valente (CS) feels it was important not to have debts: "I didn't owe anybody, so I never was broke. If I haven't got the money, I don't buy it." Mr. Christian Jespersen (CS) talks about his future: "Sometimes I think I'd like to take a trip to Denmark, but I know I won't because I'd feel bad if I spent all that money at once." Miss Bertha Schaeffer (CS) also prides herself on conservation of her financial resources: "I'm not complaining for myself, because I'm a good manager. Maybe I'm a little boastful, but I have a lady friend whose earnings are very much like mine and she never saved a dollar. It looks like she'll have to go and work. She can't manage. I was never extravagant. I was always complimented on my business attire, but they were always inexpensive."

Perhaps Mr. Butler (CS) is the most articulate subject about this particular value-orientation: "When you are young and struggling to get ahead, you are out to impress people and achieve success. When you get older, you become more security-oriented; you begin to coast a little. You have to be careful, otherwise you will lose everything you have tried to achieve. I doubt if I'll change any more, so I must be content with what I have, to remain in good health, and to be able to handle my problems as they come up. I don't want to be plagued by a series of financial upsets. I'd like life to be smooth and peaceful."

By contrast, the mentally-ill members of the intensive sample more frequently reflect a view of life as a state of unlimited resources and new opportunities for every American citizen, regardless of age or condition. They seem to feel that *acquisition* of new resources is possible for anyone, if only one has the intelligence and drive to seek them out. A failure to do so is often perceived as a character defect. This view often leads to a prodigality in the management of health, social relationships, and financial resources. For example, Mr. Avery Jackson (HS) explains his lack of money in this way: "Well, I came out of Mendocino State Hospital; I tried to get on a pension and they told me I had too much money and I'd have to spend some—so I spent it *all*." He went on to say, "The world would be my oyster, if I now had the opportunities that young people have today." Mrs. Harris (HS) regards awareness of physical and economic changes as a weakness and tries to put them out of her mind: "I am conscious of every little change in myself, but then I feel I am giving in to my baser elements. For a time I get fussy about my physical condition and then give up. I still don't worry. I just won't let myself think about things that I won't worry about. I suppose I still have a stubborn streak. I'm a little wasteful. I don't buy too sensibly. If I want something, I buy it—don't look around for bargains. I have the ability to do a lot of little things to pull myself out of the hole —ingenuity. I collect junk—Scotch, I guess." Mrs. Rena Trocopian (HS) has always thought of herself as a woman with exquisite taste; even in the face of diminishing resources in old age, she clings to this view of herself: "I'm not envious, but I want what I want. I'm hard to please; I just don't like anything and everything. Choosy, I guess. I have a very, very rich spirit and a poor pocket [laughs]."

Community subjects often express pride in being as well off or better off than others of the same age, sometimes attributing their good fortune to inherent strength and stamina, and sometimes explaining it by their care in maintaining health regimes—eating properly, getting exercise, not drinking too much, and avoiding other immoderation. Routine, regularity of habits of living, and self-discipline take on positive values for conservation of physical, mental, and economic strengths. More hospital subjects, on the other hand, would like to believe that "there's plenty more where that came from."

Ability to Cope with External Threats or Losses

To some extent, the value-orientations in this sphere overlap with those just discussed, but we are treating them separately because they relate logically to somewhat different life problems. In the preceding topic, conservation and acquisition emerged as contrasting attitudes toward personal resources and proper ways of getting one's physical needs met. The orientations discussed here have to do with conceptions of appropriate ways of meeting and coping with external threats and losses.

In this area of life, the characteristic value-orientation of the mentally-well group is a set of attitudes that we have called *resilience*. It is best characterized as "rolling with the punches," making the best of things, or making a virtue of necessity. It includes qualities such as endurance, forbearance, and stamina. The source of self-esteem in this area for the mentally-healthy aged derives from the skill and strength to find contentment in the face of adversity. These people express the belief that old age, with its accompanying changes, is natural, predictable, and reflects on the worth of the individual only to the extent that he permits himself to feel defeated by it. If one cannot bend with the years, one is broken—there is nothing to be gained in fighting the inevitable, but if one remains flexible, one can snap back to some extent even after the hardest blows.

Mr. Samuel Wheeler (CS) puts it this way: "In aging successfully, you must realize you can't control things, and live as it is given to you to live. Make the best of it, and that's all." Mr. Ed Hart (CS) expresses the belief that the whole of one's past life determines the nature of one's present, and it is foolish to think you can somehow change the present by tinkering with the past. "Since I spoke of the incident of my change of philosophy, let me be specific: I have learned to refuse to be unhappy. I take life as it's handed out to me and I am happy. I refuse to worry for the simple reason that worry is a habit and a habit can be broken down. You take worry, hatred and anger—they cause more disease than anything. They only depreciate your ability to meet a problem when it arises." Mr. Hokusai (CS), a man who has always prided himself on his energetic aggressiveness, was able to make a change in this value-orientation as he reached old age: "I think I am more likely to accept ineffectiveness in myself now. When younger, if I couldn't do what I wished, I'd be irritated. Now I say I can't go so fast, and I accept this much easier. In general, I accept things much more than ever before. I have lost the energy for aggressiveness in my activities—I have to accept things now. I made this change maybe around sixty-five."

The mentally-ill subjects seem to feel that acceptance of things as they are is a personal defeat, that a "good" person should always meet life's difficulties with aggressive action and attempt to control the environment. This philosophy was well articulated by Mr. Spenser, a former state hospital patient now discharged and living alone in San Francisco. He says, "The best way of getting along in life is doing things to help yourself. There are hundreds of persons not deserving, because they go against the laws of nature. God helps those who help themselves. Pick yourself up— how does that song go? Pick yourself up, brush yourself off, start all over again. Always try, try again. The more people tell me I can't do something, the harder I try to prove I can. That's me all over." Mr. Hopland (HS) also reports difficulties in accepting losses of any kind: "I'm angry when I'm beat. I try to just forget about it, but I can't. Next time it happens, I get angry as usual." Miss Potter (HS) has become increasingly concerned about her physical appearance since she has grown older. She cannot accept these changes in appearance as inevitable, but constantly attempts through aggressive action to control these outward manifestations of old age; she spends a great deal of time and money on hair-styling, facials, cosmetics, and other beauty treatments. Her failures to change her appearance appreciably are a source of chronic frustration: "I'm always seeking self-improvement. I think I've gone farther with that than a lot of my friends. I've never been satisfied with myself, always trying to improve. To me, I look old as Methuselah. I'd like to change, but I can't change enough to like myself. I look in the glass and look one hundred—haggard. I keep using the cream they advise. Guess I'm not faithful enough."

This, then, is another major difference between the mentally-healthy and the mentally-ill aged: The healthy don't "fight city hall" and the disturbed do.[4] It should be remembered, however, that we are here discussing patterns of coping with the *inevitable,* with irreversible changes or irretrievable losses. Actually, the difference between the two groups in coping behavior seems to grow out of an inability or unwillingness on the part of many of the mentally ill to distinguish between circumstances which can be changed and those which cannot.[5] The mentally-healthy aged seem able to meet unpleasant but alterable circumstances with action, and inalterable ones with flexibility and forbearance. The mentally ill, by contrast, value *aggressiveness* as such; they are instrumentally-oriented, valuing action for its own sake. They feel

---

[4]This finding is confirmed in part by an analysis of reactions to stressful events in old age and how older people responded to them. In that study, Anderson found that, among the hospital sample, there were two principal kinds of behavior directed toward an external stress: "Behavioral adjustment was directed either toward doing something about the stressor, that is, toward removing, resolving, or alleviating the stressful circumstance itself; or it was directed toward the assuagement of the felt *strain* resulting from these happenings . . . . For our sample, old age is therefore a period during which stressful events are adjusted to by strain-directed activities . . . (p. 207). For our chronic brain syndrome subjects, the alternative to active engagement was no activity at all (p. 212)." This analysis, however, did not attempt to differentiate between stressful siutations which *were* amenable to outside intervention and those which were irreversible in nature (Anderson, 1964, pp. 190-217).

[5]This observation is reminiscent of the practical psychology of Alcoholics Anonymous, as reflected in their motto: "God grant me the strength to change those things which I can change, the courage to face those which I cannot, and the wisdom to know the difference."

that they must *do* something, and they are less likely to admit that there are circumstances beyond their control, and if the difficulties persist, they become self-condemnatory, seeing themselves as weak and ineffectual. The results are often loss of self-esteem, helpless rage against a threatening and uncontrollable environment, and sometimes serious depression, as we will discuss in a later section of this chapter.

Ability to Cope with Changes in the Self

The majority of the self-image responses included some volunteered statements about how the individual believed he had changed or not changed in recent years. Responses included phrases like the following: "Up until the last three years . . ."; "there have been changes . . ."; "I've always been the kind of person who . . ."; and "I haven't changed one single bit." These responses, in part, were a reflection of our general emphasis throughout the interview on change itself. Furthermore, we had been specifically interested in comparing the current self-image with the individual's view of himself during middle age. Specifically, we asked our total survey sample: "How would you describe yourself when you were about fifty—the kind of person you were then?" Consequently, for eight-tenths (N=563) of the total self-image study sample of 700, we have information which enables us to determine how the subjects perceived themselves in relation to time, i.e., the time-orientation of the self-image.[6]

We were able to distinguish four patterns of self-image in relation to time: continuous, evolving, deteriorative, and retrospective. The most common pattern within this elderly sample was continuous, i.e., emphasizing long-standing traits which can still, realistically, be characteristic of the subject.[7] In this mode no

---

[6]This discussion does not pretend to be a systematic analysis of time-perception among the aged. That topic is the subject of two project reports by George M. Burnell and Majda Thurnher (publication pending) and Donald Spence (publication pending).

[7]For example, the following response would have been coded as a continuous self-image: "I've always been ambitious, and I'm still trying to make a success of my business." On the other hand, the following response from an eighty-year-old woman would have been classified as retrospective, rather than continuous, in spite of the subject's insistence: "I'm seventeen, have a wonderful mother and father, and have always been very popular with the boys."

particular distinction is made between past and present. The
personality is stable and unaltered. Time alone moves and
changes: "I've always been the same person." A retired housekeeper of eighty-two, born in England, reports such a continuous
self-image: "I'm a clean, respectable woman who likes fun." At age
fifty, she was "the same—just the same. I clean and cook and
make the best marmalade you ever tasted."

Second, an *evolving* image describes the current self as being
in some ways better or more than the earlier self. The image presented is one of a still-evolving personality, substantially improved
over the past one: "I am a better person now in some ways." Mr.
Janisch (CS) reports a positive change in himself as he has approached old age: "I think a man is still a boy until he is forty-
five or fifty. With time, I have become mellow and I saw the evil
of my ways. I was intolerant, not only toward my wife but towards
others as well when I was younger. I was hasty and had a bad,
bad temper. After fifty years, there comes a slow realization that
man has to change. The only way to arrive at that is to realize
that others have feelings the same as you do."

A third type of image we found in our sample was a *deteriorative* one, in which the emphasis is on loss and decline in personal
attributes: "I'm a worse person now in some ways." An eighty-
year-old woman, Miss Susan Roth (HS), describes herself in this
mode: "I used to be efficient. Now I'm just careless and let everything take its own course, which is wrong. I have a 'fraid feeling.
It holds me back. They don't let me have twenty-five cents to get
a piece of candy. It is as if someone owns me—I've got no say."
The theme of normalcy or superiority of the former self compared
with the present one is reiterated by Mr. Helmut Kreisler (HS):
"I have no real hope other than to become my old self. I used to
be cheerful, agreeable, active, with a desire to do something. Now
I'm mentally much older than I should be, uninteresting, lazy.
I would like to get back to normal, but I don't have the confidence
that others have that I'll do something for myself. I've lost confidence in myself and God. I have changed; at present I'm restless
and useless—isn't that awful?"

The fourth type of time-orientation we found was similar to
that of the deteriorative image, but differed from it in that the

subject seemed unable to perceive himself at present at all, but existed for himself *only* in the past. This we have called a *retrospective* orientation; this image focuses the "real" identity upon the past and ignores, minimizes, or denies the present: "I used to be somebody, but I'm nobody now." One eighty-eight-year-old woman says, "I certainly would not describe myself now as a person, but I used to be one—a very busy person—happy—very busy." Often in this mode, the self is perceived in terms of roles long obsolete or in terms of relationships with others who have been dead or removed from the person's world for many years. Terminated activities and characteristics are conceived as still persisting into the present. For example, one woman, a long-retired school teacher of seventy-five, describes herself now in terms of her former role as teacher: "I believe in work more than talk, and I like to help people in trouble. I worked in a school where children were poor—in Shanghai. I got clothes for them and tried to help them in other ways too. I try to be a good teacher, I miss my pupils."

When we examined the differences in frequencies of these four patterns of time-orientation between the mentally-healthy and the mentally-ill aged in our total sample, we found highly significant differences in all types. An image of the self as continuous or evolving is related to mental health, whereas a deteriorative or retrospective self-view is more likely to accompany mental illness (see Table IX).

TABLE IX
TIME-ORIENTATION OF SELF-IMAGE FOR TWO
MENTAL STATUS GROUPS

	Community Sample %	Hospital Sample %	Total Sample %
Time-orientation of Self-image			
Continuous	70	41	62
Evolving	16	10	14
Deteriorative	11	31	17
Retrospective	3	18	7
Total	100	100	100
N	(406)	(157)	(563)

Since we had a large enough sample of data on this dimension of self-image to permit statistical study, we were able to examine the extent to which certain personal characteristics other than the diagnosis of mental illness influenced these orientations. First, we expected to find some age-differences within the sample, since a popular conception of identity among older persons is of a self more and more retrospective, living increasingly among reminiscences and mementos. We found, however, that increasing age within the two samples (either community or hospital) made no difference in time-orientation. For each group, distributions among the four modes of self-perception were similar for all five-year age groups from sixty on. There were no sex differences in time-orientation within the mentally-well sample. Among the mentally ill, however, men were less likely to have a continuous self-image and more likely to be retrospective than were the women of that group. As we have noted in Chapter IV, data from the intensively-studied subjects suggest that men in the hospital sample feel the loss of occupational role more keenly than do men in the community sample and are more likely to mention former work in their self-descriptions. Loss of work roles in connection with self-image is not so frequently reported by women patients.

We thought that perhaps a deteriorative or retrospective perception of the self might be related, among the mentally ill, to memory loss, disorientation, and other cognitive malfunctions associated with organic brain disease, and that, among those free of cerebral pathology, these patterns might not be so common. Therefore, we examined the hospital sample to determine whether differences in time-orientation were dependent on the nature of psychiatric diagnosis. No differences were found: those with only functional disorders as well as those with varying kinds and degrees of organic deterioration showed similar distributions among the four patterns of time-orientation. Both of these diagnostic groups, however, were notably different from the mentally well.

Also, no significant correlations were found to exist between these self-image patterns and Wechsler Adult Intelligence Scale scores, ratings of physical status, socioeconomic status, occupation, education, religion, or native *versus* foreign birth. The patterns did vary, however, with the level of social activity. No person in the community sample with many social contacts and activities viewed himself retrospectively; most reported a continuous self-image, and many others described themselves as evolving personalities. Subjects with meager social contacts, by contrast, were more likely to have retrospective or deteriorative views of themselves.

We expected to find that poverty and physical disability would influence this dimension of self-image, if the community and hospital samples were examined separately—but they did not. What proved to be the case, as we have shown in earlier parts of this report, was that mental illness has a leveling effect on many functions within the personal system and that this effect often overrides other considerations, such as those of health, wealth, education, or other assets. But equally important is the fact that the nature of the social system which provides a context for the lives of the aged has a strong determining influence on personal attitudes, regardless of the level of mental health. This is clearly indicated in the relationship found between time-orientation and the level of social interaction. This general theme will provide the subject matter of Chapter VIII of this report—but it cannot be overemphasized even in this discussion, which we have tried to limit to the intrapersonal factors in adaptation to aging.

We were fortunate in our study of the time-orientation of self-image to have some information from a large sample of aged subjects, data which could be examined quantitatively, as we have just done. But, as we have found to be true in our analyses of other dimensions of self-image, a more detailed and dynamic explanation of the observed differences between the sick and the well aged was more fruitfully (albeit less rigorously) approached through a study of intensive case materials.

Among the intensively-studied community subjects, we see the same general pattern that emerged from the quantitative analysis: i.e., the mentally-healthy aged overwhelmingly think as well of themselves now as they did in middle age, or so they say. They describe themselves as more often happy than unhappy, relaxed than agitated, and optimistic rather than depressed. Thus, thinking well of oneself is a general trend among the healthy aged, and although the inroads of time are recognized, they are not dwelt upon. But a new topic comes out in the content analysis of the intensive case material which the quantitative study did not disclose: there are two somewhat interrelated attitudes characteristic of the mentally-healthy subjects, which distinguish them from the mentally ill.

First of all, the mentally well conceive of life as a "holding action." They emphasize what they still have, rather than what they have lost. And, perhaps more important, they are able to *substitute* a new set of achievable gratifications and sources of pride to replace old ones which are no longer functional for them. Community subjects are far from being indefatigable Pollyannas— they are well aware of the numerous problems facing the aging American. But they are able to be somewhat manipulative of their perceptual world in order to find backdrops against which the self may be most favorably regarded. Often this is accomplished with little modification of the middle-aged view of the self. And it is generally both a plausible and a successful undertaking because the perceptual point of departure is an asset of proven worth. Sometimes appearance is emphasized: Mr. VanDamm (CS) says, "I am still attractive to women. Yes, for the social life I lead, I can still find women." And Mrs. Bruzinsky (CS) reports, "Some men I know speak about how pretty my eyes are and how young my figure is." This woman, except for "white hair and more wrinkles, of course," regards herself as much the same person she was twenty years ago. Then she adds, "Maybe sometimes a little fatter or a little thinner, but pretty much the same." Mr. Hart (CS) is another excellent case in point: unlike the two community subjects just quoted, Mr. Hart, well into his nineties, has faced the fact that he is no longer attractive in any romantic sense. When we asked him if he still felt attractive to the opposite sex, he replied, "No, I don't believe I am—not for several years now." However, he did not linger over this loss for a single moment; he went right on to say, "However, I have quite a high rating of pride. This [as he was dressed up for the interview] is the way I go day to day; even just sitting at home, I have my necktie on. I have to apologize for my shoes today; haven't had energy to polish them this week. I always had a sense of pride in personal appearance. I think it makes you feel better."

This ability, then, to find new substitutes for old sources of satisfaction is an invaluable, perhaps crucial, skill that appears highly developed among the mentally-healthy aged. These substitutions may be introduced into any sphere of life and are clearly related to the perpetuation of a desirable view of the self. Mr. Van-Damm (CS) gives another typical example of this process: "I'm not physically capable of spending my time in the same way as I did when younger. Then, I could play sports such as bowling and basketball. Now I fill this time by reading or watching TV. I also play poker and meet with a group of my friends for a small party. We have more fun now than at any other time. We all enjoy the same things. However, we are not night owls anymore; now on weekends we cut things short. I guess we all agree that we can't take staying up as late as we used to. We all realize that we are not as young as we used to be. Overall, I'm enjoying life now more than ever before. Not as active, but I have good friends and a stable life."

The mentally-ill group characteristically fail to perceive alternatives or substitute sources of pride and satisfaction. They dwell instead on limitations and losses. It is as though, if they cannot have things the way they want them, they are categorical failures, and there is nothing to be gained by trying anything else at all. For these people, introspection in old age is a painful exercise—a reminder of the good that was and is no longer.[8] Many of these people seem to be in mourning—sometimes grieving for a lost intimate who gave meaning to life, sometimes unable to recover from the loss of employment and the significant activity accompanying it, and, most poignantly, sometimes inconsolable over the partial death of something within themselves. In all these cases, pride is dependent on recapturing the middle-aged self. The dilemma created by such a definition of the task of old age is illustrated by Mr. Apostolos Phidrios' self-description (HS): "I was a different person when I was fifty. My energy was different. I wanted to work and had the ability to." His only response to the ques-

---

[8]Although Robert Butler (1963) has emphasized the positive benefits to be derived by mentally-healthy aged in reviewing their lives, this is not always the case among the mentally ill.

tion on current self-image was: "Now I'm a pensioner." Today this man's sense of personal worth is dependent upon criteria which distinguished him in middle age: his only desire now is to be what he was at fifty, but—by his own testimony—he was a different person then. There is no road back, and little hope he can create one. He must either resurrect his "real" defunct self, or come to terms with the unwelcome stranger he sees as his aged being. When we asked him how he felt about old age, he replied, "Angry!"

As we suggested above, sometimes the self cannot be perceived as existing outside of an occupational role: the image of the working former self is vital; the unemployed self has a moribund quality. This attitude was what underlay Mr. Phidrios' anger with aging. He could not get beyond this description of himself: "I was a waiter *in my life*" [emphasis ours]. By clear implication, for Mr. Phidrios, life is no more. Or, as Mrs. Ada Bevin (HS) says, "Now? I don't care. I feel I've lived my life. There is no more life for me—no place to go."

When the image of the self is bound up with family role performance or simply with kinship status, the dissolution of these sources of identification, without some form of substitution, can result in a devalued self. This is a difficulty for many of the mentally-ill aged. Asked what she was like in her middle years, Mrs. Doris Tillford's (HS) immediate response is: "I think of my husband; he was so nice. Oh, I hate to think of him [gasped]. Children would flock around him like bees." Urged to talk about herself rather than her husband at that period, she replies, "Well, I would say I was a person like this: you could rely on me, if I told you I'd do something. House full of friends all the time. My family stayed around me. I did church work, mission work, visiting, helping." She recalled her stature then as an individual: "People thought much of me: 'That's a woman you never hear a bad word of—every time you see her she is a good wife, at work, minding her own business, not making trouble.' " In describing herself now, this woman can only say, "Oh man, I'm breaking down, but I try not to let it get me." Today, with her husband dead and her children scattered, Mrs. Tillford reports, "I catch myself snapping, not knowing how to be kind, raising my voice. It's just in me—I'm used to helping out."

Failures in substitution, then, characterize the hospital sample and lead to a retrospective or deteriorative view of the self. Skill in this task characterizes the mentally-healthy aged, and evokes a view of the self as a continuous or evolving personality.

We found a second major difference between the community and hospital intensively-studied subjects which seems to be dynamically related to the time-orientation of the self-image. There are notable differences between the groups in *level of aspiration*. Whether or not one's image of oneself is favorable, and whether or not one comes to happy terms with aging, seems to depend to some extent on what one expects from oneself and from life. Thus, mentally-healthy subjects seem to be at an advantage in maintaining a healthy evaluation of themselves because their goals were more feasible or their expectations of life more modest. Santayana has said, "True vice is human nature strangled by the suicide of attempting the impossible." Mentally-healthy subjects seem able to avoid this vice. For example, we asked Mr. VanDamm (CS) whether or not he had gotten what he wanted out of life so far: "Yes, I've done a fair job. I haven't asked for much and I have even gotten a little more than I expected I would get." When he was asked what he expected to accomplish during the rest of his life, he reported, "Nothing more—I'm content the way I am." Mr. VanDamm also had been prepared for poorer health in old age— his relative freedom so far from pain and suffering has come as a happy surprise—almost as a bonus: "Things have turned out better than I thought. I didn't think I'd be in such good health. You see old people who are sick and I thought I'd be like that." Mr. Mark Janisch (CS) makes a similar statement: "I've changed. I want to say that I'm quite satisfied now. I don't have to worry about the day after tomorrow. I feel safer than I did when I was young. My old age has been much happier for me than I thought it would be."

From reports such as these, we conclude that many mentally-healthy people do not expect all the rewards of life nor all the virtues of age. "I learned a long time ago," says Mr. Butler (CS), "that you get nothing for free. I'm reasonably happy—I'm pretty well satisfied. I sometimes think I could be a lot worse off. I'm by no means a rich man. Many of my friends are rich, but they are also dead. I hope that I will enjoy my retirement, so really, maybe, I'm better off."

The level of aspiration among the mentally-ill group, on the other hand, tends to remain high; there seems to be an expectation among them that the future should remain bright with promise. They seem to goad themselves to keep striving for perfection. They sometimes admit verbally that nobody can hope to achieve perfection, but they act and speak as though its continued pursuit were an appropriate major life goal: "I'm a perfectionist, but I did not have any opportunity. Deep in my soul I am not happy"; "I am a perfectionist in anything I undertake . . . no weaknesses—none"; "I'm always seeking self-improvement—never been satisfied." The problem here seems to be an earlier anticipation that old age would be a "golden" period, in which the individual would be at least as well off as he was in his middle-years, and probably much better off—the expectation was that old age would be a time for reaping the rich harvest of a lifetime of striving. The inevitable assaults and losses of old age, then, come as bolts out of the blue; since they have not been anticipated, they are not viewed as natural, but as cruel and unpredictable blows from a capricious destiny. Thus, when Mr. Hopland (HS) found himself physically disabled in old age, he felt devastated and beaten: "It all came back to me that I was such an able man and here I was all busted up. Made me kind of want to die." Compare this statement with the following report by Mr. Hokusai (CS) who also had developed a serious physical disorder: "Well, nature takes its toll on the body regardless of how well you take care of it. You can't help it—it's from getting old, you know. I'm trying to take care of myself the best I can. I take it easier and I try not to worry too much."

Related to this idea of high expectations of the self and the future is an accompanying tendency among the mentally ill to fail to anticipate changes in their future, or even to speculate about the future at all in realistic terms. Mr. Raymond Coffman (HS), for example, although he has experienced drastic life changes within the previous few years, responds in this way when asked if he expects any change in his life in the next few years: "No. Not any more . . . ." Mr. Hopland, the man mentioned above who described himself as "all busted up," was asked if he thought younger people should look ahead to being older; he answered, "I don't know. I don't know. I didn't myself. I don't like this life. I would rather be back living my old life." And Miss Louise Potter (HS), who finds it exceedingly hard to accept aging as a fact, reports that her major weakness is "always this lack of looking ahead."

This group of mentally-ill people seem to feel that life has somehow cheated them; they anticipated great things and they are bitterly disappointed with either themselves, life, or both. This attitude explains in part the different orientation to time we have seen between the two groups of subjects. People in the emotionally-disturbed group find it difficult to come to terms with the past; they feel either that the past has not given them enough, or that they themselves have failed to use past time to proper advantage: thus they tend to become preoccupied with ruminations and guilt about what might have been. Mrs. Powers (HS) says, "Each year you can see mistakes and opportunities you have missed when they were right in your hands." And Miss Miriam Christiansen (HS) describes herself in this way: "The principal part of my life today is memory. There haven't been many bad things in my life except disappointment in not being able to accomplish more. I'm a very mediocre person." Or, as Mr. Helmut Kreisler (HS) says, "I never make any plans—they all go flat anyhow."

The present, too, is unrewarding to the mentally-ill aged, because they can find no recompense for the loss of the past. Present time drags along, ticking off the slow, painful minutes—hours—days of emptiness. If old age is perceived as a time when the joys and satisfactions of life are eroded away, one by one, then the present can only be reluctantly endured. As Mr. Kepler (HS) says, "Well, I suppose you could say time hangs heavy. I am anxious for time to pass. Time doesn't mean much to me. It goes slower now; it drags. Every moment is difficult to face. Every little move I make takes a lot of energy. Just existing and enduring is a strain.

I'm not actually living—only going through the motions and routine of living." Mr. Jackson (HS) expresses much the same idea: "Time? That's the thing that passes—just passes slowly. It's when you have nothing to do—worst life in the world, and the hardest. So I'm just living along here and it isn't a very pleasant life."

For the mentally-ill aged, while the past is either disappointing or viewed with poignant nostalgia for lost youth and if the present is empty, meaningless and dragging on endlessly, the future holds real terror. As we will discuss later in the section on morale, the spectre of death begins to loom ever larger. Some want to stop the inexorable advance of time. Mrs. Frieda Caldwell (HS), for example, suffering from severe loss of memory, tends to forget how old she is, and when reminded of the fact that she is eighty-seven, is greatly troubled: "I'm not eighty-seven—not that old! It's a mistake. I'm fifty-seven. No that's wrong, too—I'm fifty-four. I know you think I'm a crazy woman, but I don't want to die." Mr. Jackson (HS) shows some insight into the relationship between failures to substitute activities and interests and the fear of death: "I *could* go to the show, although I haven't for years—I just don't do it. And this hotel life is awful, awful, awful! I don't make the effort to get to know people. I was happiest when I was working hard to keep my mind busy—had something to look forward to. Now there's nothing to look ahead to; now all I have to worry about is dying. Well, I have a shrewd idea that my thinking is brought on by dwelling on death—that's the cause of me doing a lot of things I shouldn't. I'm erratic; sometimes little things disturb me quite a bit—little things that shouldn't matter one iota one way or another."

The mentally-healthy aged are not oblivious to time—sometimes they seem acutely conscious of its transience—but neither do they see it as a threat. Mrs. Langtry (CS) explains it this way: "Being on time is very important to me. I used to do things in a rush when working and younger. Now I do things slowly—that way I can do them right and enjoy doing things. I don't want to be rushed. That's why I get up so early. I'm up before 7 a.m. Don't even sleep late of a Sunday. Seven a.m.—I get up." Compare this with the statement of Mr. Charles Leveritt (HS): "Sometimes I don't want to get up, because then I'll just wish it was time to go to bed."

Mr. Butler, a man who is in the mentally-well sample, but who has been quite articulate about those of his attitudes which he recognizes as "unhealthy," describes well the two contrasting time-orientations discussed above, adding that he tries to sustain a positive orientation, but sometimes lapses into the other: "Time —it's going too fast. When you reach the age of retirement, you begin to realize that there is a limit to the amount of time you have left and it begins to go by all too quickly. Until recently, I never thought there was an end to time. I thought that I was ageless and never considered anything else. However, time has gone fast since I've been sixty. When I was in high school waiting for graduation to come and for me to go into the Air Force, time went slowly." Asked why he felt time goes faster now, he says, "Well, in some ways you want to stop time, for you know you're on the way out. On the other hand, you want it to hurry, for then you can retire and do things you want to do but had no time for before. I think it's the beginning of ambivalence toward life and death."

In summary, our content analysis of intensive-interview materials on time-orientation and self-image disclosed that: (1) Mentally-healthy subjects tend to view life as a "holding action" which can continue to provide pleasure if one can substitute other sources of pride and satisfaction for those that become unavailable in old age. Mentally-ill subjects fail to perceive alternatives and lack skill in substitution. (2) Mentally-healthy subjects tend to have more modest expectations of life and a lower level of personal aspiration. Thus, if old age has any pleasures and satisfactions, they come as happy surprises and the older person considers himself fortunate. The mentally-ill aged, on the other hand, are more likely to strive for perfection in themselves, and seem to believe seriously in the Cinderella legend—for them, life should have a happy ending and all dreams come true. If these things do not happen, they are bitterly disappointed and feel either that life has failed them, or that they have failed themselves. (3) For the mentally healthy—perhaps as a corollary of the two above-mentioned perceptions—time is not an enemy, but an old friend who will leave them all too soon. What time remains, however, is to be cherished and enjoyed. Among the mentally ill, by contrast, time often seems to be perceived as a harsh task-master, proctoring the final critical examination of one's life. Many of these aged people have had such high aspirations that they fear not having enough time to complete their life-tasks; they desperately want that achievement, for they see no other way of proving their worth and so gaining a measure of remembrance after they are gone. Some, as we have shown, have given up hope of meeting their own inflexible standards of excellence. Then time drags on with nothing to fill the days. As Mrs. Trocopian (HS) puts it: "I have always been active and ambitious, all my life—I was like an electric clock. Whatever I did, I did with vitality if I was accomplishing something. The past few years have not been the same—I do things to pass time. That accomplishment and automatic quality—those things are gone. This present life—I don't know what it is. Actually, life does not have any value for me. I wanted to live and die with respect. Now I want to cut life short. I'd rather die—there is nothing much to look forward to—just the same routine."

Having Significant Goals or Meaning in Later Life

Self-esteem among this group of older people is influenced also by a search for meaning in one's life in the later years. But, in this search, community and hospital subjects, again, have characteristic orientations.

The mentally well take pride in a cluster of personal characteristics which we have called *relaxation*. They describe this relaxation as a positive and desirable state of being, enjoyed by people who have the ability (and they think of it as an ability) to appreciate certain of the compensations of old age. These men and women take pride in gaining greater control over certain drives, impulses, and emotions; they speak gratefully of release from the compulsion to compete, to produce, to succeed, and to hurry. Problems do not loom so large; inconveniences are no longer so important, and one need not be so disturbed by them. Community subjects describe a new and broader perspective, which they call by different names: wisdom, maturity, spirituality, humanitarianism, peacefulness, or mellowing. They feel less "driven" and are able to take real pleasure in allowing others to excel. They feel released and freed to develop new thoughts, new concerns, and new interests. They claim to be less excitable and in greater control of themselves and their reactions. This attitude is a source of great satisfaction and self-esteem for those who have been able to achieve it. Many of the community intensive sample make reference to one or several of such characteristics.

For these people, old age does not represent the bleak terminus of a downhill slide from mature status. It is a new life period, with the compensations and liabilities that are a part of *any* phase of life. Mrs. Manx (CS) says, "My age has its compensations. You mellow and become a little more intelligent and peaceful." She views herself as a better person, "more relaxed," than she used to be. Mr. Janisch (CS) also feels he has improved as he has aged: "My nature is settled for the better. I tolerate things better than when I was a young man and in my middle age. I managed to overcome even grief—something I could not do when I was young." Mr. Knight (CS) agrees that he has become more appreciative: "You learn as you grow older—learn from experience. You become wiser, more tolerant, patient, more easy-going. You are able to enjoy life and make it happy, for now you have more time to do the things you like to do." Mr. Ebenhauser (CS) approves of the "maturity" he has achieved: "I began to get more mature thoughts and I'm satisfied. I've become more spiritualistic maybe—more humanitarian." Mrs. Burbank (CS) reports changes for the better in her personality: "I don't have that drive. I can take things day by day—no great drive to excel. That's a terrible thing, and I would like to add, confidentially, that sex drive is something to get rid of, too. I expect all this to be of benefit."

Although the value placed on relaxation might seem to be the result of withdrawal from active roles, this is not the case. More often than not, community subjects who pride themselves on their ability to find relaxation in old age are still actively involved in a number of roles—but the quality of that activity has undergone a subtle change—it has become less *competitive*.

The mentally-ill group are still driven to compete, ambition is still a central value, and inability to achieve leads to self-recrimination. Whereas simply getting along in life and having the appreciation and opportunity to enjoy it is a source of satisfaction to many community subjects, Mr. Ableson (HS) finds it reprehensible: "I see nothing spectacular about myself—average plugger, plugging along, getting nowhere. I wouldn't want my son to be like that." Mr. Carelli (HS) says, "I used to be a fighter. Now I'm just playing pinochle and poker. Just a gentleman of leisure. You could put it down as a tramp or bum, or something like that." Mrs. Harris (HS) speaks of her declining energy as a personal weakness: "When I was young—I was a real go-getter then. Now I take the line of least resistance—let things go until tomorrow."

Other people in the mentally-ill group make a special point of denying explicitly any evidences of what they perceive to be failures in competitive achievement, productivity, or capability to excel in some activity. Miss Caldwell (HS), for example, a woman rendered quite dependent by severe and progressive memory loss, says, "I'm a different girl from probably what you think I am. I'm capable of doing anything. I've handled more things, thanks to God." Mr. Hopland (HS) in one interview admitted to serious physical disability and then vigorously denied their limitations: "It's not very easy what I'm going through. Can't walk but a couple of blocks and have to lean on buildings. I still believe I have the ability to do things; I want to think I still have strength to do a lot of things I'm not doing. I have no weak points." Mr. Ritter (HS) finds most other people "boring" and "ordinary." He expresses the idea that he is not like them: "I'm just like normal people; I'm active still. I don't go too much for conformity, live and let live, or the Golden Rule. There's still energy in the old system. I've always been impulsive and aggressive—and when things didn't break right, I never gave in—I worked day and night to make it a go." Mrs. Bachstein (HS), a discharged psychiatric patient with a massive loss of memory and now a resident of the county home for the aged, says, "I don't feel that way [not very useful] at all, because anything I tackle I make a go of. I can handle anything."

One theme that runs throughout a surprising number of the intensive interviews is the desire of older people, particularly men, to create some new product or perfect some invention. This was true among both hospital and community samples. One community subject claimed to be one of the inventors of a particular new and very popular type of watch-band; another man in the community sample was working on a "perpetual-motion water wheel." He says he had conceived the idea for it many years before, but then had put it aside as "too foolish." After his retirement, however, he once again began to work on it. In these two cases, however, the inventing appears to serve practical ends—in the first case, to make extra money, and, in the second case, to engage in a pet hobby to fill time. In the mentally-ill group, however, would-be inventors seem driven by some competitive urge to prove themselves at least the equal of other men, and preferably superior. In their accounts of their creative endeavors, there is an underlying tone of hostility and fear. Thus, Mr. Czernich (HS) reports: "Well, I want to create something—something that will be here when I am gone. I have more than half a dozen inventions that I am sure would sell. I haven't made any success yet, but they will work—I will *have* to make something out of them. I always have different ideas, always try to improve myself, always try to organize myself. Lots of patents. If I tell about my inventions to anyone, there are lots of people who would take it away from me." Mr. Spenser (HS) considers himself "a creative artist. I am a man of many trades. I am out of the ordinary. Ideas unlimited, that's me! I'm a designer. I have new and novel ideas. I am a creative person. I have new skills, techniques in art, too, now, that haven't been invented except by me. I am trying to help humanity on one hand and I am persecuted on the other."

Mrs. Trocopian (HS), who is not an inventor but does consider herself particularly gifted intellectually, discusses her talents with the same underlying tone of competitiveness and hostility toward others: "I have a brain to overcome and conquer the weak. If I were a physician, I would help a lot of people. I have lots of talents, you know, but I am not the bragging type. There are some who appreciate me as a capable person—artistic, alert. A lot of them are jealous. They think I am nervous and stuck-up. People try to hurt you when you are more talented, creative, or something—they get jealous instead of appreciating it."

These attitudes contrast strongly with statements by mentally-healthy subjects such as the seventy-seven-year-old man in the community sample who says, "I feel content and adjust myself to the necessity of growing old. I receive satisfaction from seeing *others* in active life." Or Miss Bertha Schaeffer (CS), who reports, "I'm not the life of the party that I used to be—I let somebody else take my place, and I enjoy letting someone else take my place. I don't know whether it happened gradually or suddenly—but occasionally, when I'm out with old friends, I resort to old tactics. I still give them a fancy dance."

The mentally-ill group, then, seems to be characterized by a continuing value-orientation toward competitiveness, achievement, and a continuing need to prove themselves somehow exceptional and worthy of note. And it is as if they fail to see there exist other paths to the discovery of some meaning in their lives—of making others aware that they still exist, as significant human beings.

ADAPTIVE AND MALADAPTIVE VALUES AMONG THE AGED—A SUMMARY

We are now in a position to draw together from the foregoing analysis a set of personal value-orientations (i.e., those serving as criteria in self-evaluation) which characterize the majority of the mentally-healthy aged in our intensive sample, and a comparative set that we found more typical of the mentally ill. Expanding our earlier schema, we find that such shared goals as independence are actually generic, or broad areas of concern, to both groups of aged subjects in our sample. These generic concepts might better be labelled "principal goals," under each of which we have discussed particular value-orientations. Those value-orientations which are more often held by the community sample we will call "adaptive," and those more common to the mentally ill we will call "mal-adaptive." A revised schema, then, may be shown as follows:

DIFFERENCES BETWEEN ADAPTIVE AND MALADAPTIVE PERSONAL
VALUE-ORIENTATIONS IN AN AGED AMERICAN SAMPLE

Principal Goals of Both Groups	*Adaptive Value-orientations: (Mentally-well group)*	*Maladaptive Value-orientations: (Mentally-ill group)*
Independence	Pride in autonomy and concern for freedom of others	Avoidance of dependency out of fear and mistrust of others
Social acceptability	Congeniality Consideration (Love)	Commanding respect through status and achievement (Power)
Adequacy of personal resources	Conservation	Acquisition
Ability to cope with external threats or losses	Action if appropriate; resilience if loss is inevitable Harmoniousness Emphasis on the existential	Aggressiveness, regardless of the situation Control Emphasis on the instrumental
Ability to cope with changes in the self	Emphasis on continuity and development Skill in substitution Reasonable level of aspiration	Emphasis on progress, with retrospection and deterioration if progress fails Continued pursuit of earlier goals High level of aspiration
Having significant goals or meaning in later life	Relaxation Cooperation	Ambition Competitiveness

In concluding this discussion, there are two observations that should be reported. First, this content analysis of intensive-interview materials had as its goal the description of central tendencies or characteristic configurations of value within each of the disability groups. Certainly not all the community subjects espouse adaptive value-orientations in each and every area of concern; nor do all members of the hospital sample manifest uniformly maladaptive patterns. Unfortunately, the intensive samples are small, and statistical distributions, therefore, somewhat meaningless. Also, because our larger sample had been surveyed *before* the intensive interviewing was done, we lack any specific data on value-orientations for this larger group.[9] However, something of the range of adaptation within each of the intensively-studied groups can be roughly estimated. By our best guess, about three-fourths of the community subjects manifest adaptive value-orientations in most areas, while probably not more than two-out-of-five of the mentally-ill group do.

Second, we were struck by the fact that the value-orientations which seem to be maladaptive for the aged in this sample are strikingly similar to values found to be characteristic of American culture generally by a number of other observers.[10] It seems to us that the major orientations of American culture, then, while they may be eugenic enough for a young population, probably aggravate the particular problems which confront the aged in our society. We will have much more to say on this topic in Chapter IX.

COMPONENTS OF THE GOOD LIFE

Each culture and every social class has its own unique image of the "Good Life"—its own recipe for that elusive estate called human happiness. Among most Japanese today, for example, to be surrounded by one's descendants in old age, treated with deference and honor, is the vision of the "Good Life." For these people, entering the last stage of one's life means earning the serene consummation of a lifetime spent in assiduous, uncomplaining toil. At last, one can be free of tedium and economic necessities. Dependency upon the younger members of the family to fulfill

---

[9]This unfortunate chronology was not a flaw in research design, but was rather the result of a changing purpose in the overall program and the development of new interests among some of the staff. The original study was designed as a descriptive, comparative survey of the major physical, psychological, and social characteristics of a large sample of mentally-ill and mentally-healthy aged, as well as an exploration of the decision making process involved in the commitment of older people to psychiatric facilities. These findings are reported in other publications of the project (cf. Lowenthal, 1964a; Lowenthal, Berkman, and Associates [1966]; and Simon, Lowenthal, and Epstein [publication pending]). It was only after these original purposes of the overall research program had been achieved that staff interests turned to studies of the dynamics of aging, such as the current volume reports.

[10]These include Kluckhohn (1949); Williams (1959); M. Mead (1943); and Riesman in his several works, particularly *Individualism Reconsidered* (1954).

these functions is no cause for shame or self-blame. Indeed, caring for one's elders is a source of family pride. Accordingly, old men and women of Japan value unfettered time for *sakura*-viewing on holidays, tea ceremonies, and contemplation (Keene, 1959). Among the poorer classes of many peasant societies, the "Good Life" is making the most of one's opportunities to secure the future of one's family, but always within the structure of one's own fixed social class level. As one older Mexican worker has put this:

There's nothing better in this world than upright work. . . . I'd be happy, it would give me the greatest satisfaction, if [my children] could be like that. . . . I have my happy moments with my grandchildren. It is first for God and then for my grandchildren that I'm on my feet, plugging away. . . . I want to leave them a room, that's my ambition; to build that little house, one or two rooms or three so that each child will have a home and so they can live there together. . . . I asked God to give me the strength to keep struggling so I won't go under soon and maybe finish that little house (Lewis, 1961, pp. 481 and 499).

In "Sun City," a newly developed retirement community in Arizona, the "Good Life" for older, middle-class Americans is based not on contemplation or work but on play. As one recent observer of this community has noted:

Sun City's claim to influence is based on its phenomenal growth and on its having devised an "Active New Way of Life." Billboards on the highway from Phoenix proclaim that ". . . Sun City" is "where Active Retirement originated." It takes a visitor only a few hours to realize that the Sun City formula for happiness — or "pure happiness," as the man who speaks between renditions of the advertising jingle puts it — is, roughly that happiness equals activity plus friendliness . . . playing shuffleboard, golf, canasta, and bridge, going to club meetings with other retired people, and being generally friendly. . . . (Trillin, 1964, pp. 120-121).

Since our San Francisco sample permits us to view a wide range of cultural and social contexts, we suspected that formulae for satisfaction in old age would be equally diverse, despite the communality of the urban setting. We already know from our analyses of Chapter IV that mentally-ill subjects have lower morale than community subjects, but even among the mentally healthy, we found a wide range of reported morale levels. Likewise, as we have just seen, criteria for self-judgments vary greatly as well. In this analysis, we shall turn to the sources of satisfaction and dissatisfaction with life in old age, endeavoring (as we did with the sources of self-esteem) to codify the anticipated variety of perceptions into a continuum of adaptive and maladaptive patterns. These patterns added to the others will form the basis of the adaptational model reported in the final chapter.

We examined the sources of high morale separately from those of low morale because we suspected that not all items would be the converse of the other. For ascertaining the sources of high morale, we asked the intensive sample such questions as follows:

1. In general, how happy would you say you are these days? (*Probe*: Why is that, do you think?)
2. What have the main satisfactions been in your life so far?
3. What are the most important things in your life today?
4. What would you say gives you the most pleasure these days?

Sources of low morale were, in part, tapped with the following questions:

1. If you could change the way you are living today, how would you change it?
2. What have been the two hardest things you've had to face since you were sixty?
3. Most people feel low or depressed sometimes. Do you? (Probe for reasons.)

These as well as other related questions provide the source of the findings reported here.

SOURCES OF HIGH MORALE

For the questions relating to high morale, we have complete responses for only sixty-five of the seventy-nine in the intensive sample. The other fourteen either declined to answer some or all of the questions, reported that they did not know, or seemed unable to grasp the meaning of the inquiries. Some of these latter subjects were in the inpatient group. Understandably, attitudinal data derived from seriously disturbed people will not be amenable to any deep content analysis. However, there were also people in the community subsample—usually in a nursing home or the county home for the aged—who failed to respond. In all, we had usable information on thirty-three community and thirty-two hospital subjects. For this subsample of sixty-five, seven major sources of satisfaction were referred to by at least a fifth of all subjects. Sources of satisfaction less frequently referred to are grouped together in an eighth (miscellaneous) category. In rank order of frequency of mention, these categories were:

Rank Order	Sources of High Morale	Per-Cent of Intensive Sample Reporting the Factor
1.	Entertainments and diversions	69
2.	Socializing	57
3.	Productive activity	54
4.	Physical comfort (other than health)	52
5.	Financial security	46
6.	Mobility and movement	40
7.	Health, stamina, and survival	20
8.	Miscellaneous	38

Entertainments and Diversions

The most frequently mentioned source of satisfaction among these subjects is the enjoyment of various kinds of entertainment. Watching television is mentioned perhaps more often than anything else, with the exception of reading—also a source of considerable pleasure. Subjects enjoyed attending the theater, movies, baseball games, or lectures, as well as playing cards. Quite a few said they enjoyed listening to the radio or playing records, but fewer, going to concerts or visiting museums. But reading and watching television—essentially home acitivities—are mentioned by almost two-thirds of the subjects. Mr. Monroe Abelson (HS) claims that the most satisfying period of his life is ". . .right now, I believe. I don't have no worries. I watch TV, go to bed; I'm very well satisfied." Mrs. Bruzinsky (CS) reports, "Usually my spirits are very high. I play bridge and go to shows and movies. Sometimes I get low spirits because, every time you look in the mirror, you see you are old. It doesn't last long—and when something nice happens, I'm glad again. Sometimes I just say 'Ech!' and forget it. I play bridge—this makes me feel better." Mr. Jespersen (CS) says that "reading is very important" to him, but he also mentions that part of the pleasure he derives from it is "being able to discuss a book you have both read with a friend. It gives you some common interest—something to talk about."

We were rather surprised at the functional value people place on viewing television. Williams and Wirths (1965) also found that their elderly study subjects watched increasingly more television, and "most of them expressed the attitude that watching television was something they just seemed to enjoy more as they grew older" (p. 196). We knew from our survey data that most subjects do watch television, but assumed it was actually enjoyed less than proved to be the case. The reports seem to suggest that television-viewing is a type of "passive socializing" for some older people whose range of movement is somewhat restricted and whose social world has consequently atrophied. Television is thus "company" of a sort. Old people—especially if they are disabled—may find it harder to go out into the world, but, through television, they can bring a segment of that world into their homes. They can "keep up with what's going on" and not feel so isolated from the events and concerns of the larger society. Mrs. Langtry (CS) reports that, during her post-surgical convalescence, she became very much interested in certain television programs and felt almost personally involved in the dramas she watched: "My husband laughs at me, because I sit there in front of the TV and laugh and cry just as though it was really happening."

Reading the newspaper, too, keeps older people "in touch." Mr. Ritter (HS) reads the newspaper avidly, and keeps a steady stream of letters going to Senators, Congressmen, and other government officials, because he enjoys being an interested and participating citizen. This is a preoccupation which he has developed much more since his retirement: "I'm just as happy as I've ever been. After I got the kids through college, I relaxed completely and I watched the world go by. Watch them whirl and where they are going. I participate only occasionally—when I feel like it. I just sit on the sidelines and watch it go by, but I interest myself in letting them know in Washington what I feel."

The responses in this category of entertainment and diversion also suggest what might well be a problem specific to American aged—"filling time." We have already made the observation in Chapter I that time for our culture can have concrete, saleable value. Unlike the Japanese aged who can value contemplation for its own sake, our subjects seem to derive great satisfaction from "doing something" with the time they abundantly have, and, quite obviously, involvement in our ubiquitous mass communication network offers a handy solution for this uniquely American problem.

We have included playing bridge, poker, and other games as entertainments and diversions, although, in most cases, the social interaction with fellow-players may be just as important as the pastime itself. Therefore, in cases where both the game for its own sake, as well as the associated socializing were mentioned, we included the subject in both categories of response—this and what follows.

Socializing

Personally-motivated social contact was mentioned as contributing to life satisfaction by 57 per cent of the intensive sample. Visits with friends and relatives, chatting with neighbors, or even making casual acquaintances in parks, restaurants, and shops, provide older people with a great deal of pleasure.[11] Some of the subjects mentioned that they enjoy people more now than they did earlier in life. Miss Potter (HS), who described her life during middle age as one of constant preoccupation with work, competition, and achievement, was asked in the intensive interview to name the important things that had happened to her recently: "It seems lately I've been finding more pleasure in other people. I'm getting amusement and fun out of crowds—even strangers

---

[11]For a thoroughly intensive study of friendship patterns among the aged of Cleveland, the reader is referred to Rosow (1964). Specifically, this writer found five different patterns of socializing: the Cosmopolitan (least contact with neighbors, no desire for more friends, many outside interests) ; the Phlegmatic (low degree of contact with neighbors, no desire for more friends; no good friends at all) ; the Isolated (low contact with neighbors but do want more friends) ; the Sociable (high contact with neighbors but do not want more friends) ; and the Insatiable (high contact with neighbors and want still more friends) .

lately—like saying 'Merry Christmas' when you're shopping—all that. People used to annoy me—now I enjoy them. My friends seem friendlier. I guess that's my own attitude that's changed, don't you think?" Mrs. Dillon (CS) reports a great deal of happiness in her life: "A lot—it's being around other people." Mrs. Tillford (HS) reports that company always cheers her up: "I don't know when I had such a happy time—a pleasant, restful time. Sometimes people come in; they lift you up."

Mrs. Reinhart (CS), whose rapidly deteriorating physical health—and concern for sparing her family the burden of her helplessness—has even made her contemplate suicide from time to time, says, when asked how often it seems that life is not worth living, "Never, because I have a lovely family and friends. I find a great deal of happiness because of the love of my husband and children. I don't think I ever feel blue—except when I realize my condition."

Productive Activity

The older people we interviewed intensively still derive a great deal of satisfaction from productivity. Fully 54 per cent mentioned it as a major source of satisfaction. In some cases, the subject was still gainfully employed, and this served as a source of high morale. In other cases, activity had been shifted to another sphere, such as a hobby. These subjects mentioned sewing, gardening, repairing clocks, photography, upholstering or refinishing furniture, doing chores for neighbors, making home improvements, woodwork, painting, and creative writing. Women in the sample who are not too physically disabled spoke of their enjoyment of household tasks—cooking, shopping, and housekeeping. For example, Mrs. Burbank (CS) says, "I'm having a wonderful time. I like my present way of life. Of course, it's good for a person to feel that you are achieving things every day, and I do. My work is never done. I would probably have an 84-hour day, if I could change things. Make some jewelry too—all kinds of creative things." Mr. Spenser (HS) reports that old age has been the most pleasant period of his life because "I am involved with such things as my artistic ability—products which I myself have created." Mrs. Sandusky (HS) reports that she derives a great deal of pleasure out of doing housework: "I like it, believe it or not." However, in this woman's response there is an underlying sense of *having* to be useful in order to be socially acceptable. She goes on to say, "I'm never happier than when I'm helping, so—that way—my children like to have me around." As we will see later, the *compelling* quality in activity is an underlying difference between the community and hospital subjects.

Physical Comfort

Fifty-two per cent of the intensive sample mentioned the satisfactions they derive from simple physical comforts—having a comfortable place to live, enjoying meals, being able to sleep soundly, and having a place to sit in the sun. Mrs. Valente (CS), for instance, takes great pleasure in having an apartment of her own which is enjoyable to her: "I'm very much at home here; I've done the painting myself. What I got is my own and very comfortable. Everything's so handy—transportation, shopping."

A number of subjects mentioned the importance of light and heat to their psychological well-being. Mrs. Bennington (CS), for example, reports, "I have a comfortable apartment. I think I have a lot to be thankful for. Everybody in this building has plenty of heat and sunshine. It's not a dark apartment, and when you get along to my years, that's very important." Even very simple things often provide pleasure. As Mr. Wheeler (CS) says, "I take snuff. You can put that down—it's very important to me!" And Mrs. Roth (HS) says, "I've got everything I want—I had my bath twice this week. Everything is O.K."

Reference has been made in other studies of aging to a tendency of old people to exhibit "regressive narcissism."[12] Our data

---

12Fenichel (1945) defines "narcissistic regression" as when ". . . the object relationships are replaced by relations within the personality; the patient loses his object relationships by regressing into a phase where no objects yet existed" (p. 402). Zinberg (1963) sees this inward movement among the aged as both pathological and egosyntonic: "The weakening of the synthetic function of the ego and the reinstatement in part of primary-process and pleasure-principle functioning are exemplified best in preoccupations with bodily needs. With all these changes, which are a retreat to earlier developmental states as well as to libidinally invested objects from the past, the state of the aged person shows elements of both what we have discussed as pathological regression and as regression in the service of the ego" (p. 148). Reichard, Livson, and Peterson (1962) found a sizeable group of regressed older men in their San Francisco Bay Area sample and these they called "the Rocking Chair Man" (see Chapter 9, pp. 129-135).

give no evidence one way or the other as to whether this phenomenon is "regressive," but it is clear that physical comfort is very
important to our subjects, ranking even a little higher than financial security. It seems as though, with age, these people have
stopped taking physical comfort for granted; it is no longer
viewed as the natural state of affairs. Perhaps, with chronic aches
and nagging pains increasing, with strength and energy waning,
and sometimes with sight and hearing failing, the simple fact of
being comfortable seems almost like a special gift.

Financial Security

About half of the intensive sample made special reference to
freedom from economic worries as a source of satisfaction. Mr.
Lewissohn (CS) attributes his good spirits to freedom from such
anxieties: "I have no fears. Most of the time a man used to worry
about who would support him. I have investments, cash." When
Miss Barton (CS) was asked to name the most satisfying period of
her life, she answered, "I think it is about as satisfying a period
now that I'm sort of settled. Unless something unusual happens,
I think I have enough money to take care of me the rest of the
time. I certainly hope so. I made some money on the stock market
and, of course, I have a pension." Mr. Jacques Sablon (CS), a
man quite physically disabled and requiring intensive nursing
care, expresses great satisfaction in having been able to pay in
advance for care he now gets at a convalescent hospital: "I will
be here for life. This room I have for life. What worries do I
have? [Is anything difficult for you these days?] Nothing whatso-
ever; whatever I have, it's paid for. If I am sick, I am taken care
of. I got everything I want. The future I got assured." The pre-
Medicare subjects of this sample expressed considerable concern
about high medical expenses. Since they could not foresee how
much medical care they would need in the future, having pre-
paid hospital and medical coverage was often mentioned as a great
relief from worry. "We have Blue Cross, and it is a real source of
satisfaction to us," said Mr. Janisch (CS).

There is some indication that a good deal of the satisfaction in
financial security actually derives from the great value we saw
placed on independence. Mr. Markrinos (CS) made this clear:

"I got that money I get from my pension. I make out all right. I'm not hungry and I pay my room rent. I don't ask anybody for one penny."

Mobility and Movement

An occasional change of scene seems to be something that older people both need and appreciate. Forty per cent of the sample mentioned this category as a major source of positive morale. They speak of the enjoyment of traveling, of drives into the country, going downtown on the streetcar, walking in the park, or just getting out of the house for a while to sit in the sun, looking at flowers, trees, or people walking by. Several of the men (and one woman, too) mentioned the pleasure of fishing trips: "It's not so much the fishing—it's just the chance to get out in the fresh air and see something different."

Movement has often been listed as a basic human need. As people age, the need persists, despite the fact that its satisfaction becomes increasingly difficult in many cases. Our society is so dependent on the private automobile that we sometimes assume everyone has a car and can drive anywhere he wants to go. In old age, this is rarely the case. Many of our subjects do not have enough money to maintain an automobile, and even those who could afford one are not always physically capable of driving. There is, therefore, a great dependence on public transportation or on one's own legs. Those with ambulatory difficulties, general weakness, or failing eyesight may have problems in walking even a few blocks. They become, then, quite dependent on the consideration of friends or relatives with cars, for the rare excursions they can take from the confines of their own quarters. These opportunities are greatly appreciated by many subjects.

Health, Stamina, and Survival

As Mrs. Bennington (CS) says, "I think I have a lot to be thankful for, having good health and being able to just go along." Mrs. Vinnie Ackley (HS) was asked to name the most important thing in her life today, "Health," she replied. "It's important to know I'm living and got my health and strength. I can get up when I get ready and lay down when I get ready. And I'm thank-

ful I have the strength to do things for myself." When we asked
Mr. Albert Jay (CS) when he is happiest, he said, "If everything
goes all right and if no one is sick—then you feel free and happy."
Mr. Butler (CS) listed as one of the main satisfactions in his
life ". . . that I've lived this long and I've kept my good health."

One-out-of-five people in the intensive sample mentioned this
area as being a major source of satisfaction. Even among some of
the physically disabled subjects, stamina and simple survival are
rewards not to be discarded lightly. Mr. Ableson (HS) reports
that he is satisfied with life as it is, although he has serious health
problems: "I decided I'm still kicking and you've got a lot of
things to be thankful for. I'm thankful I could live this long."
When we asked Mr. Ritter (HS) what the most important thing
was to him these days, he said, "Breathing—just to continue breathing. I don't worry. I just enjoy myself." Or, as Mr. Jespersen (CS)
sums up his satisfactions: "I have no reason to be jealous of anyone now. I've enough money to get along on. I have friends now,
I'm not a burden upon anyone, and I'm still alive. What else can
anyone my age ask for?"

SOURCES OF HIGH MORALE, COMMUNITY AND HOSPITAL SAMPLES

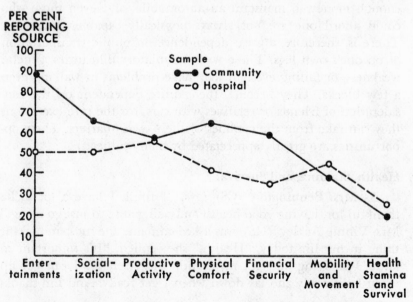

Figure 1. Sources of high morale, community and hospital samples.

COMPARISON OF COMMUNITY AND HOSPITAL
SUBJECTS

Figure I shows how frequently community subjects mentioned each of the seven categories (other than the "Miscellaneous" items) just discussed as sources of high morale, compared with the mentally-ill group. The two resulting profiles are somewhat different in two respects. First, mentally-healthy subjects simply find more things in life to make them happy. In five of the seven areas, proportionately more community than hospital subjects reported that they found some satisfaction. The two exceptions were satisfactions from movement and good physical health, which were more frequently cited by the mentally ill.

A second difference between the two groups lies in the relative importance of the various categories. If we examine the order in which each group ranks areas of satisfaction, the four categories more frequently mentioned are:

Rank	Community Subjects	Hospital Subjects
1.	Entertainments and diversions	Productive activities
2.	Socializing	Entertainments and diversions
3.	Physical comforts	Socializing
4.	Financial security	Mobility and movement

While amusement and social contacts are high on both lists, the mentally ill place productivity at the very top of their hierarchy of life satisfactions. This finding is readily understandable in the light of what we have just discussed about the major value-orientations of the mentally ill—most of them place high value on achievement, competition, and recognition, and they tend to see productive activity as the only pathway to those goals. Among the community subjects, productive activity is in fifth place. When it is mentioned by the mentally healthy, the reference is usually to a creative avocation—pursued for the pleasure it gives the subject rather than for the hope of public acclaim.

Community subjects are more concerned with physical comfort and financial security than are hospital subjects. For this sample, at least, we find an enjoyment of creature comforts to be adaptive rather than maladaptive, i.e., it is more characteristic of elderly people in the community than it is of those with a recent history of mental disorder. However, both the concern with physical comforts and the emphasis on financial security may be more than a symptom of regressive hedonism; it may be an indication of a present-time-orientation—an ability to enjoy life as it is, rather than a striving to make it something other than it is.

The emphasis placed on mobility and movement by the mentally ill may be related in part to their value of instrumentality—moving about may be thought of as "doing something," a very important thing to hospital subjects. But, in addition, it must be remembered that the mentally ill have lived through periods of time when their movement was forcibly restricted—at the time of our baseline study, they were all confined to a psychiatric ward, and many are still in state hospitals. We would expect this history of forced confinement to make them prize more highly what mobility they do have.

Another factor in the difference between community and hospital subjects may be the fact that a larger proportion of the hospital sample are physically disabled. If we examine the ranking of sources of satisfaction for two *physical* status groups, we see the following order among the more frequently mentioned categories:

Rank	Physically-well Subjects	Physically-impaired Subjects
1.	Entertainments and diversions	Physical comfort
2.	Productive activity	Entertainments and diversions
3.	Socializing	Socializing
4.	Financial security	Movement

It is clear, from this ranking, that movement is more important to the physically disabled—those who have more difficulty in its attainment. We also see that, while entertainment and social contacts remain important to both groups, the physically ill place less emphasis on productivity—no doubt out of necessity; remaining as physically comfortable as possible under the circumstances is highly prized by them. Financial security is fairly important to the healthy, but things other than solvency assume greater proportion in the presence of physical disability; serious illness among the aged often makes economic self-reliance an unattainable luxury.

SOURCES OF LOW MORALE

The range of sources of dissatisfaction reported by the intensive sample is much greater than that of sources of satisfaction. The subjects we interviewed seemed more specific about their woes than about their pleasures. We originally thought that we might be able to group the sources of low morale into the same categories as the sources of high morale, with the area mentioned in one case as a deprivation and, in the other, as a satisfaction. We also expected to find a similar rank order of importance. However, the factors which lead to depression, we found, are not always the simple converse of the factors cited as sources of satisfaction. In some cases, people did not perceive what assets they really had—until they were lost. For example, almost no one in the sample mentioned the pleasure of having good eyesight or good hearing, but those who were beginning to lose sensory faculties found it frightening and demoralizing. The same situation held for loss of memory, impulse control, or orientation. (Who would think to find happiness simply in knowing where he is?) And, except for a few women who expressed pleasure in the continued health of their husbands, very few people perceived the well-being of familiar others as a source of satisfaction, although a number of subjects whose intimates were having serious problems mentioned this fact as contributing to their depression.

In other cases, we found that some circumstance was conceived as having a unique value of its own in promoting happiness, when actually it was a common means to several ends—although these different ends only became explicit in the absence of the factor producing the high morale. Thus, productive activity was seen to have both a personal and a social function in the data on low morale—in some cases, inability to engage in such activities was linked to the personal problem of boredom, and, in other cases, to the social problem of loss of status and respect. Matters of health, also, which seemed to be somewhat unique in the high morale data, appeared to be related to at least three underlying dynamic factors, as people spoke of the problems created by poor health: physical discomfort, dependency, and fear of death. To some extent, it was also related to the major source of depression—

boredom (lacking the physical strength to keep oneself occupied)—
and boredom, in turn, was also influenced by lack of entertainment and diversion, movement, and productive activity.

In other words, while there may be some common themes
underlying both high and low morale, the two are perceived and
articulated in somewhat different terms by our sample. In order,
then, to do the least damage to the phenomenological point of
view, we will attempt to describe these reported sources of low
morale, using the same framework as that provided us by the
sample. Following that, we will identify the underlying concepts
that serve to integrate the two sets of data.

In rank order of frequency for the total intensive sample, the
expressed sources of depression or dissatisfaction were as follows:

Rank	Sources of Low Morale	Per Cent of the Intensive Sample Reporting the Factor
1.	Dependency—financial or physical	60
2.	Physical discomfort or sensory loss	57
3.	Loneliness, bereavement, or loss of nurturance	50
4.	Boredom, inactivity, immobility, and confinement	38
5.	Mental discomfort or loss	18
6.	Loss of prestige or respect	12
7.	Fear of dying	10
8.	Problems of others	8

Dependency

Once again we are struck with the enormous value placed by
elderly Americans on independence—its loss ranks at the very top
of the list of sources of dissatisfaction with life, having a higher
frequency (60 per cent) than either pain and suffering (57 per
cent) or social isolation (50 per cent). We expected loss of prestige or respect to be mentioned more frequently, since this often
seems to be the fear underlying dependency, but the two factors
were not directly associated in our sample. It may be that independence is such a strongly internalized value that, regardless of
social consequences, its loss cannot be tolerated by the individual.

Physical Discomfort or Sensory Loss

Mr. Hopland (HS) describes this source of depression very
simply: "Well, I can't be happy because I'm sick." Mr. Jackson
(HS) reports that the hardest thing in his life is ". . . ill health.

It's very rough on me. You have no idea how rough. I may just forget myself and run upstairs and then I have an attack of angina. And I have pain on account of the cancer. I never have a pleasant day because of that." When we asked Miss Mabel Wimsatt (CS) if she ever felt low or depressed, she replied, "We all do—with me it's my physical condition. The only way of overcoming it is to take extra rest." Mr. Angus Pillsbury (CS) reports that his illness has left him so depressed that he doesn't care whether he lives or not: "I have very little happiness in my present life. Down in the dumps. I feel useless and blue all the time since I had the stroke. You don't know just exactly what is going to happen to you. You worry this way. I'm afraid I'm going to pull a boner—the condition I'm in you've got to watch every move you make. The thing I fear most is falling. I just don't tie my shoelaces or anything since my stroke. I've had close shaves crossing the street in the past two or three months. You can say it this way—I'm afraid of the future."

Even subjects who are in reasonably good health have an underlying dread of falling ill. For example, Miss Barton (CS) reports, "I'm not especially afraid of anything at the present except that I might be in an accident, where I fall on a curbing or something like that. I try to be more careful and I try not to think about it." Mrs. Valente (CS), who describes her general health as "excellent," tells the following story: "Sometimes my spirits are kind of low. When I'm sick, that worries me. About two months ago I had a nightmare. Right arm giving me trouble. I thought that something was coming toward me. I was not awake. When I woke up, my heart was pounding. I said 'Jesus, help me!' The second time the same night it happened again, and I called a friend and she came over and stayed with me. I had a fear something would happen to me. It started a third time but I didn't let it happen. A heavy feeling in my right shoulder and arm. Just my arm paining me so terribly. I caught a cold, must have pulled ligaments. I haven't been scared since."

Perhaps even more than the pain and suffering involved in physical illness is the accompanying helplessness which is greatly demoralizing. For example, Mrs. Viet (CS) reports the following: "Since I had my stroke, I don't even cut the meat. I'm alone. I need help though—I can't cut the meat and I have a hard time opening cans sometimes. I almost cry. My hand, since the stroke, doesn't hold things. Sometimes I hold it with both hands and try, and things fly right out of my hand. I don't cut the meat—I use my hands to pull it apart."

Sensory loss was reported by several people in the sample as a source of dissatisfaction and low morale. Failing eyesight is more frequently mentioned than hearing loss, although both occur. Thus, Mr. Sablon (CS) describes himself as a man who had worked very hard during his life, but has now "completely run out of steam" and is "finished." His gradual loss of eyesight was the final blow. When we asked him what makes life most unpleasant for him, he replied, "My failing eyesight, that's all. Nothing more to my life now—I'm all finished." Mrs. Gertrude Miller (CS), a furrier all of her adult life, and a woman with strong values on work and productivity, was asked what she thought she would miss most when she retired: "I've got an absolute horror of it. I'll go mad. That's why I'm so worried about my eyes." Mrs. Powers (HS) speaks of being demoralized by the helplessness her encroaching blindness is inflicting on her: "I'm not very happy nowadays. My eyes—if I had my vision, I'd be very happy and content. I can't sew and all I can do is be bored by TV much of the time."

Loneliness, Bereavement, or Loss of Nurturance[13]

Loneliness is a major problem for the elderly people in this sample. Among the hospital sample and among the physically ill in the community, simply being housebound often produces a sense of loneliness. For example, Mrs. Kramer (CS) makes the following statement: "I get very lonely. Oh, I have peace of mind. I have TV and a robe and everything to wear and read—but I get very lonely." Mrs. Alida Trumble, a hospital inpatient, reports, "I suffer most from being left alone at night. I don't like that." Mr. Charles Cambry (HS) was also asked from what he suffered most. He says, "Loneliness, being here, locked up and

---

[13]Readers are referred to a recent study of death and bereavement based upon our hospital sample (Anderson, 1965). This paper also contains a review of the literature relevant to this topic.

not knowing what's going on. My wife is supposed to be here today."

Sometimes the loneliness is a result of confinement and immobility. At other times, as in the following examples, it is the result of alienation from one's kin, particularly children. For example, Mrs. Miller (CS) discusses the advantages and disadvantages of having been a business woman: "It's the loneliness. You know your children don't want you around. In the business world, you don't have any social life and when you get older, well, I don't know what's going to happen. You know, when you take away the feeling that you can't be of use to anyone, that's awful. I had a family that depended upon me a lot. Now they're grown and have other interests and no one depends on me anymore." Mrs. Miller went on to tell a story of a wealthy woman who lives downtown in San Francisco and sees no one but her maid. "Her relatives in town never see her, although they know they'll get her money when she dies."

In some cases, the loneliness reported by members of this sample resulted from a disruption of an earlier pattern of living, with the loss of meaningful roles for the subject. Mrs. Lois Willoughby (CS) discusses the main problems in her life lately: "I think mostly myself. At times I feel sorry for myself. Then I get mad at myself for the rest of the day. This living alone is killing me off. I get depressed. I often wonder what in heck I'm waiting for. How am I going to end up? I never used to be like that when my husband was alive—I never had time to be—just these last five years I've been down in the dumps. When I feel sorry for myself, I go around kicking myself. Self-pity is a terrible disease!"

In some cases, bereavement leaves an older person almost devoid of a social identity. Several of our subjects seemed devastated and broken by the disruption of their intimate social world. It was almost as though the people that they were could not exist out of a familiar social context. Miss Christianson (CS) gives the most poignant example of the catastrophic effect bereavement may have on some of the elderly: "My biggest problem is loneliness. Nothing to look forward to. I'm all alone in the world now. I'm homesick—I miss my mother and sister. I'm feeling all right, except I'm terribly unhappy. I want to be at home. My life is just shot to pieces. My mother died—my sisters died—Adele, my older sister, died—I don't know where my sister Sylvia is. There really isn't nothing more to tell. I'm really up in the air. I don't know what to think or what to expect. My sister Sylvia died. Did I tell you that? Also, my sister Adele passed away. Well, I don't know what to do. Perhaps the Department of Welfare would have some place to put me in until I can get on my feet. Well, I don't know what I'm going to do. I know the Department of Welfare will look out for you. My sister Adele died. I think my mother died also. I don't know what to do or what to say. So that's my life history so far."

In some cases the bereavement seems less related to problems of identity or the disruption of a familiar pattern of life than it is to the loss of nurturance, support, and care from others. Thus, Mrs. Tully (HS) was not only left feeling lonely after the death of her husband, but also anxious about her own welfare in the future. When we asked her about her worries, she said, "How to get along; what I'm going to do in the future. I don't know how I'm going to get along without somebody—where I'm going to live—what I'm going to do. Of course, it will be different when I get my glasses and I can see better. My friend passed away too, but I've always managed to get along, in a way."

Mr. Boris Mersky (CS) reported in an early interview that he had developed a serious drinking problem after his wife died. At that time he was ". . . down; I don't care about life. I see no future now. I feel bad about the loss of my wife." When we interviewed this man again two years later, he gave the following report: "I began to feel sorry for myself after the death of my wife in 1960. I was grieving and started drinking very heavily. Then one day I almost felt I had a heart attack. I had terrible pain in my chest. I went to the doctor, but he gave me nothing for the pain. He talked to me for two hours and he told me my main grief was feeling sorry for myself and not on account of losing my wife. While he was talking, I felt better. After that talk, I slowed down my drinking. As I thought of it at home, it was true—just sorry for myself."

Boredom, Inactivity, Immobility, and Confinement

Boredom ranks lower on the list of sources of depression than we had anticipated (38 per cent of the intensive sample mentioned this area), since entertainment and diversion, movement, and productive activity had all been frequently mentioned as sources of *high* morale—and all of these are cited by members of the sample as inversely related to boredom. However, a number of both community and hospital subjects found inactivity to be a demoralizing state. They made comments such as the following:

> "The main problem older people have to deal with today is an empty life. Sitting around is no good for anybody. Sooner or later you're going to sit there for good."
>
> "What happiness can I have? It's tough to resign work — nothing to do."
>
> "I feel so stagnant sitting around here, doing nothing. Maybe it's just a case of being bored, do you ever think about that? Maybe it's just sitting around. It just seems to me the thing I keep thinking about all the time is I would like to be active and do something."
>
> "There's not much to do and that's what makes me tired."

Mental Discomfort or Loss

A number of the hospital subjects are made extremely unhappy and demoralized by their mental symptoms. In some cases, they do not perceive these as being psychiatric symptoms but refer them to some objective or physical reality. For example, Mrs. Harris (HS) says, "I want to make sure I can get this over to you—in case you can do something about it. I am in extreme pain, and they won't do anything about it at the clinic. They said it was psychological, but something in me is flying around—that is as near as I can describe it—and it is causing me extreme pain. My spirits are about the same. Naturally, I'm discouraged about my pain, but otherwise I enjoy life. I can be contented within myself—except for my pain." Mr. Leveritt (HS)—as we have already described—lists as his main source of depression the fact that he has to spend all of his time and energy in manufacturing elaborate mechanical devices to defend himself against the influence of the brain-controlling machine which is directed toward him.

Other people in the intensive sample find it difficult to cope with confusion or memory loss. For example, Mrs. Tillford (HS) was asked if she ever feels low or depressed. She replies, "Oh Lord yes, sometimes my mind leaves me—it gets on me so hard. I try to do the best I can. If it gets too rough, they'll take me into the hospital again. They [son and family] say, 'Mama, lay down, take it easy.' I try to, but I get so nervous, I can't rest." Mrs. Willoughby (CS) is also demoralized by her loss of memory: "It changed. I don't know—lately I can't remember things as well, and to go to the grocery store, I must write down a list. That bothers me terribly, to think my memory isn't as good as it once was. I noticed it a little more than a year ago. It's a little frightening. Sometimes I think I'm losing my mind; it really bothers me."

This area was not mentioned frequently—only 18 per cent of all in the intensive sample listed mental changes as a source of low morale. People without other psychological distress sometimes mention occasional lapses of memory, but seem to accommodate to them quite well. However, in the presence of serious emotional disturbance deriving from other sources, the added assault of cognitive loss is frightening and demoralizing.

Loss of Prestige or Respect

Twelve per cent of the intensive sample mentioned loss of prestige or respect as an underlying cause of dissatisfaction. There is one aspect of this area that should be commented upon further. A few of our subjects realize that aging has brought with it a tendency toward social withdrawal, and that this social withdrawal is simply a defense against a fear of criticism. Mr. Butler, a schoolteacher (CS), describes it in this way: "You sort of lose confidence in yourself and you begin to condemn yourself very much. This self-condemnation process and loss of confidence is much greater now than ever before. I don't know, now almost anything will set me off. Any time a kid wants to give me a hard time, I guess. Well, you sometimes get the impression they think you're old-fashioned and not competent; then I sound off at someone or say something harsh that I feel sorry for, but I'm stubborn enough that I don't want to apologize. I guess there are guilt feelings about this. I've always *felt* sorry, but I never apologized. In many ways my friends are criticizing me much more than ever. I don't enjoy being with them as much as in the past." Mr. Alioto (HS) ·puts it much more succinctly: "I don't care what they think. People don't like me, I don't like them—don't care to see them."

This seems to suggest that, at least in some cases, voluntary disengagement[14] is actually a defensive maneuver on the part of the subject who would rather avoid people than run the risk of possible critical attacks upon his already floundering ego.

Fear of Dying[15]

One out of ten members of the intensive sample mentioned fear of dying or death as a source of depression. Fear of death seems to range from a vague discomfort (more akin to regret than to fear) to an attitude that amounts to stark terror. Mr. Hokusai (CS) expresses attitudes of the former type. Discussing his dissatisfactions with life, this subject mentions that he is old and can't do much any more: "Also, I won't be in this world much longer. My only regret is I wish I could have done many more things during my lifetime. You know, I had that operation ten years ago. The doctors didn't tell me it was cancer, but I knew it was. At any time it might act up and then I would be a goner." Mr. Makrinos (CS) is less afraid of death itself than he is of dying and having his body

---

14This subject of voluntary disengagement is extensively discussed in Cumming and Henry (1961). In another study (Lowenthal and Boler, 1965), based on our community sample, it was found that "the voluntarily-withdrawn ranked as high and sometimes higher than the not-withdrawn/not-deprived on a number of social interaction variables . . . [and] [o]n morale measures, the voluntarily-withdrawn tended to rank nearly as high as the not-withdrawn/not deprived...."

15An excellent compendium of articles dealing with the subject of death and its impact upon those approaching it or suffering from bereavement can be found in Feifel (1959). In Christ (1961), readers can find an analysis of attitudes toward death as expressed by our hospital subjects at the time of our first encounter with them. Specifically, Christ found a marked denial of death, 87 per cent stating that "they had never talked about death or dying before," but although fearful of death, on the whole, these patients were willing to discuss it with the author and even, in some cases, were "relieved to discuss it" (p. 59). See also Feifel (1955; 1956; and 1958).

lie undiscovered for a period of time. This subject, a very religious man, states that it was very important to him to receive the last rites of his church before he died. He says, "I can't sleep in the bed. I sleep downstairs in the lobby till 5 or 6 a.m., then come up here to my room—I lay down on top of the bed and then sleep two hours. Haven't slept in bed for six months. You know, sometimes I'm scared. You can't tell. One friend of mine, he was all right; then we found him up in his room—dead two days. I got scared."

Miss Jernigan (HS) seems quite ambivalent toward the prospect of death. She says, "I'm always sad. I'll be happy when I go to God, but I don't want to die here [in the state hospital]. I'm afraid here, because we're Catholic—I'm afraid here. I don't want to die here—oh, I'm afraid to die! I'm afraid of August [the month she was scheduled to undergo a surgical operation]. It's unpleasant here. I'm scared here."

From responses such as these, it becomes clear that the *circumstances* under which one will die seem to be more important for many people than the inevitability or imminence of death itself.

Problems of Others

Several people in the sample mentioned as depressing the difficulties experienced by relatives and friends, particularly their illnesses. If it became clear in the interview that the primary concern was the threat of loss of nurturance and care for the patient himself, those cases were included under that heading. However, eight per cent of the intensive sample seemed to be genuinely concerned with the difficulties of people they cared about, quite apart from thir own needs. Mrs. Sandusky (HS) states, "Well, I'm worried about my boy's condition, about his eye. Sometimes I go to bed at night and it comes up to me. I can't do anything about it and there's no use to break down my own health lying awake all night worrying. Of course, I wish I could do something about it." Mrs. Langtry (CS) was asked what the main problem in her life was lately: "The problems of my family—concern for my family. My daughter lives in New York and had difficulties. And my sister lives here and I worry about her being alone now that I'm married."

Mrs. Miller (CS) reports one of her major problems at present to be the condition of her youngest daughter: "I have a reason for feeling low. My daughter's drinking too much—it's a horrible situation. I keep busy so I won't think of it—especially as it affects my two grandchildren. I think my daughter drinks more than she should, and I just can't see any neglect to those youngsters. I'm kind of a stickler for meals for children. I can't see sitting over a bar and letting children wait at home. I keep busy so I won't think of it." Mr. Jay (CS) says that he is thoroughly dissatisfied with his life because of his wife's condition: "In 1959, she had a stroke and has been paralyzed a little ever since, and then she had diabetes too. She gets crying spells once in a while. She gets lonesome. Can't be very happy living like that."

COMPARISON OF COMMUNITY AND HOSPITAL SUBJECTS

If we look at the way mentally-healthy and mentally-ill subjects rank these eight morale factors, we see some striking differences. The first five ranking categories in each sample are these:

Rank	Community Subjects	Hospital Subjects
1.	Dependency	Loneliness, bereavement
2.	Physical discomfort, sensory loss	Dependency
3.	Loneliness, bereavement	Boredom, inactivity
4.	Boredom, inactivity	Physical discomfort, sensory loss
5.	Problems of others	Mental discomfort or loss

While dependency and physical discomfort are the first two ranking factors in low morale for community subjects, they are listed second and fourth respectively for the hospital subjects. Loneliness and bereavement, on the other hand, are the most demoralizing problems for the hospital subjects. The mentally-ill aged seem to have considerable difficulties in establishing and maintaining relationships. Also, as we will see in Chapter VII, their range of social contact is much smaller than that of the mentally healthy. The loss, then, of even one or two intimates may leave them completely isolated. Under these circumstances, they are fearful for their own survival.

Boredom and inactivity are fairly important in both samples, but there are qualitative differences between the two samples in the sources of this problem. While mentally-ill subjects often can simply find nothing to occupy themselves once having lost the instrumental roles of middle life, boredom for community subjects is more the result of physical inability to engage in interesting activities. This difference is, we are sure, related to the problems in substitution which we have previously seen to characterize the mentally-ill aged.

It is interesting that physical discomfort and sensory loss should be mentioned more frequently by community than by hospital subjects, since hospital subjects are more often physically impaired, and the severity of their illnesses is usually greater. However, physical discomfort ranks only fourth among hospital subjects in sources of low morale, while it ranks second among community subjects. The mentally ill, apparently, have life problems of greater impact. In other words, their psychiatric difficulties outweigh their physical ones. Thus, mental discomfort or loss is specifically mentioned as a source of depression by 32 per cent of the hospital intensives, and only by three per cent of the community sample.

Only one subject from those in the intensive sample who listed their concern with problems of others as a source of low morale was a member of the hospital sample. Also, not one who mentioned this area as impinging upon him personally was physically disabled. It seems that if one's own problems are serious enough, those of others make no added assaults on personal morale.

With respect to the other two areas, equal proportions of mentally-ill and mentally-healthy subjects mentioned loss of prestige or respect as a source of dissatisfaction, but twice as many hospital as community subjects mentioned fear of dying.

SUMMARY OF FACTORS UNDERLYING THE MORALE OF THE AGED

Looking back at the analyses of both high and low morale, there seem to be six underlying themes which we might interpret as the major perceived needs of this sample. Satisfaction of these are the components of the "Good Life":

(1) Sufficient autonomy to permit continued integrity of the self;

(2) Agreeable relationships with other people, some of whom are willing to provide help when needed without losing respect for the recipient;

(3) A reasonable amount of personal comfort in body, mind, and physical environment;

(4) Stimulation of the mind and imagination in ways that are not overtaxing of physical strength;

(5) Sufficient movement to permit variety in the surroundings;

(6) Some degree of passionate involvement with life, to escape preoccupation with death.

These, then, seem to be the basic requirements that this sample of older people ask of life, of themselves, or of the society around them in order to maintain an adequate level of morale.

Chapter VII

DYNAMICS OF THE SOCIAL SYSTEM: SOCIAL PERCEPTIONS OF THE AGED

> *Consciousness arises from the interrelation of the [person] and the environment, and it involves both of them. Hunger does not create food, nor is an object a food object without relation to hunger. When there is that relation between [person] and environment, then objects can appear which would not have been there otherwise.*
> —GEORGE HERBERT MEAD
> *Mind, Self, and Society*
> (1934), p. 333.

INTRODUCTION

IN ANY STUDY OF adaptation to transitional life stages, social considerations will always occupy a place of central importance. As the first chapter has emphasized, the life cycle is conditioned not only by its biology but also by social and cultural "meanings" which become attributed to these stages. It is for this reason that problems of personal adaptation become especially acute during these periods.[1] We know from studies of other societies that these transitions can be very simple or extremely stressful, depending upon how well the culture rallies support for those members moving through the metamorphosis. At such times, the availability of social supports becomes crucial to the success or failure of the adaptation. Reference-group theory has pretty well demonstrated that individuals lacking such supports are more vulnerable to low morale and other psychological difficulties. Benedict (1953), for instance, writes of the need for a "solid

[1]These periods of transition, in which individuals drop one set of sanctioned statuses for another, are often marked by formal rituals and awesome ceremonies (cf., for instance, the anointing and crowning of royalty, the swearing in of new inductees into the army, the cliterectomies of nubile maidens in certain African tribes, the increasing popularity among modern upper-middle class Jews of elaborate Bar Mitzvahs for their thirteen-year-old sons, etc.). Called *rites de passage* by van Gennep (1909), these ceremonies render formal, official recognition of the new status-set acquired by the individual and offer to the one *in transitu* the mobilized assistance and moral support of the entire community.

phalanx" behind individuals undergoing conflict and change. So, too, Rollo May (1950) underscores the necessity of "relatedness" to others, if individuals under stress are to avoid the "anxiety of the defiant and isolated."[2] Sensory deprivation experiments and accounts of extreme social isolation substantiate May's point by showing that schizophrenic and other equally alarming symptoms develop rapidly under conditions of extreme social deprivation.[3] Quite literally, man needs his fellow man to keep his sanity.

In studies of the aged, social considerations are especially important, and this for reasons which ought to be immediately apparent. Social losses are greatest at this time of life, and many social statuses, such as parent or worker, drop away or become no longer viable. The resulting social alienation poses one of the greatest difficulties old people have to face in our culture. In fact, when preliminary analyses of the hospital sample were inaugurated, we learned—much to our surprise—that half of the patients had been living alone. This finding has led us to explore the role of social isolation and mental illness in an attempt to learn if a lack of relatedness to others might not be one of the causes of the high incidence of mental breakdown among the elderly. Findings from our preliminary explorations into this problem (Lowenthal, 1964b; 1965) do not unequivocally support this thesis but do indicate a close association of the two factors.

The social background of our hospitalized subjects is especially important since, as has been stated in the first chapter, we are here defining "mental illness" as a consensual judgment placed upon these people by whole sets of interested individuals and institutions—from landlords to judges, families to physicians. Also,

---

[2] Cited in Cohen (1961), p. 180.

[3] The literature, both scientific and otherwise, bearing on these two topics is extensive and fascinating, but, unfortunately, space does not permit as complete a listing as we would like. Readers interested in sensory deprivation findings are referred to Charny (1963), Lilly (1956), and Ziskind and Augsburg (1962). In addition to numerous studies of loneliness (Moustakas, 1961; Wood, 1953; Fromm-Reichmann, 1959; and Zilboorg, 1938), there are many autobiographical accounts from individuals subjected to prolonged social isolation, such as solitary confinement, monastic seclusion, shipwreck, and the like. See especially Bartek and Pardue (1943), Bernicot (1953), Buhl (1956), Burney (1952), Ellam and Mudie (1953), Gesell (1941), Holliday (1964), Itard (1962), and many others.

their very institutionalization represents an organized attempt on the part of society to modify their behavior so that it will better accord with social norms.

The social system is also important for the reason alluded to in the epigraph from George Herbert Mead: self-identity does not exist but in *relationship*. We have seen how a sense of individual value is necessary for mental health, but it is a *social* validation of this worth that makes possible a sturdy self-esteem.[4] As one discharged patient attempted to describe herself: "I don't see anybody any more to know what kind of a person I am." In this sense, society is a mirror reflecting back to us the only notion we have of ourselves. We need not ask with Robert Burns for supernatural powers to perceive ourselves "as others see us"—self-awareness must be, by definition, a social ratification. In view of this need for a social acknowledgment of our very existence, we must also consider seriously the consequences of a system of values that would withhold this ratification of the self from large numbers of people in one segment of society, essentially denying them the very right to *be*. Here the old share the same fate with many minority groups: invisibility, a paucity of available roles, the social devaluation symbolized by poverty, eroded self-esteem, and the futility of ineffectual living.[5]

---

[4] The hypothesis that self-concept is dependent on social interaction has had numerous exponents. In psychiatry, one of its chief advocates has been Harry Stack Sullivan, who summarized his position as follows: "Personality is made manifest in interpersonal situations, and not otherwise . . . . Psychiatry concerns itself with the way in which each of us comes to be possessed of a self which he esteems and cherishes, shelters from questioning and criticism, and expands by commendation . . . . We know that these self-dynamisms, clearly the referent of a great part of our conversation and other social behavior, are by no means inborn, relatively immutable, aspects of the person. Not only do they show significant differences between people from various parts of the world, and between the siblings of one family, but they change their characteristics in a more or less orderly fashion as one progresses from childhood to maturity . . . . Much of the praise and some of the blame that has come from [those] with whom one has been significantly related, have been organized into the content of the self" (Sullivan, 1949, pp. 98-102).

[5] Barron (1953) has discussed some of the parallels between majority attitudes towards the aged and those prevailing towards the Negroes and other racial, religious, and nationality groups. He speaks of the tendency to stereotype the aged, to discriminate against them in the labor market, and he cites the growing fears

In the following pages, we shall explore in detail the perceptions of the social relationships entertained by our subjects. This analysis will attempt to identify certain patterns of social relatedness which are characteristic of the elderly. Some of these patterns we see are sustaining individuals into their old age while others create problems and conflict.

KINSHIP STATUSES AND ROLES

Husbands and Wives

After the age of sixty, only about a third of the elderly (at least as indicated through our intensively-interviewed subjects) can depend upon the companionship and nurturance of married life. The others must cope with the problems of widowhood or separation or face growing old as a single person. There are more married men in our intensively-interviewed sample than married women: out of seventy-nine subjects, thirteen men were still married (at the time of baseline) in contrast with only six women. These married women span all the decades we are studying, but the married men tend to be in their sixties. Also, while only one of these marriages among the women was contracted late in life, five of the thirteen marriages among the men were instigated after the age of sixty. Three of these late marriages had followed shortly upon the death of the first wife, one was a first marriage, and the fifth occurred after sixteen years of divorced status. A few of the unmarried men in the intensive sample had contemplated marriage, and, in fact, had proposed in their sixties but had not been accepted.

The Happily Married. Several of these marriages were of long duration and of great comfort to the partners. Mr. Mark Janisch's (CS) marriage was one of these. "People who are married for a long time," he says, "they become almost one. My wife is

---

of younger people that the aged somehow represent a threat or a menace to the remainder of society. He quotes a public statement equating "the new class war between the young and the old" with other mass movements such as Marxism. In view of these social attitudes, Barron finds it useful "to regard the aged thus as an emerging quasi-minority group. [This] may well enlarge our understanding of the problems of aging and the aged and hasten their resolution" (p. 67).

closer to me than anyone else. My wife is like my mother was to me as a child. We have learned to live in intimate contact." He elaborates upon this theme: "The only thing that keeps me going is my wife. We've been married forty-nine years. She I feel like living for." Mr. Janisch also believes he has become "more mellow and tolerant with age" and in relation to his wife "more thankful, more thoughtful, and more attentive." Mr. Harry Hokusai (CS) also alludes to this deepening of affection in his own marriage: "As you get to know your wife better and you have children together and raise them, you become more united—you become closer together over the years."

In some cases, this enhancement of the marital relationship is a godsend. Mr. Horace Kepler (HS), although suffering from an extreme depression, was especially thankful for his wife: "I really don't know where I would be now, if I hadn't met my wife. There's a word—'uxorious.' I looked it up. The definition is 'being too fond of one's wife.' Maybe you can say that about me. But my wife wouldn't." Mr. Kepler loves to sing praises of his wife who, according to him, is the living embodiment of all virtues. To a great extent, he does this to emphasize his own worthlessness, but while this praise of her might serve masochistic needs, there can be little doubt that he would, indeed, be helpless without her.

This case also illustrates what we have frequently observed in these successful marriages in old age—an almost symbiotic interdependency of the partners, especially when one or both partners need the care and support of the other in the presence of illness. Mr. Selma Reinhart's (CS) difficulties with multiple sclerosis have been already mentioned and something of her dependency needs *vis-à-vis* her husband suggested (Chapter V.). This woman claims that among all her personal relationships she feels closest to her husband, and this because of "his love and devotion" and also because she sees "more of him than anybody else." With much pleasure, she comments further: "I know positively I am uppermost in his mind, and he thinks of me first, last, and always." Mrs. Ellen Powers (HS), introduced in Chapter II, must also rely heavily upon her husband. Despite very poor eye-sight and an assortment of physical illnesses, this woman leads a very active social life, both within her own home and on the outside in clubs and church. That she can keep up such activities is largely due to her husband's help. "If I didn't have him," she explains realistically, "I wouldn't know what to do. My husband has to be my eyes."

Especially among the men, this symbiotic quality in some old marriages suggests a perception of the spouse as something more than just a source of warm affection. For these men, their wives are more "pillars of strength" without whom they would be significantly worse off. Such men indicate a need for a stable person to discipline them, guide them, and take some of the responsibility for their actions. In fact, these subjects are looking to their wives for assistance in adjusting to the changes accruing to them in old age.

In this way, Mr. Boris Mersky (CS), briefly introduced in the conclusion of the last chapter, relies upon his wife for his own impulse-control. This man experienced the sharpest discontinuity in his life with the illness and death of his first wife, when he was sixty-four. Always a heavy drinker and extravagant host, his intake of alcohol increased during her illness and, following her death, got so out of control as to cause him concern. To save himself from ruin, he married again at the age of sixty-five. The first marriage had been a good match: "She was one hundred per cent what a person can expect. I liked her, tried to please her, but she never doubted me or asked what I did. I loved her, respected her. She had a good disposition, true, not demanding. When we didn't have anything, she tried to comfort me, instead of asking, 'Why don't you do this or that?'" Describing his bereavement, he says, "It was a big blow to lose my wife. For at least ten months, I lost myself. I pretty near lost this place too [his cigar business]. I was spending much more money than I was making." Recalling her death, he says, "Never took anything so hard in my life. Cannot forget it even now." Living alone had been unbearable. He thought he had had a heart attack and went to a doctor who talked to him for two hours. He told Mr. Mersky that "my main grief was feeling sorry for myself." The "heart attack" turned out to be "psychosomatic." Since his second marriage, there has been an occasion when he felt he was going to have a nervous breakdown. "I was too nervous," he says. "Went to the doctor and got some pills. Still take them." This subject quite frankly appraises the man he had been the year before: "I realized I was going to the dogs." He did seek medical help for his drinking problem. That he did manage to bring this problem under control he mainly attributes to the help of his second wife: "Stopped suddenly, the day I met my second wife. She said she's been married to an alcoholic and wouldn't marry anyone who drank at all. I made up my mind to quit."

Mr. Mersky's drinking bouts have now been replaced by quiet fishing trips with his wife. Mrs. Mersky has succeeded in keeping him away from drinking, and he is still working up to ten hours a day in his store. Unfortunately, while his marriage has enhanced his physical and economic survival, it has not brought him much happiness or contentment. Apparently, there are disputes, but despite these, Mr. Mersky still feels that his wife is the one person who has the most influence over him currently: "Because what she wants, I do!" and she is also the one person closest to him: "We live together." He admits, "She is not a bad person. At first I thought we were in love, but now I realize that this foolish old man got married to a lot younger woman." He does not feel she "cares too much about him," and believes she is too dependent upon him financially, regarding him as little more than a "meal ticket." Nevertheless, he is afraid to leave her because he might return to drink and squander his money as he formerly did. To a certain extent, his new wife can serve as a scapegoat, for even though life is now rather dull and widely different from what it had been in his younger years, he can blame not his own good common sense which has made his life a bit humdrum now—he can blame Mrs. Mersky and, thereby, preserve his self-image as a *bon vivant* who had once lived high.

It should be noted that many of these cases of mutual dependency and deepening companionship in marriage quite often present reports of the obverse of these feelings—nagging fears of losing the spouse one is so desperately dependent upon. Understandably, Mrs. Powers (HS) admits that one of her greatest fears today is the thought that her husband's death might precede her own. Sometimes she gets depressed at the thought, for she poignantly asks, "If I were left alone, what could I do?"

Finally, happy marriages present another interesting feature —a greater equality in the companionship of the partners. Rather than the feminine subordination to a husband, characteristic of romantically-generated marriages for child-bearing in the younger years, husband and wife appear more as social equals, dividing up the labor of the household, blending the masculine and feminine into one tight little social unit. As Mr. Lawrence Southern (CS), at sixty-nine, expresses it: "We live together closely. You never see us alone, and I guess this closeness affects the way I live and act. Yes, she influences my decisions." In like manner, Mr. Edward Hopland (HS), at seventy, remarks about his third marriage, contracted at the age of sixty-four, shortly after he had lost his second wife: "She's more of a companion to me than the others were. We're here in the apartment together, day after day, and we go everywhere together. She's closer to me than my children are. She stands with me forever." This last statement is literally true, for, shortly after this most recent marriage, Mr. Hopland suffered a severe automobile accident which left him crippled and reduced his income, formerly satisfactory, to extreme poverty.

The Unhappily Married. As a countertype to these happy marriages, a few in the sample report prolonged unions marred by rancor and bitterness. Such has been Mrs. Rena Trocopian's (HS) marriage. This subject has already been introduced in Chapter IV and allusion made to her early marriage. In fact, Mrs. Trocopian was hurriedly brought to this country at the age of fourteen through the offices of a marriage broker in her native Armenia. This permitted her to escape certain persecution had she remained in the homeland, but since Mr. Trocopian was twenty years her senior and hardly in tune with the problems of his child-bride, the marriage seems to have been a poor remedy for the earlier distress. This subject was hospitalized in her sixties for a severe involutional psychotic reaction, with paranoid

and depressive signs. In her perception, it is the hated Mr. Trocopian who is the cause of all her unhappiness in a life barren of
any fulfillment. "My husband and I are entirely different people.
He's old-fashioned, and I'm modern. The trouble is this marriage
has been lasting so darned long. It's lasted fifty years. Same old
way goes on and on, never ending. You see, even talking about it
is not good for me. When he goes away for a few weeks, I begin
to feel better." Despite the intensity of this hate, other statements
in the case materials suggest an ambivalence. On the one hand:
"For ten years or more I was hoping for his death"; while on the
other: "But if he would die, I don't know whether I could carry
on." In this case, dependency has thrust this woman into an ex-
asperating conflict of hostility and fear.

In like fashion, Mr. Sylvester Kahn's (CS) marriage has suffered from incompatibility and especially so in the last five years,
since the onset of his wife's mental illness subsequent to her retirement from school teaching. "For the last five years, it's been
hell!" Mr. Kahn reports. Since his wife's commitment to a state
hospital, this subject, friendless and depressed, broods about his
long dependency upon a woman he never really loved. "I spoiled
my wife," he says, "and that was wrong. It's wrong to let a relationship get started that way. I let her determine where we lived,
where we took trips, our friends. People I liked enormously she
just cut off the list. I haven't had a man friend since I got married." Still, without her presence in the home, Mr. Kahn does
not know quite what to do with his time. "What do I do presently? Well, I eat supper. Then I go for a walk, and I go to bed
at 8:15 at night and get up at 4:00 in the morning. And that's my
fascinating life." During one interview with him, Mr. Kahn re-
counted three times that his wife had wanted to be converted to
Catholicism but that he had told her: "You'd better be a good
Catholic, because if you're a Catholic and you're a bad one, I will
hate you more than I hate you now!" It is highly probable that
a religious orthodoxy is preserving the marital relationship in
both of these cases, but, at the same time, Mrs. Trocopian and
Mr. Kahn serve to remind us how the need for mutual assistance

and interdependency in these long marriages may outweigh the long-endured strains of persistent recriminations and hatred.

In the case of Mr. Albert Jay's (CS) unhappy marriage, the difficulties are not due to incompatibility but adverse circumstances. Mr. Jay, a former merchant seaman and warehouseman, married late: "I was around fifty when I married. It was my first marriage. My wife was married before." Like many of the subjects who took this step so late in life, one gains the impression that Mr. Jay was, by this move, preparing for the day when old age would make him more dependent and in need of someone to look after him. Unfortunately, his wife's sudden stroke in 1959 forced Mr. Jay into the position where he has had to do the nurturing. At seventy, he must continue working (as a janitor) and has had to move into cheaper quarters so that he can be near his wife and nurse her, a woman who is incapicitated ("My wife can't walk") and subject to frequent crying spells. "I'm not satisfied with my life," he says in depressed tones. "If she were well, life would be different, but we've got to make the best of it."

Late-life Marriages and Remarriage. In general, those in our sample who had delayed their marriage until the later years manifest in their early histories either: (1) a strong personal identity based exclusively on work or family of origin, or (2) evidence of longstanding psychosexual difficulties which would make a mature, intimate relationship with the opposite sex problematic. However, with the encroachment of old age, these subjects have turned to marriage as a refuge and a buffer from fears of oncoming helplessness. Unfortunately, any marriage in later life runs the grave risk of being short-lived because of the greater possibilities of one partner becoming ill and dying.

Mrs. Sarah Bennington (CS), our "Aging Lady of the Lamp" in Chapter II, is an example of a woman who postponed marriage because of strong parental family ties. She did not marry until she was fifty-five. Mrs. Bennington came from a strongly-forged family of Swiss dairy farmers. Not only were parents and children cemented by a clan spirit, but the children themselves long faced the world as a solid group of kinsmen. In addition to this,

Mrs. Bennington firmly resolved at an early age to be a competent, efficient nurse and remained dedicated to her profession
through all her mature years. For much of this time she shared
a common household with her brother, "because he and I were
the only ones left in the family." It was the death of this sibling
which precipitated her marriage. This brother's demise was, admittedly, the worst thing she had ever had to face in her life, "because then I was alone." Her primary motive for making this
change in her life had been to gain some companionship and security in her old age. "I guess when I first married," she says, "I
thought I had a husband to take care of *me* and that—financially—he would pay all the bills—that I wouldn't have to worry
about that." At first, the plan worked and she enjoyed her marriage, especially entertaining their mutual friends: "I enjoyed
being married at first, being entertained, having friends visit us,
having company. It's always pleasant when you are inviting
people, cousins, congenial friends." But her freedom from worry
was short-lived. During the last two years of her marriage, she was
burdened with the nursing of her husband, who became very ill
and died, leaving Mrs. Bennington, at sixty-three, a widow from a
very brief marriage. Luckily, this subject was able to pick up the
strings of her former life where she had left them. After her husband's death, she was able to return to her former employer (a
private physician) and her former friends (other nurses) in San
Francisco. Although she was in her sixties at that time, the Second World War was in progress and her professional help was
welcomed, despite her age.

Mr. Axel Schwann (CS), also introduced in the second chapter, illustrates the second reason we have given for a long delay
in marrying. Up until he was sixty, Mr. Schwann's life history
shows many features of the Repressed Bachelor. He talked at
length about his strict upbringing in a small Swiss town which
had a shrine to "the Blessed Mother" and to which many pil-
grims came. Recalling his early education, he was led to reminisce,
"All the schools in the village were Catholic schools. The teachers were all men. The girls had some sisters [nuns], but we had
all men. The girls were in one wing of the school and the boys in

the other." When asked about his early sexual experiences, Mr. Schwann was embarrassed and evasive: "I didn't know anything about sex. I had no girlfriends. Most of the boys and girls were not interested in one another. When you're eighteen or twenty years old, there's plenty of time to think about that." Upon the death of his parents, Mr. Schwann came to America and settled with his aunt and uncle in a small Swiss-German community in the Midwest. Here he worked hard at farming and thought of little else. "I was never much interested in girls," he says. "Until I came to San Francisco, I had no dates and no girls. I was friends with them, but I was not interested to get married. I had not much sexual experience—a little—I don't know. Sex did not create much problems when I was young."

Mr. Schwann is distinctive in our sample for the sober and realistic preparations he has made since he was fifty for the approaching adjustments of his old age. These preparations included accumulating sufficient capital and changing his occupation from that of farmer to janitor. Finally, at sixty, he decided to marry a woman he had known for twenty years. "I met my wife at a friend's house," he narrates. "I took her out sometimes. I don't know why I ever married. I thought it was nice to have a little company now that I was getting old"—thus incorporating the marriage into his Master Plan for Late Maturity. "It was not so nice alone," he continues. "She thought the same thing. Being married was a nice improvement." They were married at a quiet church wedding and took a modest two days for their honeymoon. Mrs. Schwann then hired herself out to a wealthy family as a cook. The following year, Mr. Schwann made up for the modest honeymoon with another—this time a longer one—"in Idaho." Mr. Schwann is well satisfied with his marriage: "I need her and she needs me." They have few friends and seldom go out, but he would not change this for the world. Their main diversion is playing cards, which they do "every day for a couple of hours as a rule." He admires her for her "cleanliness," as he puts it, at the same time appreciatively scanning the apartment. Furthermore, she is an excellent cook.

Affluence is another consideration in whether these older

people will marry or not. A close look at the financial condition of
those who do or do not marry or remarry indicates that those who
do usually possess high socioeconomic status. Some older men do
not feel they can support a new wife on limited post-retirement
income. This is not to imply that people at lower socioeconomic
levels never attempt to solve some of their old-age problems by
some sort of "teaming up," but the prevailing pattern in such
groups often encourages nonlegalized conjugal unions. Two of
the subjects in our sample who proposed marriage but were not
accepted came from a low socioeconomic group; both suggested
that they might have succeeded had they had somewhat more to
offer financially. These class differences in remarriage could also
be a reflection of Social Security regulations prevailing at the
time the sample was drawn. Specifically, the sum paid to married couples was less than that paid to two individuals. This policy has since been changed, but it can be readily seen how it
had tended to inhibit remarriages in lower-income groups.

Also, it should be pointed out that these late-life marriages
or remarriages plainly favor the men. Since they tend to marry
women younger than themselves, they obviously have a larger
pool to draw from than similarly-aged women. Likewise—as we
shall presently see—widowhood is a greater financial blow to
women, so women are at an economic disadvantage in comparison
with men for whom a spouse's death does not pose as drastic a
change. Reviews of the case histories suggest that these are at
least some of the reasons why we find more men than women
marrying or remarrying late in life. However, those cases that
best illuminate the problems of remarriage are found among the
women.

As found with women who married late, Mrs. Rita Viet's
(CS) remarriage was also brief and burdened with nursing responsibilities. Mrs. Viet had a short and unfortunate marriage at
seventeen and did not marry again until she was sixty-six. Regret-
tably, this second marriage was also cut short, lasting only two
years. "My second husband was sick all the time," she says. "I
was married to a blind man. We were the first couple married in
the Blind Center. We had a big reception there and then at his

house also. Getting married was nice. We lived in a dump. He got a blind pension and I worked. I liked him and I didn't have anything to lose, so I married him. Married eleven years ago. He died nine years ago. We were together only two years." Mrs. Viet is bitter, for though she did take her husband's blindness into account, she did not reckon with his diabetes: "I knew he was blind. I didn't know he was a diabetic too, or I wouldn't have married him." Once again alone, Mrs. Viet now complains that she is "kind of lonesome, depressed, not enough company." Today she lives very much as a social isolate, angry with the world but, by her own admission, difficult to get along with.

Others in our sample have been more successful in compensating for the loneliness and isolation of the widow or widower estate in old age through a remarriage. We have observed in the reviewing of these cases that this loneliness and isolation is especially acute where the relationships with one's children have been unsatisfactory, where there have been no children at all, or where the social system has always, in some way, been unsatisfactory, such as in a paucity of intimate friends or in certain social habits causing disruptions in interpersonal affairs. Considering the urgency of the need, it is thus no surprise to find that not a few of the widows and widowers in our sample would welcome the setting up of a new household, even when they already have the security of a home with a child or sibling, and even with the disadvantages of a second possible loss and bereavement. In some cases, a woman's chance to be returned to the status of wife and mistress of a home is welcomed with a mixture of joy and relief —if not downright elation—as in the case of Mrs. Edna Langtry (CS) whose case has been sketched earlier (Chapter V) — although the circumstances here are somewhat idyllic and, one might add, highly romantic.

Mrs. Langtry presents herself as the epitome of the Southern Lady, embodying the highest ideals of Southern womanhood. She manifests great social skill, and despite a rather calculated naiveté, has a charming manner. "Gracious living" has always been her ideal, and when she moved from the "Southland" to San Francisco at fifty, she brought with her the traditional love for warm Southern hospitality. Her greatest enjoyment in life was cultivating a circle of friends and acting the charming hostess for her husband. Widowhood at sixty brought an end to this very important role, and the fact that co-residence with her married children did not work out could well be attributed to her lack of opportunity for performing this role in their household.

Subsequently, she found a home with her single sister, who —fortunately for Mrs. Langtry—was a professional woman with little time for entertaining. This responsibility she therefore relegated to her ever-willing sister. In spite of this, Mrs. Langtry's morale dipped very low while she was residing with this sister. Depression, several severe illnesses, and hospitalizations began to plague her, until, at the age of seventy-two, she made a decision which transformed her life. Mrs. Langtry decided to remarry— this time to her childhood sweetheart. Her joy was so genuine and infectious that one interviewer was led to comment: "This interview was a real pleasure! To find a seventy-two-year-old woman so happy and bubbling! I had the feeling she was pinching herself to see if it was true. She is surely enjoying life and getting a high charge out of remarrying at seventy-two." Others who have met her also described her as jubilant. The examining psychiatrist noted that her mood was one of elation and that it has "persisted probably from two and a half to three years—since she has remarried."

Mrs. Langtry is now more secure financially, has regained her prized role of "lady of the house," and at last found a male companion she can cook for and look after. After a repressive, very religious childhood and a sedate first marriage, she finally has full license to act the "Southern Belle"—a long-cherished desire which had been strictly curtailed by her Baptist parents. Her current life seems quite clearly to be a belated fulfillment of this adolescent fantasy. She is fully determined to enjoy life now, as much as her physical frailities will permit, and she will not allow any negative thoughts to obtrude very long into the comfortable world she has created.

Mrs. Langtry's reinstatement as mistress of a household and helpmate to a former lover has not been marred by the fact that her spouse has deficits in two areas of great importance to her: conversation and cooking. "I chatter incessantly, and he is deaf." (One interviewer has noted how she has collected a large repertoire of humorous anecdotes which she is "happy to tell and re-tell.") Then, too, "he is on an ulcer diet and it isn't as much fun cooking." But even the threat of encroaching illness is something to be shared; they truly regard themselves as a twosome, steering their way through the increasing perils of old age. They appear to derive much comfort in progressing through such difficulties together.

Widows and Widowers. With approaching old age, it is inevitable that one member of each conjugal union will have to undergo the loss of the other and the consequent bereavement. Among the very elderly—where couples are usually very similar in age—the thought of one's own death often involves a moral dilemma: should one hope to die first, thus escaping the aloneness of widowhood? Or should one wish to spare the beloved mate this same anxiety? Whose last days must bear the burdens of "going it" alone?

Because of the greater longevity of women, our intensive sample shows—as expected—more women than men suffering the state of widowhood. Also, case materials make it clear that the blow of losing a spouse has more serious consequences in morale for the women. In fact, if one were to look for an equivalent among females to retirement among males, one would find it in the aging woman's loss of the set of roles she plays as spouse. Her losing the status of mother is not at all comparable. By the later years, in American culture, her maternal functions have already become attentuated, since children by this time have grown up and are raising their own families, but widowhood will often create the severest break in the continuities of her life. Most importantly, she must usually suffer an economic loss in her widowhood equivalent to what many men must suffer when they retire.

One-third (18) of the female subjects in the intensive sample are widows. This number represents three times the number who are married (6). Furthermore, all but one of the eighteen experienced widowhood between the ages of fifty-seven and sixty-eight—while they were still comparatively young and well. Let us look at the significance of this state of widowhood, as perceived by these women.

To begin with, many were widowed only after the husband's long, financially-taxing illness. Thus the rupture of relationship was doubly stressful. Recollections of the loss and grief are often tinged with accounts of lingering illnesses and the strains of nursing. One widow recalled her husband's illness of two-to-three years' duration: "I did everything I could for him while he was sick. I had nurses around the clock the last three weeks and it cost thousands of dollars." Another woman also recalled the strain of caring for a husband with a terminal illness: "I took care of my husband until the last thirty days, when I had to call in my sister. It was hardly any use when I was nursing him to go to sleep at all. He was paralyzed, and even the three of us—my sister, my brother-in-law, and I—could hardly lift him." Perhaps not as obvious in the narrative accounts but equally as important is the shift in patterns of dependency which these illnesses foisted upon the women. As one respondent phrased it: "When my husband's health broke down from the stroke, *I* did the pampering and nursing. Instead of him taking care of *me,* I had to take care of *him.*" However, once the break occurs, widows must face the hardest fact of their new status—loss of companionship.[6]

Even where a marriage had been a stormy one, the loss of the husband's presence in the home can nevertheless be experienced acutely. Mrs. Gertrude Miller (CS) was widowed ten years before our interview—at the age of sixty—and her account of her mar-

---

[6]In a recent study of the perceptions of stress in our sample, Anderson found significant sex differences in those perceptions where the death of a spouse was considered as the most stressful event in life. "For the women in our sample, loss of spouse was a matter of grave and encompassing consequences making immediate demands upon them. Heavy emphasis was given to the disappearance of the breadwinner occasionally in periods when wives had dependent children or were themselves at an employment disadvantage because of age or because they had never worked for a living. For the men, personal loss and emotional trauma were seldom compounded by the threat of economic privation. It was not that the women cared less but rather that they could not afford the luxury of undiluted sympathy. There was more immediately at stake for them and few cultural supports" (Anderson, 1965, p. 189).

riage centers on the lack of common interests between the two
and on her husband's unwillingness to give due credit to her
financial skill. Contrary to her husband's wishes, Mrs. Miller
started a small furrier business on her own when in her mid-thir-
ties. Apparently, Mr. Miller "never figured I would ever need to
go anywhere or need money. That was our main 'discussion' [she
might have said 'disagreement']." She complains that all her husband was ever interested in was mining (". . . a hole in the
ground") and ores. One gains the impression that Mr. Miller's
lengthy illness during the last years of his life was somewhat mitigated by his wife's ability to handle finances. As far as Mrs. Miller was concerned, the relationship changed for the better at that
time: "I handled the finances the last two or three years he was
alive. I think he figured I wasn't as dumb about finances as he
thought I was. Nurses told me that everyone in the sanitarium
knew that he worshipped the ground I walked on. I don't know
why he said that. Perhaps because of the way I handled the
finances."

Despite the altercations in her marriage, Mrs. Miller was nevertheless interested, ten years later, in "having a companionship,
having complete companionship and understanding. It's that loneliness. You just have to have companionship. The majority of the
trouble with older people is that you don't have anyone depending on you." Mrs. Miller does find some measure of escape from
this dilemma during the working hours of the day in her home-
workshop, but in the evening there occurs a "letdown." As she
puts it: "When the dinner hour comes, I feel sorry for myself, and
I'm not the only one. So sometimes I take the bus downtown and
have coffee and dessert. As I said before, it's not being needed.
That's the bugbear of all us widows."

Mrs. Mildred Tully (HS) attempted to resolve her problems
of widowhood by moving in with her son and his family. (This
adaptational maneuver is described in greater detail in the forthcoming discussion on relationships with children.) Mrs. Tully's
efforts to establish a home with her son were unsuccessful, for
she soon found herself an intruder in conflict with her daughter-
in-law. We have in general found that the patterns of American

family life do not tolerate this kind of extension of parental roles into an already-established nuclear family.

However, Mrs. Tully had previously tried to cope with her widowhood in other ways. After the death of her husband, she lived for a while on relief until Old Age Assistance became available to her. During her early sixties, she tried to earn additional income as a babysitter or as a kitchen-helper in small neighborhood restaurants. Finally, Mrs. Tully is one of the few widows in the sample who was able to find a gentleman friend. During one of our interviews with her, she spontaneously mentioned she had one, but he had unfortunately died not too long before. She had known him "almost ever since my husband died. He was a good fellow. Had an awfully good heart. He was company, you know. He took me to the show, to dinner once or twice a week. When I started to go with him, my brother-in-law's wife said that was the best news she had heard in a long time [indicating that it had met with the approval of her husband's family]. We used to have awfully good times together. He was working—making good money, I guess. But it was the companionship, you know."

Mrs. Tully's insistence upon the platonic nature of this relationship is echoed in the other reports we have from widows who desire male companionship. The chief value of such relationships lies more in the escort service these gentlemen can provide than in any required ardor in affection. As one subject expressed it: "You need a male companion to go places where you can have fun."

As Mrs. Tully suggests, femininity is not discarded with old age. Many of our female subjects still appreciate getting dressed up and being seen in public. In this regard, we have been especially struck by the importance ascribed to permanent waves by many of these women. Often the reimbursements offered by the study project for the interviews were spent for permanent waves. Grooming is particularly important for Mrs. Ada Bevin (HS), and she speaks with pride when she tells how a twenty-year-old girl, living in the same hotel with her, has helped her maintain her appearance: "She cuts my hair and gives me permanents. Just gave me one for Christmas. She bought me this dress."

Several recent studies in gerontology (e.g., Cumming and Henry, 1961; Blau, 1961) have uncovered groups of widows with high morale and a wide social milieu. These aptly-named "Merry Widows" have evidently made a successful adaptation. There are widows in our sample who sustain desires for looking their best and enjoying the years left to them; they have lost little of their zest for a full life. One lady of seventy-seven is quite firm about this: "Some young people think if you get older, you don't enjoy life. They have to get older to learn that at my age you can still enjoy things—you can still enjoy life!" We have already seen how Mrs. Bennington (CS) takes delight in her appearance, her sunny apartment, her friends down the hall, and her charitable work in a nurses' association. Mrs. Clara Bruzinsky (CS), a woman of seventy-eight, described as having "shining and sparkling blue eyes," is still working several hours a day in her son's gift shop and still keeps up her active social life with fellow Viennese expatriots. Blau (op. cit.) has emphasized how an advantageous economic standing makes such good adaptations to widowhood possible. A relative affluence seems to enable these women to avoid a complete restriction of social activity to subcommunities of widows. Rather these women can afford to entertain relationships with others which are more along ethnic or former professional lines.[7]

Finally, the "Merry Widows" and their attention to grooming hint at another aspect of growing old which is common to both men and women. In general, this is the problem of the retention or readjustment of the lines of social power. In the case of the women, this revived interest—almost hedonistic or regressive—upon prettiness and charm arises out of the shift in social control which comes with the attrition of mother and wife roles. Losing the social leverage provided by these roles, one finds it necessary to develop congeniality and attractiveness in order to retain the

---

[7] In the Cumming and Henry study cited in this paragraph, the authors found in a Kansas City sample of oldsters that "widows have a ready-made peer group in other widows, and there is reason to believe that they join this very happily" (p. 157). Because we do not find this to be true of our San Francisco sample of widows (and certainly not among the more affluent of these women), we suspect regional differences in the patterns of collateral-group formation.

affection of others, even within the nuclear family. Since one can no longer command the social control legitimatized in the child-rearer role with its critical and disciplinary functions, one must (or can, at least, try to) command the same kind of respect and control through an appealing personality. The real center of social control lies now in the hands of one's children.

The impact of loss of spouse upon the men is not as grave or disruptive: they appear to suffer no radical change in economic status because of it, and although bereavement is a problem for some men, opportunities are better than for the women to replace the lost spouse with a new wife or, at least, a "girl friend." The latter alternative was Mr. Jackson's choice.

Readers will recall the summary of Mr. Jackson's pre-hospital experiences at the conclusion of the last chapter. Upon his return to the community, however, Mr. Jackson met Hilda, "a hard-headed little German girl," who was eleven years younger than he at sixty-four. Through her ministrations, he was able to bring his drinking under control to the point of abstinence: the merest suspicion that Hilda might withdraw from him if he drinks is sufficient sanction. Although feelings of isolation, rootlessness, and futility still remain, Mr. Jackson's relationship with Hilda seems a close and satisfying one. She is sincerely concerned for his welfare and is dependable and level-headed. Since she lives at some distance, he must wait for her to come to him. "Killing time is the hardest work in the world," he says, because he is acutely uncomfortable when left alone with his thoughts and suffers keenly any loneliness. In fact, the only enjoyable hours in his life are those spent with Hilda. "As a rule, we get along just wonderful. I care for her a lot, although I can't marry her, and she treats me nice. She treats me like a brother now."

Despite the terminal cancer which now plagues him, he makes every effort to get out of his room with his friend. He speaks with animation of a picnic he is planning with Hilda. Discussing their social activities, he says, "Hilda and I go out on Sunday and visit various points of interest. We went up that 'bug' [a glass elevator] outside the Fairmont Hotel. We were out the night the Giants finished the pennant." In addition to this, he meets Hilda every

Thursday night for dinner. Because of her, he has begun to attend Mass again—now every day—and he also finds self-discipline and edification as a reactivated member of the Holy Names Society. It is doubtful that Mr. Jackson would have reestablished these former contacts on his own.

In summary, our discussion of the roles allied to the spouse status, whether present or lost, shows that, generally, men seem to be more successful in getting their dependency needs met in old age than are women. Many of the cases we have cited would indicate that these dependency needs are stronger in men than in women, but we do not think this is so. Rather we feel sure we are observing here an artifact of cultural conditioning which forces women by and large to deny many of their dependency needs throughout their lives.[8] In other words, what we see here is not in any sense a male developmental pattern specific to the process of aging but the culmination of long-held, mutual expectations between the sexes. In looking at the difficulties widows undergo in replacing lost husbands and the comparative advantage men have in replacing lost wives, one might be led to suppose that the widow's lot is the more psychologically expensive. But, in fact, widows often find their earlier, now atrophied roles as mothers and wives have been good practice for the self-care and independence now required of them. In many cases, these advantages are enough to offset the possible effects of the personal loss and the subsequent loneliness. The widower, on the other hand, usually lacking such "practice" in self-maintenance of personal needs, is impelled either to deny his dependency needs or to seek their appeasement in others. Failing to succeed in the latter, the wid-

---

8Often we can see these sex differences expressed in the forms of popular culture. In a recent television commercial for aspirin, a husband, sick with a bad cold, is portrayed as put to bed by his wife, where, through her ministrations, he recovers. His virility and working power restored, he then expresses his gratitude for his recovery to the aspirin. However, the wife, attempting to combat her cold in the same way, is portrayed in bed, futilely attempting to hide from her children clamoring at the door of the bedroom. "When a woman gets a cold," says the announcer, "her world doesn't stop." Forced to get back on her feet again, she expresses her gratitude to the aspirin company for enabling her to "carry on" in spite of her cold. Compare this entire discussion of perceived sex roles in old age with Neugarten and Gutmann (1958) and Neugarten and Associates (1964).

ower often runs the risk of developing some form of self-destruc-
tive behavior, as we saw in the pre-hospital experience of Mr.
Jackson. In the case of Gerald Spenser (HS, see Chapter II), we
see an example of a still-married man attempting to deny dependency drives in a frantic effort to retain the productive, instrumental male role of his full maturity. Because Mr. Spenser compelled his whole household to revolve around this struggle of his,
he finally forced his wife out of the house altogether and alienated
himself from his children. In short, it is hard to assess which status is the more burdensome—widow or widower. Each sex has its
own special set of adaptive tasks to perform when death dissolves
the marital union.

   Old Bachelors and Spinsters. Proper to any discussion of
marriage and widowhood in old age is a brief look at those who
never married. How do these lifelong bachelors and spinsters fare
in coping with the stresses of old age?

   We have uncovered in both hospital and community samples
a small group of men who have lived all their lives as social isolates. Now in their old age, these former vagabonds, day-laborers,
ranch hands, lumbermen, and merchant seamen haunt the bars
and cheap cafeterias of the geriatric ghettos. Mr. Elwin Ebenhauser (CS) is typical of these men. As a very young man, he
was the victim of a brutal punishment which he considered a
gross injustice. He has never been very close to people since.

> It all started when a friend played a trick on me. My
> mother, my brother, my sisters, and me was staying at this
> house. My father died when I was five in an accident. My
> mother had a dry goods store then. Well, this friend put some-
> thing in the landlord's closet that fell on the landlord when
> he opened the door. I got blamed for that. That night I got a
> terrible beating from my mother and oldest sister. They tied
> me to a lath in the cellar and beat me till I got welts on my
> back. They left me in the cellar and locked the door and about
> twelve o'clock I went to bed on the wood shavings they had
> down there. And I made up my mind that when I got old
> enough to make my own living, I wouldn't be around home.
> I'd be pretty independent. You see, they were afraid that they
> would be evicted because of that joke on the landlord. After-

wards, they told the landlord they had beaten me. That was a pretty expensive beating.

As he had promised to himself, Mr. Ebenhauser left home as soon as he thought he was capable of making his own way. For the rest of his life, he pursued an itinerant existence, working at temporary jobs, hopping freights, and never staying in any one place longer than a year or two. "I just wanted to be free," he explains. "Whenever I went with a girl and thought I was going to get married, I'd get out of town. When people start dictating to me, I ain't there anymore. When people don't get along with me, *I* do the moving. That's one reason I didn't stay at home—I don't want no discord." At seventy-nine, Mr. Ebenhauser is still employed, now as a dishwasher. When he is not at work, his time is completely taken up with his many solitary pursuits: inventing a perpetual-motion water wheel which will "convert one unit of power into fourteen times as many," reading upon spiritualism and telepathy, repairing his own shoes, and taking sweat baths in tubs of hot water and five pounds of epsom salts. Mr. Ebenhauser is scornful of the people he must associate with in his hotel and at work: "I try to avoid the slum elements which I see and understand. I seek intellectual stimulation." Accordingly, Mr. Ebenhauser regularly attends meetings of the Spiritualism Society, "a vegetarian club," as well as the Interplanetary Society, a "flying saucer club." He even claims to have talked with beings from outer space. "I get lots of information from people on other planets," he insists.

This man's morale is high and he impressed all the interviewers as a cordial, cooperative informant. By a curious irony, many old bachelors like Mr. Ebenhauser, who have maintained a social distance from others throughout their lives, often appear to function well, as though they have had a lifetime of practice in the self-reliance and autonomy required of many old people. Since they have never been close to others, they are spared the grief and loneliness of those who, having invested in and been intimate with others, must suffer the loss of a cherished relative, spouse, or friend.

Other single men in the sample do not seem to have been as much traumatized into bachelorhood as forced into it by circumstances resulting from a particular choice of vocation or life style. Mr. Grant VanDamm (CS), the retired Marine Corps officer introduced early in Chapter V, would certainly qualify as this type of bachelor. This subject was attracted to military life very early. After a stint in the Army during the First World War, he thought of settling down, but decided to join the Marine Corps instead: "Well, civilian life is fine, but I couldn't see going around in a small town. I wanted to travel and do things, and I knew that if I settled here at home, I would be stuck there." Mr. VanDamm's many tours of duty throughout the world did not disappoint his hopes for an exciting life with the Marine Corps. "I spent thirteen years in the Far East, in China, in the old China coast. Most of the men—whether officers or enlisted men—lived off the base in a little home they'd rented by the month. They'd have their permanent girl friends there. Liquor was cheap, women were easy to get, the life was a good one. There was always enough excitement." This pattern of living was to remain virtually unchanged throughout Mr. VanDamm's many other adventures in Nicaragua, in Haiti, in the Mediterranean with the Sixth Fleet, and during his long stay on Guam. Now, Mr. VanDamm seems quite content with his life: "I found it much easier to adjust to civilian life this time, because I'm older and more stable, I guess. For the past twelve or thirteen years, I've fallen into a routine that I find enjoyable. It's not too exciting, but at my age [sixty-one] you can't expect much more." Several other retired military men present much the same pattern of contentment in their retirement as Mr. VanDamm appears to do.

Mr. Bertrand Venable (CS), however, appears to have adopted a mode of living which has made sustained intimacy with others difficult. This man, a retired accountant at sixty ("I was retired on disability"), lives in the lonely splendor of a superbly decorated apartment near the Nob Hill district of the city. Covering all the floors are expensive Persian rugs and judiciously placed about the room are numerous classical Oriental and Italian *objects d'art*. Several fresh floral arrangements complete the picture of an epicure's lodgings. Intelligent, sensitive, and himself an artist, Mr. Venable indicates with his well-manicured hands a mosaic table-top which he has executed. "My work is good but not too original," he says in mock self-deprecation. Asked to describe himself, he says, "Well, I am egotistical, selfish, and rather self-centered. You want me to be frank, don't you? I'm interested in a wide variety of things, and I have a great deal of curiosity. I have good taste for the finer things in literature, drama, and art." Also, Mr. Venable is tall, well dressed, and younger looking than his actual age—perhaps because of his crew-cut hair and impeccable grooming.

Apparently, the only person admitted into these exquisite quarters is his maid, whom he describes as "very good and very black." [So, then, you never married?] "I have always lived alone. I wouldn't have it otherwise. I couldn't live with anyone." His only social life, he confesses, is in bars which he frequents almost nightly where he "just mingles with the crowd." He is frank to admit that this behavior has produced some problems of physical depletion: "For the last few years I have dissipated a good deal. The result of all this is that, probably, I am younger mentally but older physically. I guess I am a little more debilitated because of it." In order to quiet his nerves at night ("I'm moody, irritated—old age is creeping up"), he must take sedatives prescribed by his psychiatrist, "unless I go to bed inebriated. I drink wisely but not too well," he adds, paraphrasing a line from *Othello*. [Any other changes with age?] "Well, I'm getting more crabby and resentful. I talk to my psychiatrist about it. I can't stand other people's stupidity. Little petty things bother me more. I just worry because I am sensitive. Sometimes my friends offend me when they don't mean to." With this, Mr. Venable diverts the conversation to something a little more pleasant—his many trips to Europe and their relation to his art work. "I admit it, I admit it," says Mr. Venable with another touch of self-mockery, "in the best sense of that word, I am a dilletante."

We find that career-choice has also created several of the spinsters in the sample, but—something we see rarely among the men —so does a strong orientation to family of origin. Miss Myrtle

Manx (CS) illustrates both these conditions in her life history but also had to endure early stresses similar to Mr. Ebenhauser's —her traumatic childhood could hardly endear to her the opposite sex. Fortunately for Miss Manx, a devoted older sister ("she loved me so") was able to protect Miss Manx from some of the worst effects of abandonment in childhood. "Mother died when I was six," she recalls, "and I was farmed out for three years. Then I came to San Francisco to live with Father, but it didn't work out. He was a good man but very irresponsible, so I was put in an orphanage at nine. As a young girl, my sister went to work for a dentist. She didn't go to the orphange with me. There was no one allowed by court action to remove me." Here Miss Manx suffered the usual abuses of such institutions of that time (cold custodial care, harsh punishments) until her sister was able to remove her for medical treatment of emphysema, which Miss Manx contracted when she was twelve. From this time on, her sister was her unofficial guardian and protector. Her hospitalization for "water on my lung" introduced Miss Manx to "the romantic side of nursing." She resolved to become a nurse herself. In thinking back now upon that choice, she says, "I have never regretted it." Miss Manx fails to mention here that nursing was also her adored sister's career. For the rest of this sister's life, these two women lived together. "My sister really acted as my mother," Miss Manx admits. Their interests, friends, and activities were shared. Everything they did socially they did together. "I thought of marrying. People proposed. Time slipped by. Harry worshipped me, but he was an older man. I met him when I was in private duty. I felt we were just good friends. Yes, there were people I fell in love with, but different things came up in life—quarrels, I don't know what. My sister was not opposed to my marrying, but we were satisfied as it was. I wanted children, but my sister and I were too close to be separated."

Today, at sixty-five, Miss Manx is content with her retirement. Her comfortable apartment in an exclusive new housing development permits her to escape the dangers of downtown living: "I don't feel safe downtown, but here I feel quite safe. There's very close screening and they take no trash." Her sister's will provided very handsomely for Miss Manx. "All my stocks are blue chip," she says. She looks back on a life well spent in service to others. Her only regret is that with children her life might have been fuller. "We realized as we got older," she says, speaking again of her sister, "that we should have married."

In contrast with Miss Christianson (HS), characterized in Chapter II as a "Citizen of the Past" (who was also a career-woman and highly dependent upon other family members), Miss Manx is aging well in her single status. In many respects, she resembles Mrs. Bennington (CS), also a retired nurse, in the way she has carefully prepared for her old age. Then, too, her early misfortunes appear to have strengthened her sense of inner-reliance—much as we saw with Mr. Ebenhauser—so that, given continuing good health, she is likely to remain for some time independent and autonomous, despite her spinsterhood.

Sexuality in Old Age

Marriage in the later years—as at any other time of life—cannot be fully understood without reference to its sexual component, which persists in terms of mutual expectations long past the child-bearing years. Accordingly, we asked the intensive subjects several questions relating to actual and ideal sexual performance in old age and, although many found such questions somewhat embarrassing, subjects generally responded well in this area—"for the interests of science," as one informant put it. We were especially desirous of gathering as much substantial data as we could on this topic in order to dispel (or affirm, if such were to be the case) the many myths and preconceptions entertained about sexuality beyond sixty.

We found individual variations in sexual attitudes and reported behavior to be as widely ranging in the later years as in any other period of the life cycle. There are, for instance, elderly people in the intensive sample who claim to have lived all their lives as confirmed celibates, and there are others whose tales of prowess are of truly epic proportions. There is, however, one general characteristic that prevails: sexual contact is not sought as frequently as in earlier life—according to almost all our subjects, both men and women. But, among all subjects who were still married and living with a spouse, half (seven out of four-teen) reported having a viable sexual relationship at the time of the intensive interview. These seven subjects ranged in age from sixty-six to seventy-eight at the time.[9]

As pointed out in the previous section, some of these fourteen marriages had endured since early adulthood, others were marri-ages contracted late in life. We suspected that these latter liaisons would be nonsexual for the most part, but this did not prove to be the case. Recently-married subjects were just as likely as those who had been living with the same spouse for several decades to have an active sexual interest in the partner. However, these sexually-active subjects tend to characterize their late-life sexuality as a quiet, pleasant experience rather than the consequence of a compelling, driving force. For example, Mr. Janisch (CS), who still has—at seventy-eight—a sexual relationship with his wife after almost fifty years of marriage, gives the following description: "Sex has a great deal more influence on youth than in later years. The discovery and the joys of sex is more delightful when you are young. In later years, you take things for granted and that's all. I just feel nonchalant about it. If I see a beautiful woman in the street, I still look at her—but with no ulterior motive. Now, a good-looking woman is just like a work of art. But I have always enjoyed sex throughout my lifetime. I still do, but it is not as frequent."

Mr. Hokusai (CS) is similar to Mr. Janisch in that he has been married for over forty years to his present wife, with whom he still resides. Although he is four years younger than Mr. Jan-isch, he reports that he and his wife have had no intimate relations for many years. Moreover, Mr. Hokusai acknowledges that differ-

---

[9]Regarding frequency of coitus or other sexual outlets, Kinsey, Pomeroy, and Martin (1948) and Kinsey *et al.* (1953) —probably the best sources for frequency data— report the following for the 126 males past sixty whom they interviewed: "At sixty years of age, 5 per cent of these males were completely inactive sexually. By seventy, nearly 30 per cent of them were inactive. From there on, the incidence curve (as far as our few cases allow us to judge) continues to drop. There is, of course, tremendous individual variation" (Kinsey, Pomeroy, and Martin, 1948, p. 235). For women, they report: "There is little evidence of any aging in the sexual capacities of the female until late in her life" (Kinsey *et al.*, 1953, p. 353). Readers interested in a fuller discussion of sexuality in the later years are referred to Rubin (1965).

ences in temperament and health were involved in their early cessation of sexual contact: "My wife was not very sex-minded, and I was never strong towards sex, and, since I'm not strongly built, we have had no sex relations since I was sixty-five years old. Sex was never really important to me, but it depends on every individual. All ages have sexy people. It depends on people's nature and health and if a person is morally minded. I don't think after seventy you need it any more."

Late-life marriages differ, too, in their measure of sexual love. Mr. Schwann (CS), introduced in Chapter II and further discussed in a preceding section of this chapter, did not marry for the first time until he was seventy years old. He reports that this marriage is entirely platonic. Although Mr. Schwann was extremely reluctant to discuss this aspect of his life, he would admit that he had been somewhat sexually active during his late twenties and thirties: "I had some women I knew when I was younger. I had no sex in my middle years. I didn't have much time for girls. I was a foreman on a ranch and I had no time. When I was seventy, I married. I don't think much about it. It's all too late now. I was never so hot about sex anyway, and now I guess I am too old for that."

Mrs. Langtry's (CS) marriage, on the other hand, is different. This marriage is clearly a romantic love-match for both partners, as has been indicated in a previous discussion. When we asked Mrs. Langtry how much sex a person her age should have, she was seventy-one. She was somewhat abashed by the question: "Oh, my Lord! I don't know the answer to that, but about two times a month, I would guess. My husband and I don't have it quite that often—because of his health, you know. I don't know how to explain. I think women ought to have it and need an outlet just like a man should. I don't think she should discourage it. Both men in my life have been very conservative—not to excess is what I mean."

As Mrs. Langtry suggests, loss of physical health in one or the other partner seems to be the most frequently mentioned reason for terminating sexual activity in those marital relationships which no longer have a viable genital component. For example, Mr. Albert Jay's (CS) wife suffered a grave stroke prior to our intensive interviews, leaving her with serious mental and emotional impairment. Mr. Jay claims that she has had a "nervous breakdown" and often has "crying spells—just like a little child." At the time of the stroke, their intimacies ceased. "To tell you the truth," he says, "we haven't slept together for ten years—not since she got so sick." Mr. Jay seems very sad about this turn of events, but he has not sought any other sexual outlets. Instead, he escapes through retreatism of various sorts. He claims that his main satisfactions in life these days are ". . . beer, TV, and—to tell you the truth—sleeping. I sleep a lot."

Mrs. Reinhart's (CS) marriage also illustrates this. Now completely disabled because of advanced multiple sclerosis, she reports that she and her husband had a sexual relationship "up to the point of my physical incapacitation." Asking her to characterize her sexuality through the various phases of her life, we learn that, although her feelings about the matter have not changed much in later life, she did notice a gradual increase of interest "starting when I was about twenty-eight years old." Her sexual life had not been "very satisfying when I first married—I was too young and too busy having children. But when I was around thirty, I had an operation, so it was not possible to have more children—so I had no more worries about *that*."

Mrs. Reinhart's avowal of sexual inhibition during her young adulthood because of her fear of too many pregnancies makes us aware that some of the sexual problems in marriages of later life may be related to sex differences in the times men and women experience the peaks of their sexual drives. The men of our sample report that, for them, these drives were strongest during the twenties and early thirties. In contrast, the women more often report that they did not really enjoy sexual relationships until they were thirty-five or forty. Among couples where the husband is several years older than the wife, this temporal disharmony in the phases of psychosexual development and decline may pose serious problems in marital adjustment, which then can carry over into old age. For instance, Mrs. Trocopian's (HS) marriage—already described as an unhappy one—is an excellent example of this problem.

At the age of fourteen, Mrs. Trocopian was married to a man twenty years her senior and one she had never seen before. At the time of her marriage, she had not as yet experienced the onset of her menses, and, considerately, Mr. Trocopian waited to consumate the marriage until this occurred one year later. Even at that time, however, this very young girl was totally unprepared for assuming the sexual responsibilities of her marriage: her parents had been killed when she was quite young and her old grandmother, who had taken her in and reared her, provided her with no information on this subject. "I didn't know anything about sex," she says, "and all my grandmother told me was that, when you are married, you have to do what your husband tells you. It always bothered me. I believe my husband was too big—it always hurt me. As long as we are talking like this—perhaps if he had been quieter and more refined about it—that's got a lot to do with it. It wasn't very satisfying—I just had to please him. I never would ask and he would—and he asked too much. He would have to beg and ask me and often I would refuse, but you can't do that all the time." Also, because Mrs. Trocopian had had great difficulty in bearing her two children, she was fearful of any additional pregnancies after these births. "I had to be repaired after each childbirth," she confesses.

However, during Mrs. Trocopian's middle years, she began to experience a change in her attitudes. When she was forty, she had a hysterectomy, thus eliminating the possibility of any more pregnancies. With this, she began to notice an increment in her sexual appetites. For a few years, this couple had an opportunity for a fairly free physical relationship together, but this, unfortunately, was marred by reactivations of Mrs. Trocopian's early resentments against her husband as well as by her husband's waning physical powers. "I have never felt in love with any man, because I just do not trust them," she reports.

Then, when Mrs. Trocopian was forty-eight and her husband in his sixties, he suffered a heart attack. This calamity brought all sexual intimacies between them to an abrupt halt, but for Mrs. Trocopian such precipitous termination was painful and premature. "We haven't had any relations for fifteen years now," she says somewhat ruefully. "My husband has been sick. Since then there hasn't been any marriage actions at all. I didn't care, because I don't care too much for it. Oh, once in a while I do have feelings. They come and go. If I had a younger husband, maybe I would be interested two or three times a month. They claim it is good for us, but there isn't any sex for me now. My body is healthy, functioning—but for fifteen years we've been nothing like husband and wife. He had thrombosis—I told you that, didn't I? He was going to die, but he didn't. I wouldn't go outside my marriage for it though. I'm modest and then—I'm scared of syphilis. I just have to suffer desire, I guess. My sexual feelings are much stronger now than when I was younger. They get strong, especially when I'm idle."

In 1959, twelve years after her husband's heart attack, Mrs. Trocopian made an attempt to reopen marital intimacies with her husband. In a collateral interview, he reports, "We tried a few times and she seemed to be pleased, but I couldn't do much, and she talked about it too much." About three months before her hospital admission, Mrs. Trocopian began to develop dark suspicions that her husband's declining virility was not genuine but actually the result of extramarital affairs he was secretly entertaining on the side. She first accused him of going with other women, then of having incestuous relations with their daughter and with his brother's daughter. Finally, she accused him of wanting to kill her and so threatened to kill him first. This was the behavior that led to her hospitalization in 1959.

Since her discharge from the psychiatric ward, however, Mrs. Trocopian seems to have sublimated her sexual desires fairly well. After two years of living again in the community with her family, she reports: "Most women need a man and their happiness is around men. They die very soon though, if they are too sexy that way. I could be happy with a beautiful flower—my happiness is very simple. I don't have to have a man—I can just enjoy nature. I'd rather keep away."

The male counterpart of Mrs. Trocopian's problem can be seen best in the case of Mr. Arnold Ritter (HS). Mr. Ritter's fears of "lost virility" are by no means universal in the sample, but his dramatic way of coping with this problem would suggest that for some older men this loss is very threatening. Before Mr. Ritter's admission to the psychiatric ward in 1959, he was receiving treatment at a veterans' hospital in follow-up care for an earlier arrested case of tuberculosis. At the time of his psychiatric admission, Mrs. Ritter explained the events leading up to it in this fashion: "Well, I think he thinks he's losing his manhood. He's seemed slightly worried about that. He wore a beret down here, when he was living in San Francisco. He'd take walks along the Bay, and he said other men were wearing berets, so he got one too to keep his head warm. But he wore this at the Veterans' Hospital. They teased him and called him 'a fairy,' and he's very sensitive about this now and keeps talking about it." At the veterans' hospital, Mr. Ritter became convinced other patients were trying to castrate him. He complained to the doctors and had himself moved to another cottage. But, when his fears of castration persisted, he took absence without leave. A court order was then issued to have Mr. Ritter picked up and taken to the psychiatric ward.

After two months in a state hospital, these delusions of sexual threat abated and Mr. Ritter was discharged to his home in San Francisco. At the present time, he seems to have no problems and even reports an active sexual life, although he denies ever having been sexually preoccupied: "No, sex was never uppermost in my mind. I didn't worry about sex." However, he can now at least face the fact of some decline in sexual function without too much emotional turmoil. His feelings about sex, he says, have not changed ("can't get along with women, can't get along without them"), but he can see that his desire is waning: "Old Father Time is taking his toll—the machine wears out. But I'd rather *burn* out than *rot* out! Sex, like religion, has its place in a well-ordered life—it's personal and private." Mr. Ritter is seventy.

The foregoing subjects have attempted to maintain a viable sexuality into their later years. Others have not tried to do this—at least, according to their reports—for the following reasons. For Mr. Phidrios (HS), sexual continence is a kind of loyalty he wishes to give to his deceased wife: "For twenty-three years after I got married, I had a nice wife, sex, companionship. Sometimes I'd go to another woman—sometimes—very seldom. But then she died, and

I didn't want it no more. Funny thing—but in those fifteen years I never bothered about women no more." For Mrs. Tillford (HS), other men are poor specimens beside her idealized late husband: "It makes me want to cry just to think about the blessings I had through my marriage. My husband, he was so nice. Older than me, but really nice. He'd say, 'Mama, I want *you* for my wife, not the whole neighborhood.' He never went out sporting. Now I look at other men and they get on my nerves. They come in gruntin' and kickin' over the furniture—sit down and eat your food. And when they're through with you, they go out clownin' somewhere else. So I don't fool with them. If they want to come to my house, I say, 'Don't forget that bottle of liquor you're gonna bring,' and when they get here, I say, 'I better stay right here in my chair.' If I found a nice man like my last husband, that'd be different." Mrs. Tillford is sixty-five.

Mr. Harold Lewissohn (CS) was an eighty-year-old widower when we interviewed him in this area. Married at the age of twenty-seven, he was blessed with a full and happy union until his wife's untimely death, when Mr. Lewissohn was forty-eight. He reports that he had wanted "nothing to do with women" for five years after that. "When you love anybody," he says, "that's where it all originates. If you don't love anybody, you don't want them. And after my wife died, at first I didn't want anybody—I was still in love with her, you see. Even later, they had to be good-looking. I always went out with very good-looking girls." From fifty-three until he was seventy-nine, he engaged in several affairs: "Anytime I had sex, I enjoyed it, because, if you don't enjoy a person, you don't have no affair with them. I've been quite active all my life, except right after my wife died, but for the last year it's been different [since age seventy-nine]. Now I like the opposite sex to talk to, but I don't get involved any more."

It has never been clear why Mr. Lewissohn never remarried. In part, it may have been a fear of upsetting his children, but he also seems to have some frightening notions about late-life sexuality. He has cited several stories of old men who did remarry only to die shortly thereafter.

Such fears of a physical depletion if sexual activities are continued into later life are expressed by other male subjects too. Mr.

Fox (CS), for instance, a man who divorced his first wife during his middle years, now at eighty-four has a regular "girl friend" with whom he sustains an intermittent sexual relationship. However, he says, ". . . it ain't like it used to be. Sometimes I want to be with a woman, but not very often. It changed when I got to be eighty years old. I'm eighty-four now. It's just not there—the Old Man Above didn't give us the ammunition. Living with a woman, sleeping with her every night, would kill an old man. I only see Louise every three or four weeks."

Among some of the widowed and divorced men, abstinence is practiced in later life, not because of impotence or fears of depletion, but because of anxieties about venereal disease. Mr. Knight (CS), widowed many years, expresses such fears: "I had a lot of dates before marriage and I still go around. But I have no sexual experiences—if you mean sleeping with a date. It was my training as a child. It was the bugaboo of picking up a disease. This, and my responsibilities, were quietly mentioned at home when I was a child."

Widowed and divorced women often convey a thinly-veiled relief at the now-afforded respite from the sexual demands of the marital relationship. These women express strong belief in the inherent virtues of Victorian morality. Many claim to have never enjoyed sexual activity, except as a necessary means for the conceiving of their children. Asked if she ever had premarital sexual relations, Mrs. Miller (CS) replied indignantly: "*I'll* say I didn't! You know, when I was raised, if a fellow talked about a corset or a garter—well, that was just unheard of! I sure was fortunate being born when I was—a girl on her own like that. I'd be ripe bait for some of these vultures today. I don't think my feelings about sex were very prominent. And, of course, they've changed a great deal [*sic*], which doesn't bother me a bit. I don't have any desire at all. It's just blank. Maybe I'm a freak, but I hear other women say the same thing. I don't think I ever was so crazy in love with my husband—or *any* man. Maybe it was because my father was so strict and rigid—I guess I thought all men were the same. My husband was pretty close."

Mrs. Bruzinsky (CS), a widow whose recollections of her long-deceased husband are now gossamer romantic fantasies, reports that sex was never an element in her love for her husband: "You know, in my young days, you never talked about this with your mother or sisters or your friends. Sex was a very matter-of-fact part of our marriage and I never really thought about it. In the early part of our marriage, it was important to my husband, but I wasn't too happy about this. It really isn't too important between two people who love each other. Well, you know, there is a saying women tell their husbands: 'If you're hungry, eat.' This I would tell my husband. To me it really didn't make too much difference."

As one might expect, the single people in the sample—particularly the women but some of the men as well—express strong inhibitions deriving from a stern sexual morality inculcated in early life. For example, asked if she ever married, Miss Bachstein (HS) is outraged: "No, of course not! We always went to the best schools and that—and this kind of talk, I don't believe in it. Live just straight all the time—always close to religion, to home." It should be noted that Miss Bachstein was one of nine siblings and only one of them, a brother, ever married. Miss Karen Jernigan (HS) practically exploded when we broached the subject of her sex life: "My God, I never, *never* went with a man! I'm not that kind of woman! *Beware of men!* Gee whiz, I'm not married—I can see you don't know me very well. I'm not a good Catholic if I do that. Why, that's a disgrace—a mortal sin! That's why I didn't get married—I'm afraid. A boy asked me to marry him once and I said, 'I'm too young,' because I didn't want to go to bed with him. Gee, that's shameful! I never did want to go to bed with a man."

Although the single women in the sample are more articulate about their prudery, some old bachelors were equally so. Mr. Kreisler (HS), for example, reports that all his life he has been, sexually speaking, ". . . backward. I wasn't as forward as the other ones were. This is embarrassing. I never fooled around. We never ran around like that. I don't think that I ever kissed a girl until I was twenty-five. I only met one girl I liked very much. She passed away. She died of an auto accident. I think sex before marriage is terrible, myself. Parents should be more strict. It's the parents' fault, I believe. Of course, now it don't interest me any more."

As these last cases suggest, mental illnesses in late life, although perhaps having other etiological components, sometimes derive in part from sexual anxieties or, at least, take on the form of sexual aberrations. In this regard, Mr. Marcos Antonelli (HS) was admitted to the psychiatric ward following an attack on his daughter-in-law, accusing her of sexual infidelity and then trying to strangle her. An analysis of this case by our staff psychiatrists has revealed that this man's fears of impotence had driven him to infidelities of his own whereupon he projected his subsequent guilt on to his daughter-in-law.[10] In another case, Mr. Forest (HS) suffered a terrific blow with the death of his wife, since he had always believed that she was the only woman who would have him. He claims to have always had difficulties with women: "I always did like girls, but they didn't like me. I don't know why my wife cared about me—no money, no looks." Following his wife's death, Mr. Forest became convinced that his brother's wife was sexually interested in him, and jealousy of his brother's good fortune became a serious preoccupation. He began making advances to his sister-in-law, and this behavior resulted in the suggestion that he enter the county home for the aged (he had been residing in his brother's home). At the county home, he came to the attention of the psychiatric staff when he was discovered making homosexual advances to other patients. For this reason he was transferred to a state hospital, where he was still an inpatient at the time of the intensive interviews.

In a similar fashion, Mrs. Amelia Harris (HS) developed psychopathological symptoms upon the death of her husband. This woman reported bizarre physical sensations in her abdomen and the feeling that appendages were growing from her pelvic region in a way suggesting phantom male genitalia. She came to the county hospital seeking relief from the severe pain she was suffering as

---

10Actually, this case is much more complex than indicated here, but a full presentation is beyond the scope of this present discussion. It should simply be noted that our statement in the text is an oversimplification. Among other factors was an intense sexual rivalry with the patient's son.

a result of this appalling transformation. It is beyond the scope of this report (and the skills of the authors) to attempt the elucidation of the psychodynamics underlying the development of sexual aberrations of later life, but it is of some interest to us as students of culture and personality that this woman was an early rebel against a double-standard of sexual morality. She repeatedly emphasized her resentment of the sexual freedom customarily granted to the men in her family and community and the rigid prohibitions inflicted upon her and other women. She was determined to have some of this license for herself and, rebelling against a strict Protestant upbringing (her father had been a clergyman), she engaged in several premarital affairs. When she finally married, she dominated a rather weak-willed husband, considering him a sorry specimen of virility. She was ever a strong advocate of women's rights and once said to us: "I'm all for women and I've always resented everyone assuming that God is a man." In the last analysis, however, she must have acceded to the belief that males are indeed the superior sex—if imitation be the sincerest form of flattery.

To summarize our findings on sexuality among older people, we have found that half of our intensively-studied married subjects who were still living with a spouse were sexually active, although in all cases the activity had changed somewhat, both quantitatively and qualitatively. In cases where there was no sexual relationship in the marriage, one of the spouses was usually eighty or older, or there was some physical illness which made sexual activity difficult or fatiguing. In some cases of late-life marriage, sexuality was present, but, in others, subjects manifested a long history of sexual repression or conflict, waiting until they could be reasonably exempt from sexual responsibilities on the grounds of age before contracting the marriage.

The most common cause of termination of sexual activity is loss of spouse. Grief reactions often persist for many years following widowhood—for both men and women—and, in some cases, sexuality is never resumed. We suspect, from the case material, that age has brought a loss of sexual self-confidence to many widowed subjects. As long as the spouse is alive, long-familiar patterns of intimacy may be comfortably pursued; but widowhood in old age forces many into the sidelines of romance with little chance to counteract the enforced continence. Making overtures to others is often threatening to an already wavering self-esteem—and diminishing drives do not provide sufficient motive power to overcome the uncertainties of such a hazardous new enterprise. Although some of the men reassured themselves of continued potency through an almost compulsive promiscuity (see, for instance, the case of Mr. Fox discussed earlier in this section) , others accepted a premature celibacy for fear of embarrassment. The emotional tortures of an uncertain sexuality, easily inferred from the intensive interviews, are highly reminiscent of adolescent problems. In fact, some subjects are quite explicit about this parallel. Mrs. Burbank (CS) , for example, speaking of recent changes in her own sexual attitudes, says, "It's just like adolescence—you just don't know what's happening to you." In some cases, sexual attitudes seem to be almost reactivations of preadolescent ones. One subject, Mrs. Tully (HS) , reports observing behavior between the elderly men and women who are also residents of her apartment-hotel: "There are no men I dislike—except those downstairs. Why, they don't treat women right. They've lost their desire for women and got it against them all, I guess. In the lobby, all the women go with their heads up and won't talk to them." The scene easily conjures up the postures so frequently seen in popular calendar art: a gaggle of ten-year-old boys grudgingly forced to admit the presence of "girls," while, strolling past them, the young ladies—noses in the air, dolls in hand—studiously ignore the "dirty, little things."

Some of the widows expressed relief with the cessation of sexual activity, thus, at long last, escaping the turmoils and guilt generated by a lifetime of Victorian attitudes. Some widowed men, too, escaped blind fears of depletion and physical breakdown in the belief that continence was best.

In the most poignant (and sometimes the most colorful) cases, the declining years bring serious sexual aberrations, thereby provoking unacceptable social behavior, and, finally, commitment to a mental hospital.

Aside from sexual problems and conflicts—many of which can occur at any age—there seems to be one factor in cessation of sexual activity largely unrelated to nonbiological factors, and that is advanced old age itself. Between the ages of seventy-five and eighty, on the average, sexual desire (and potency among men) diminishes almost to the vanishing point. For some subjects, this time comes a bit earlier (Mr. Janssen [CS] reported loss of virility at age seventy-three); for others, a few years later (Mr. Lewissohn, at eighty-one, and Mr. Fox, at eighty-four, could still be interested occasionally). Eventually, however, the time comes when there is no longer an active sexual interest, even among the mentally and physically healthy elderly who are living with a spouse. Mr. Southern (CS), at sixty-nine, has not reached this point in life yet, but he feels it approaching. "We still do it," he candidly reports, "but, boy, it's getting to be work!" Mr. Ed Hart (CS) was ninety-three when we last interviewed him. This man had sustained sexual relationships with his second wife through his seventies. The relationship with his third wife, however, commencing in his early eighties, was entirely platonic. Musing about this, he says, "It's just deterioration, I presume. But it's certainly nothing to get upset about. This seems to be what happens to all male animals as they grow older—but you don't stop loving or living!"

Parents and Children

Reports from the subjects of our intensive sample indicate that the role of parent is, generally, an active one. Twenty-nine of these sixty-four subjects are parents and, of these, twenty-four have at least one child living in the San Francisco Bay Area or its vicinity. Of the five who do not have children living in the area, one finds that contact with the children had been severed at a very early period of life, the estrangement usually resulting from a divorce of the parents. This is true in three of the five cases; a fourth case is an illegitimate child who lives in Europe and is supported by the parent here. Of the twenty-nine parents, we find seven living with adult children. None of these seven is a spouse in a viable marriage. In our sample, at any rate, it is only the widowed or separated parent who makes his home with his adult children. (The only exception where both spouses are living with a child is in the case of a Japanese-born subject, but here the daughter is single.) In this sample, we simply do not find two married couples of differing generations living in the same household. Again, the best relationships between parent and child are found to exist in the two rare cases where both parent and child lack a mate. These particular relationships are marked with a high degree of mutual dependence and self-sufficiency, where the presence of the parent is a definite asset to the child. However, this type of adjustment is atypical. The pattern in the remaining five cases is one marked with friction. Where it is a mother living with her married son, we note the mother's resentment of her daughter-in-law for a real or imagined alienation of her son's affection. The mother will hold on to the belief that her son still loves her best, despite overt signs to the contrary, and that he would be more affectionate were it not for his reluctance to displease his wife.

In several cases, we have also noted the curious effect that regulations on welfare payments have upon these patterns. We suspect that more of the parents in our sample would be living with their children but for the restrictions ordinarily placed on these payments. In these cases, the child inviting the parent to live with him is a resident in another state and, thus, the parent is prevented from moving for fear of becoming ineligible for this aid.

A good relationship with children in old age depends, to a large extent, on the graces and autonomy of the aged parent—in short, on his ability to manage gracefully by himself. It would appear that, in our culture, there simply cannot be any happy role reversals between the generations, neither an increasing dependency of parent upon child nor a continuing reliance of child upon parent. The mores do not sanction it and children and parents resent it. The parent must remain strong and independent. If his personal resources fail, then conflicts arise. The child, on the other hand, must not threaten the security of the parent with requests for monetary aid or other care when the parental income has shrunk through retirement. The ideal situation is when both parent and child are functioning well. The parent does not depend on the child for nurturance or social interaction; these needs the parent can manage to fulfill by himself elsewhere. He does not limit the freedom of his child nor arouse the child's feelings of guilt. The child establishes an independent dwelling, sustains his own family, and achieves a measure of the hope the parent had entertained for him. Such an ideal situation, of course, is more likely to occur when the parent is still provided with a spouse and where a high socioeconomic status buttresses the parent and child. These ideal conditions prevail in the case of Mrs. Selma Reinhart (CS).

Mrs. Reinhart states that her relationship to her three children —two daughters and a son—has not changed through the years. Two of them live in the San Francisco Bay Area and visit her frequently. They form the core of the social circle that visits Mrs. Reinhart almost daily, bringing her company and comfort. "All have a sense of humor and we have fun together," she says. "My younger daughter told me she admired me so much, she thought she would never come up to the picture she had of me. Well, let me tell you, I may be good at keeping my hair in place, but she's Phi Beta Kappa. I couldn't have done that. Norine is the best integrated—both feet on the ground." Mrs. Reinhart also emphasizes a mutual respect between the generations: "No barriers of age or respect between us. We are just like friends." But Mrs. Reinhart had a special adjustment to make while, earlier, she observed her children raising their own. "I learned not to be critical of their ways of bringing up children," she says. Despite this mutual acceptance, equality, and friendship as well as her awareness that her children would willingly provide a home for her should she ever need one, she affirms, "I can't imagine a fate worse than that!"

Mr. Phillip Knight (CS), at seventy-one, a retired successful businessman, and widowed since the age of forty-eight, has raised two sons and a daughter who are all living in the Bay Area but not in the family home. Mr. Knight lives there alone. Active and alert and occupied in many activities, he is on excellent terms with his offspring. His children come by at least once a day and he often drops in on them for visits. In the telegraphic style characteristic of Mr. Knight, he describes his relationship with his children: "Same interest in them. Not sitting on top of them. Same relations. They're mature. I don't interfere with them. Now, they are attentive and don't do it from duty. Good relationship. See them daily." There is approval of his sons: "Older one does the thing I'm interested in. Younger one, I'd have said eight to ten years ago, was a big mistake. Now, he's a howling success. They're well on their way." He is very satisfied that these sons have become independent and he is well aware that the values of his own generation might not be suitable for the future his offspring will have to face: "There are things I could wish different, but they might be just right for their times. Why should I elect what they should do? They are independent as a hog on ice." Also, Mr. Knight is well aware that his relationship between himself and his children might be specific to his particular social class and circle of friends. He would not generalize as to the position of older people in their families but merely stated: "The ones [aged parents] *I* see are wanted, desired." He, too, is of Mrs. Reinhart's persuasion: "Relationships with your children are always O.K., if you're not living with them."

At issue in these relationships with their respectable distance is not so much a withdrawal from intimate social contact but a shrinking back from the potential contest of power and control that is inherent in the relationship between old American fathers and their grown American sons. In our culture, older men must learn to defer to youth in order to avoid incurring the competitive hostility of younger men. We have already touched upon the perceived necessity of some older male subjects to step aside and "enjoy" watching someone younger succeed. Commanding power over others from the vantage point of a patriarch simply does not work in modern American society. But Simmons (1960) has shown how, through a continuing hold on property rights, government, ceremony, magic, and education, the old preindustrial or peasant societies maintain a gerontocracy.[11] In the rural dis-

---

[11]Simmons concludes this study by accounting for the preeminence of the elderly in these societies as well as the devalued status of older generations in industrial societies such as our own. He writes: "Here is one way to express the general principle: in the long and steady strides of the social order, the aging get themselves fixed and favored positions, power, and performance. They have what we call seniority rights. But, when social conditions become unstable and the rate of change reaches a galloping pace, the aged are riding for an early fall, and the more youthful associates take their seats in the saddles. Change is the crux of the problem of aging as well as its challenge" (p. 88).

tricts of many modern Mediterranean societies, in Central and South America, and in Old China, the family homestead is always and firmly in the hands of the old patriarch, and the young who do not obey (or do not, at least, pretend to obey) have negative social sanctions brought to bear against them, losing thereby the respect of others and becoming stigmatized as "bad sons" and "bad daughters." In fact, we can visualize many of the mentally ill in our sample as a group of older Americans who have broken themselves on the horns of this dilemma of power and control. We can even see among the emotionally disturbed of the community sample signs of this same frantic effort to retain the discipline and influence formerly exerted over their children. The mentally healthy seem best able to accept substitutes for this lost power, and a loving respect from their children is the most preferred compensation these old ask for their "stepping aside" and "staying out of the way." We see almost touching instances of this in the pleasure many of our subjects take in the turning once again of their children to them for advice.

Mr. Lawrence Southern (CS) was especially articulate about this: "Naturally, they grow up and their love naturally goes to their own families a lot instead of just to you. They think of you the same way, but maybe they don't show it as they once did." There is deep satisfaction when his child turns to him: "My daughter puts me on a pedestal. Whenever anything comes up, she calls me. I say, what does your husband want to do? She says he doesn't know and that you would know better. Makes me feel good that she feels that way." Any indications of respect are appreciated by the old since, in our society, such feelings are offered as free gifts, dependent upon the social skills of the old and gallantry of the children.

Within the minds of all the fathers and mothers in the sample is the thought that maybe a day will come when one might *have* to move in with one's children, but it is the men who show the greatest reluctance to do this. They consider it a weakness and an imposition upon their children and, prizing autonomy for as long as it can last, they hope to avoid the frailties, illness, and deterioration that might make such moving an absolute necessity. Even Mr. Hart (CS), a ninety-three-year-old gentleman who impressed every interviewer with his intelligence, charisma, and serene wisdom, expressed such views. This man, who lives alone in San Francisco, is on excellent terms with his married daughter living in Portland, Oregon, and he tries to visit her at least twice a year, often staying for a month, but he insists he will not ever throw himself upon their sufferance and care. "My daughter—a very lovable person—and her husband want me to come live with them in Portland, but I won't go until I positively have to. My son-in-law pleads with me, but, at my age, with Social Security and all, I might be bedfast and I wouldn't want them to take care of me when I have security here." Mr. Hart is afraid that taking such a step would result in "disrupting their happiness." On the other hand, he is courageous enough to face that unavoidable time when he may not be able to care for himself, but he faces this thought with feelings of sad resignation: "I can see a time may come when they will have to step in and tell me what to do and I'll have to do it, but I hope that time doesn't come." This subject holds strongly to the belief that when children marry they form a "separate unit": "After their marriage, their attachment to their parents was given up. I did, with my own feelings, long before. I knew what was going to happen, so I just relinquished my right and wished them godspeed."

Underlying Mr. Hart's reasoning is also the suggestion that he recognizes an incompatibility between the values and goals of his own generation and that of his daughter. Many of our subjects are keenly aware of these differences, and these, too, must be taken into account when exploring the reluctance of our subjects to move in under the same roof with their children. Strikingly enough, the drinking patterns of the younger generation come under the criticism of the old more often than any other complaint they are wont to level against their juniors. Generational differences in standards of housekeeping, child-rearing practices, manners and etiquette, as well as religious apostacies figure also in those statements we might categorize as "views with alarm." However, it is the women who seem to voice their disapproval of these things more than the men.

In much the same way, our male subjects seem less sensitive to perceived slights they may receive from their children than are the women. This is true to the general pattern we wish to adumbrate here: less emotional dependency on the children among the men and, hand in hand with this, their already-noted advantage over the women to seek and find adequate substitutes in their collateral relationships for any losses of affection they may suffer. Women, on the other hand, tend to be more sensitive about the alienation of their children, undoubtedly because they have invested more time and attention in them. So, too, widows are often forced to seek substitutions for their lost husbands in their children. Here one can readily tap the wellsprings of old, familiar intimacy and respect—ratifications of the ego seldom available in the exclusive company of old maids and other widows. Also, in contrast with the men who still want to be able to advise their children, women are more willing to take the counsel of their offspring, thus transferring the authority and judgment of the husband to their own children. It is not so much counsel they wish to give but consolation, especially to the sons.

Mrs. Nella Sandusky (HS) illustrates this well. During her third interview, she—a widow of three years—was dividing her time equally between the households of her two sons. She could rely on her eldest son: "I go by his judgment in most things. If I wanted advice pertaining to financial matters, I'd talk to him. I think he has more influence on me than anybody else." Still, Mrs. Sandusky is split in her desires to be of use and yet not become so intrusive into her children's lives as to merit their rebuke. Thus, speaking of an out-of-town friend who comes to visit her from time to time, Mrs. Sandusky states: "My son and daughter-in-law like her very much, but I don't want to ask her without checking with my son first." Evidently, she is comfortable only with visitors of whom her children would approve. "I don't want to take that much for granted," she says. "I try not to impose or take advantage of my privileges any more than I can help."

The ideal female of Mrs. Sandusky's generation was embodied in such figures as the Gibson girl and, later, Mary Pickford—females who would easily defer to the executive functions of the male. Such a woman was taught to live vicariously through her husband, viewing him as the authority in all matters pertaining to the truly "serious" business of life. In Mrs. Sandusky's case, we have already seen how such a dependency became perilous after her husband, injured in an automobile accident, became intermittently delusional. In effect, Mrs. Sandusky was seduced into her husband's syndrome and nearly developed with him an alcoholic *folie à deux.* Because, since her husband's death, she has had to seek satisfaction for her dependency needs in her sons, she is again in a vulnerable position—this *vis-à-vis* her daughters-in-law. Mrs. Sandusky is especially sensitive on this subject. She praises their goodness inordinately: "I don't think my own daughters would have been as good to me as these two daughters-in-law," but somewhat later she is noted to say: "I don't want to upset them in any way at all about anything." This woman needs to continually justify her stay with her sons and their families. A bit coyly, she says: "Of course, I have my family a little spoiled. I always make noodle soup out of the turkey carcass after the holidays. You know, grandmas always make pies and things. They look forward to my pies and homemade noodle soup."

Mrs. Gladys Dillon (CS) is also trying to cope with the problem of juggling her needs to lean on her children and yet stand free of them. Following a rather unhappy marriage, Mrs. Dillon divorced her husband when she was fifty-three. Now, she is living alone in a rooming house but is satisfied with the attention her two daughters are giving her. She is, above all, very appreciative of their financial support, but, then wasn't she largely responsible for rearing and providing for them while they were growing up without a father? "I don't have to work now, because my girls are good to me," she says proudly. "They each send thirty dollars a month and I'm drawing a hundred and thirty dollars Social Security each month." She is "very proud" of them. "I pack a bag and go out to my daughter's place on weekends." Often she is taken with them on excursions or weekend trips to Lake Tahoe. Mrs. Dillon willingly admits that her children's marriages have brought inevitable changes: "It's now close contact but not like it used to be. I realize my position and I do not try to push myself on them. I want them to feel they can depend on me. At the same time, when I go to their houses, I like for them to invite me over."

This last remark is not as offhand as it might sound. We have been struck by the frequency with which formal invitations are used to signify the new relationship between aging parents and their grown children. One subject, in fact, was quite explicit about this. She differentiated sharply between special trips to visit upon invitation and the more spontaneous "dropping-by" whenever the route might take one through the neighborhood. "I appreciate the invited visits more than just the passing-by," she says. For these older subjects, a formal invitation has the double virtue of offering deference and respect to the older generation but also of clearly marking off the boundaries of the newly-adjusted relationship.

To demonstrate that dependency upon one's children can be stress-provoking, we turn anew to Mrs. Langtry (CS), in whose case lies the proof of this in the way her relationship to her children improved once her dependency was removed. This woman's late-life remarriage appears to have benefited the morale of everyone concerned. Now happily mated to Mr. Langtry, she can turn once again to her son with pride in her role of parent: "My son is quite happily married. He is progressing in Sacramento. He has a nice little wife. Walter and I talk to them about once a week. They come over often and we go over often—at least once a month, I'd say. They love to come over and we love to go over." Now that she is no longer dependent on them, she can afford to view them sentimentally: "Whenever they feel like they need anything, it's always Mama they come back to. I have no doubt of their devotion." She no longer dwells on the time, following her first husband's death when, at sixty-two, bereaved, and financially insecure, she had tried unsuccessfully to set up a home with her son. She even speaks of her daughter-in-law with kindness now, recounting with pleasure how it was she who had pointed out this woman to her son as a potential bride for him. The strains of the old relationship are forgotten: "My little daughter-in-law did not want me to live with them. It was my house, but I went to live with my sister. That's all over now. She was too young. I don't think it's a good plan to live with your children, but I think that as long as all the furniture and things were mine, I had the right to ask it."

In the case of Mrs. Mildred Tully (HS), we have dramatic evidence of the raw sensitivity which can frequently develop between a mother and daughter-in-law living together under the same roof. At eighty-four, Mrs. Tully now lives by herself in the city, as self-sufficiently as any person her age—with loss of energy and a memory deficit—can do. During interviews with her, she turned almost obsessively to the topic of her son and daughter-in-law's "lack of concern" for her. Once she even complained that her son did have the means to help her find better quarters but stubbornly refused to give it. Her relationship to this daughter-in-law is doubly malignant: both have been hospitalized for mental illness and Mrs. Tully is an especially rigid person. Mrs. Tully can never forget that evening twenty years before, when her daughter-in-law came home while Mrs. Tully was babysitting for her. "She just screamed at me: 'Get out! Get out!' She's nervous. She's had all her female organs out. I haven't stayed all night since. She hasn't asked me. They've got a big station wagon and a big boat and they never take me with them. I told them a while ago I would just love to come down sometimes—besides Christmas and Thanksgiving, Mother's Day, and my birthday—but they just pretended I hadn't even said that. My son never calls—or hardly ever." A rapprochement is all the more unlikely since, upon Mrs. Tully's return from the hospital, she has begun to develop an increasing hypersensitivity: "A while ago, when I was visiting them, I wanted to have a picture—four generations, you know. My daughter-in-law was going to take the picture. She was mad because she spoiled the flash, but *I* think she did that on purpose, because she wanted *her* mother to be the greatgrandmother in the picture." This rivalry with the daughter-in-law is interesting because it extends even to the younger woman's mother.

Imported cultural expectations for the aged, different from those now current in the United States, can also create difficulties in the parent-child relationship for the foreign-born (or for those first-generation Americans who are still strongly identified with the parent culture). On the whole, native-born aged subjects appear to grant greater independence to their children and even insist that their parental roles remain only peripheral in their childrens' lives. The nature of interaction between the generations seems to be somewhat formal and dispassionate: they are welcómed visitors in the households of their children; sometimes they will render financial assistance; sometimes they will perform services such as babysitting or cooking special "grandmother treats." For their part, the children will often take the "old folks" out for a Sunday ride or chauffer them to bridge parties or church socials, or they will periodically phone and chat with their parents, offering them at the very least a *signe de vie*. The cultural expectations for most aging Americans thus seem clear: recognize that the children have a right to lead their own lives; be not overly demanding and thus alienate yourself from your children's affection; above all, do not interfere in their normal pursuits. We have already seen that such expectations work best when the parent and child are still functioning well, physically and mentally, and when financial resources are intact enough for separate residences.

But other cultural systems program old age differently. Some of the immigrants in our sample come from areas of the world where kinship ties are the *major* sources of support and comfort in old age, where devotion and warm affective bonds persist, becoming even more intense, with advancing years. For some, such as those with Latin or Oriental backgrounds, the continuation of the family line is of prime importance, so, in consequence, being a grandparent is equivalent to heading a dynasty. Among other ethnic groups, even grown children are denied mature rights and responsibilities—as long as the parents are still alive.

Mrs. Marta Valente (CS), at seventy-one, is alienated from her two sons and at war with their wives. This woman was born into a Mexican-American family in the Southwest and, because of an extremely deprived childhood and even more wretched marriage, has separated herself from her past and her subculture to the point where she has adopted as her own many of the "Anglo" values of old age just discussed. This process of acculteration has been all the more effective since, for over twenty-five years, Mrs. Valente has supported herself as a housekeeper and practical nurse, often living in the homes of her Anglo employers. Now retired and living on Social Security, Mrs. Valente takes particular pride in her current life: "Now I'm boss of my own life. I have a home ready-made here." She can only reflect with pain upon her twenty-five years of marriage to a brutal, alcoholic husband. "I never enjoyed life with him," she says. "He'd go away for two or three days, come back when he wanted to. He scared me—I wouldn't dare speak to him. 'Where you been? Why not come home?'—none of that was my business. I don't think he cared for us at all—come home, get clean shirts—no responsibilities. He just wanted a servant." However, when Mrs. Valente's oldest son was seventeen, he was able to challenge this tyranny: "My son opposed his father. He was going to whip his father. His father would tear my clothes off when he come home from playing at a dance, to make me get up. My son wouldn't let him hit me any more." Up to this point, Mrs. Valente had been fearful of leaving her husband because "I was afraid if I'd leave him people would talk." But her son's defiance of his father gave her the strength to make the separation. "I left with not a dollar to my name. What money we made working in the fields he'd put in his pocket." In leaving her husband, however, Mrs. Valente took the first important step away from the complex network of fictive kin supports available to members of her subculture. "We piled up a few rags, the kids and me, and went on to Denver. I did housework for Jewish people. They'd give me old shoes. I was destitute. He left me nothing." After a variety of similar jobs, she came to San Francisco: "I'm thankful I'm here. Been pretty lucky. Buy what I want to eat—no fancy clothes, but good enough."

Mrs. Valente has fought hard for her independence in old age and will not brook any challenge to it, such as recently happened from one of her sons. Encouraged by his wife, one of Mrs. Valente's sons went to his mother for money: "She had Frankie come here for a few hundred dollars for wall-to-wall carpets. They must have thought I was loaded. I said, 'I don't have that kind of money. If it was in need of sickness, it's a different thing, but not for luxuries.'" This refusal was made, evidently, with mixed feelings, for, as a good Mexican-American mother, she would have liked to help her son as much as she could, but she is also indignant at the inconsiderateness of this demand: "You don't have to buy friendship from your children. You learn not to give too much."

In this case, it appears that Mrs. Valente's children continue to hold expectations of their old "Mamacita" which Mrs. Valente herself has long repudiated. There is also too much of an echo in this son's behavior of the draining, exploiting husband from whom she withdrew thirty years before, so, since the demand for money, Mrs. Valente has begun to drift away from her sons: "They're not mine anymore. I'm not worried about what they think, or even if they never think of me. I look after myself."

In contrast, Mrs. Trocopian (HS) is loud and clear in her demands upon her children. She has an insatiable need for demonstrations of kindness and appreciation for her talents and worth. The slightest suspicion of rejection must be assuaged by soaring flights into her supposed superiority. And not only does she require admiration and appreciation but expensive material contributions and gifts as well. For instance, she feels that her son and daughter should have rendered more financial assistance while she was in the hospital so that she could have prolonged her stay there. This was "their duty." She also feels that her son who lives on the East Coast is sufficiently affluent to provide her with the gift of a car, even though she does not drive. Despite his refusal—so far—this son is closest to her: "He appreciates you. He will tell you how nice you look. He's so thoughtful and considerate. When he is around, I'm very happy. If I was with him, or someone like him—not that I want to stay with him—I would be better. He has about seventy-five per cent of my nature." Mrs. Trocopian sees this son only once a year because of the distance at which he lives from her. Even so, "my son could be a little friendlier, write more often, also be of a little help financially. If I only had money to get a little car! That would give me independence and pleasure. In that way, he could be of help. He has a good position now."

On the other hand, Mrs. Trocopian's daughter does live nearby and it would seem that she is of much service to her mother. Mrs. Trocopian does "appreciate" her daughter and regards her as her "best friend." Furthermore, she is assured that this daughter "has love for me" and that "she performs her duty." But, unfortunately, this daughter has only "twenty-five per cent" of the mother's nature. "She's not as simple and generous as she could be," Mrs. Trocopian complains. "Inherited *that* from her father! There are some things—if she had more hospitality, not be so tight with money. Well, if she were more appreciative and expressed her appreciation, I would be happier." Furthermore, "she could be with me two or three hours a day. That is all I want." Earlier discussions of this case have already suggested how Mrs. Trocopian's expectations for her older years differ radically from the usual American pattern, because her birth and early experiences in Armenia still exert a strong influence upon her hopes to crown a lifetime of subservience and thwarted desire with great achievements.

In the cases of both these women, we find a generational conflict due to acculturation, but in the first case, it is the *parent* who is more acculturated than the children, while in the Trocopian case (more to usual expectations), it is the *children* who have embraced the American mode of treating their aged parents. Mrs. Valente is more marginal to her native culture than her sons, possibly because of her more intimate exposure to Anglo ways. Her sons, however, remain in the subculture, apparently reluctant to surrender any of the advantages conferred there on male status. For her part, Mrs. Valente is only too glad to relinquish the dependency required of females in the parent culture, while Mrs. Trocopian is desperate to revive the prerogatives reserved for women in hers.

Mr. Harry Hokusai (CS) is also caught between two cultures in his old age. Born in a rural village of northern Japan in 1890, Mr. Hokusai was adopted into the prominent Hokusai family, because the "real son" was "physically and mentally weak." As the chosen heir of his adopted family, Mr. Hokusai was raised in a prosperous, progressive household. His foster-mother spoke French and his foster-father was involved in international trade. Mr. Hokusai was exposed to Western culture early through tutors who trained him intensively in French and English. Between the ages of eighteen and twenty-two, he studied at Kyoto University, majoring in political science and economics in preparation for a future position in his foster-father's business concern. "My parents were very proud of me," Mr. Hokusai says. "They thought I was showing them much respect with the grades and praise I attained." In 1913, his foster-father sent him to San Francisco with the inten-

tion of his gaining business experience with a foster-uncle before
returning to Japan. Shortly after his arrival, however, Mr. Hokusai
suffered the sharpest discontinuity of his life: his foster-father at
home in Japan went bankrupt and, soon thereafter, suffered a
stroke from which he died. Almost immediately after this, his
foster-mother died. Short of funds, Mr. Hokusai could not return
to his homeland to perform the proper obsequies of the dutiful
son. Because of this, he is acutely conscious that he has failed in
his duty to his adoptive parents, considering this failure the greatest blemish on his otherwise honorable existence.

In 1921, Mr. Hokusai married after a period of apprenticeship
in his foster-uncle's import-export house. During the next five
years, he sired three daughters whom he dearly loved ("It is the
fulfillment of life to have children—to have children is the fruit
of a married tie and of life"), but he would have more dearly
loved to have had a son. For a time, he contemplated adopting
one from Japan, but finally decided against this. In effect, he is
allowing the Hokusai name to die out in this country in a way
which seems a poignant acquiescence to American values. However, as we shall see, a grandson has since been born and this has
been the greatest fulfillment of his life: "To see your fruits produce new fruits and enrich you! Another addition to my fortune
in life!"

As a member of the Issei (first) generation of Japanese in
America, Mr. Hokusai has been very anxious to preserve Japanese
culture and traditions within his community. "Betterment of the
community" is, for him, a natural outgrowth of his desires for
"the betterment of the family." He would like to see the perpetuation of "respect," "proper behavior," "betterment," and "success"
—the noblest ideals of his life and culture—into the Nisei (second)
and Sansei (third) generations of Japanese in America, but he is
also aware that intergenerational differences are rapidly widening
under the influence of American folkways. While he is immensely
proud of his daughters and despite the importance of his grandchildren, he foresees difficulties were he to live with them: "If we
lived with them, my wife and I might hurt their feelings, for we
might act and behave so different from them because of our
Japanese ways." The obverse of this would, of course, be equally

true. In the last analysis, the Hokusais have resigned themselves to the American pattern of separate households for the generations.

We shall conclude this discussion of relationships with children by looking briefly at those in our sample who have tried to renew contact with offspring they rejected, abandoned, or neglected in earlier periods of their lives. Within this group, we also include those without progeny (mostly men) who have developed keen regrets at this time for never having had children at all. Both of these wistful types seem to have been individuals early animated by strong drives for achievement which, still unfulfilled after a lifetime, have aroused yearnings for "something real to leave behind," as one subject explained it.

As noted, Mr. Butler (CS) was a man of several ambitions—scholar, schoolteacher, real estate entrepreneur, and master-mind of "big-deals"—but, also, he has been consistently blithe in his responsibilities as a husband and family-man, preferring the thrills of amorous conquests over the rewards of paternity. He is very frank about his cavalier approach to life: "Up until recently, I never thought there was an end to time. I thought I was ageless and never considered anything else." Mr. Butler waited to marry until the age of forty-three and, even then, did not reside with his wife (seeing her only on weekends) until he was fifty-eight. This couple never had children: "Not having children is really my tragedy—one way I really missed out." However, Mr. Butler's thoughts are reverting more and more to a child in Europe, reputedly sired by him while there on a study-trip. He is not absolutely certain that this girl is his daughter, but, as he says, he now wants to play the role of father so badly that he has finally decided to send her some money, put her through school, and openly acknowledge his paternity. He describes her in glowing terms as a very slim, attractive, young lady now, and Mr. Butler has recently been making efforts to find out if her immigration to the United States is possible.

Mr. Avery Jackson (HS), also introduced in another context, had shown in his past great resourcefulness and flexibility in his pursuits, tackling whatever work came his way with high interest and energy. He has worked as a salesman, a promoter of charitable

organizations, a labor contractor, and a member of a chamber of
commerce. So important to him were these pursuits that he almost casually abandoned his first wife and two children somewhere in the Midwest. During his middle years, he turned his
hand to more stable employment in a municipal department.
Upon the death of his second wife, when he was fifty-nine, Mr.
Jackson's drinking habits became uncontrollable. Brought low by
this alcoholism and a severe deterioration of his physical health (a
liver ailment, cancer, and heart trouble), he voluntarily sought
treatment in a state mental hospital. When interviewed in 1963,
he was a desperate man, tortured by thoughts that he had wasted
the one life given to him, that he had not made the most of his
potential and had not planned wisely for his old age.

Though his downhill progress began only in his late fifties, he
now condemns his whole existence, minimizing his achievements
and repudiating his former pleasures. As a terminal cancer patient, he is keenly aware of imminent extinction. But, despite a
loyal woman friend and his increasing participation in church
activities, Mr. Jackson is distressed by feelings of isolation, rootlessness, and futility. His thoughts now turn to a son he sired
in his first marriage whom he has not seen in forty years. He is
determined to locate him and reestablish parental ties with him.
He feels he will then and only then be able to come to terms with
life and his own impending death. This alone will resolve his
isolation and the harrowing thoughts that he has accomplished
nothing at all with his life. "Well," he says, "I sure would like to
see those kids I left while they were still little tykes, I can tell you
that!" Then he adds, "Yessiree, I'd sure like to contact those kids.
You know, I haven't seen them for more than forty years. I'm
going to do something. [What about expected changes in your
life?] Well, that's the only thing that would make any real change
in my life right now." Somewhat later in the interview, he makes
the decision: "Yes, I'm going to contact my son." He is curious to
see how this stranger, his son, has developed: "I'd like him to be
a decent man, and I hope he has a family. I hope he's not a politi-
cian. I hope he has the ability to speak as well as I can, or to write
a speech." But, curiously, Mr. Jackson has so far made no realistic
effort to reach his son, which suggests some ambivalence under-

lying his fervently-expressed desires. He cannot dismiss the nagging thought that he might possibly be an unwelcome stranger in his son's home. After all, he had abandoned him. Then, again, he fancies that his son would "most certainly" insist upon his father's going to live with him at his home in New Orleans, and Mr. Jackson would not want that. In discussing his burial plans, he states categorically that he is going to be buried in San Francisco, "unless, of course, my son gets hold of me and takes me back to New Orleans." This, then, is his excuse for not contacting his son: "That's why I'm afraid to write him."

The pathetic efforts of these aging prodigals to reconcile themselves with their castoff children remind us of the frequent efforts the elderly make to round out their lives, resolving old worries, and closing up long-open wounds. We have repeatedly encountered in these reports statements such as: "I'd sure like to hear from old Charlie before I die," suggesting that reminiscence among the aged often springs from a deep-seated need to make of one's life a comprehensible whole.

Grandfathers and Grandmothers

Much to our surprise, the status of grandparent appears to be a largely inactive one. But in light of our findings that an ever-widening gulf separates elderly parents from their own mature children, an even greater distance from the third generation seems a natural consequence. Another thing contributes to widening the distance: often the very old and the very young do not make good company. For the very old, young children about for too long a time can become irritating and confusing. In the case of adolescent children, an intense interest in peer-group relationships isolates them from both parents and grandparents. Because of these factors, grandchildren figure but slightly in the narrative reports of our subjects.

Mrs. Langtry (CS) witnesses to the fact that grandchildren can be rather exhausting at times for older people. She partially attributes her good relationships wtih her grandchildren to the fact that "we are not in the same town. If I lived in Sacramento with them [as she did at one time], maybe there would be more things to find fault with." She does, however, see them on occa-

sions ("every six weeks") and it is "a delightful experience,"
though she will admit she gets easily ". . . worn out. They're very
good children, but in a small apartment . . .!" Mr. Knight (CS)
describes his experiences with six grandchildren as "perfectly
wonderful," but he makes it clear that his encounters with them
are brief: "My relations are very casual—just whenever I'm there
visiting their parents. Then I see them for a few minutes. Just
happy experiences. How can you get cross with *that* kind of deal?"
Similarly, Mr. Ritter (HS) claims he has always enjoyed his association with his grandchildren but admits: "The older I get, the
less I like to see them—not too often." He explains the reason
why: "Well, they're very active, you're inactive, and there's a
clash—inevitably." As a final instance of the stresses inherent in
the grandparent-grandchild roles, we cite a little episode in the
life of Mrs. Tillford, who, at sixty-five, was babysitting with her
granddaughter when we came to call on her for an interview. She
was quite harassed with her job: "When you have grandchildren
around, you've got to keep moving! [Here subject went to rescue
fifteen-month-old granddaughter from falling off a porch (*interviewer's comment*).] I wonder why my hair's not as white as this
white sweater. They scare the breath right out of you!"

The even further estrangement of the old from their adolescent grandchildren is attested to by Mr. Southern (CS), who says
at sixty-nine: "As you get older, you like small children more,
because the older children don't like to be bothered with older
people." As these children advance in years, the earlier aura they
might have perceived to surround the awesome personnages of
their grandparents begins to dim. The grandfolks do not seem to
be as competent as they were. The youngsters begin to notice
their old-fashioned ways and might even begin to think of their
grandparents as "old fuddy-duddys." Thus, Mrs. Burbank (CS)
complains of her granddaughter. Mrs. Burbank lives with this
granddaughter and her own daughter who is divorced and blind.
"I still love being a grandmother," she says, but she adds that
she was happiest in this role only up until the girl turned twelve.
"I used to enjoy taking her places," she says, "and she was very
companionable, but in high school she was very difficult." Often—
as in this case—when a relationship with a grandchild had been

deeply felt, estrangement during the child's teen-age years can be experienced as a serious loss: "My granddaughter was a very warm outgoing young child, but now she doesn't even know me. There was a time when I was home with my grandchild all day. We were very close, but her mother was jealous of me. Now, whenever she comes home on a weekend from college and I try to ask her how she's doing in school, sometimes she doesn't even bother answering me. I realize there is a large difference between her age and mine, but I have gone through many things and I could help her in some of her problems, but I don't have the chance to do so. She seems more like a stranger than a grandchild." During later interviews, Mrs. Burbank's granddaughter had even ceased to drop by on weekends: "She used to write once a month and now it's only holidays. She doesn't say much about herself." Mrs. Miller (CS) concurs: "As grandchildren grow older, they have other interests. They forget about you. They figure you're old." Sometimes, even the grandfathers complain of the widening distance: "They know I am 'grandfather,' but that's about all. They don't see me often enough to play with me."

Not all members of our sample, however, fare so poorly with their grandchildren. Some find in them a source of pride: "I love them as much as before—in fact, more now—because, as they grow up, you really enjoy them. The girl, aged twelve, is very smart. My relationship with all of them has stayed the same and is improving all the time." Others seem to find a deepening of the relationship through the years: "As time goes on and they are more understanding, I enjoy them more and like to sit down and have a discussion with them."

Our male subjects tend to feel that the happiest time of being a grandparent is at the birth of their first grandchild. One subject put it succinctly: [Happiest time when being a grandfather?] "When they were born." Another speaks of the moment with almost a sense of awe: "The most satisfying time of my life was when I first touched my first grandchild." Another speaks of the event as something like love-at-first-sight: "When the first grandchild was born, she was the most beautiful-looking child you have ever seen: beautiful red hair, small mouth, small nose, pretty face."

As for the grandmothers, one outstanding trait of theirs is to live vicariously through a granddaughter. In some instances, the granddaughter assumes the most significant role in the older woman's relationships. She is the one person the grandmother feels closest to. Frequently, this intense a relationship develops when others are not of the best. Mrs. Trocopian (HS) says: "But Lillian [granddaughter, aged nineteen] is different—appreciative, thoughtful. I look forward when she comes for lunch. She began to appreciate me after fourteen. Lillian means the whole world to me today. She fills the whole world for me. She's about ninety per cent me." So, too, Mrs. Sandusky (HS) is eager to list the accomplishments of her granddaughter and comments: "I guess my grandchildren are my life. I let my heart rule my head sometimes." She hopes that this favorite granddaughter will go to a college in the vicinity and live with her. Mrs. Sandusky considers her to be the one person she feels closest to, next to her sons. As she says with pride: "All her life I've been able to see her and all her accomplishments."

This close relationship between grandfather and grandson does not seem to obtain, probably because the instrumental accomplishments and technical knowledge which elderly men can impart to today's youth are outdated. This, however, is not as true for the emotional and interrelational concerns of women. Cultural changes in these areas of life come much more slowly and, consequently, grandmothers are better able to be useful and give guidance to their granddaughters. Mrs. Miller (CS) points up all these aspects rather well. Increasingly isolated and lonely, this woman shrinks from imposing herself on her own children but does feel quite close to her youngest granddaughter, aged seventeen. "I can see her going through some of the same things I did. She is interested in sewing and some of the same things I am. I like Betty coming here the best. I think she is more dependent on me. The rest of the grandchildren are more self-sufficient."

Brothers and Sisters

By far, the most common kinship status sustained by our subjects is that of sibling. We have already seen that, in our community intensive sample, only 38 per cent have living spouses and

61 per cent have children, but fully 93 per cent have living siblings. (Proportions in the hospital sample are not as great but parallel.) However, the specific nature of these sibling relationships, the degrees of intimacy and mutual support or dependency and interaction show great variation, ranging from almost complete estrangement to a pivotal relationship, crucial to the individual's well-being. Almost all subjects were able to list the whereabouts of their siblings and, even where communication was minimal—either because of geographical distance, diversity in life styles, or separations in young adulthood—subjects managed to keep themselves well informed and were especially aware of the time of their deaths. The old keep close watch on the depletion of their ranks.

During young adulthood and the middle years, the family of orientation fades in significance with the formation of a new nuclear family. With the advent of old age, the earlier loyalties are frequently reactivated and sought after. One advantage here is that these relationships do not require continued validation. The closest alliances with siblings occur when both lack an immediate family. Examples of the co-residence of siblings (six in the intensive sample) are only between siblings who have been single, divorced, or widowed. Otherwise, interaction with siblings in old age is dependent on marital status and the closeness of either sibling to his or her own children. Generally, siblings are of lesser importance to the elderly married or to the widowed individual who has a positive relationship with his or her children.

Many of the same objections that enter into residing with one's married children also enter into the decision to take up joint residence with one's married siblings. In American culture, any co-residence with a married couple—be it with one's child, sibling, or friend—becomes an unwieldy *ménage à trois,* an intrusion into basic privacies. The troubles with sons- and daughters-in-law can be equally matched in sister- and brother-in-law conflicts. For the most part, widowed aged subjects first turn to their married children for comfort and support, but when this is impossible, they will turn to their siblings.

In old age, more effort is made to visit siblings, even when they live at great distances. We have been struck by the relative frequency of contact with them within the five-year period preceding interview. The majority of those subjects who have siblings living outside the state—often in the Midwest or even further away on the East Coast—have seen these relatives within the five-year period preceding the interview. And this has not been limited to only those enjoying higher socioeconomic status. We lack systematic data on the frequency of contact before this period, but we are led to suspect that this frequency represents an increase. To a certain extent, this frequency is related to retirement. The increase in leisure time permits lengthier trips than one could afford to take earlier. But the motive for these trips is mixed; siblings alone do not provide the spur to travel. Extended trips are probably the singly, most valued diversion reported by our sample. For many, a restlessness follows upon retirement, an urge to break through the boundaries circumscribed by the duties of work and the raising of children. Many experience a revivification of youthful needs to explore the farthest reaches of their environment. Visits to relatives can often afford anchoring points on these extended trips and, incidentally, buttress the motivation so that these odysseys will not be undertaken for purely hedonistic reasons. It is a "duty" to visit one's relatives, but also one "had better" for the chance may never come again. For these reasons, there is much visiting back and forth across the continent during these years.

Siblings are mentioned in the interviews more spontaneously when current social horizons are narrower than usual. Even where siblings live at great distance and personal contact has been little, subjects will mention that, in case of dire need, a sibling could provide a permanent home. In this regard, siblings were mentioned more frequently than friends and less frequently than children, but there seems to be not as great a feeling of "being a burden" with siblings. Thus, Mr. Butler (CS) at first states that he wouldn't ask his relatives to provide him with a home, should he ever be in need of such assistance, but then recalls that there is a brother he could go to. Similarly, Miss Mable Wimsatt (CS), when asked if there is anyone she could turn to if she were ever to need care for a long time, responds: "Yes, a younger sister has a room. I could go there." There are indications that siblings will often extend invitations to their widowed brothers and sisters to come and stay with them, but these are unwillingly accepted if the sibling happens to be married. In this fashion, Mrs. Bruzinsky (CS) reports: "In the last two years, I went back to see my sister in New York. She and her husband live there now with their daughter. They were wonderful and happy, but they have each other and I felt odd being a third person around them, so, in a way, I was glad to leave"—this, despite the information that she feels closest to this sister. The same feelings are expressed by Mr. Alioto (HS) at seventy-seven: "I have a brother across the Bay. They want me to live with them. But I hate to butt into their married life." In both of these cases, the individuals have withdrawn from any deepening of the relationship at great personal sacrifice: Mrs. Bruzinsky lives in the household of her married son where she feels unhappy and unwelcome; Mr. Alioto was, at the time, living alone and isolated in a shabby hotel room.

Some reports suggest that a sibling enmity might be influencing this reluctance to reside with brothers or sisters. Mrs. Harris (HS) hints at this. Following the death of her husband, Mrs. Harris spent three years in a county nursing home and, after a brief subsequent sojourn in a state hospital, she was returned to the community where she now lives alone. This woman has lived as a rebel against her narrow, middle-class, dogmatically religious background. By contrasting herself with her siblings who remained within the confines of these values, she insists that her life has been more enjoyable. She derides her relatives for their stuffiness and their preoccupation with home and possessions, but, at the same time, she traces all her misfortunes, shortcomings, and ill-considered choices of action to her abiding resentments against her family. At sixty-six, she muses: "I think both my sisters believe I would like to live with them, but I would rather go back to an institution. Not that we don't love each other, but we wouldn't want to live together. I think I'll write my one sister. She will be happier if she knew I don't want her to invite me over to live with her."

Cases of sibling rivalry are not rare in our sample and are often voiced with resentment against parental favoritism or injustice or jealousy because of a difference of socioeconomic status:

"My sister in St. Louis—I wouldn't cross her door-step"; or: "My own brother, here in San Francisco—I dislike him"; or: "Older sister, she's all right, but the younger one—ugh! She's stuck up. She don't bother with us and we don't bother with her."

In contrast with these examples of enmity and estrangement are those where siblings draw close in old age, usually where subjects now lack intimate bonds. Sibling solidarity occurs especially when one is having difficulties with the environment, and the stronger or more fortunate will generally offer a home to the less fortunate, though there is often reluctance to accept such an offer. We have seen how Mrs. Langtry (CS) was quite unprepared for living alone or earning a living for herself when she was widowed at the age of sixty-four. Attempts to live with either of her two married children proved to be very stressful and she was lucky to have a single sister, ten years her junior and drawing a good salary, to come to her aid. While her sister was overseas, Mrs. Langtry took care of the apartment and later, when her sister returned to the city, Mrs. Langtry stayed on and set up a division of labor with her—Mrs. Langtry doing all the housework while her sister earned the livelihood. Despite a vast difference in economic status and age between the two sisters, self-respect and closeness was maintained by these individual contributions to the home. This period of Mrs. Langtry's life lasted for eight years.

Perhaps Mrs. Langtry was able to accept this dependence willingly because, in her youth, she had had to take care of her sister. According to her, she was largely responsible for raising her sister: "I was ten and just the right age to look after my sister when she was born. Mama took me and my sister to a resort and I was the nurse. I just felt like she was mine. I brought her up almost." For her part, the sister seemed honor-bound to reciprocate these early favors: "It seemed wise to establish this home for her." When Mrs. Langtry was considering remarriage, she told her suitor that she had to consider her sister's wishes in making of her decision: "I told him I felt obligated to look after my sister."

Mr. Monroe Ableson's (HS) siblings also came to his rescue in a desperate hour. This man had pursued an earlier pattern of life characterized by frequent changes of locale, job instability, and an early divorce after a very brief marriage. By the time of his forties, he had lost all track of his siblings. These lived in San Francisco and, when Mr. Ableson was fifty-nine, they made a concerted effort to reestablish contact with him. They found him in Los Angeles, "living all alone," alcoholic, and anxious for his survival. His siblings—a brother who ran a shoeshine concession and a divorced older sister—begged Mr. Ableson to abandon his life in Los Angeles and live with them: "My brother kept asking me to come up here to San Francisco. Came on a vacation and never did go back. I didn't know whether I was going to stay or not. My brother said he wanted me to help him in his shoeshine business. I came up here and went to work for him." Mr. Ableson's difficulties were not completely resolved with this move. His drinking persisted and eventually led to his voluntary commitment to a state hospital. It was during this crucial period that his brother and sister benefited him most with their continued loyalty and financial aid. Once Mr. Ableson became eligible for Social Security, his morale improved and he stopped drinking—an achievement he extolled continually during all of his intensive interviews. After a life of exertion and movement, he seems happy today to settle into a life of inactivity, passivity, and relative comfort. Though he never expressed missing his siblings during his young-adult and middle years, it is plain that Mr. Ableson welcomed the reestablishment of these ties in his later life. He appreciates now the affection they had maintained through the years.

Another exceptionally good example of family solidarity can be found in the case of Mr. Helmut Kreisler (HS). A bachelor for all his life, Mr. Kreisler, at sixty-five, is currently living with his brother and the latter's divorced son and grandsons. For the past sixteen years, this group has lived in separate units of the same apartment building. Mr. Kreisler spends much of his time in his brother's more spacious quarters, even taking his meals there: "We watch TV together. He does all the cooking and we split the bills."

Where a sense of family solidarity prevails but, for one reason or another, the more fortunate sibling cannot come to the aid of an unfortunate brother or sister, guilts develop. As one subject has phrased it: "I worry an awful lot about both of my sisters. I can't help it. I don't talk about it. I don't say things because both of them are in much poorer health than I am. I'm really bothered more by what I feel is my inadequacy to do something. I feel very much that I neglect the sister down the Peninsula, but I can't be there very long. She gets upset about things and I get upset to see her like that. I never know how she will take an innocent remark of mine. She is just miserable, I know. She sleeps in traction for months and has arthritis."

The death of a sibling may often shock an aging individual more deeply than the death of any other kind of kin, especially where the bonds of relationship had been strong. Such a loss brings home one's own limited existence with greater immediacy. One subject found this to be especially so: "Three years ago I lost my sister. She was close and helped me financially. There is just one sister left in a family of six. I am very alone. After my sister's funeral, I came back and took out all these things. I've tried to simplify my life as much as I can. I've done away with what I thought I had to have and had to do. I was never for material things too much. They are just in the way." This pruning away of material goods and simplification of one's life carry the buried suggestion of preparations for her own death. Something like this seems to be operating in the case of Mrs. Ellen Powers (HS), who, since seventy-three, had undergone a series of brief hospitalizations for depressive reactions. When probed on stressful events experienced after sixty, she replied, "My sister's sickness and death. I indirectly feel that was the beginning of all my troubles. She was the last member of my family." Somewhat later, she is reported to have said, "I haven't really gotten over my sister's illness. She died in 1954 when I was sixty-eight." Mrs. Power's husband is still alive and she comments expansively on his large and "wonderful" family—brothers, sisters, nephews, nieces—many of whom she likes very much and gets along well with: "My husband has oodles of them and they are lovely." However, when discussing how pleasant these in-law relatives are, she will add: "But I feel awfully lonesome sometimes. I have no one but one nephew, my sister's son, and I don't know his address." Since this subject is more than commonly proud of her ancestry, one can little doubt the sharpness of her distress at having so few consanguine kinships left.

To the foreign-born, sibling ties are especially important, particularly to the single, the widowed, or the childless. It is reassuring to think of siblings still living in the home country, when retirement, loneliness, old age, and isolation begin to haunt the immigrant to a new land. These relationships are always potential avenues for possible change or escape, should matters take a turn for the worse. In many instances, the immigrants have kept in touch with the home-country relatives, often assisting them financially, and, for this reason, they sometimes feel they would be well received there. Mr. Jacques Sablon (CS), at seventy-nine, recalls his native French village: "I write every month to my sisters and I get letters from them. That way I know if they need anything and I can help them. They are eighty. If I go back, I could go to the same house—just the same as I left it." Likewise, Mr. Louis Czernich (HS), a seventy-three-year-old Yugoslavian, dreams of home: "If I ever get sick and cannot take care of myself, I can always go to the Old Country." He, too, has been helping his brother and his brother's children in Yugoslavia. Despite the fact that Mr. Czernich is retired, he continues to scrape together enough funds not only to assist his brother but to donate money for the repair of the village church. In like fashion, Mr. Apostolos Phidrios (HS) feels the pull of his native land, Greece. Following the death of his wife in his late fifties, Mr. Phidrios turned to a close attachment with a brother who had immigrated with him, but this sibling, too, became ill and died eight years before our first interview with Mr. Phidrios. Now at seventy-seven, lonely, in very poor health himself, and suffering from a marked impairment in mental functioning, Mr. Phidrios' only expressed goal in 1961 was to return to Greece to finish out his days in the home of his only remaining brother. "Before I die," he is reported as saying, "I am going to see him." By 1963, this wish had come true, for the social interviewer assigned to this interview found him with plane tickets and traveling documents in hand, ready to depart for Greece. Mr. Phidrios had little doubt of his brother's good reception, but he was somewhat preoccupied with the living arrangements possible in his new home and was worried how he would get along with his sister-in-law. His brother had made Mr. Phidrios' stay contingent upon his getting along with his wife.

Summary of Kinship Roles

In our study of kinship roles in old age, we have found the possession of a spouse to be an asset in successfully maintaining an active, open interest in the social world. Through their wives, men can keep in touch with workaday activities, while women can draw from their husbands the emotional support they need in sustaining the living relationship. In fact, a spouse is the major social asset an individual can have at this time of life, but, unfortunately, it is a social advantage highly vulnerable to attrition, with consequences often disastrous for the ones who survive. Where a spouse is lost, an ability to substitute through remarriage is probably a sign of good adaptability (no hospital subject, in the intensive-study sample for example, was able to so replace a lost mate), but once again, women run a high risk in such marriages of undergoing anew the trials of nursing and bereavement. To a large extent, however, remarriage is not the usual mode of spouse-substitution—platonic relationships with "boy" and "girl" friends are. Where a well-functioning marriage has been perpetuated into old age, the capacity for erotic intimacy is likely to be sustained (albeit with some abatement of drive) even well into the late seventies. Where circumstances have earlier prevented the exercise of this function, we are likely to encounter either loss or disinterest in it entirely or—especially with the men—disturbances in other systems of the personality. A viable sexual functioning beyond eighty is rare.

Three factors seem to account for the intergenerational distance we have observed in this sample: (1) the high value placed on personal independence in American culture, with the result that the aged are encouraged to maintain households separate from their children and to revive relationships with collateral kin that more than likely had been left to lie fallow during the child-rearing years; (2) the rapid cultural change which modern society has undergone since the years when today's older generation were in their prime, with the result that the elderly of 1966 seem very "old-fashioned" and "obsolete" to the younger generations; and (3) the process of acculturation which, in first- and second-generation American families, can create conflicts of expectations in behavioral norms.

FRIENDS AND NEIGHBORS

Because the ties of kinship can be either nominal or strongly binding, they are a poor index of an individual's optimum functioning in the social system. Occupancy of the status of friend, however, provides an excellent indicator of one's articulation with social reality. This status is occupied with as great a frequency as that of sibling, and these two occur with significantly greater frequency than any of the other six statuses studied. Theoretically at least, the possibility of friendship remains open to older persons long after the roles of spouse, worker, churchgoer, and organization member have been closed to them through illness or disability. Certainly, being a friend requires less physical energy than is required for these other statuses and may allow for much greater passivity. While it may not always provide security, it is often a source of greater companionship than is provided by any of the other social positions except that of spouse.

In the intensive sample, female subjects have significantly more friends than male subjects: of the twenty-two female subjects, half have either no or few (one or two) friends and a like proportion have three or more; among the thirty-two males, over three-fourths have no or few friends. Assuming that the ties of friendship are more crucial for individuals lacking kinship support, number of friends was examined in relation to the availability of kinship support. We found that the availability of kinship ties does not affect friendship patterns: there is no greater cultivation of friends where marriage or kinship ties are absent. On the other hand, while the presence of kin often makes for a sense of security, it does not necessarily satisfy all needs for companionship. Eighteen subjects (slightly better than a third) expressed dissatisfaction with the nature of their social interaction and, included in this group are a number of individuals who are married and also some whose degree of social activity with other kinsmen is high.

How do our older subjects define friendship? We asked them

to describe actual friends and to specify their criteria for friendship and, in both instances, stress was laid upon two qualities: a friend's readiness to be of assistance and certain other worthwhile personality traits. Friends were defined as persons: "who will come to your aid whenever you need help . . . who will come forward when needed . . . who will come and do some thing for you . . . who are very good about running errands for you when you are ill . . . who loan you money . . . who are good to you." Other types of response emphasized not so much what a friend could *do* but what he could *be*: "pretty good characters . . . sensible—have their feet on the ground . . . interesting, amiable, congenial . . . real good company, nice people, have a good time together." In the main, sensibleness was the most favored quality and congeniality second. In general, subjects stressed either the dependability for support when in distress or the pleasing companionship with like-minded individuals—few referring to both at the same time.

These descriptions, however, emphasize ideal conditions and do not necessarily reflect the actual friendships made by the subjects of our sample. Within the limits of circumstances, our subjects, when asked to cite friends, showed an enormous elasticity in applying the term to actual people. Some were relationships that were quite obviously close, marked with mutual understanding and concern; others more like acquaintances gathered at semi-formal affairs for the sake of sociability; others no more than persons one had known by name for a number of years in brief and frequent encounters, exchanging friendly banter and congeniality. As an example of this last type, we can cite Mr. Merton Fox (CS), a lifelong itinerant, who now, at the age of eighty-three, still has a part-time job selling newspapers on a street corner. His customers come to mind when asked to name his friends: "When they see me, they say, 'Hi ya, Foxy—think you're gonna live to be a hundred years old!' " Another friend "comes up to see me once a week at the stand." When asked to name the person he feels closest to, he names the owner of a jewelry store: "He likes me," he says. "He'd go to bat for me any time. He comes by the newspaper stand and talks to me all the time." Similarly, Mr.

Helmut Kreisler (HS) will speak of the tenants of the apartment building in which he collects rent as "friends" and will add, "I have quite a few men friends, but I never associate with them." These attitudes are generally typical for single males of low socio-economic status. A contrast is Mr. Knight (CS), an alert and affluent subject who is prominent in community affairs and very conscious of the responsibilities of his wealth. Mr. Knight has great freedom of choice in the amount of social activity he will participate in and places a very circumscribed meaning to the term, "friend." He denies he has any: "Never had bosom friends that you can call up in the middle of the night. Plenty of associations—wonderful always. I like people—don't expect anything of them, nor should they expect anything of you. Only maintained when it is convenient all around. When people hear you have pneumonia, they will call up and will do anything. But I don't call that friendship, though some would." Mr. Knight's attitude, however, is atypical for the majority of our subjects who cannot be as indifferent as he to friends. For them, the presence or absence of friends has great bearing upon their enjoyment of life.

Behind these two definitions of friendship lie some very interesting sex differences in the perceptions of "friend." For example, female subjects speak at greater length of their friends and appear to place greater value on such relationships. They are frank in expressing their dependency on friends, the importance of having them, and their loneliness without them. Mrs. Bruzinsky (CS) has a number of friends and many social engagements and freely admits: "Yet now I feel I need more friends than ever before. I am lonely now and could use some real close friends." For Miss Potter (HS), dynamic, youthful friends are important for reflecting the youthful image she has of herself: "People who want to be on the go." Women place high value on their friendships and strive to continue the contact. As Miss Potter put it: "I used to take friendship for granted as my due. Now I have to earn it, if I am to have it." After losing her friends, Miss Wimsatt (CS) "realized you have to make an effort to meet people more than half-way." In contrast with these attitudes, elderly men rarely express such feelings and their attitude toward friends, on the whole, appears to be considerably more passive. In part, their lesser need for friends may be due to the greater number of them who are married. Conjugal status permits them to reserve active social interaction for their wives and to participate—perhaps only passively—in the social activities their spouses might design. Yet this social reticence is not without its misgivings. Men, particularly, are somewhat embarrassed to reveal their isolation, implying, perhaps, feelings of stigma at the absence of friends. As we have already seen in the case of Mr. Knight, elderly men will sometimes feel compelled to justify a lack of friends by indicating that such is of their own choosing, or that they are highly selective, or that they prefer to devote their time to other things, or merely that the people within their reach do not meet their high standards. Finally, narrative material relative to friendship indicates that older women will express their sociability more via the telephone or letter-writing than will the men. Men are more apt to lose contact with old friends through their reluctance to keep up correspondence.

There appears to be little exploration for new friends among these aged subjects. When asked to name friends and specify the duration they had known them, the majority of our subjects listed persons they had known from ten to twenty or more years. Very rarely was any individual listed as a friend who had been known for a shorter period of time. A certain pride is involved in having known the friend for so long a time and, again, the reason is trustworthiness. And while the satisfaction with old friends eliminates the necessity of forming new ones, it also suggests that elderly subjects are, on the whole, not very able to form close relationships in old age. On the basis of these many friends of long duration, it appears that friendship among the aged is largely a matter of carrying over the relationships formed during the middle years of life. Additionally, whatever new friendships are made during the later years tend to be with individuals considerably younger than the subject. This is possibly a reflection of the older person's need for someone capable of handling the environment, but we believe it also mirrors the rather negative attitude some of our subjects have toward the "average" aged individual. Thus, Mrs. Miller (CS), at seventy-three, remarks: "I'm not too anxious to mingle with people my age. They just talk about aches and pains. I feel I can't learn anything from them. They don't know about anything else." Only a minority of subjects comment on the preferred age of their friends, but those who do are likely to prefer people younger than themselves. Very few would agree with Mr. Welton Spicer (CS) who, when sixty-four, said, "As you grow older, you like to associate more with people your own age. Some people, as they grow older, associate only with a younger crowd. They don't want to admit that they are growing old. Not me. I'm no longer a young man and I know it."

When aging individuals lose the ability to forge new relationships with others, attrition in the ranks of friends results, even as kinships are lost and unreplaced. For almost half the subjects in the sample—men as well as women—death is the thief of friendships in old age. They go unreplaced and reports of the loss carry a certain burden of finality. These things are to be expected. To be left without friends is an inevitable concomitant of growing old. The women say: "Two of my best friends passed away this year . . . I had good friends until they moved away or passed away. . . . I just have my sister's friends." The men take up much the same refrain: "I haven't any close friends. We had about four, five, six friends, but they all died in the last year or so. . . . Right now, I have the smallest number of close friends I've ever had." Mr. Louis Czernich (HS) was quite philosophic about it: "If a friend dies, you can see him no more. For some friends who have died, I feel sorry. But it is no use to feel sorry. We all have to go some time and time changes everything."

Replacing friends lost through death is generally acknowledged by these old people to be difficult. Many would like to but —because of a decrease in energy or restrictions on mobility or shrinking funds or the shortage of time—they find they cannot. Nonetheless, they admire those who do. Miss Mildred Barton (CS), a retired schoolteacher, remarks at the age of sixty-nine that she is "simply appalled" at the number of her pupils who have died. She feels that her sister has the best advice about replacing these friends: "My oldest sister says you have to cultivate friends of a young age too, because those you have known for a long time die, and it's very hard on some people." Miss Barton admits not "cultivating" her friends sufficiently of late and marvels at her sister's "remarkable" ability to do so.

Elderly people make other kinds of apologies to themselves and others for their decreasing interaction with friends. It is because they often live in "different parts of the city" that friends are "scattered all over San Francisco." Some subjects complain about the problems of transportation or their reluctance to expose themselves to lengthy trips, mounting and dismounting buses and streetcars and transferring to other lines across the city. The single and widowed express their reluctance to visit friends who still are married: "To their homes I don't want to go. They have their own families." One single man is quite uncomfortable in such situations: "I could go visit a married friend of mine, but if there's a husband and wife, you're a third party. Husband doesn't want you around." Among friends the distinction between the married and unmarried becomes keener with age.

Also, we note rationalizations of a change in economic status, usually for the worse. This drop in purchasing power results in a forced reorientation in patterns of entertainment, an inability to reciprocate social invitations, the breaking of ties with those who have not experienced the same kind of change, and a limiting of new friends to those in the same status. Mrs. Miller (CS) is losing friends because "my place is so shabby now. I hate to have people in. Being a friend is a little more difficult now because the only way I can reciprocate is to take them *out* to a dinner." Mrs. Bennington (CS) also finds it difficult to keep up her end of a friendship: "If you're invited out, you should reciprocate. You just don't accept as many invitations, because you're not able or don't feel like it and you can't afford to. If I go out, we each pay our own way." Thus, inadequacy of living quarters often forces older people to restrict their meetings with friends to public places. Lowered income forces a restriction on entertainment of one's friends. Under these circumstances the social horizons of the old become delimited.

Finally, the elderly excuse attrition in their friendships by pointing to changes in style of living brought on by illnesses or accidents resulting in self-devaluation as someone who is unworthy or too old to have friends. In this regard, Mr. Hopland (HS) has drifted into social backwaters because of an accident which left him slightly crippled and lost him his job. He thinks of the old days when he "always had good friends" in contrast with now when he has "no friends since I got hurt. We moved so much nobody knows where me and my wife live." In similar fashion, Mr. Mersky (CS) is very bitter now about his former friends: "They were friends when I was rich. I don't believe in friendship anymore. I don't want anybody."

Mr. Butler (CS) was quite candid with us on how his decline in self-esteem since recognizing his age and failures has served to make him want to withdraw from friendly contacts. He wrestles with these problems in morbid introspection and self-condemnation: "Since I've gone through a period of self-evaluation, I think I never felt less important to people as a friend than I do right now. I think my desirability as a friend has diminished in the past two or three years. They see me as a disappointment, for they think I could have amounted to more and made more money than I did. This may be a projection on my part, but I feel they see through my phony dress, the false front that I present to the world."

For the very reasons that Mr. Butler wants to disengage himself from his circle of friends, others feel impelled to seek out new and fresh friends—to escape from oneself, to flee from dissatisfaction with one's environment, to find someone to reaffirm one's worth. This reaching out for a new social milieu is often articulated as a desire to move into a completely new setting: a trailer court or a retirement community. One woman mentions a "lonely" friend of hers who had the "happiest time" after moving into such an intentional community of old folks: "I know a woman who went there and loved it. Now she goes to dances, plays cards, and she's seventy-two!"

Ofttimes a decrease in interaction with friends is not necessarily felt to be a painful loss. Gerontological research has come to

tag such people as "voluntary disengagers" (see especially Lowenthal and Boler, 1965) and most of them consider their withdrawal
as part of the normal course of events in growing old. Miss Barton (CS) is one to feel the loss without regret: "I admit I haven't
kept up with my friends as much. Suddenly I noticed I was just
seeing people less." So, too, Mr. Hokusai (CS) has limited his
activities in community welfare organizations in order to allocate
his decreasing energy more efficiently to the family business. "To
have good friends, you must meet frequently," he states. This
drop in his social contacts, however, does not bother him overly
much. In this context, it should be pointed out that these individuals who disengage voluntarily are not necessarily social isolates. Frequently, they have always entertained large numbers of
friends, have enjoyed a solid family life, and are blessed with a
wealth of personal and economic resources. They are not individuals at a loss to know what to do with themselves.

In summary, intensive community subjects, both male and
female, list greater numbers in their inventory of friends than do
the hospitalized. So, too, the mentally healthy seem to be the only
subjects capable of making new friends. Several of the community
men exemplify great flexibility at winning new friends in their
old age. Many of the women, too, entertain large circles of friends,
sometimes despite severe physical limitations. Community women
are also more articulate about loneliness or their lack of companionship.

In contrast with community males, *not a single discharged or
hospitalized man in the intensive sample can point to a close
relationship with a friend.* Whenever these men speak of their
social interactions, the liaison seems purely tangential or circumstantial; however, a large proportion of them have wives or relatives to whom they could turn in cases of emergency. The hospitalized or discharged women appear to do a little better at
maintaining a set of friends; some report few friends but rely
heavily upon relatives for social sustenance. Miss Potter is the
only woman in the sample who approaches the kind of social isolation we have seen with the hospitalized or discharged men.

ORGANIZATION MEMBERS AND VOLUNTEERS

One of the most outstanding features of modern American social organization is the proliferation of voluntary associations. So pervasive is this pattern that foreign visitors to this country have been led to believe that American democracy is built upon these voluntary associations in much the same way as patrilineal clans structured the society of old China or as caste groups do today in India (Hsu, 1963). In fact, we shall see that America's aged also feel obliged to participate in the social world through these clubs and associations and the mentally well and ill among their numbers are distinguished by the degree in which they do this.[12]

Occupancy of the status of organization member in the intensive-study sample sharply differentiates the community and hospital subjects (both inpatients and dischargees). While the discharged tend to occupy a midway position between community and inpatient subjects for the majority of the eight statuses, in the occupancy of organization member the discharged more closely approximate the inpatients and differ significantly from community residents. Additionally, organization membership varies with sex and marital status: almost two-thirds of the male community residents are organization members, while only two-fifths of the community females are; and similar proportions prevail between the married (almost two-thirds) and the unmarried (almost two-fifths). The sex differences seem largely attributable to union membership, for if we examine membership in organizations other than unions, these differences tend to disappear.

These differences between the psychiatrically well and ill represent lifelong patterns of nonaffiliation *vs.* affiliation, rather than changes occurring with the onset of old age. Significant differences were found in earlier affiliations: three-fourths of the community males had participated in nonunion organizations

---

[12]A good survey of recent research in this area of voluntary associations and the aged can be found in Rose (1960). Wilensky (1961) casts his study in terms of some very intriguing hypotheses relating life cycle and participation in formal organizations.

earlier than age sixty as compared with only about half of the discharged males; nearly three-fifths of the community females had participated as compared with only half of the discharged females.

Memberships do decline with age, however, and this holds for union and nonunion memberships, for men as well as women. The drop in nonunion affiliations with age seems to be more marked among men than among women; that is, we find that women at this age tend to drop out of organizations less frequently than men at this age.

But there are some who *increase* organizational affiliation in old age. In our intensive-study sample, six people did so—five community subjects and one hospital dischargee. These late-life joiners, as well as those who devote more time in old age to such activities, are the better educated, or those of higher socioeconomic status, in other words, middle-class people. All had participated—not necessarily regularly and sometimes briefly—in organizational activities during earlier periods of life. One gathers the impression that renewed interest in this avenue of social interaction followed close upon the loss of an occupation and its resulting increase in leisure. Reasons for the change were primarily social and recreational and, in some cases, the increase was welcomed for the change in routine the meetings and lectures provided. A few felt that club premises offered better facilities for entertaining friends than could be mustered in the home.

With few exceptions, subjects discharged from the hospital tend to shrink from associations with clubs, lodges, and the like. The very few who retain affiliation are inactive in their memberships. Mr. Ritter (HS), when seventy, explained his inactive status in the American Legion as follows: "I don't have to go down there and listen to somebody tell me a lot of stuff that I already know about politics." Mr. Ritter joined this organization in 1921 and his special contribution was in the area of "rehabilitation work for bedridden patients." In his old age, he reads *The Congressional Record* daily and is extremely interested in legislation related to the aged. He is very well informed on the problems of the old and can toss off statistics and hold long discussions on the remedies that should be taken. However, despite his continuing interest in national affairs and the welfare of the aged in particular, he chooses to remain aloof from political parties, community welfare organizations, or any direct exposure to Senior Citizens' groups. He acts alone: "I take occasion, depending on the legislation, to let them know my views in Washington." Mr. Ritter keeps a safe distance from other old people—perhaps he does not want to admit that he is one of them. For, while he energetically pursues the cause of the aged, there is no evidence that he has any particular liking for them. In fact, his abstract concern may actually serve to widen the gulf which he intends to keep between them and himself.

Mr. Ritter's attitude of "I never was much of a joiner-upper" is echoed and reechoed in our hospital sample. Such reserve is almost totally absent in the responses of community people. "I never joined anything," says Mr. Kepler (HS) , at sixty-six. Others reiterate the theme: "I wouldn't care for it. No, I'm not a joiner." Mrs. Harris (HS) balks at joining women's clubs because, "I don't like groups of women. They are too catty, just too gossipy." Miss Potter (HS) recalls how she joined the Rebecca Lodge in her early twenties, but she was throughout indifferent: "I was never interested in it much. I'm not a joiner." She disliked the "jealousy among the women" and the fact that "at that time the members were all older than I was"; so, ironically, age still plays a role in keeping Miss Potter from affiliations, but now it is her present age which holds her back. Entertaining as she does a desperate attitude toward her own aging and a horror of old age in general, she insists that she would never belong to any "clubs for older people." She could not bear to be so reminded of her own advanced years (or worse still!) to rub elbows with women who were still "older than I am." In all these statements of the erstwhile mentally ill, one catches a whisper of uneasiness about social contacts in general.

A few of these former patients do not express a negative attitude towards organizations, but half-heartedly report instead that they plan to join some kind of organization but have not yet done so. This is the way Mr. Ableson (HS) puts it: "I've been figuring on joining the American Legion over in Oakland." Mr. Ableson had been a member of this organization for seven or eight months in his young adulthood and had enjoyed "the card games." By the time of our last interview, however, he had still not joined. (These statements of good intentions are utterly lacking in community reporting.)

Only one hospitalized subject (Mrs. Powers) was highly active in various organizations and, in her case, it has been difficult to avoid thinking of her involvement as compulsive or defensive— even, perhaps, a bit frantic. We have already seen in Chapter II how she leads a merry round of club and other social activities. At one time, she was a member of the Women's Auxiliary of the Longshoremen's Union, but she complained: "I did not like it, yet I am a past president." Currently, she is a member of this union's pensioners' group: "In March, we will have a large party and luncheon—one hundred to three hundred people. I am active in all their activities and assist in all ways. I know what to order and how to order and when to get things done." She participates in this activity despite the fact that she feels "more antagonistic" toward this group's political orientation than she did formerly.

In contrast, community residents display a more realistic attitude toward organizational memberships. When obliged to curtail such activities, they express regret, attributing the decline to physical incapacitation or illness. Sometimes, changes in the composition of the membership—good friends drifting away and younger members coming in—is the reason given for the lesser involvement. For a number of elderly persons—especially those without immediate kin—organizational activity provides a structured arena for new social contacts as well as welcomed changes in the daily routine. Mrs. Bennington and Mr. Wheeler, both from the community sample and introduced in Chapter II, have a large number of friends. Mrs. Bennington has joined no new organizations but merely increased her activities in those to which she already belongs. Mr. Wheeler had not been as active socially before his retirement as he is now. Although he has immersed himself in many social activities in his old age, he differs from Mrs. Powers in that he has readily adjusted to the necessary attenuation of them. While he enjoys human companionship, he is not lost without it: "I've lived alone most of my life. I'm used to it and I like it. I don't believe I miss things. I'm content being retired, getting along without people I don't miss. Naturally, you enjoy life more when you're younger, but you don't demand as much when you're older and, consequently, you don't put out as much."

Mrs. Bennington does not lack friends and relatives but derives the greatest of satisfaction from her continued affiliation with the Retired Nurses' Association, within which organization a certain prestige adheres to seniority. Mrs. Bennington is eighty-three. She speaks with pride of her thirteen years' service in her office with this association as chaplain: "In that way, I'm kept busy. I get on the bus to visit these sick nurses at army hospitals as well as at the old age home for nurses and the association pays my traveling expenses."

A parallel case of a satisfying and long affiliation with a group is the case of Mr. Jespersen (CS) and his membership in the Socialist Labor Party. Mr. Jespersen joined the party in the 1920's and it has continued to provide him with an ideology and a purpose in life. "Although the party is still small," he explains, "we are a pretty active group. We meet more than twice a month sometimes, and we all do what we can. Like me: I distribute the Socialist newspapers to the Geary Street district. I don't get paid for this. I do this because I still believe we are the voice that should be heard." Mr. Jespersen has formed all his friendships within the party.

Mr. Knight (CS) spends about three hours a day on various community projects and has done so for the last ten or twelve years. He enjoys directing large-scale social welfare programs impersonally and at a distance from the individuals in distress. His contacts are essentially limited to the professionals administrating the community programs, but some of our less affluent subjects also appear to find some worth in performing more direct service to others in worse straits than themselves. For example, Mr. Ebenhauser (CS) has recently lent his helping hand to an aged couple. Six years before the first round of interviewing, Mr.

Ebenhauser discontinued his membership in the Odd Fellows and the Moose lodge: "I quit paying dues and going to lodge meetings. I'm not a subject for formalities and rituals." Now, at seventy-eight, his interests have turned to the more esoteric cults, which either tend to set mind over matter or promise unusual achievements in physical and mental functioning. To a vegetarian society, Mr. Ebenhauser has donated three to eight hours a day of free work, thereby helping a crippled old couple he has met at the meetings.

Visiting the sick and doing other services for those worse off —either momentarily or permanently—than oneself is an activity frequently mentioned by community subjects. They repeatedly refer to visiting friends in hospitals. They seem to do this as something of a duty or obligation the healthy aged owe to their sick compeers—thinking, perhaps, that they might find themselves one day in similar straits.

As one would expect, those subjects who express their primary satisfactions as contributing services or collaborating in some good cause are usually the still active and energetic subjects. The other, more passive, subjects stress the opportunities for sociability and the breaks in monotony which their belonging to organizations affords. Miss Barton (CS) is a member of the Vistas Club and attends their lectures ("we had the man who started the Peace Corps give us a lecture"). Upon her retirement from teaching school, she joined The Daughters of California and considered their "lovely lunchroom" to be the best advantage in her membership. "It's a lovely place to take people that you want to pay back social things."

A decrease in organizational participation is most frequently traced to illness and the decline in energy accompanying old age. For instance, Mrs. Valente (CS) has discontinued going to the Dalewood Community House for the past few months, but, she says: "I will go back when I feel better and the weather warms up." So, too, Mrs. Viet (CS) reports that she has always enjoyed being a member of the Klondike Girls' Club, but had to discontinue: "After my stroke, I couldn't go to meetings."

The women have another reason for cutting down in their

participation—fears of going out at night. "I belong to the Eastern Star and the D.A.R.," says Miss Wimsatt (CS), "but I don't go to either one now because you don't go out late at night in San Francisco any more." Mrs. Tully (HS), at eighty-three, is similarly reluctant: "I'd go to the lodge meetings now if I were able, but I don't feel like being out so late. There's kind of a run-down bar and a service station on the corner where the lodge is, and I see a lot of funny-looking types hanging around there, so I'm afraid to go. There's a lot of women like myself." Since she is no longer able to attend, she maintains contact by reading the lodge paper.

Had Mrs. Tully the funds, she would probably take a taxicab to her lodge; decline in income also restricts the frequency of using the organization's facilities, their dinners, the entertainments. Mrs. Miller (CS) would be eligible to join a number of high-prestige organizations, but she "can't afford it," and Mrs. Bennington (CS) lists the raising of dues as the only undesirable aspect of membership in her alumni association. While Social Security benefits remain constant, an increase in dues often forces the older person to drop these organizations in favor of more modest memberships.

Lastly, there are often unwelcome changes within an organization, making participation less satisfying for older members. Organizations are often specifically geared to certain age groups and accord seniority status in ways other than according to age. As a case in point, Mr. VanDamm (CS) reports that he had formerly been more active in his club and gives as his reason for this: "Now I feel it's more for youngsters. Old timers are passing away and no one there you know anymore." Miss Barton (CS) has other reasons for her decline in interest. She is no longer satisfied with the club for business women she has belonged to for twenty to thirty years because "it has changed so much. I do like a drink but everything they do there is so much liquor. Yes, as years go by, you get a different set of people in."

Seven of the community men and two of the hospital men retained union membership. In many cases, the motivation is largely economic, but we do find some appreciation for union activity.

Mr. Mersky (CS) emphasizes that favorable insurance rates are the sole reason for his having joined the union. "Only belong on account of the insurance. The agent told me their insurance scheme, so I joined and that's that." He never goes to meetings, but Mr. Janisch (CS) remains an inactive union member because: "I feel I got many benefits from the union I wouldn't get otherwise."

Only in the minority of cases does union life signify to these older individuals anything more than a measure of security, such as identification with a group or a cause, or a field for social action. Mr. Czernich (HS), single and seventy-three, likes to go now and then to meetings of his union's Pensioners Club to see and chat with some of his old friends. A borderline social isolate, Mr. Czernich finds that his union membership provides him with one of the few opportunities he has for social interaction. When hospitalized in 1959, he turned to the union and its representatives appeared to be the rare individuals he could finally trust. Membership for him is also one of the major sources of self-worth, providing him with a sense of accomplishment. In his narrative account, he repeatedly dwells on the achievements of the waterfront strikes in San Francisco during the 1930's. In his estimation, they appear to have been the single great achievement of the union movement. "I was one of the first to join the union," he says proudly. "Where would we all be if it were not for unions?" Mr. Makrinos (CS) also resorts to the union—to which he has belonged for twenty-seven years—whenever he finds himself in difficulty. It was through his union lawyer that he established eligibility for disability payments at the age of sixty-two, and it was the union he turned to when, later, he was anxious to be released from a medical hospital where he was faced with oral surgery which he wished to avoid. "I'm a working man," he states. "You have to protect working people." Mr. Makrinos is today a very ill man who will never work again, but he still faithfully participates in union meetings: "I go to meetings three times a month, pay my dues, make friends. Four or five months ago they wanted to elect me to the executive board."

In general, these older subjects turn to organizations primarily because membership affords them excursions into a structured social milieu. The activities planned by these organizations are not as important for them as is the opportunity to interact with others in a convivial, reliable setting. A free, easy-going atmosphere, suitable for informal exchanges of conversation, is more appreciated than high-powered programs for self-improvement or social service (although some healthy aged are still devoted to a great cause and can muster up a warm concern for overcoming deficiences within themselves and others). Yet these desires for a setting which stimulates interchanges of ideas and feelings are not alloyed with any great love for play and games in themselves. The competitive spirit that so often draws the young into sport has abated within the old. What brings these older members to meetings is rather the implicit desire to remain within the flow of humanity, perhaps no longer playing as important a role there as before, but there nevertheless, to be of use again if called upon, still a functioning social unit, still interested, talking, alive.

WORK AND RETIREMENT

Already in this report, we have met some people for whom loss of employment has posed serious problems of adaptation in later life. Although only one member of the study sample specified retirement as the single most stressful circumstance of his entire life (*cf.* Anderson, 1965), it has been nonetheless an unwelcome event for many. For some, like Mrs. Dillon (CS), unemployment has been the most troublesome event of life after sixty: "Not having a job, not getting out and being with people—I miss that. There is nothing I can do about it. People say you could do volunteer work, but they're not paying, and some people are being paid. I've registered at five or six agencies. Every time I go, they start shaking their heads. These machines keep people out of work, even younger people."

Attitudes toward retirement vary greatly among our subjects. At the time of the baseline interview, community subjects (study sample) were asked to tell how they felt about retirement. The results are as follows:

	Per cent
Still employed	31
Do not miss working	28
Miss working	26
Have never worked	15
	——
N=260	100

These figures show that almost one-third of community subjects were still gainfully employed at the time of the baseline interview. The proportions of hospital subjects in the study sample who had been working just prior to their hospitalization was much lower: only 19 per cent of those who were later discharged and 6 per cent of those who remained as inpatients had been employed during the month prior to their admissions to the psychiatric ward. As we have already reported, hospital subjects were older on the average than community subjects, and they were also more likely to be physically disabled. These seem to be the reasons, along with emotional disturbances, for the higher proportion of retired persons among the mentally ill. In both samples we found employment related to these two factors: four times as many healthy as impaired subjects were working, and four times as many people under seventy had jobs as those seventy and over. Employment rates were also higher among men and among those with some college education.

Among the 141 retired people in the community sample, there were just as many (73) who claimed that they did *not* miss being employed as there were those who claimed that they did (68). Mrs. Kramer (CS) is one happy not to work any more. This woman had been a milliner in her early years, but gave up her job when she married. Then, when she was widowed in her early fifties, she was forced to seek employment again. She tried to resume her earlier occupation, but found that there was little demand for custom-made ladies' hats: "They were all buying hats out of factories in New York. You couldn't get any customers." After making this discovery, Mrs. Kramer found employment at the Post Office, and, later, as a sort of "girl Friday" to the manager of a taxicab company: "I got it in 1953 and that job saved my life. That was the last job I had. Then I was eligible for Old Age

Assistance, and I was glad to take it because I didn't want to work any more if I didn't have to have the money. Frankly, I got tired. With my rheumatism—ooh! If I had to work now, I don't know what I'd do."

Miss Barton (CS), a former school teacher, retired at sixty-four, one year before the mandatory retirement age in her school district. She explains that she felt too old to cope with the children any longer. She became frightened of them and unsure of her ability to control and discipline them: "I thought for my own peace of mind, I'd quit. When I retired, I tell you, people were very nice. You know, the only thing I missed when I retired was the faculty."

Miss Barton is not the only one whose major regret about retirement is the loss of contact with people. When we asked the community subjects what it was they missed about lack of employment, the most common response was loss of companionship and social contacts. We obtained the following distribution of reasons for missing work:

	Per cent
Companionship or contact with public	28
Routine, keeping busy	23
Salary	17
Interest in content of work	16
Other	16
	100

For many like Miss Barton, loss of employment had the consequence of a serious attrition of social contacts. Miss Christianson (HS) reports that she retired from her secretarial job with the federal government but, "I was completely alone. I wasn't enthusiastic about retiring. I enjoyed working, being around and seeing people."

Mr. Lemuel Bauer (CS), a retired railroad machinist, misses most the stimulation of the work itself: "I don't know—when I was working, I was always happy with the job. I always liked trains, machinery, that was it. Now, however, after eighteen years of retirement, he feels "all right" about not working: "I'm well satisfied as it is. At first, it got on my nerves—not having anything to think about. But now it doesn't bother me a bit. I got plenty other things to do."

For many subjects—particularly those who are forced to retire during their early sixties because of failing health—loss of income is a matter of real concern. For example, Mr. Ableson (HS) had been working in a shoe-shine parlor until about a month before we saw him at second-round follow-up interview. "This is one of the hardest times of my life," he reports, "because I've got no job and no money. Up until about a month ago I worked, but then I started to feel so bad that I couldn't work. It was my high blood pressure, and not being able to sleep. I don't feel so good—my money's run out and the bills are piling up. I worry about those bills. I wish I could get into the veterans' home where I could rest for about six months or so. Maybe then I could come back and do better."

Mr. Kreisler (HS) worked as a janitor and handyman just prior to his admission to the psychiatric ward in 1959. His commitment, following a round of drinking and violence, was related, in part, to a series of conflicts with his employer (who was also his landlady). He claims she was taking advantage of him because of his age: "When I first started working for her, she gave me two hundred dollars a month, then she cut it back to a hundred and fifty, and now to a hundred. I can't live on that. I'd like to move out of that place and find another job, but I know I can't find one at my age. I don't belong to the union, so it's hard for me to get another job, and my age is against me. When I'm sixty-five, I'll get a veteran's pension and also my Social Security—I could live on that all right. But it's the next three years that worry me—I'm just sixty-two now."

Mrs. Viet (CS) worked as a seamstress for forty-five years and retired about eight years ago following an illness. She had always been poorly paid ("sewing is the lowest paid work you can get"), and her small savings were depleted during forty-five days of private hospitalization after her stroke: "It cost me plenty. All my own money. No one helped me. Now it's all gone. I'd like to work as before—I didn't feel good about retiring. It's okay if you can live in style and come and go as you please. I can't—I've got nothing. Oh, well, some have a good life, some haven't." Clearly, the disability and impoverishment of her old age are more oppressive to Mrs. Viet than her retirement *per se*. Mr. Jespersen (CS) reports that it is the money he missed most when he retired: "My eyes were going bad and I thought I'd be blind. I had to retire and I thought I'd become a burden on people." For him, the fear of a dependent old age is the most serious consequence of retirement.

When Mr. Lewissohn's (CS) wife died, he found his contacts at his place of business one of his few bulwarks against the loneliness of his bereavement. He reports, "I was so discouraged I didn't care what happened. Fortunately, I was still active in business; I had four people working for me, and that kept my spirits up. I used to eat out in restaurants and was friendly with the waiters. I went to a show, went to bed, and slept soundly. The following morning the same routine over again, just to shake it off. And finally I did shake it off." Mr. Lewissohn's comments suggest that one of the important functions of work is to provide some routine, some structuring of one's time. Sometimes, with retirement, all the meaning and order goes out of life. As Mr. Forest (HS) says, "Time went fastest, believe it or not, when I was working. You're occupied almost every minute of the day. The best time of your life is when you're working, for the simple reason that you have some incentive—not like sitting in a room doing nothing." Mrs. Tillford (HS) expresses the same feeling when she speaks of retirement from her employment as a domestic worker: "One thing that presses the life out of me is not having a job—when you've been used to it, it's the only thing that makes you lively. I try to do things around the house—folding clothes to entertain me. I guess that helps me."

Mr. Antonelli (HS) is very bitter about his forced retirement: "In 1961 my employers told me, 'Out! That's it!' I go to the union every day, five or six times a week. They tell me, 'That's all.' They don't need you after you're forty or fifty. That's no good. You've got to have work, keep busy, see people, talk, get out and do your work and take care of your family. Staying home, doing nothing, that's no good, boy, I tell you for sure!" Mr. Antonelli mentions almost all the major dissatisfactions with retirement that members of the sample expressed, but he also suggests, by his manner and by the phrase "they don't need you" that in some cases there are deeper emotional reasons among some of the elderly for clinging to employment than those most frequently articulated.

Under the category of "other" in our tabulation of things missed in retirement are the responses given by some of the most seriously troubled people in our intensive sample. These people are those whose self-esteem has been so strongly tied to work that retirement represents a serious threat to the organization of the personality. One such person is Mr. Hopland (HS), whose reaction to the accident that forced him to retire, has already been discussed in Chapter IV, but Mr. Alioto (HS) attests to how profound a dislocation in one's life a retirement can be.

By the time Mr. Alioto was forcibly retired from his last job as a Navy guard, fifty-eight of his seventy-three years had been spent in work. By far, the largest block of his working experience had been as a caretaker-chauffeur to a single family—a position he had initiated in his teens and left when he was sixty-four, outliving his employers. According to the baseline testimony of his "dearest friend," the seventy-nine-year-old "girl friend" who advised his hospitalization: "Well, Al had been drinking heavily for many years, but just last week was the first time I'd ever seen him like this—to extreme, I mean. It was because he'd lost his job at Treasure Island. That same day he came home to the hotel and he commenced to cry and I said, 'My God, Al, cut that out—get some guts into your system!' because I thought it was just self-pity."

Mr. Alioto's work severance had not been entirely unanticipated. He had been given notice, but—again, the "girl friend": "He had trouble sleeping, I know. The doctor gave him sleeping pills, but they were 'too weak,' he said. Why, he'd drink as many as twelve cans of beer at a sitting! And he drank brandy, too. He liked that, and sometimes he'd mix it with the beer." Finally, Mr. Alioto decided to commit himself for treatment. "He's like that—one to solve his own problems," said his "girl friend."

Now, in describing his hospitalization, Mr. Alioto denies any depression or anxiety, claiming instead that his institutionalizaton had been based on a misunderstanding—that he had been drunk because he wanted to "celebrate a happening" involving his brother. He was very indignant against the psychiatrists who, he claimed, were keeping him incarcerated against his will: "Well, I just kept telling them that I had to get out and look up some jobs I've got lined up. I told them that if I didn't get some kind of work, the city'd have another boarder at the County Home for the Aged. But," says Mr. Alioto confidentially, "I'll have to be pretty darn crippled—almost creeping—for *that!*"

But, once discharged, Mr. Alioto found no opportunities for reemployment. "When I see all those young men at the employ-ment department, I can tell that an old man like me doesn't have much of a chance. I tried to find a janitorial job, but I'm too old. I inquired about getting a newsstand, but the man who was going to help me died. Old, too." Since his forced retirement, he has begun to suffer "blue moods. Well, naturally I began to feel blue—anybody feels blue when you're put out of action. After I retired, a change took place. I didn't like being sociable any more. I liked my job. Hell, I was *active,* but if you're not active, you're not good for anything." [But do you think you could do anything to remedy this situation?] "Hell, no—just sit back and be quiet. Be a 'good, old man.' Do the best you can do. But sitting around is no good either. Sooner or later you're going to sit there for good. It all started when I had to retire because of my age. It broke my heart."

Since moving away from the family he served as a chauffer, Mr. Alioto has resided in a residence hotel on the fringes of the Ten-derloin district. He is desperate to find activities to keep himself occupied: "Well, most of the time, I just sit around, go for a walk or lie down. I don't talk to people very much any more. I sold my car. I feel lost without work to do. Oh, I talk to people in the lobby—baseball, horses, things like that. One day is pretty much like the last. I just get up in the morning with a blank mind and wonder what I can do to keep busy for the rest of the day."

Probably because he has always had only a marginal social adjustment, Mr. Alioto's whole life has been so thoroughly orient-ed to the work role that, with retirement, he can see little purpose remaining in the days left to him. Asked what he has done best in his life, he replies: "I don't know of any 'best.' Just satisfaction in my work. I never got fired or anything. I always held on to what I got." In answering question after question, he harks back to the crushing blow of this retirement. [Can you explain why you had to be hospitalized?] "It was because I was retired, that's why, which I didn't like very much. That annoyed me. Like a horse being put out to pasture. Why, I was in *good* physical health! And then the government retired me on a lousy pension. The only thing that worried me was being retired." [Have you any plans?] "Now? No. Just death."

Except for extreme cases as Mr. Alioto's, Americans generally appear to face their retirement with mixed feelings: many welcome the leisure, considering it well earned but where one's major articulation with the social world had been through work, retirement can serve to alienate such a person from the only meaningful ratification of the self available to him. We shall have more to say in the final chapter on the necessity of substitution for work in such cases, once opportunities for it have been withdrawn from the individual.

RELIGIOUS ATTITUDES AMONG THE ELDERLY

In undertaking this study, we expected to find that, as our subjects grew older, their interest in religious matters and church activities would be accentuated. We based this expectation on two factors: first, ceremonialism and ritual have provided a traditional social role for the elderly in most cultures. High ecclesiastics in most organized religions are generally senior churchmen: popes, patriarchs, and archbishops are seldom recruited from the ranks of the young. Religion seems to be one sphere of human activity where the wisdom and experience of age remains an asset, if not a necessity, for those in positions of responsibility and leadership. We saw no reason why this should not also be the case among laymen. Second, we expected to find among our subjects an increasing concern with their shortening span of years. We foresaw that older people, because they are closer to death, would consequently express a greater need for spiritual comfort and the assurance of immortality.

In our intensive study, we therefore included a set of questions having to do with current religious activities, beliefs, and interests, as well as changes which have occurred in these areas within the later years of life. We made inquiries relating to five general topics: (1) To what extent do older subjects have a belief in a Diety or some supernatural power? (2) To what extent do they believe in personal immortality or an afterlife? (3) Do they express a fear of death? To what extent does religious faith provide an antidote to such fears? (4) Do older people attend religious services regularly, and has attendance increased in later life? (5) Regardless of frequency of church attendance, do they consider religious belief an important factor in their lives? And, in those cases where religion is cited as important to the subject, what is its primary contribution to his psychological well-being, as he perceives it?

It is clear from the nature of these questions that our interest in religious attitudes is only, in part, related to the social supports that may be provided the elderly by church affiliation and religious group membership. We recognize that, whatever may be the social functions of religion, it also has a strong personal component that is also potentially important in adaptation to aging. Both aspects, then, will be discussed here.

At the time of the baseline study, both community and hospital subjects were asked if they had a religious affiliation or preference. Most of them did: only 10 per cent of the baseline community sample and 4 per cent of the baseline hospital sample reported that they had no religious identification. Religious affiliations for the two samples were as follows:

	Community Subjects Per Cent	Hospital Subjects Per Cent
Protestant	38	42
Roman Catholic	29	40
Jewish	10	4
Other	13	10
None	10	4
	100	100
	(N=592)	(N=515)

The only notable difference between the two samples was that there were proportionately fewer Catholics in the community sample, a fact probably related in part to the differences in socio-economic status between the two groups of subjects.[13]

We did not, however, find any large difference between the two samples in proportions of subjects reporting some religious affiliation—90 per cent of community subjects and 96 per cent of hospital subjects claim some religious identification.

Religious activity in the form of church attendance, however is another matter.[14] We have already seen, in Chapter V, that more community than hospital subjects in our larger study sample occupy the status of religious person (that is, reported participating in religious observances at least once a year). According to this criterion, three-fourths of the community sample were in the status of religious person compared with only about one-third of the hospital sample. However, looking at more detailed information on church attendance among members of our intensively-studied sample, we see quite a different pattern. In the intensively-studied group, a *minority* of the subjects reported that they regularly attend religious services as frequently as once a month. Among the sixty-seven subjects for whom we have information on voluntary church attendance (the remaining 12 in our sample of 79 are hospital inpatients, and their attendance at services is not entirely in their own hands), we find that twenty-seven attend services regularly and forty do not. Looking at the community and hospital subjects separately, we get the following comparisons:

Attend Church? Monthly or More	Community Subjects	Hospital Subjects
Yes	13	16
No	26	12
No information	—	12

13In our sample, the hospital subjects tend to have a higher proportion of Catholics, and, in this, are more representative of the population of San Francisco as a whole. Our designation of certain census tracts for selecting our community sample (those with high proportions of elderly residents) seems to have screened out many of the districts of the city with large concentrations of Catholic families.

14A good review of recent studies of religious activity among the elderly is found in Maves (1960). In general, current research in the United States reveals "no support for the notion that religiosity increases as a function of age" (p. 739).

In these figures it is clear that regular and frequent church attendance is more characteristic of the mentally-ill than of the mentally-healthy subjects, in spite of the fact that more of the latter attend on special occasions from time to time. Mrs. Viet (CS) is one of the subjects who attends services at least once a year; however, she does not regard herself as a religious person: "I never had a religion, but I attend services about once a year, for weddings and funerals—never very often. I listen to religious programs on the radio every Sunday, but I don't belong to any church. As a child we used to go, but I just remember the singing, not the sermons. As a teenager, I didn't go at all. When I got to be middle-aged, I would visit a synagogue or the Catholic church with a friend once in a while, but I get disgusted when I see people come out of church—some are such hypocrites! They talk a lot about Christian charity, but they wouldn't go two steps out of their way to help anybody. My religion now is very simple: I believe in the Golden Rule and I believe in God. I don't do any wrong to anybody, and I say prayers every day." Mrs. Viet was therefore counted as a "religious person" in our status index, but it is clear from her intensive interviews that she is not a regular participant in organized church activities, nor does she conceive of herself as particularly pious.

Mrs. Viet is thus one of a fairly large group of subjects who show some interest in religious matters, although remaining unaffiliated with a church. However, there are twenty-seven people in the intensive sample who find regular services a source of help, support, or interest. Some of these subjects have been active in religious observances all their lives. One of these is Mrs. Langtry (CS), who says she was ". . . just born and bred a Baptist—and I'll live and die a Baptist. I know very little about the beliefs of others. I'm satisfied, so I will never change." Of the thirteen people in the community intensive sample who are regular churchgoers, ten—like Mrs. Langtry—have always been participants. Miss Wimsatt (CS) reports that she ". . . was born and raised in generations of Methodists. I don't talk about it, but I'm glad I'm a Methodist. We're a liberal church. The only thing we ask is that you take Christ and turn away from sin. You should live a life that will honor God. I always find something in church services I can get out of it. The church is lovely, and in the congregation you feel that the people share feelings with you—I guess it's crowd psychology. I think as we grow older our idea of our relation to God changes—becomes more of a bulwark to us."

Similarly, Mr. Schwann (CS) has remained an active and devout Catholic all his life. It has never occurred to him to be otherwise: "I was born a Catholic and stayed that way. You don't think about anything else because everyone in that part of Switzerland had the same religion. There was no one in the whole village who was not Catholic. My religion has always been very important to me. We do our duty for the church. We go to church every Sunday and help out and pay what we can for charity."

Mrs. Bruzinsky (CS) also says that religion has always been important in her life: "I feel I am a Jew and I am proud of it. I take pride in the long history we have and I like the rituals, for they have deep meanings. It is a long tradition that Jews follow, and you know that if you do the right things, God will always help you out of difficult situations." Mrs. Bruzinsky did not always find it easy to be a Jew, however. "When Hitler came to Vienna, being Jewish was bad. But I was in Italy then. When the Italians became anti-Semitic openly, I wanted to get out of the country. People told me that I couldn't get across the border to France if I were a Jew. I was afraid and so I went to a priest and I was baptized a Catholic. I remember that when the priest was baptizing me, I kept on repeating to myself, 'Hear, oh Israel, the Lord our God, the Lord is one!' I know I am forgiven for this sin, for in the Talmud it says a person can do anything in order to live so that he can worship God and keep the Jewish life. I have never lost my pride in being a Jew. If anything, because of what happened to the Jews in Europe, one becomes more of a Jew than ever before."

There are three subjects in the community sample whose interest in religious matters is of fairly recent origin. One of these is Mr. Ebenhauser (CS). Although his parents were church-going people and he was sent to Lutheran Church and Sunday School when he was a child, he was disinterested in religion until recent years. "Religion didn't mean much of anything to me when I was a child. I went to church because I had to. And in my teens, my parents sent me, and it was just routine, I guess. Then, when I was eighteen I started moving around and just stopped going. I figured there was a difference between good people and bad people, but I never went to church." However, when he was in his early sixties, Mr. Ebenhauser went with a friend to a Spiritualist meeting. There he discovered the existence of the spirit world and found that the living could communicate with the dead. Mr. Ebenhauser now attends meetings regularly, and seeks advice from the spirit world for his own actions. He obtains predictions of things to come, and, as a result of this guidance, has started working on an invention: "About two months ago I began working on my patent again. I was told at a Spiritualist meeting out of the clear blue sky what I should do."

The other two community subjects who have experienced a renaissance of religious interest in late life have also discovered new sects which they feel offer them much more than their former religious affiliations.

Mr. Wheeler (CS), although he early in life rejected his family's Protestant teachings as "superstition," has also developed a late-life enthusiasm for spiritualism: "I've always needed a religion, but I had to work it out for myself. Now this one is my own."

Mrs. Kramer (CS), once an inactive Presbyterian, began "shopping around" for a different church when she was in her late fifties. "I just didn't see anything in the Presbyterian Church. You got nothing there. Who cares about the future? They tell you nothing there for your life today." For a while she attended Christian Science meetings, but "didn't like the man who runs it. He was too immature, so I started going to the Unitarian Church where there is a more intellectual pastor. They have brainy lectures. Of course, Christian Science goes right along with the teaching of Unitarianism, and I got a lot out of Science." Mrs. Kramer reported that, as a child, she had found "Presbyterian ritual boring—I didn't like to go to church. When I was a teenager, I really hated it. Then, when I left home, I didn't go hardly at all. I wish I had know about a religion like the Unitarians sooner. With them, I can be free to be outspoken—say just what I think. In my church, we have Catholics, atheists, Jews. It's interesting to be among them and learn their side of things."

So far, we have been discussing the third of the community intensive cases who attend church services regularly. What about the religious attitudes of the remaining two-thirds? In a few cases, the subject was active in church participation until he became physically incapacitated. This is the case with Mr. Sablon, a life-long Catholic. He is now in a nursing home and not well enough to leave the grounds. However, he does receive visits from a Catholic chaplain in his room at the hospital.

By far, however, the larger number of nonchurch-goers either have never been associated with a church, or have developed some antagonism to church organizations at an earlier period of life, usually in adolescence. Mrs. Miller (CS) is one of the former subjects. Asked about her religious background, she replies, "That's difficult for me to say. I was never baptized. I never joined a church and I have never been a church-goer. My mother's parents were Lutherans, but we never went to church—maybe once a year." Most of the community subjects, though, had some religious indoctrination as children, but the interest has not carried over into adulthood. Mrs. Willoughby (CS) said, "I'm a Protestant, brought up in the Wesley Methodist Church. I don't know whether there is one anymore. No, I'm not very religious, and I'll tell you why. As a small child, my grandmother was very religious and she dragged my sister and me to church. We had it practically crammed down our throats. I was about twelve when I realized this. I don't think church hurts anyone, if they're not *forced* to go. I say my prayers every night, but I don't believe you have to go to church to live a good life."

Mr. Lewissohn (CS) says, "I feel that I belong to the Jewish faith and will never change that." However, in contrast to Mrs. Bruzinsky's feeling that religious persecution merely strengthened her faith, Mr. Lewissohn reacted differently: "Being religious, that's a different matter. Religion just isn't important to me, although I'm not an agnostic. I don't oppose religion, but I was persecuted too much as a child because of mine." Although Mr.

Lewissohn has not been in a temple since his own Bar Mitzvah, he does express a wish to be buried in a Jewish cemetery.

Some subjects, like Mr. Jay (CS), associate religious observances with an unhappy or deprived childhood or youth, and are glad to have left religion behind, along with the miseries of the period. Mr. Jay reported that, as a lonely child in the back bush of Australia, he was beaten regularly by his violently authoritarian father (he finally ran away from home to escape this ruthless treatment). He describes his religious training in this way: "I had a little religious training at that time. The preacher came out to the sheep ranch once in a while. My mother was on the religious side—she tried to teach us. But after I ran away to sea, that was the end of that. Now I'm not overly religious, but I always have a little religious feeling in me. We listen to church on the radio sometimes."

Mr. Jespersen (CS) is one of the two professed atheists in the intensive sample. This man, born on a Danish farm, also had a pathetically brutalized childhood and youth. Frail and sickly, he was bullied by his older brother, fearful of his father, and tormented by the belief that Hell and early death await the wicked and ungrateful child. Now seventy-eight, he says, "Some of the people in my family who were very religious were also the biggest hypocrites I knew. All the time they were out to screw their fellow man, but went to church every Sunday. Religion is just a bunch of superstitious nonsense. It doesn't mean a damn thing to me!"

Some subjects find the strictures of their religion difficult to reconcile with the events of their adult lives. Mrs. Valente, whose unhappy marriage we have described earlier in this chapter, had been born and reared in the Catholic faith. When she finally decided to separate from her husband, she decided as well to take the teachings of her church less seriously. Now she says of religion: "It's all right, but there's lots of things I don't like about the church. Catholics should let the other fellow live his life. I am religious in a way, but I don't go to church too much any more. I'm Catholic—I feel there's only one God—but how you live is most important, not going to church. The creed doesn't mean much."

A number of community subjects expressed outright anti-clerical attitudes which they associate with their lack of religious activity. For example, Mr. Makrinos (CS) reports: "I'm still Greek Orthodox. The church is all right, but I'm not much for the priest. I don't like priests because a poor man died years ago that I knew. They collected seventy dollars to bury him. I called the priest and he refused to come up. He asked us if we had any money. I said, 'Listen, priest, if you come, you get paid.' He says, 'Want money first.' I hung up. I went to the Russian Orthodox one. The Russian priest came around and buried him. I got mad at the Greek Orthodox priest, but the religion is okay. That priest, he ain't around here no more."

Mr. Hokusai, a Roman Catholic, said that in one way he prefers his wife's Buddhist faith: "I'm not too happy with Catholic priests—they are too strict and not at all kind." Mr. Hart (CS) reports that he had been an active member of the Methodist Church ". . . up until the time I was thirty-six. I held every office in the church that a layman could. But then I got sick and was in a sanitorium for a long time. I had nothing to do but think. That's when I resigned from every organization I was a member of. I'm a very devout Christian, but I don't believe in any religious organizations any more. I don't want any preacher to dictate how I serve my Master."

Church-going is more characteristic of the mentally-ill intensive subjects: as noted, 16 out of 28 for whom we have information attend religious services regularly. There seem to be two primary reasons for this greater preoccupation with religion among the mentally ill, compared with the community subjects. First, the mentally-ill aged are, by and large, fearful and unhappy people, looking desperately for whatever sources of consolation and strength they can find—and many find it in religious observances. Second, just as the mentally ill may become delusional about *any* facet of life—whether it be in the form of sexual aberration, delusions of great wealth or power, or whatever—they may become obsessed with religion. There are some members of the sample who have had a history of religious delusions or fanaticism. (As an example: The first author was one day greeted by an elderly psychiatric inpatient with a cheery, "Good morning, Jesus!")

Religion provides consolation and emotional support to Mr. Jackson (HS). Mr. Jackson, a second-generation Irish-American who was admitted to the psychiatric ward with a diagnosis of alcoholism, is a life-long Catholic. He was not particularly devout, however, until—during his hospital stay—he was found to have an inoperable cancer. Since that time, daily attendance at Mass has enabled him to remain sober and face his inevitable death with some degree of strength and dignity. "I'm a strong Catholic now," he says. "As a rule I go to twelve o'clock Mass every day, whether I can walk or not. I'd crawl if I had to. Back in the days when I was drinking, I forgot about the church, but they didn't forget about me. Once I was out stiff in my hotel room. Boy, was I sick! The only thing I remember is the priest coming in to see me—I guess the manager called him. I remember he took one look at me, saw the bottle of whiskey on the bureau, and poured it down the sink. So when I got out of the hospital, I thought I'd better get to church and maybe that would help me." Also, Miss Potter (HS), a woman who is quite concerned about growing old, and particularly despondent about the accompanying physical changes it has brought her, has developed a strong interest in Christian Science since recovering from her "nervous breakdown": "I'd been to a number of churches, but somehow I didn't get too much out of it. I don't know what was the matter with me. But then I got interested in Christian Science—I've gone to a lot of lectures. People think our religion is easy, but we aren't even supposed to *think* wrong! 'As ye think, so ye believe'—that's true. I was looking for something new, and this religious science came along. Some of it is too deep for me and some of it kind of gives me the creeps, but it *has* helped. Without it, I wouldn't have any faith or hope or anything to look forward to or to work for. I think it's changed my whole attitude."

Mrs. Tillford (HS), aware of the mental changes she is suffering as a result of progressive deterioration of the brain, finds her religion a great consolation: "My family was always Baptist. You can be anything you desire—if you can go on with that, it's fine. For me, it's food for the hungry soul. Who gave you this beautiful day? I think it's wonderful to be in service for the Master—He helps me keep my mind when some are losing theirs." Mrs. Trocopian (HS), a member of the Armenian Apostolic Church, reports, "I am a great religious person. It helps me as much as medicine does. Religion is good for our well-being, makes us more hopeful. I need consolation all the time." Mr. Cambry (HS), secure in his lifetime membership in the Church of England, put it very simply: "I'm a church man. I don't fear anything, sir!"

There are, however, subjects in the hospital sample who are just as skeptical of organized religion as many of the community subjects. For example, Mrs. Harris (HS) was a bit condescending about Christianity: "Religion probably does some good. Of course, I think the truth would be better, but Christianity will have to do. I wouldn't claim to be religious, but I don't discourage it in others—in fact, I try to help them along. There's a very devout lady next door. I say, 'God bless you,' and tell her I will pray for her. I even try—I don't believe it will do much good, but I try."[15]

We have found that, in general, hospital subjects are more concerned than community subjects with the emotional support religious belief may provide. Community subjects, on the other hand, see more real or potential value in the social aspects of church-going than do the hospitalized. For instance, when we asked Mrs. Burbank (CS) what means the most to her in her religion, she replies, "The social aspect and the feeling that there is someone to turn to. It is a good discipline and a source for an older person for acquaintances and friendships." Also, Miss Barton (CS) reports that she is well satisfied with her church affilia-

---

[15]The problem of religious delusions, fanaticism, or religious preoccupation as a symptom of mental disorder is a very complex issue, and one that is somewhat beyond the scope of this discussion. We can only say here that our hospital sample seems to contain several such cases: the Greek Orthodox woman whose paranoid delusions are accompanied by beliefs that she has been visited on several occasions by the Virgin Mary; the Irish Catholic spinster who converted to Protestantism when she believed she saw her nude cousin hung up by her heels in the cathedral and raped by the priest; the Episcopalian man who believed that his personal Hell had inexplicably arrived in this life when he began to feel himself controlled by invisible and malevolent supernatural forces; the Bavarian Catholic who attempted suicide and is now obsessed with uncontrollable fears that his soul is damned forever; the Christian Scientist, faced with progressive blindness, haunted by recurrent nightmares that God has deserted her and left her alone in an abyss. These are all part of the tragic world of the mentally ill.

tion because, "I think they are fine people. I am considering putting my membership in the church." Likewise, Mr. Butler (CS) reports: "Even today my wife and I think about joining the Unitarian Church, for there's no dogma there. Well, another reason is that maybe we will meet some new friends there. This might fill a gap in our life—new friends and interesting people." Community subjects also emphasize the ethical and moral principles in religious belief; for most of them, this is the most important aspect of religious life. Mr. Butler goes on to speak about this aspect: "Religion gives you standards which most people are in accord with. It gives us a moral basis to live by." In like fashion, Mrs. Bennington (CS) says, "Religion means quite a lot to me—'do unto others as you wish to be done by'—helping your sick friends. When you have thoughts of religion, you like to do things for other people, but you don't always consider the religious part of it—it's just the idea of doing some good."

In spite of diverse attitudes towards religious organizations and church attendance among members of our intensively-studied sample, they display much greater agreement about the existence of God. Seventy-one subjects provided such information, and sixty-one of these asserted that they did believe in the Deity or some supernatural power; two subjects stated firmly that they were atheists; and the other eight reported uncertainty in their beliefs. Attitudes ranged from powerful conviction of the existence of an anthropomorphic, omnipotent personal Deity, to a positive denial of any other than natural forces in the universe. There are no major differences between the two samples on this basic issue, as shown in the following figures:

Belief in God or a Supernatural Power?	Community Subjects	Hospital Subjects	Total Intensive Sample
Yes	29	32	61
No	2	—	2
Uncertain	4	4	8
No information	4	4	8

However, there is a noticeable tendency for the mentally healthy to conceive of God more in terms of His creative, benevolent aspects, while the mentally-ill subjects are more likely to emphasize the judgmental and punitive aspects. For example, compare these two statements: Miss Wimsatt (CS) says, "The most important thing there is is the fact that God created us and loves us. He is always present—how could you live without Him?" Mr. Kepler (HS), however, says, "I worry about meeting God, because of the punishment I may have to go through. There's only two places—Heaven and Hell, and one goes to either one or the other. Being a selfish person, I worry about punishment."

There is much less agreement among our subjects on the matter of immortality. Although there were only two subjects who denied the existence of the Deity, and eight who were uncertain of the fact, forty-five subjects either stated that there is no life after death or confessed that they were uncertain about immortality. Only twenty-three of the sixty-eight subjects who provided information on this topic were reasonably assured of immortality. Although differences between community and hospital samples were slight, there was a slight tendency for community subjects to be more doubtful on this point than hospital subjects. The figures were as follows for the intensively-studied sample:

Belief in Immortality or an Afterlife?	Community Subjects	Hospital Subjects	Total Intensive Sample
Yes	10	13	23
No	10	4	14
Uncertain	19	12	31
No information	—	11	11

Among community subjects, as many do not believe in immortality as do, and as many were uncertain as had some definite belief, one way or the other. Among the mentally ill, however, only four deny belief in an afterlife, but thirteen are confident of immortality. Proportionately fewer of the total in the hospital sample were uncertain.

Among the mentally-healthy aged, there seems to be a greater tolerance of uncertainty about death than there is among the mentally ill. The most common response in the community sample to the question: "What will happen to you after you die?" is much like that given by Mr. Knight: "Nobody can answer that question —nobody knows." Mrs. Willoughby answers in much the same way, but a little more negatively: "I don't really know. Many people argue about it. I wonder, but I don't think the dead come back to life—when you're dead, you're dead." Mrs. Miller concurs: "After death, I think you're just plain dead, that's all. I don't feel there's a hereafter. There may be, but I don't know. God put us all here for a while, then He takes us away, just like the flowers die."

Mrs. Bruzinsky (CS) states that she doesn't really care, one way or the other: "The body is nothing and we return to ashes, like the Torah says. I don't know if there is a life after death, but, as long as we're alive, we will never know for sure. It doesn't make any difference to me—just so I have peace and quiet."

Mrs. Kramer (CS) expresses a belief in some other plane of existence, but says she does not believe in the orthodox notions of Heaven and Hell: "I try to think realistically about it, and I know that death can be no worse than life. I think that death is another dimension, but I don't know exactly what it is. I do not believe that there is a Heaven, but Dr. Schweitzer says there's hope of a future existence." Miss Barton (CS) is a little clearer about her concept: "I think there is a hereafter. Have you ever looked at a beautiful sunset? I think it must be something like that— some kind of a spiritual world that we will enter."

Mr. Bauer (CS), a life-long Catholic, is even more specific, but he finds it necessary to modify the traditional views of his church a bit to meet his own conceptions: "I've had the last rites of the church three different times. They say after death you go to Heaven, Hell, or Purgatory. Of course, I don't believe in this hellfire business. There must be some other punishment besides a burning eternity. I think you're going to a better place than you've got here on the earth—no worries, no sickness, nothing."

Among the mentally-ill subjects, much the same range of attitudes towards immortality were expressed, except, as we noted, there was a bit less tolerance of uncertainty. The following responses indicate something of the wistfulness of these people that there will at least be escape from the tortures they have suffered in life: "Well, I think I will descend into an abyss of nothingness— I don't believe in life after death." One hospitalized subject is especially eloquent: "Well, that's where the end of the line is. I went to my friend's funeral last month, and she looked like she was just asleep. Wish it could be like that—nothing hurting you—

oh, Lord!" Another former patient says, "I don't know what happens after death. One time my priest asked me. If I think scientifically, the body goes to dust, and the soul to Heaven. The spirit should remain forever. Perhaps there is something like that, but all I can think about is just restfulness—don't feel, don't worry, just peace."

Some of the hospital subjects are dubious, but seem to want to believe in personal survival after death. Miss Potter, for example, says, "I don't know what happens after death—only I never could see the idea of me being nothing. I don't think I'll ever cease to be, but I don't believe in Heaven or Hell the way the preachers tell it."

Miss Bachstein (HS) espouses the rather unique notion that whatever an individual believes will determine his fate after death: "Well, after death, people go according to their religion. If they believe in it, they go to Heaven; if not, they just die dead. I'm pretty sure what will happen after *I* die: they'll bury me."

We asked the members of our intensive sample if they were afraid of death, expecting that there might be some correlation with either religious affiliation or beliefs concerning immortality. Neither proved to be the case. Neither church-going nor a belief in an afterlife provides immunity from fear of death. However, fear of death is somewhat related to mental illness. In the total intensive sample, forty-seven out of sixty-eight subjects for whom we have such data asserted that they were *not* afraid of death; eleven confessed that they were afraid, at least sometimes; and the remaining ten stated that they were not afraid of death now, but sometimes worry that they will *become* fearful when the time comes. The distribution for the two samples is as follows:

Fear of Death?	Community Subjects	Hospital Subjects	Total Intensive Sample
No	29	18	47
Yes, or sometimes	5	6	11
Fear of *becoming* afraid	5	5	10
No information	—	11	11

For the mentally ill, fear of death seems at times related to the low tolerance we have noted for uncertainty or ambiguity. They need to *know* what is going to happen to them, and if they are uncertain, they often express a great deal of anxiety. For example, Mr. Phidrios (HS) states, "I think a lot about dying, and I'll be honest—I'm scared of it, too—because, how do I know what it's going to be? I'm no prophet." In some cases, a conviction of one's unworthiness coupled with a firm belief in the hereafter produces near-panic among some of the mentally ill: "I don't want to die; I pray to live. I know I'm lost forever. Seems like I'm going straight to Hell. [Are you afraid of death?] You bet your sweet life!"

Of course, not all of the mentally ill are afraid of death. As we have suggested above, some long for death as a release from the burdens of physical and emotional illness. As Mrs. Powers puts it: "I'm not afraid of dying—I only hope it is quick. All I can think about is peace. I'm just hoping everything will be peaceful and quiet soon."

Some of the mentally-ill subjects are clear in their expressions of reliance on religious beliefs to sustain them as they must face death. Mr. Jackson, as we have seen, is such a person. "Religion means everything to me," he says. "It means that by living up to it, I'll die a good death—whether I go to Heaven or Hell. I don't want to die a coward like some people."

Attitudes of the mentally healthy are sometimes fearful ones, but as often as not, the fear is much like that of Mr. Jackson—they worry about becoming frightened as death approaches. As Mrs. Viet says, "I sure hate to die, but afterwards I'll probably never know I was ever born. Everybody goes the same way. [Are you afraid of death?] Not now, but I won't want to die, I know—maybe I will be then."

By far, the most typical attitude of mentally-healthy subjects was one of acceptance of this inevitable fact of life: "I'm not afraid; it happens to everyone at one time or another"; or as another phrases it: "Let 'er rip! I don't think it'll be half as bad as they say." Or another: "I'm ready to go when the Lord wants to take me—I'm not a bit afraid." So, too: "Let it come when it will. I'm going to live till I die." Perhaps Mr. Janisch epitomizes this acceptance-of-the-inevitable characteristic of the community subjects, when he says, adding his own dash of healthy curiosity:

"Death? Well, darling, I know from nothing about death. But one thing I'm sure of—I'll look back on it as an experience!"

THE SOCIAL LIFE SPACE OF THE ELDERLY POOR

Miss Manx living in her modern apartment in Park Merced and Mr. Knight within his seaview baronial mansion—and even Mr. Bauer and his daughter in their cozy Sunset-District bungalow—are living now in no way very different from that of their prime of life. In their immediate neighborhoods are young married couples with their children and successful middle-aged couples, as well as a sprinkling here and there of people similar to them, in their seventies and eighties. They have not had to suffer any serious restrictions of their spatial mobility which, because of physical, mental, or financial decrements force many aging individuals to move in ever-narrowing circles of possibility. For people such as these, declining resources will often make impossible the upkeep of an automobile, thus forcing them to use public transportation, and illness and disability will often make even this mode of travel impossible. For those who lack family and friends or who are too proud to have others do favors for them which cannot be reciprocated, the immediate neighborhood sets the boundary to their realm of social action. These factors help to explain that phenomenon which is fast becoming a common landmark in American cities—the "geriatric ghetto." These little pockets of elderly residents usually spring up on the fringes of downtown commercial districts where—because the redevelopment bulldozers have not yet arrived—rents are cheap and shops handy. In San Francisco, day-to-day existence for most of the denizens of these quarters of the city is severely restricted to the blocks of these neighborhoods. Often the only alternatives to remaining in one's lodgings are short trips to restaurants, libraries, parks, and shops in the vicinity. Thus, the immediate neighborhood is of great importance to many old people—as important as their own living quarters. Those who can find pleasant habitation within such a low-rent area are fortunate, and even luckier are those who can find such an area that is also safe. According to the elderly themselves, safety is very important, for many—limited to public transportation and often slow in locomotion—do not like to stray too far from their own streets at night. When the aged must leave these areas, it is usually only for special appointments to a doctor or for pressing business affairs. One rarely sees an oldster strolling alone very far from home base.

Any necessity compelling the older person to move to other lodgings can be very threatening. During the seventies and after, such movements tend to be restricted to new locations within the same block of buildings or, sometimes, even within the same apartment building. Generally, our older subjects have demonstrated great reluctance to shift residence. Many will remain in the same hotel from the first days of their retirement. Also, in their discussions with us, many have indicated that they sense very keenly this forced retreat into marginal areas. Under the circumstances, one can readily understand why they zealously seek to resist change in these neighborhoods, keeping a sharp eye out for the alien newcomers who threaten their well-defended territories. Of course, many of these newcomers hail from foreign and minority groups, and the old often find the greatest difficulties in living side-by-side with such people and their strange ways. Given their general reluctance to move and their need to guard carefully their dwindling resources, it is small wonder we have found so many older people socially isolated, almost hiding out from the rest of the world, locked away in many a forgotten cell in the urban beehive.

For another reason, the old resist uprooting themselves: they cling to the familiar in a world that is rapidly changing—the old friends and the dear, familiar haunts. The patterns of a familiar routine can protect the aging urbanite from the modern flux, There is a deep security in being able to move about one's own neighborhood, recognizing familiar faces even though one may not wish to be drawn into conversation. Many would choose not to escape from these ghettos, even if given the opportunity. The women seem to be especially on the *qui-vive* for housing bargains, but when they find them, they are generally within the radius of the same little community. Their friends usually live in the neighboring buildings.

Mrs. Tully (HS) is a typical resident of these downtown geriatric communities. She lives alone in a residence hotel and limits her activities to within a few city blocks. At eighty-four, she survives on Old Age Assistance ($1400 a year) which permits her to reside in a shabbily genteel hotel with other permanent guests of about her age. Mrs. Tully moved into this hotel seventeen years ago, at the time of her husband's death. This move was forced upon her, however, not by her widowhood but because of a serious disagreement with her former landlady. For a short while, she had to make a number of moves within the general neighborhood until she found her present location which is, interestingly enough, only five blocks from her former residence.

Mealtimes appear to be the only thing preventing her from remaining holed up in her room: "I go out to eat every day. If it weren't for getting out and eating, I wouldn't know what I'd do." The rules of a local restaurant encourage her to be up and out of the hotel quite early in the morning—if she wants to have breakfast: "If I don't get there on time, they raise the prices before eleven." Following her various excursions downtown, she will usually return to the hotel in the afternoon to take a nap.

Her encounters with people are friendly but slight. She meets one friend regularly for dinner. To several others, she will call on the telephone for long, one to one-and-a-half hours' conversations. Sometimes she will talk to a friend on the telephone before arising in the morning. The hotel also provides social contacts. Every so often she will sit "in the hotel lobby for maybe an hour" watching television. Most of her associates are barely nodding acquaintances: "There's one fellow there who asked my friend if I ever get enough to eat, but the other men in the lobby don't even know you're there." [Do you like to make new friends?] "Oh yes, I like company. I like to go as much as I can." She doubts, however, that she is very adept in social situations: "Lately I'm with people that I don't know very well, and I'm not a very good mixer." Nevertheless, she still tries to make new contacts: "The other night I ate at the Happy Hour Cafeteria at Fifth and Mission. I met a nice lady from the Wilmington Hotel. Once in a while I do meet people I can talk with." Other contacts are not as pleasant: "Just recently, maybe seven months ago, I knew this woman, but I found out she was a drinking woman. I couldn't get rid of her. I go up to Polk Street a good deal and I run into her."

Mrs. Tully lives within five blocks of Polk Street and yet considers that another district. Having lived there formerly, she yearns to go back. "I take the bus to go up to Polk Street. I have three or four friends there and we always eat together." She prefers the Happy Hour Cafeteria in that district and frequents it whenever she can, but she considers it a bit too far away for her to eat there regularly, although it is only two blocks away from her residence hotel.

Mrs. Harris (HS) is another subject for whom a diversified and pleasing neighborhood is important. She is dissatisfied with the location of her present apartment as it is somewhat removed from the center of town: "I'm not satisfied because I'm stuck here on Mission Street. I want to move downtown where I can get to a decent restaurant. I would move right down to the middle of town, have a small apartment, get out to eat twice a week—two dinners out. Eat Sunday dinner once and maybe a lunch. Move downtown on a bright street where I could go out at night."

This strong interest in good restaurants reminds us, of course, that the enjoyment of food is one of the few sensual pleasures left to the very old, but Mrs. Harris reminds us as well that it can serve a number of other functions: "I get tired of eating at home and I go across the street and have bacon and eggs on Sunday mornings. Just to get out and eat in a public place and see people! I get tired of staring at four walls. I eat out one meal a week—lunch—just to get away." For many of the metropolitan elderly, restaurants may afford the only place where they can observe the bustle of life from a sitting position. Often the parks are, again, "too far" or nonexistent. City fathers do not usually take into account these needs of our aged citizens, but Mrs. Harris would like to remind them. When asked about the problems of the aged, she responds: "Well, there are no benches where you can sit on the street. You have to leg it. I feel deeply about this subject." Mrs. Harris says she will vote for the candidate in the next municipal election who proposes "benches by bus stops—I'm voting for him." She has a further practical suggestion: "Wish there was a wagon that would go around with books from the library."

Restrictions in territoriality may be an inconvenience even for those whose living quarters are pleasant and the neighborhood essentially a good one. The problem in the following case is one of transportation. Mrs. Trocopian (HS) loves the apartment in the house she and her husband have bought but mentions: "I feel lonesome and too congested. I feel very much tied down and very much in one place." She feels the one great advantage to her present location lies in the fact that she lives half a block from a park, visits to which are the only excursions she takes alone. Above all, she regrets not having a car. Her present location is quite far from her church which she used to attend very frequently for it meant much to her: "I used to go to church a lot and come back and make dinner on Sunday, but now I tire easily when I have to go out and take the bus and come back." She has had to drop her membership in the Clarion Club because "I have to take three busses to get there." Finally, she wants an automobile so she can visit her many friends who are scattered about the city: "If I had a car, it would take me a month to round up all my acquaintances. I just stay all the time in the Richmond district."

Mr. James Janssen's (CS) circumstances also provide an illustration of living arrangements among the elderly—this, however, in contrast with Mrs. Trocopian's world. Mr. Janssen, at seventy-six, has been living in Skid Row for the past fifteen years. For twelve years, he lived on Fourth Street and, since, has moved but a few blocks to his present address on Sixth Street. Now his life circles around this one street where he does his shopping and visiting. In earlier years, he found a number of drinking companions in the area and these were individuals from whom he could borrow money. "Then we got drinking and I don't know where the money went, but I will borrow some from people I know." Mr. Janssen's neighborhood is "pretty rough. That's why I put a lock on the front door, and now I padlock this one in the kitchen." He has lost most of his former friends through death, through their moving to other neighborhoods, or merely because, if they lived at too great a distance, contact ceased. "I used to have friends up on Eddy Street, but they don't come down here any more—not to this part of town." Yet a few friends remain:

"I go to see the Swede about twice a week, but sometimes two or three weeks, I don't see him, but he does come around here sometimes." Then there is the owner of a garage on Fifth Street: "When I feel better, always some work to do there. I saw wood for Frank. He runs a parking lot. He's a good man." Finally, there is a woman who comes to his room: "She's supposed to come and cook. I give her a dollar."

Mr. Janssen's neighborhood is changing and he considers this a misfortune. "I had quite a few men friends. We used to live here in this building—the whole bunch of us, all single men. There was a bunch of us. We played cards, talked, and one would make a pot of stew." However, the landlord began renovating his place and "got them all out." With his new neighbors, Mr. Janssen does not "get along at all. Different people altogether—colored, Filipino. I can't even speak to them. Only one white man here and he talks too much. Talk your ear off. He can't write or read, but he talks your ear off." He almost wishes he had married: "You get lonesome all alone, especially now with all these niggers and Filipinos in the neighborhood. Before, we were all pals."

Other hotel dwellers in our sample report problems similar to Mr. Janssen's. Mr. Jackson (HS) has found it difficult to relate to his neighbors living in the same hotel with him: "Well, it's strange, because I'm not used to the kind of people who live here in the hotel. [Probe] Well, they were raised in a different environment. Even at Mendocino [State Hospital], I associated only with the nurses and techs. But here! None of them [residents of the hotel] know anything. Even these sailors here can't discuss how a ship is built and how it isn't built." In this instance, a change in economic status brought on with old age has thrown Mr. Jackson into a social milieu he finds difficult to adjust to.

Many of our subjects who live in the cheap hotels of the "geriatric ghetto" are forced into at least some kind of mutual interrelating for the sake of self-protection. A large proportion have made certain contractual arrangements with their neighbors to help out in case of illness or to perform certain necessary services. Very frequently, payment is tendered for this Good-Samaritanism. For example, Mrs. Harris (HS) has a friend who comes over on weekends: "She sleeps here, has her meals—doesn't charge me for the work she does." Also, her tenant does her grocery shopping for her. Mrs. Kramer (CS) mentions a lady in her apartment "who gets groceries for me when I am sick. I pay her for it." Somewhat later she adds: "The lady down the hall helped me when I was sick. I paid her five dollars for what she had done. I don't want for anything. She brought me groceries." Quite clearly, the reimbursement soothes the embarrassment in asking for help and preserves one's sense of self-reliance. In like fashion, some of the men will mention women who come and occasionally cook for them—again, for reimbursement. Also, from those who have been through the psychiatric-screening-ward experience, we learn how, during the period of worst psychological stress, some friend in the building had been providing them with food, or that the illness had been brought to the awareness of the hotel manager by some "friend down the hall" who had shown concern. Many of these "loners" who had to be hospitalized were pleasantly surprised by neighbors who came to visit them during their distress. They frequently mention that they "never knew" they had such friends, but, touched as they have been by such gestures, they usually drift back into isolation upon their return to the community.

In Chapters VIII and IX, we shall explore the wider issues involved in the trend observed here to segregate the elderly into their own sub-communities. At this point, we only wish to take note of the living arrangements that prevail when the elderly poor are left to their own resources when solving their problems. Widows and spinsters, for the most part, appear to value some not-too-secluded, safe little place of their own, where their "nesting" impulses will continue to be satisfied. Lifelong isolated males will, of course, favor this mode of living too, but, in certain cases, we have been struck by the revival of "barracks"-type, all-male households. These appear to be mainly attempts to institute some sort of a mutual-aid society to handle emergencies. Above all, the old ghetto dwellers seem to ask for a measure of privacy in inexpensive quarters which are not too far from the bustle of the city's heart.

Chapter VIII

SELF AND SOCIETY IN OLD AGE:
BEYOND DISENGAGEMENT

> *It is . . . expedient to enable the individuals, by their own foresight, prudence, and industry, to secure to themselves in old age a comfortable provision and asylum. Those now employed at the establishment contribute to a fund which supports them when too ill to work, or when superannuated. This fund, however, is not calculated to give them more than a bare existence; and it is surely desirable that, after they have spent nearly half a century in unremitting industry, they should, if possible, in the decline of life, enjoy a comfortable independence.*
>
> —ROBERT OWEN
> *A New View of Society*
> (1817), pp. 119-120.

INTRODUCTION

THE NOTION THAT the aged should exist socially and economically independent of their juniors has a long history in Western civilization. The Utopian social essays of Robert Owen, from which we have drawn the epigraph, contain one of the first published pleas in English for public assistance to the aged. As a matter of additional interest, this same essay proposed that there be built special housing tracts reserved for the retired elderly.[1] And here in the United States, a century and a half later, such "retirement communities" have become an accomplished fact; many already exist and more are being built all the time. The value of self-reliance has been a part of America's earliest heritage. Historically, there has existed in this country a preference for

---

[1]Owen goes on to suggest: "To effect this object, it is intended that in the most pleasant situation near the present village, neat and convenient dwellings should be erected, with gardens attached; that they should be surrounded and sheltered by plantations, through which public walks should be formed, and the whole arranged to give the occupiers the more substantial comforts. . . . [T]hose still engaged in active operations would of course frequently visit their former companions and friends, who after having spent their years of toil were in the actual enjoyment of this simple retreat; and from this intercourse each party would naturally derive pleasure" (pp. 120-121) .

the transfer of responsibility for the care of the elderly from family groups to the elderly themselves (through early life inculcation of "habits of industry, temperance, and foresight"), then finally aided, if necessary, by the state.

However, early nineteenth century Utopians were proposing some nonfamilial means of *economic* support of the aged ("comfortable provision and asylum")—not *social* independence (*cf.* footnote 1). Owen took it for granted that there would continue to be frequent social intercourse between the generations, and that one could benefit from contact with the other. In twentieth-century America, however, the value of financial autonomy has been extended into the social sphere. There now exists in contemporary American thinking considerable discussion of the question as to whether the aged are happier and more content if they are "disengaged"—this is to say, only minimally involved in the social life of the community. It is this notion we should like to examine in the light of our study.

On the basis of statistical evidence, we will show how each of our measures of *personal* function—self-evaluation and morale —relate to our two measures of *social function*—the status index and level of social interaction. The questions we are asking here are these: (1) To what extent—if any—are self-esteem and high morale in old age dependent upon an individual's continued occupancy of adult *social statuses?* (2) Does his *level of social interaction,* regardless of the number of formal social positions he occupies, affect his self-esteem and morale? If so, is it more or less influential than the number of statuses he occupies? (3) Are these two social factors—statuses and amount of social contact—*additive* with respect to healthy attitudes towards oneself and one's way of life? (4) Finally, which factors are most likely to be associated with *confinement for mental illness* in late life— personal factors such as a disturbed self-image and a state of depression—or social factors, such as attrition of roles and social isolation? Or, is there some combination of these problems that makes for an emotional disturbance of sufficient gravity to warrant psychiatric hospitalization?

Answers to the last question have significant implications for the elderly. It may be that old people who suffer mental illness in late life simply have developed personality disturbances for which no degree of social support can compensate. There is some evidence in our case materials suggesting that this may be so: for example, Mrs. Trocopian was far from socially secluded prior to her admission to the psychiatric ward. She had a husband, children, grandchildren, many friends, and was an active member of a church and voluntary organizations—yet, in late life, she began to suffer such severe disturbances of thought and behavior that she had to be locked up, lest she carry out her threat to murder her husband.

On the other hand, it may be that there are old people whose self-esteem and morale are intact, but who are hospitalized for relatively benign conditions (such as mild memory loss or fainting spells) simply because there is no one but a public institution who will care for them. This certainly seems to have been true in the case of some of our subjects, including Mr. Angus Pillsbury, who was getting along fairly well until his sister—his last remaining relative—died and left him without any source for the minimal assistance he needed to maintain an independent existence.

A further question can best be explored with our intensive case data: Does the *quality* of social interaction influence the world of the self in old age? Is the role that the aged perceive themselves to have in American society inimical to happiness and self-esteem? Do the elderly consider that younger people devalue, avoid, or resent them—and, if so, do these perceived attitudes affect their views of themselves?

Finally, we will examine the notion of social disengagement of the aged in some detail: its distribution, its relationship to mental health, and its value for some in the process of adaptation to aging in American society.

SOCIAL STATUSES AND THE PERSONAL SYSTEM

The number of statuses an aged person occupies is correlated with mental health (Chapter V) : those occupying a sizeable number of social positions are much less likely to be psychiatrically

impaired. In this section, we will examine the relationship between number of social statuses and two elements of the personal
system: self-evaluation (what one thinks of oneself) and morale
(one's spirits or sustained mood).

TABLE X

RELATIONSHIPS AMONG DIMENSIONS OF PERSONAL AND SOCIAL FUNCTION
FOR TOTAL STUDY SAMPLE

	Self-evaluation Positive %	Morale High %
Number of Statuses Occupied		
7-8	73	81
5-6	67	69
3-4	57	54
0-2	52	16
Total N	(331)	(287)
Social Interaction Levels		
1 (highest level)	77	89
2	68	73
3	65	40
4	50	31
5 (lowest level)	44	27
Total N	(407)	(351)
Social Function Groups*		
1 (highest)	72	80
2	70	75
3	69	50
4 (lowest)	48	26
Total N	(292)	(261)

Group 1 is high on both number of statuses and level of social interaction;
Group 2 is low on statuses—but high on interaction; Group 3 is high on statuses,
low on interaction; and Group 4 is low on both. (High on statuses means occupying five or more; high on social interaction means having a score higher than
three, i.e., leaving the dwelling unit in order to socialize.)

As shown in Table X, the greater the number of statuses occupied by members of the study sample, the more positive the
self-evaluation. Fully 73 per cent of the group occupying the most
social statuses as compared with 52 per cent of those having two
or less report a positive self-image. Even if we simply divide the
sample into those with few statuses (0-4) and those with many
(5-8), 14 per cent more of the latter group render positive self-
reports than do the former.

A number of subjects seemed to have difficulty in describing themselves in any terms *other than* their social roles. One community subject gives the following response:

> Well, describing yourself, eh? That's hard — to make a description of yourself. Rather difficult to describe yourself. How would *you* describe yourself? Well, I enjoy good company, friendship. My relatives are all in the east in Chicago and Vermont, but I have no relatives living out here. I had cousins here that died.

This man, retired at the time of the interview, had much less difficulty describing himself as the kind of man he had been at age fifty: "Well, I was more active then. I was teaching school and keeping books." Note, however, that—even retrospectively—this man perceives himself exclusively in terms of past statuses—specifically, his former occupation.

Another community subject similarly bases his self-image almost entirely on work and kinship roles:

> I don't worry much as long as I can keep busy. I work four days a week at the store. I feel good all the time. Oh, I get kind of lonesome — all my brothers and sisters are gone. We all lived here in San Francisco. Now they're all passed away, so I'm alone. But as long as I'm healthy and able to work, I'm cheerful all the time — even if I am lonesome. I go to visit my son and his family nearly every week.

A widow in the community sample describes herself as "a well-adjusted grandmother and a darn good worker." She describes herself at age fifty in terms of her role as a wife: "I was about the same then. Anxious about a sick husband—faithful and kind to him, I hope."

There is not only a positive relationship between self-esteem and the subject's degree of involvement in social roles, but, among the mentally healthy, there was also a greater tendency for reference to those roles in self-descriptions. Members of the community sample *do* occupy more social roles, on the average, than hospital subjects. The interesting thing here, however, is that social relationships clearly provide a significant portion of the content of a perception of the self—and, furthermore, the more such relationships, the more likely is the self-view to be a positive one.

In old age, one's inventory of social relationships is even more highly related to one's morale than it is to one's self-esteem. Significantly, 81 per cent of all subjects with seven or eight social statuses had high morale scores (Table X). Among those with no more than two social statuses, only 16 per cent had high morale: nearly five out of six such older people were demoralized. With every decrement in social relatedness, the likelihood of depression is increased.

However, when these figures are assessed in terms of the intervening effect of mental illness their impact is less dramatic. The mentally ill are both more socially deprived and more disturbed in their personal function (Chapter V). Some of the differences just described, then, are simply reflections of mental status differences in the total sample. In order to examine the exclusive influence of wealth or dearth of social statuses on personal function, we must examine community and hospital subjects separately. We have done this, and the results are presented in the first part of Table XI.

TABLE XI

RELATIONSHIPS AMONG DIMENSIONS OF PERSONAL AND
SOCIAL FUNCTION FOR TWO MENTAL STATUS GROUPS

	Self-evaluation Positive		Morale High	
	Community Sample %	Hospital Sample %	Community Sample %	Hospital Sample %
Number of Statuses				
5-8	71	68	77	43
0-4	69	51	73	24
Social Interaction Levels				
High	72	53	80	48
Low	56	50	45	28

These figures show a curious pattern: the number of available social statuses has a discernible influence on self-evaluation and morale *only* among the mentally ill. Community subjects, regardless of the number of social relationships, show no differences on these two dimensions of personal function. This seems to signify that there is a stronger reliance upon social supports in the event of emotional disturbance in old age, but that among the mentally healthy, formal social positions are not relevant to either self-esteem or level of morale. In other words, if the mentally-ill aged can point to some established relations with their society, these may enhance a floundering self-esteem and alleviate personal depression. But, among the community subjects, a positive self-view and satisfaction with life seem to depend on something other than formal social positions—for them, personal function has been divorced from continued occupancy of traditional social roles.

Perhaps having available kin, friends, and membership in churches or clubs is something like having money in the bank. As long as things go well, it is other aspects of life that bring pride and satisfaction. However, when life becomes trying and painful—when mental or emotional problems begin to take their toll—then, having a reserve of potential sources of support and help relieve one of considerable anxiety. The mentally ill in our study sample have already been forced to take stock of these sources of support—they have reached a crisis point in adaptation to aging. For them, the availability of social supports is a matter of vital importance which can affect their welfare in very realistic ways. Willing kinsmen may provide them a home when they can no longer maintain one for themselves; helpful friends and neighbors may provide assistance with the tasks essential to life; if their health permits it, even the most menial and occasional work or participation in any organization may give them a sense of purpose; and a religious faith may help to carry them safely through moments of black despair. It is then that social assets become crucial for their satisfaction with life, and even to their sense of self-worth.

LEVEL OF SOCIAL INTERACTION AND PERSONAL FUNCTION

Our second measure of social function is the social-interaction score (described in Chapter V). Table XI indicates regular and dramatic associations between social interaction levels and both

self-evaluation and morale. Morale is more highly influenced than
is self-evaluation by the level of social interaction. Of those subjects at the highest level of social interaction, 89 per cent reported
high morale. Only 27 per cent of those at the lowest level (the
social isolates) have high morale scores. In the area of self-evaluation, 77 per cent of those at the highest level of social interaction
reported positive self-images, compared with only 44 per cent of
those at the lowest level.

Once again, however, mental status is an intervening factor
in these relationships. Table XI examines these associations independently for the community and hospital samples and presents a very different picture from that provided in our analysis
of formal social statuses. Community subjects, it will be remembered, were neither demoralized nor self-critical as a result of occupying few formal statuses. However, as Table XI suggests, they
are affected in both these areas by social isolation. Among community subjects, there are regular and appreciable differences in
self-esteem and morale, depending on the level of social interaction. Among the socially active, 72 per cent have positive self-
views; among the socially inactive, only 56 per cent. Morale
scores show an even more marked response to social contact:
among the socially active, 80 per cent have high morale; among
the inactive, less than half—only 45 per cent. Among the mentally-healthy aged, then, it is not the formal social statuses one
occupies—the usual roles of earlier adult years—that provide satisfaction with life and a feeling of self-worth. It is rather the utilization of those relationships one *does* have—the preservation of a
high level of social interaction—that promotes a sense of personal
well-being in later life.

Many community subjects are quite explicit about the importance of contact with others. One man living in the community describes himself as "a pretty fair person. I never harm nobody. I go all over the neighborhood and keep busy; that's why I
feel so good." Another community subject reports: "At fifty, I
was like I am now. It's being around people. I always liked people.
Not to see people is no good. I lived in an apartment alone once
but it was no good—no people. After my wife died, I went to
live with friends—then things were better."

Conversely, other subjects relate negative personal attitudes to meager social contacts. Mrs. Miller (CS), for instance, attributes some of her unhappiness to social isolation. Asked to describe herself, she says, "I don't know. I have the reputation of being set in my ways. I get angry—I get hurt easily. I think it's because I'm alone so much."

The case of Mr. VanDamm (CS), whose social life we have already sketched briefly in Chapter V, is a good example of the importance of sociability. This man, now in his mid-sixties, has very few formal social statuses. He is employed, belongs to a club, and has a group of close friends, but he has no other formal positions in his society. He never married, and has outlived most of his close kin; he never joined a church. Yet, as we have seen, he is a very active man, replacing lost relationships, making the most of the few roles he does play, and living a rich and rewarding life. His self-esteem is intact and his morale excellent.

The influence of social interaction on the mentally-ill aged, however, is somewhat ambiguous. Self-evaluation among hospital subjects is independent of the level of social interaction; almost as many of the inactive as of the active give positive self-reports (50 and 53 per cent, respectively).

This is a rather curious finding, but an understandable one if we recall the case of Mr. Leveritt (HS) presented in Chapter V. The events of this unhappy man's later life indicate that it is sometimes only by "a retreat into anonymity" that assaults to the personal system—and even psychiatric hospitalization—may be avoided. Certain kinds of elderly people, like Mr. Leveritt, spare their self-esteem through a defensive social disengagement, which insulates them from social criticism or intervention. Ernest Becker (1962) has described the impact of social interaction on the self-image in the following way: "In the social encounter each member exposes for public scrutiny, and possible intolerable undermining, the one thing he needs most: the positive self-valuation he has so laboriously fashioned. . . . '[F]ace' is the vital self-esteem exposed to the public. . . . Nothing goes deeper than the exposure of the self-esteem to possible intolerable undermining of the social context. . . . [T]he self must submit to being socially engaged, if this engagement is done with proper deference to the self-esteem" (pp. 94-96). We would go one step further and point out from our study of the aged that, if there is not proper deference given to the self-esteem, the aged person may disengage from his society.

Although the self-evaluation of the mentally ill may be sustained independent of social interaction, those who do interact more frequently show considerably higher levels of morale. In other words, among the mentally ill, social isolation may preserve "face" and thus self-esteem—but it is nevertheless demoralizing. Retreat in the service of pride is often effected at the expense of life satisfaction.

COMBINED EFFECTS OF SOCIAL STATUSES AND INTERACTION

To determine whether or not status and amount of contact are, in effect, *additive* in promoting good personal function, we examined their combined influence by dividing our sample into four social-function groups: (1) those high on both number of statuses and level of social interaction; (2) those low on statuses but high on social interaction; (3) those high on statuses but low on interaction, and (4) those low on both. In terms of self-evaluation and morale, we found that it is only the very lowest of these four groups who report significantly less self-esteem than the rest of the sample. Table X shows that high function on either or both of the social function measures allows for preservation of a positive self-image. About 70 per cent of subjects in each of the first three groups gave positive self-reports, but only 48 per cent of those in the last group did so.

This finding suggests that, while the maintenance of former social roles enhances self-esteem, an individual may compensate for role losses by preserving a high level of social activity. Conversely, even an elderly person whose social world is restricted to his own four walls can place a positive value on himself, if his existence is defined as having social meaning to other people. Thus, Mrs. Cox, a ninety-two-year-old widowed resident of a home for the aged, too infirm to leave her bed and long separated from family and friends, still finds good things to say about herself: "I'm a religious person of good character and good family." Although Mrs. Cox believes she is "lost to the rest of the world," her family and friendship roles, although inactive, remain vital to her self-image: "I'm not lost to my children. They come; they think of me. I have the reputation of being a pretty good wife and mother. I got a nice Mother's Day card and some nice birthday cards. You know my daughter lives in Minneapolis. I've only got some friends here." But, as can be seen from the low levels of self-esteem among the group with the poorest social function, old people who are truly lost to the whole world are often lost to themselves as well.[2]

Data on morale for these four social function groups show that while the most socially-involved subjects have high morale in 80 per cent of the cases, and the least-involved in only 26 per cent of the cases, the intermediate groups are by no means identical in morale—although they are in the case of self-evaluation. Three-fourths of the second group (those with few statuses but socially active) report high morale, but just one-half of third-group subjects are high (those with many statuses, but socially inactive). Insofar as morale is concerned, we interpret this to mean that social interaction is the more critical of the social function measures. Occupying a sizeable number of roles does somewhat enhance the level of morale but role occupancy alone by no means compensates for social isolation. Self-esteem, then, can be maintained through the mechanism of nominal relatedness to others, even though one might rarely have opportunity to interact with them. Satisfaction with life, however, can be sustained only through a vital, on-going engagement with life.

RELATIVE IMPORTANCE OF PERSONAL AND SOCIAL FACTORS IN PSYCHIATRIC HOSPITALIZATION

At the beginning of this chapter, we also asked what combinations of personal and social resources are required to keep an older person out of a mental hospital. From other studies of aging

---

[2]We have not considered in this volume the relationship between duration of isolation and mental illness. For such a discussion, see Lowenthal (1964b).

it is clear that, certainly, the ways in which individuals grow old and their ease of adaptation depend to a large extent on deep-seated differences in their earlier life personalities (see, for example, Reichard, Livson, and Petersen, 1962). However, as these writers point out, "Not only may personality exercise a decisive influence on the way in which individuals react to growing older, but personality itself may change with advancing age. . . . [T]he transition from middle to old age can be assumed to have a significant impact on personality development, paralleling in many ways earlier stages of development" (p. 3). That is, personal characteristics of the aged must always be viewed in the light of the social setting within which they occur. For while personal thoughts, feelings, and behavior are individual constructs, they assume meaning and value only in terms of the social matrix within which they occur. For the old of our sample, individual character is tied up with past and present role systems and the influences of the behavioral environment (Chapter II). The position of an aged individual, then, is not entirely dependent on his personal characteristics. He exists within the web of inter-acting personal and social systems, and their joint consequences will determine his success or failure in adaptation to aging.

In this volume, we have limited our examination of quantitative measures of function to just a handful of dimensions—and these are somewhat global measures. Nevertheless, we can get some notion of the relative influences of personal and social factors in the mental health of the elderly by looking at groups of subjects who vary in relative strengths of one system compared with the other. Thus, in Table XII we have divided our study sample into three groups based on personal-function measures, Group I having the highest level of personal function and Group III the lowest. Each of these groups has then been divided into three subcategories, depending on the strength of social support. Subjects falling in Column A have the highest level of social function and those in Column C have the lowest. In this way, we have defined nine groups of subjects showing varying degrees and combinations of function in the two interacting systems. For each cell, we have computed the proportion who were mentally well, defining the mentally healthy here as those subjects who have not been hospitalized for psychiatric problems during old age—that is, the members of the community sample. By comparing these actual proportions to the frequencies we would expect by random distribution, we were able to distinguish those cells which showed higher and lower proportions of mentally-healthy subjects than the expected frequencies. We were able then to draw a line between the cells that exceeded expected frequencies in the proportion of mentally-well subjects and those that fell below the expected values. This line might be thought of as "the threshold of social tolerance for the aged." It might just as well be labelled "the threshold of mental illness"; however, since we are dealing here with the interaction of the individual and his milieu, we prefer the connotations of group process implicit in the former term.

TABLE XII

SOCIAL AND PERSONAL FUNCTION BY MENTAL HEALTH[a]

	Social Function Measures[b] (Percentage Difference—from Expected Proportion Mentally Well)[c]		
	(A) High on Both Measures	(B) High on One Measure Only	(C) Low on Both Measures
Personal Function Measures[d]			
(1) High on both measures	+16	0	—41
(2) High on one measure only	+13	—9	—53
(3) Low on both measures	+ 6	—6	—68

[a] The total number of subjects used in this table is 261; this number includes all subjects in the study sample who could be scored on all four measures.

[b] The measures of social function used were the Status Index and the F-2 Social Interaction Level. Both measures were used in dichotomous form. Category (2) includes subjects with a low Status Index score and a high Social Interaction level, *and* subjects with a high Status Index score and a low Social Interaction level.

[c] "Mentally well" as used here refers to those subjects in our sample who have not been hospitalized for psychiatric problems during old age, i.e., the Community Sample subjects.

[d] The measures of personal function used were Self-evaluation and Morale (Depression-Satisfaction cluster scores). Both measures were used in dichotomous form. Category (2) includes both subjects with a positive self-evaluation but low morale, *and* subjects with a neutral or negative self-evaluation but high morale.

This table shows that, regardless of the level of personal function—whether high or low—a high degree of social involvement increases the probability that an individual will be tolerated in the community. On the other hand, all those at the lowest level of social function, regardless of personal disturbances, have a better than average chance of being removed from the community through the mechanism of psychiatric hospitalization.

People with serious disruptions of the personal system, as indicated by being in the lowest group, required the *highest* level of social involvement in order to have a better than even chance of staying out of a psychiatric facility. Even those with an intermediate level of personal function (that is, with either high morale or a positive self-view, but not both) had a better than average chance of remaining in the community only in the presence of strong social supports.

These figures should not be interpreted to mean that every older person who remains secluded and has relatively few social roles will inevitably end in a mental institution. It simply means that, the fewer an older individual's social supports, the more vulnerable he is to hospitalization should any small crack appear in his personal equanimity. It seems clear that American culture defines mental health as *social involvement,* and serious disruptions of social function appear to be stronger predictors of psychiatric hospitalization of the aged than are intrapsychic factors alone.

At times of personal distress, then, social interaction and the support of others are vital to the aging individual's well-being. Yet, urban American society does not automatically provide a matrix within which that interaction may occur, at least between the elderly and the younger members of society. The distance between the generations is too great, and there is no on-going cultural tradition to cement bonds between young and old.

THE SOCIAL ALIENATION OF AMERICA'S ELDERLY

Cumming and Henry (1961) have quite rightly pointed out that some writings in the field of aging have ". . . sometimes suggested that every man ages alone, in the sense of being cut off, by the fact of his age, from others. . . . It seems to be assumed that the 'one' who is the reference point is the only one doing any aging. . . . There is little indication of people aging in ranks, echelons, or generations, but rather some feeling that growing old is a solitary experience, unique to each individual" (p. 17). From the evidence of our study (Chapter VII), the elderly do indeed interact with each other, and depend upon collateral relationships (with spouse, siblings, or friends) more than they depend upon their offspring or other younger people

Yet, there are some older people in our sample (many of our subjects—unlike those studied by Cumming and Henry—are physically disabled) who do not have the necessary mobility and strength to seek out others of their own generation—others who, too, may be partially housebound. Someone must *come to them,* if they are to have social contacts beyond their own quarters, their own city block, or, at the most, their own small neighborhood. These visitors would have to be people more active and vigorous than they themselves—people almost by definition, somewhat younger than they.

Then, too, because we have some emotionally-disturbed people in our sample (the Cumming and Henry sample was confined to the mentally-healthy aged), we have encountered more older people who hate the idea of growing old—are, in fact, horrified and depressed by the passage of years. And many of these do not want to be reminded that they are growing older; they do not want older associates, particularly if those associates have serious health problems—it is too painful a reminder of their own vulnerability. As Mrs. Trocopian says, "Some older people lose their hearing and their memory. It's hard to get along with them. It's unfortunate if you lose your memory. *I* don't feel old at all! If I don't feel right, I blame it on the food; I never say it is because I am old. Most of my friends are younger."

Some of our subjects, too, have outlived all the age-mates with whom they had formerly been close. A little later in this chapter we will describe such a man, Mr. Hart (CS), who, at ninety-three, has long survived his peers.

For these reasons, many of the elderly turn increasingly to

members of the succeeding generation for social contacts, but, in this undertaking, they are often deterred by the conviction that the young despise the old, and that the old have no place in American society.

Approximately half of the subjects in the intensive sample believe that "American society is set up for younger people." They point to "the pampering of children," the movies and advertisements extolling youth and sex, the greater job opportunities available to the young, or to the advance of automation, giving trained youth the advantage in the labor market. Others merely remark that the elderly have been "put on the sidelines" or are obliged to "take a back seat." Most perceive America's preference for youth as an injustice; but a minority—those with, perhaps a greater sense of history or a greater awareness of youth's desire to take their rightful place in a productive world—feel that these conditions, regrettable as they might be for the aged, are inherently just. Mr. Jespersen (CS) epitomizes this attitude: "You have to make way for progress which the new generation brings." Mr. Kepler (HS) reasons in the same way: "I believe that everything favors younger people. I think it used to be the other way around. But I guess it *should* favor the young because it seems natural to me—they're more alert, have more ambition." As another subject puts it: "I guess that's right, because it's going to be their world."

Some, however, point to the Social Security benefits now available to the aged and the increasing interest taken by federal and state governments in ameliorating the lot of the aged. "I think they are doing all kinds of things for the aged—even this survey," says Mrs. Burbank (CS). "There are all kinds of opportunities for older people now—if you know what they are and take advantage of them." One subject is even a bit patriotic about it: "All Americans have an equal chance." Nevertheless, only one subject claims flatly that American society actually favors the old. Mr. Merton Fox (CS) believes that life in this country is "better for old people. We can go down and get meal tickets and lodgings, but not the younger people—they have to steal." Mr. Fox has accepted his life on Skid Row as a tough struggle for survival and takes a special pride in having survived there into his eighties.

Over half of the community subjects and half of the female dischargees agreed that the position of elderly people in the United States has changed for the better and confidently believe it will continue to do so. Such is Mrs. Bruzinsky's (CS) opinion: "Why, now they have Senior Citizens' groups so people can go places and do things." Some subjects, like Mr. Jespersen (CS), contrast the present with grim recollections of the past: "Now it is better than it was ever before. Before I've seen old people work until they died on the job. They had no pensions then, no money, no security, so they worked themselves to death. Now they have many benefits and can live their older years in some comfort." Mr. Lawrence Southern (CS) remarks upon the improved opportunities today for the aged to make the most of their appearance and even to disguise their age: "The beauty shop has made the difference. A seventy-year-old woman—if she has money—can make herself look like sixty. Men sort of have to keep up with the women." This man feels that old people today are "well off": "More older people travel to Europe and there are beautiful hotels where older people live in retirement." Although Mr. Southern himself is not wealthy, he does hope to retire eventually —on a more modest scale—to a trailer park.

Despite these positive comments on aging itself, our subjects believe that the status of the aged within their families is deteriorating (the eagerness of children to "shove" aged parents into rest homes was mentioned quite frequently). They perceive a general indifference and callousness of many younger people toward the aged; for these reasons, the elderly often see little choice but to look toward the government for the improvement of their plight. The government cannot, of course, raise their prestige or improve interpersonal relationships, but it can ensure minimal survival and provide some measure of medical care. Mrs. Bruzinsky (CS), for one, welcomes the change: "The government wants to give older people more things and tries to make life better for them. They will have Medicare soon and things will be better for them, for they won't have to worry about money for the doctor." But Mr. Edwin Butler (CS), who is fearful that his ambition to become a "success" will never be realized in the years remaining to him, is of a different opinion. "People should not be forced to put away for old age." Later, he complains: "People don't have to take the initiative now, for they know that the government will always take care of them."

The responses of the male dischargees, for the most part, are very negative. They rarely notice any improvement with Social Security benefits and tend to stress the low social and employment status of the elderly. Mr. Hopland (HS) comments on the lack of job opportunities: "We're not getting the same rights we did when younger. We don't have an equal chance with middle-aged men to get a job or to do things. It used to be more equal. Formerly, they'd hire an elderly man, but now they won't." Mr. Alioto (HS) is particularly pessimistic: "You know, a man ain't worth a damn after forty-five today. Or a woman either. You used to be a man as long as you could." Mr. Jackson (HS) is very indignant about the way conditions for the elderly are deteriorating: "This whole neighborhood here: they're tearing it all down and making parking lots out of it. But you can't keep tearing down hotels for elderly people, for they cannot afford to live any place better than here. Their future isn't rosy and it's getting worse every year." Mr. Jackson is incensed about many other things too: "Right now, if you're over forty and out of work, you've got a hard time getting a job. A lot of these places that *do* hire elderly people—like those charity places—don't pay them anything." He also has much to say about the state hospitals: "They're not filled with crazy people; they're filled with people nobody wants to take care of!"

Many of the subjects who perceive the position of the elderly to have taken a turn for the worse bring up the issue of decreased job opportunities, much as Mr. Jackson does. Forced retirement is almost universally abhorred, and those who do not mention it nevertheless stress the difficulties in obtaining work after the age of thirty-five or forty. Subjects with this strong an emphasis on work and instrumental values tend to be the mentally ill in the sample. A persistence of instrumental values (Chapter VI) seems to create a hostile competitiveness with the young. This attitude, in turn, creates a greater sense of alienation from younger people.

Half of the community and hospital discharged subjects, however, indicate that age does *not* affect their relationships with younger people. Community subjects also report a bit more warmth in these relationships than do the hospital dischargees. This is apparent in the replies of the following two community subjects to the question of whether age has made any difference in their dealings with the younger generation. "No, not from my point of view," says Mr. Knight, "and I'm sure not from theirs. They're nice and sweet to me." Mr. Lewissohn has equally good relationships with younger people: "I'm getting along nice with young people. Age makes no barrier, if you understand younger people and their ways." Those dischargees who deny that age has made any difference fail to specify in what ways these relationships are positive and tend to explain the lack of difference by minimizing the differences between generations. Thus, Mr. Kepler (HS) tells how he avoids the negative: "I try, when dealing with younger people, to think like they do and act like they do." Mr. Jackson (HS) insists that not his age but his "physical ability" affects his interactions with young people. The female dischargees frequently state that they "get along fine" or that they are "liked my many young people." Some responses hint that these older people wish to disassociate themselves from other aged, as we have seen in the case of Mrs. Trocopian (HS). Similarly, Mrs. Sandusky (HS) discounts generational differences: "I go along with the trend of the time. I'm not in the 1920's, because it's 1963. I don't know that my ideas are too much different from those of younger people."

The other half of the intensive-study sample admit that age does affect their interaction with younger persons. Having once made the admission, however, community subjects express greater tolerance and understanding of the perceived changes than do the formerly hospitalized. They indicate less resentment at the change and describe the behavior of younger people in less negative terms. Positive appraisals of the change occur in but two instances. Miss Manx (CS) is the only subject fortunate enough to be able to characterize the change as "beneficial" and to state: "Young people like me and I like them." The only other response we can regard as positive is considerably tempered: Mr. VanDamm says, "Young people look up to you for advice sometimes and to see how you do things." However, this subject, a retired military man, feels that: "If you do things the proper way, they lose respect for you sometimes."

The remaining responses regarding youth-age relationships fall into two groups: those who emphasize the lack of communication between the generations—a condition often recognized as unavoidable and accepted with understanding and resignation—and those who disparage the young and their assumed negative attitudes toward older people. These latter subjects report these perceptions with some bitterness and consider them a threat to their self-esteem. Mr. Czernich (HS) exemplifies the first sort of perception: "You cannot get along with young people. They talk about different things together. Usually our conversation does not mix." Mrs. Kramer (CS) has somewhat similar ideas: "I don't get through to younger people as good. I can't get on common ground with them." Mr. Jespersen (CS) emphasizes how technology has created a gulf between the generations: "Younger people have more modern ideas which, in many ways, are better than the old ones. The increased use of machines and the more education the younger ones have, the more advanced they are from the older generation." Mrs. Miller (CS) perceives younger people as moving in a separate sphere of activity: "Younger people have different things to do—different ways in life from what is mine." Those who disparage the young generally do so mildly as Mrs. Langtry (CS) does: "Reactions of young people are entirely different; some say that I'm 'just an old woman,' but some will listen," or a Mr. Ebenhauser (CS) does: "Younger people want to travel among their own age. Quite a lot have no respect for older people." Others are harsher, such as Mr. Mersky (CS): "Young people don't want to have somebody old around. Most of the time they feel that older people are old-fashioned," or as Mr. Albert Jay (CS) says: "Some call me 'Pop.' I dislike that. Some say 'old timer'— that's all right. I don't say nothing, but it gripes me!" Miss Potter (HS) accuses younger people of very unpleasant behavior toward the old: "In the offices—some places—they [younger co-workers] sort of ridicule you." In general community women report the least number of negative experiences *vis-à-vis* the younger generation.

When our subjects are asked to *generalize* about what younger people probably think of old people, they tend to draw a considerably darker picture in the abstract than they do when they describe their own personal interactions with the young. They seem to suspect young people of harboring thoughts that the old are more or less an inferior and useless class of people, essentially superfluous and—at times—a nuisance. Only two community subjects think younger people perceive older people at all benignly. These are Mr. Bauer (CS) and Miss Wimsatt (CS). "Lots of younger people have a lot of respect for older people," says Mr. Bauer. "If they think they can do elderly people a favor, they will do it. Some won't, but nice people will." Miss Wimsatt feels that relationships would be good, if the elderly were not overly critical of the young: "I think if a younger person meets an older person in a proper way, they can have as much fun [as if they were the same age]; but if older people are critical, they won't get along."

Thirty-four subjects (nearly two-thirds of the community; over half of the dischargees) mention negative attitudes only. Nineteen (a third of the community; two-fifths of the dischargees) mingle favorable and unfavorable attitudes, as is evident in such replies as: "Some take cognizance of the elderly, others think they are fogies," or: "Some will listen to your problems, others won't." In general, negative evaluations center on themes of indifference, avoidance, and on stereotypes of the aged as backward and mentally inferior. For instance, young people were thought to: "put up with" older people, "not pay any attention," "not care," or be "oblivious" to them. They were thought to consider older people as "old-fashioned" or "dumb." Mrs. Bruzinsky (CS) thinks the young regard the old as "in the way and not very up-to-date on things. That's why many of them have no use for old people." Mr. Fox (CS) thinks that younger people "want to keep away" from their elders. "They don't want anything to do with them," he continues. "I hear them talk, and they say, 'Oh, an old crowd goes there; let's not go.'" Mr. Jespersen (CS) has the opinion that the young feel "the old fogies are fools and in the way." Mrs. Tully's (HS) criticism is not as stringent as these: "Oh, they don't consider older people at *all* any more. They are polite, but they don't pay any attention to you—that's all." While some community subjects can be bitter and some hospital subjects moderate in their opinions about the attitudes of the young, it is the mentally ill who make the most devastating statements. As Mr. Hopland (HS) puts it: "They are ashamed of older people, especially when you've got white hair." Mr. Leveritt (HS) has an equally jaundiced view: "They look at you like you shouldn't be on the street. Oh, I guess they think older people ought to be shot, or half-shot anyway." Mrs. Harris (HS) points to the theme of avoidance: "Most of them don't like older people and avoid them. They just want to get away from you," and Mrs. Powers (HS), to the theme of backwardness and obsolescence: "They think we're old fossils who don't know anything." In the light of these complaints, remarks by community subjects about youth's lack of respect and politeness towards their elders seem relatively mild.

Older people do not always place the blame for unsatisfactory relationships between the generations on the young alone. Almost half the female subjects—both community and discharged—imply that the behavior and outlook of the aged themselves have much to do with poor intergenerational relationships. If the elderly would take the effort to come to terms with younger people, if they would be less critical of them, and try to understand the ways of youth, the age barrier, they suggest, could be overcome and the elderly could "keep abreast of the times." Mrs. Willoughby (CS) states very clearly that the attitude assumed by younger people depends upon the behavior of the old: "If you're going to throw your weight around and say, 'When *I* was your age . . .', why, I'm afraid that won't go over very good. Naturally, they would resent it. I used to hear that sort of stuff myself and *I* didn't like it." Older women seem more sensitive to this problem than men do; it is a rare man in our sample who expresses any conviction that the elderly themselves should exert restraint and relinquish authority when relating to the young. Their solution to the problem of intergenerational conflict is more often phrased in terms of social withdrawal and age-segregation.

To summarize the main points in this chapter so far, we have found, in our larger study sample of 435 older people, that a reasonably high level of social interaction is strongly correlated with morale, among both mentally-healthy and mentally-ill subjects. Socializing is also a source of pride and self-esteem among community subjects, but among the mentally ill, many can preserve a positive image of themselves only through social withdrawal from a society that they perceive to be critical of them. Such defensive withdrawal is demoralizing, however. Formal social supports (as measured by the status index) do not influence the personal functions we have measured among the community aged; however, they are critical for the mentally ill, correlating with both self-esteem and morale.

Although the morale levels of both samples are dependent on social interaction, data from the intensive-study sample indicate that only the mentally healthy perceive themselves on the whole as active participants in the social system. They enjoy being useful to others and having the ability to keep old friends and make new ones. Community subjects shy away from troublesome over-involvement with others, although they seek out and enjoy pleasant social encounters. The mentally ill are more likely to perceive interaction as difficult and unrewarding, even with age-mates— but infinitely more so with younger people. Both groups of subjects, with a few notable exceptions in the community group, are aware of some social alienation of the old from succeeding generations. Nearly all feel that the aged are somewhat devalued, but only half perceive this as a significant problem. Hospital subjects are particularly bitter about what they perceive to be derogatory attitudes of younger people towards the elderly. Men, especially, feel that their authority and instrumentality are threatened by younger men, and tend to see age-segregation as the perferred solution to intergenerational conflicts. Elderly women are just as likely to feel devalued (particularly if they are emotionally disturbed), but about half express the belief that social skills and graceful acquiescence to the ways and desires of the young can ease many of the strains between younger and older people. Several of the women prefer younger friends out of a seeming desire to disassociate themselves from reminders of their own advancing years.

It seems clear, then, that personal function is adversely affected not only by role loss (among the mentally ill) and constriction of interpersonal contacts (in both samples), but also by disturbances in the *quality* of human relationships; those between the generations are particularly troublesome for men and women who perceive themselves as members of a devalued class. Elderly people who have an unstable emotional life—particularly the men in the hospital sample—often prefer the demoralizing loneliness of social seclusion to the denigration they perceive in exposure to the sneering arrogance of their juniors.

SOLITUDE, SOCIAL ISOLATION, LONELINESS

In our study of intensively interviewed subjects, we have encountered some curious provocative findings that seem almost contradictory: (1) As we have already shown, mentally-healthy older people are more socially involved than are the mentally ill; yet community people are more likely to report that they enjoy being alone at times. (2) Women, on the average, have more social roles and a larger number of friends than men do; yet, women are considerably more likely than men to complain of loneliness and a paucity of social contacts. (3) Although the mentally-ill subjects in our study have lower levels of social interaction on the whole than community subjects, some of the most highly involved people in the entire sample are in the hospital group— but still these subjects often complain of loneliness.

Returning to the first finding, our intensive-study data indicate that, in general, solitude has a different meaning for mentally-healthy and mentally-ill elderly people. Despite their concern with active participation in social life, the interest of the mentally-healthy group in others is not inordinate. They are content to be by themselves some of the time. As Mr. Knight (CS) says, "Partial solitude doesn't bother me. I have plenty of entertainment—television, magazines—I can even go to the theater alone if I have to." Mr. Wheeler (CS) states, "I like to be with people, but sometimes I like to be alone, to read and work in the garden—I love nature. We all change with age, and that change is so slow from year to year that we cannot follow it. We get more from quietness as the years go by."

The mentally-healthy aged seem to feel that they can afford to structure and limit the extent of their interaction with others, if they so desire. Mr. Knight explains this: "As an individual, I keep my own counsel. I am not sympathetic to opening my life to just anybody. Not many people tell me their problems. I'm not much of a chaplain." Such reservations are not to be confused with isolation. These subjects have friends and enjoy social activity when they choose to; however, they limit the degree of involvement. As Mr. Schwann (CS) says, "I don't spend a lot of time talking to people I don't know." "I never get *too* involved," says Mr. Van-Damm. Socializing is something to be enjoyed, but not tedious, demanding, and unrewarding relationships. Earlier in life this might have been necessary—to pacify the neighbors, curry the boss' favor, please one's mate, or gain a client. Now, however, such considerations are less compelling—life is just too short.

Most mentally-ill subjects do not *seek* solitude; rather, they *avoid* others. They rarely refer to being alone as an opportunity for simply doing the solitary things one enjoys. They more often perceive it as an escape from their difficulties in dealing with others. Mr. Jackson (HS) describes his feelings in this way: "I'm getting very ornery lately—cranky. I'm very much afraid of meeting people, but I don't know why." For some of these people, retirement is a loss greater than widowhood—being out of work may mean the loss of nearly all contact with the world around them. For Mr. Jackson, for instance, having a job provided a kind of enforced socialization. It kept him in contact with people in a relationship that was defined and understood. The role-play was spelled out for him. His difficulties in dealing with people may have been due to a long-standing inarticulateness or personality conflicts, but work and family formerly provided a rampart between this subject and the world around him. With the loss of these structured supports, he became frightened and defensive. Alone now, he is afraid of becoming an object of ridicule. He says, "If I feel someone is poking fun at me, I take umbrage—very much umbrage."

We were interested in discovering if these varying attitudes toward solitude were reflected in attitudes toward living alone. Since living alone was one of the control variables in selecting our community subjects,[3] and since—willy-nilly—we had gathered quite a few social isolates into our hospital sample, we turned with special interest to those living alone. We asked them if they wanted to live otherwise. A few freely voiced dissatisfaction with their aloneness, but many more expressed the opinion that living with others had not worked out for them. Some had tried it in earlier years of their lives, driven by either loneliness or economy, but had abandoned it. A number have deliberately turned down invitations from friends to come and live with them. One male subject describes the circumstances of his refusing such an invitation: "I hesitate because I don't want to be a burden. Two guys—buddies of mine—got a house with about five or six rooms in it. They asked me to come and live with them. They said it would cost me nothing. Well, I refused, not because I didn't like them, but I like to be free, by myself." Yet, this man often complained in the interviews of increasing loneliness. His statement points to the overriding influence of a need to avoid dependency (interestingly, he thinks of this avoidance as maintaining his "freedom").

Returning to the subject of solitude, approximately a quarter of the intensive sample—report that they *do* mind being alone from time to time, that their tolerance for solitude has decreased with their old age. Of these, all but one had at sometime been married and about half were currently living with their spouses. This finding suggests what Lowenthal (1946b), in a recent study of social isolation in our baseline hospital sample, uncovered relative to a group of lifelong social isolates who appeared in that sample. She found that these extreme social isolates—"lone wolves" for all their lives—"liked being alone, and . . . rarely mentioned loneliness as a problem of their past or current lives" (p. 64). Commenting further on this group, she writes: "While such an alienated life style might in itself be culturally defined as a form of mental illness, lack of interpersonal relationships, which is one of its main characteristics, may help [in old age] to prevent the development of overt psychogenic disorder [or to prevent its de-

---

[3]The baseline community sample was controlled for social living arrangements to match the hospital sample, which had 50 per cent living alone.

tection if it does develop]" (p. 69). On the other hand, she found that "lifelong marginal social adjustment may be conducive to the development of [mental] disorder [in old age]" (p. 70). Essentially, elderly people with a marginal social adjustment—called "the defeated" and "the blamers" in the study—are those who, early in life, tried to satisfy their dependency needs with others and, because of some failure in the transaction, partially withdrew from social intercourse. These are the subjects who, according to her findings, were "more likely than the [lifelong] alienated to mention loneliness as a problem" (p. 65). In short, feelings of loneliness in old age appear to arise more often within those who have *tried* to effect satisfactory personal relationships with others during their lives, but, for one reason or another, have failed to secure the satisfaction they required. Consequently, they have retreated to marginal positions in the social system in order to better defend themselves. On the other hand, there are those who have never—in adult life, at least—really made the effort to set up a workable *entente cordiale* with others. Very early, they struck out on their own and have ever since maintained a rigid, solitary course through life. Ironically, these—the "loners," confirmed bachelors or spinsters, and itinerants—are often better equipped, when old age arrives at last, to confront the solitude and alienation forced upon so many of the old in American society today. They are well-rehearsed in this life pattern. But, as we shall see, if incapacitating illness forces them to rely on others, if the hard shell of complete self-reliance is shattered—the fragile self-system which it houses may be seriously damaged as well.

Generally, however, it is among those who have made a tenuous and inadequate adjustment to society—the hurt who still hope —where loneliness brings the greatest threat to equilibrium and self-esteem. For such as these, solitude is dangerous. One touching example of this can be seen in the case of Mr. Makrinos (CS), whom we have already met in Chapter II. He is typical of those with a marginal social adjustment. This man, living now in a squalid hotel on Skid Row, has been severely ill for a number of years. At sixty-four and ancient for his age, he resembles quite well Lowenthal's type of "the defeated." The only source of security he has is the familiar hotel in which he has lived for seventeen years. He rarely goes out of doors, rarely speaks with anyone except the desk clerk, and seems incapable of extending himself to anyone who might become his friend. "I tell you, I'm very afraid," he says. He desperately needs the presence of others—though they be strangers—to feel secure.

More often, however, it is the individual who is or has been psychologically disturbed who expresses the terrors of loneliness most eloquently. Such is the case of Mr. Jackson (HS), who, as reported previously, voluntarily committed himself to a state hospital for alcoholism and its severe physical consequences. "No one could have helped me, unless they locked me away from liquor," he explains. He spent eighteen months in this institution. When he was due for discharge, his anticipated loneliness was so intense that he begged his caretakers not to release him until after the Christmas season was over. Today, faced with inoperable cancer, poignantly aware of his imminent death, and alone in a cheap downtown hotel, he is a desperately unhappy man. He is tortured by self-recriminations for having wasted the one life given him. He finds it intolerable to remain in his room alone with his dreary thoughts. He must be around where he can hear people talk, although he is disinterested in what they are saying and takes no part in the discussions. "What else can I do?" he asks. "It's lonely here—you don't get to know people. It's a very unhappy life."

We turn now to the second finding we reported at the beginning of this section. Our case data give us some insight into why the women in the intensive-study sample, although they have more social contacts by and large, complain of isolation more often than the men do. Women in the sample are more apt to openly admit their loneliness than are the males. Many of them are even desperate for companionship. "I would like to get work," says Mrs. Willoughby (CS). "That would mean being with people and I just can't take this being alone." The women who complain of loneliness are generally widows and are further distinguished in that, earlier in their lives, interpersonal relationships were fraught with difficulties—they are either not very accepting of others or, as the data suggest, are too self-centered. Women whose relationships have always been good continue to maintain friends into their later years. Among those complaining, we catch a note of this contrariness. Mrs. Kramer (CS), for instance, remarks: "No one drops in. Maybe I'll see someone in the street, but I don't ask them in either." She, too, admits: "I get very lonely" and is trying to avoid this by seeking work, but, at the same time, she expresses the opinion: "I do not try to get too intimate. It seems to breed contempt." Similarly, Mrs. Viet (CS), who is not on good terms with her own daughter, states: "I don't have nothing to do with neighbors. I never went in people's houses to confess or gab or whatever you call it. I always stay by myself or go to the park." This woman lists two former co-workers whom she has known for many years as her friends, but her contact with them is limited to telephone conversations: "I worked with them. They know me. Nobody could say nothing bad about me to them." Mrs. Viet feels that people "don't have the interest in me they do in other people. I imagine this is so because of the way I am. They don't want to be bothered with me. When you need help, they won't be bothered with you." Apparently unable to form a close relationship, this woman goes to the park every afternoon, where on Sundays she distributes programs for the band concerts. "A lady at the concert said I was the sweetest person there is," she muses.

A note of jealousy creeps into Mrs. Miller's (CS) description of the one friend she likes to be with: "She's a dressmaker, not furs, like me. As far as making dresses is concerned, I could do as well, but I don't anymore. My line is coats." In much the same way, Mrs. Trocopian (HS) wants people but alienates herself from them, in this case because of a grandiose self-image. "Right now, I have only one friend that I am very close to," she explains. "Unfortunately—she is a good person—but her mind is not trained enough. If she were more intelligent, I would be happier with her. I have always been choosy about my friends." Mrs. Trocopian glamorizes her loneliness as the foredoomed isolation of the elite: "Other try to hurt you when you are more talented, creative, or something. They get jealous instead of appreciating it."

All of these women seem to present a state of mind summed up in an epigram by one subject who says: "I don't enjoy being with anybody or being alone either." This is a very different attitude from that held by Miss Wimsatt (CS) who describes changes in friendship as follows: "You always go through different stages with friends. Start as an acquaintance, then you begin to know they love you and you love them and can trust them."

Feelings of loneliness following the attrition of friendships among elderly males are not expressed as freely as is the case among the females. We have already touched upon the sensitivity of many men in this area and their tendencies to describe the atrophy of friendships as a deliberate choice. This reticence is particularly evident in the reports of male subjects from the lower economic statuses. It may be that the harsh social atmosphere prevailing in the Tenderloin and Skid Row districts of the city, where many of these men live, has fostered much of the mistrust and embittered withdrawal they express. The main centers of social activity for men of these districts are bars and cheap restaurants where social contacts are superficial and without any real warmth. A sense of resignation permeates their descriptions of the lives they lead. Mr. Alioto (HS), in former years, used to "go to poolrooms and sit down and play cards—used to love to go around with the boys—all that stuff," but now he has almost no interaction with friends at all: "I'm just a distant person. Don't talk too much. I worked with four hundred people. I'd say hello to them, but that's as far as my talking went. When you get to be eighty, you're no good." Before Mr. Pillsbury's (CS) stroke, he found relaxation and sociability at the horse races, but now he sits sullenly in his cheap hotel and exhibits marked contempt of other down-and-outers who share his fate: "I don't mix much. I just get disgusted with them, that's all." He lists the manager of the hotel as his only friend, but adds, "I didn't think much of him until he came to see me at the hospital." Mr. Ebenhauser (CS) has been a loner all his life and, until his sixties, rarely spent more than two or three years in any one location. He has worked at countless numbers of odd jobs: baker, team driver, barber, harvester, painter, orchard manager, and finally, dishwasher. He has never been sociable, preferring to make only the casual contacts of an itinerant. He claims to be quite satisfied with only one friend—and at that, a person living at some distance. "I like this fellow in Reno," he says. "I can depend on what he tells me. He isn't double-faced. We think similar thoughts—congenial." Mr.

Ebenhauser does not miss social interaction. He is more interested in developing himself. Strongly narcissistic, he is satisfied to contemplate his own individuality, improving himself and nurturing his yet hidden potentialities. His enthusiasm for steam baths, vegetarianism, and spiritualism keep him so preoccupied that he has little time for people. He has never questioned his abilities and retains supreme confidence in himself.

Mr. Czernich (HS), also a working-class man, perpetuates instrumental roles to compensate for a friendless old age. This bachelor, now in his seventies, strives consciously to maintain his gift for "positive thinking," while denying the need for social interaction. The core of his self-esteem rests upon his remarkable physical prowess. He exercises daily and feels he can still challenge anybody to a fight. His days are filled working on many "inventions" which he hopes to put on the market—if he can find some trustworthy individual to help him. He prides himself on his creativity and ingenuity. Chatting and visiting with friends, he says, are a waste of time which can be more usefully spent working on his inventions. At the same time Mr. Czernich is apparently insecure in social relationships these days, assiduously avoiding all of his former friends. He limits himself to casual exchanges of talk he might strike up with passers-by on the street: "If strangers talk to me, I talk to them. I talked to a fellow the other morning. I am willing to talk to strangers, but strangers have nothing to say—maybe afraid. You can notice in streetcars—nobody talks unless they're together. Most people won't talk to strangers."

That there are subjects in the study (mainly hospital sample) who are socially involved to the point of exhaustion—but who still claim to be lonely—we have already shown. We have already touched upon Mrs. Powers' frenetic social schedule. Yet, this woman complains of thoughts of loneliness, describing them as times of gloomy ruminations. "I hate being alone," she says, "even for an hour." On the rare occasions that her husband leaves the house, she phones a friend to come and keep her company. At the age of seventy-seven, suffering from considerable physical debility, this woman will exert every ounce of energy to take part in each and every social activity that comes along. Almost pathetically, she clings to old and new friends alike, and is desirous of making still others. Her very security in life appears to be based on distracting activity. Asked when thoughts of death are likely to arise in her mind, she says bluntly: "Don't you think it is something in your mind at *all* times?"

COMMENTS ON DISENGAGEMENT

Questions about solitude, social isolation, and loneliness among the aged naturally usher in a consideration of what has been called disengagement. But, before embarking upon a discussion of this process, we must examine an allied issue of great significance for older people: dependency *versus* autonomy. The successful resolution of the grave problem inherent in this issue will often mean the difference between mental health or mental illness. Since the older one gets, the more likely one will need help of some kind, old people are often obliged to admit this need and seek this help. Unfortunately for some—and especially for men in our culture—these very real and very serious circumstances often run counter to an individual's additional need for anchoring his self-esteem upon autonomy—the ability to keep on managing for oneself, to go it alone, to reaffirm that one is still a self-governing adult. It is within the crux of this primarily cultural dilemma that social disengagement must be analyzed and understood.

What in one case might seem to be a dangerous withdrawal from all social intercourse into a hermitage might, in fact, be a valid attempt to preserve self-esteem in the face of acknowledged decrements in physical and mental functioning. If such decrements are not yet so severe as to merit professional or institutional care, we are obliged to acknowledge such withdrawal as reasonably functional to the individual's culturally-sanctioned need for autonomy and self-reliance. However, in other cases—those where withdrawal from others represents a pathological denial of physical and/or mental illness—the greatest circumspection is required in assessing the disengagement as functional or malfunctional.

Among our hospitalized subjects, we have observed the most tragic consequences of this conflict between dependence and autonomy. These older people have great difficulty in reconciling within themselves what they *ought* to do (the value culture) and what, clearly, they *must* do (the reality culture). They fail in their struggle to bridge these polarities. For some—and this is especially true of subjects whose needs for dependency have been strong throughout life—being and living alone is a threatening circumstance, for the risk is great that one's emotional and physical needs will simply not be met. For those with long-ingrained impulses toward autonomy—a primary value for American males and especially those males in the generations we are now studying—disruption of one's life-space even in the interests of health may be perceived as an aggressive, hostile development—a threat to one's integrity as an adult, an event to be resisted at all costs. Thus, the feelings one entertains about one's solitude can be a good index of one's dependency needs. Contrariwise, denials of need—especially in circumstances of physical illness, poverty, and few social supports—can be a good index of the strength of urges for independence and self-reliance.

Because of the unique, often tenuous, balance each aging individual is required to make between his own unavoidable claims upon others and his personal demands upon himself, the question of the wholesale desirability of disengagement is a burning one in gerontological research.

From our various discussions of personal and social function in later life, certain features with great relevance to the so-called disengagement theory of aging should now be apparent. In Chapter V, we have shown that decreases in social function, apparently related to age, are in fact related to other factors—physical disability, emotional disturbances, and poverty are the main ones. In the first part of the present chapter, we have shown that high levels of social interaction promote high levels of morale in all subgroups within our sample, and, furthermore, we have demonstrated that mental illness leading to hospitalization accompanies a lack of social supports and involvements to a much greater extent than personal disturbances alone.

Our findings, then, seem to be in contrast with some of those described by Cumming and Henry (1961) in their study of an elderly sample in Kansas City, Missouri. Those authors have maintained, as their first major proposition, that social involvement *inevitably* decreases with age. The findings from our San Francisco sample bear this out only conditionally. The lessening of interactions through poverty, illness, or decrease of energy secondary to psychological depression we do find related to increased age— but only indirectly, through the mechanisms indicated. In very old age (past eighty), those in relatively good physical and mental health, with reasonably adequate incomes, are just as outgoing and involved as the younger members of our sample (those sixty to sixty-five).

The loss of friends and others through death is an unfortunate but natural consequence of aging. However, in our sample, the majority of mentally- and physically-healthy old men and women are capable of replacing lost relationships through a variety of substitutions. Widows or widowers sometimes remarry, or at least establish a close liaison with a friend of the opposite sex; those who lose old friends make new ones, or intensify their relationships with those remaining; voluntary associations and other activities are pursued as strength and inclination permit. There may indeed be losses, but remaining or new resources can be mobilized.

Our findings are also in contrast with the disengagement theory at the point of another of its propositions: that accepting decrease in social involvement in old age and even enhancing it with willful disengagements from the social system is adaptive and beneficial to one's morale. Although, admittedly, our measure of morale is quite different from the one used in that study, we did not find—as was found there— "a general improvement in morale as disengagement increases" (pp. 140-141). Our findings are more in agreement, however, with some later work done in the same study—the Kansas City Study of Adult Life.[4] In a series of articles, Tobin and Neugarten (1961) and Havighurst, Neugarten, and Tobin (1963) have reexamined the hypothesis explicit in the disengagement theory that there is a positive relationship between social disengagement and psychological well-being among the elderly. These investigators have developed four measures of social interaction, two of which (Role Count and Social Life Space) are nearly identical to our two quantitative measures of social func-

---

[4]While this discussion is largely geared to an examination of the disengagement theory as outlined in *Growing Old*, Cumming and Henry themselves, it should be noted, have since enlarged their theoretical views. See Cumming (1964) and Henry (1963). For a brief evaluation of the theory, see Maddox (1964).

tion. They found positive relationships between these two measures and Life Satisfaction (an index which includes self-concept as well as some other dimensions we have combined and called morale), which were greater for older than for younger subjects. In other words, the association between social function and life satisfaction *increased* with age. Our findings also support this conclusion—that, in old age, social *engagement,* rather than disengagement, is more closely related to psychological well-being. Furthermore, we found, in our analysis of the sources of high and low morale, that—at least for our intensively studied mentally-healthy subsample—social contacts are specifically named as sources of satisfaction. Without social contacts, subjects became demoralized, and anxiety and pessimism characterize their attitudes toward later life. Among some of the emotionally disturbed subjects, however, we found that social withdrawal served a positive function in insulating the self-image against critical attack.

It is not difficult to account for these differences in the earlier Kansas City findings and our own. In many respects, our hospital and community samples have permitted us to test the disengagement theory upon a broader base than was possible with the Kansas City sample. That sample was controlled on several variables which have been crucial in our own study; subjects were carefully screened to eliminate physical and mental illness and no one on public assistance rolls such as Old Age Assistance or relief was included. In effect, these screening items precipitated a sample with a more normative range of socioeconomic statuses than our own and, of course, with an absence of those conditions which would permit a controlled validation of the adaptive-maladaptive aspects of the theory. This procedure was justified because it "would allow us to investigate the nature of the aging process without being distracted by problems arising out of illness" (Cumming and Henry, 1961, p. 28).

We have no reason to deny that disengagement from the social system may be the line of least resistance for white, middle-class, Midwestern Americans between the ages of fifty and ninety—*who do not need help.* The presence in our San Francisco sample of those who have succumbed to physical and mental illness and a careful examination of the self-evaluation and morale of the ill and the healthy demonstrate that retreat from social involvement is associated with maladaptation, here defining maladaptation as that kind of functioning in mood, thought, and behavior which eventuates in a mental hospitalization. At the present point in our research, we cannot determine whether this decline in social activity is cause or result of the mental and physical difficulties manifested by our hospital subjects. It may be one or the other or both, according to the individual case. Regardless, in a comparison of our community and hospital subjects, the healthier subjects showed a deeper and wider commitment to the social milieu—they had more personal associations with others and showed greater flexibility in making new friends in compensation for those lost—than did those in our hospital sample. This finding is further corroborated by case review in the intensive sample, showing that emotionally disturbed males, in contrast with men in the community, could not point to *a single close relationship with anyone.* Whenever a friend was named, it was the most cursory type of acquaintanceship. On the other hand, community sample subjects, both male and female, reported a greater number of friends and, especially in the case of those women who had but few friends, complaints of loneliness were easily and frequently articulated. Among the males, only those in the community appeared to demonstrate any capacity for making new friends. We are left with the conclusion that relatively healthy old people—sometimes to an advanced age—cherish their liaisons with social reality and will do everything they possibly can to preserve that level of social functioning which is customary and comfortable for each individual; that mentally-*healthy* older people, pressured to disengage by personal illness or the deaths of others, will show remarkable talents for compensating and replacing these losses with renewed creative extensions of themselves into social reality; but that mentally-*ill* older people distinguish themselves by retreats and retrenchments, often to a point of hermetic isolation, where they look out upon the world with mock indifference, contempt, rigidly paranoid superiority, or mute, hopeless resignation.

However, none of this implies that our findings support the opposite of the disengagement theory—the activity theory which has developed primarily out of the philosophy of recreational and social workers who have, in the last twenty to thirty years, concerned themselves with ameliorating the lot of older people in our society. (For more scholarly statements of the theory, see Havighurst *et al.*, 1949; Albrecht, 1962; and Havighurst and Albrecht, 1953.) We have seen in some of our case analyses that an obsessive, hyperactive involvement with others in old age can itself be indicative of maladaptation. Rather than this, the key to successful adaptation appears to be a judicious assessment of strengths and resources and a continued application of these to the flux and reflux, the rhythmic exertion and relaxation which characterize social relationships at any age level.

From the earliest moments of living organisms, we can observe this systolic-diastolic movement from solitary, self-absorbing activities to those where the individual is actively engaged in meeting and absorbing the environment—from periods of rest, sleep, digestion, and homeostatic contentment to restless searching for food, animated self-assertion, and hungering for stimulus and pleasure. Our most successfully adapted subjects witness to a continuation of systolic-diastolic rhythm of engagement and withdrawal from others, sometimes under the most incredibly delimiting of circumstances.

Mr. Ed Hart (CS) will be discussed in greater detail in the final chapter, but we would like to introduce him at this juncture as an excellent example of how one man of an advanced age has been able to maintain a viable sociability in spite of disabilities. Mr. Hart has outlived three successful marriages as well as the lifetimes of his own sons. At the time of our last interview with him, Mr. Hart was ninety-three years old, maintaining himself quite satisfactorily in his own apartment, doing his own cooking, and getting about with a cane. Mr. Hart's physical impairment had—he admitted—curtailed much of his social activity, but he was certainly continuing to interact with others at his optimum under the circumstances. Following the death of his third wife, when Mr. Hart was ninety, he invited a younger man of sixty to live with him and share expenses. This man—his "roomie" as Mr. Hart called him—was his companion and admirer. When, for instance, Mr. Hart was asked to describe his own temperament, he replied: "Very even. Well, Gino has learned about my temperament. Sometimes, though, I get angry and fly off the handle quick." To this self-criticism, Gino, Mr. Hart's roommate, responded with an emphatic: "No!"

Mr. Hart has a deep love and respect for people, and, for this reason, has earned many loyal friends. When recalling friendships out of his past he says: "I cannot recall any individual I considered a close friend who ever proved disloyal." But many of the old friends are gone now and making new ones is a bit hard for him because of his limited mobility, yet "if I had a friend without having to do anything *physical* for them, it's not difficult at all." This man readily admits that, right now, he has the fewest number of close friends he has ever had in his life ("They're all passed away"), but this is not to say he is friendless ("I have lots of friends; I can't keep up with them"). He draws a fine distinction between "close" friends and merely "dear" friends: "My neighbors are very dear friends but I can't be *close* to them." When Mr. Hart was ninety-one, he stopped sending Christmas cards to his many friends: "I quit. I told them all I wouldn't be sending any more. For two reasons, one, I couldn't send to all so I send to none, then no one is hurt; two, it was too much for my strength—about 150 cards—addressing them, writing notes." This man's social charm has enchanted every interviewer and has seemed to draw people to him as a magnet. Even his neighbors and landlady are within the radius of his loving care and concern: "Even my landlady is my friend. She had me for Christmas dinner. She never comes but she grabs me and kisses me. The lady across the street who owns those four flats—if my blinds aren't up by 7:30 A.M., I get a telephone call from her. Then next door—the two ladies are spinsters. One just retired. They come in and see if I need anything. They are my immediate neighbors. Yes, I'm blessed with lots of neighbors and friends. I . . . I will say this. Lots of people love me or they're darned good actors. Hmmm, they must like my ways or something." When asked to cite the person who had the most influence on him at present, he replied: "If it were necessary, I think I would listen to my three neighbors. They treat me like a father and they're old enough to have good judgment. One's past seventy."

In comparison with other men in our sample, Mr. Hart is somewhat exceptional in that he is a letter-writer. In this regard, he mentions a long letter he must soon answer from a young woman whom he has helped with advice for many years and who has told him: "You're the only father I know." He readily awakens trust in the young who confide their problems to him: "I've had a lot of friends in my time who placed me on the spot, wanting to know what to do." At this point, he showed the interviewer some postcards he had received from a young friend. "I've corresponded with several young people. I can't do much of that now though." (His eyesight is beginning to fail.) He then proceeded to describe a young man with whom he has long corresponded, "of parentage that was not very elevating at all—haphazard, rough drinking." Mr. Hart was mentor to this young man as he progressed through army and college years: "In each letter, I'd give him a line of philosophy, but I didn't preach to him. I have a number of correspondents very similar to that one." Finally, in completing his roster of friends, there is "Hank, who is on the staff of the Senior Citizens. He's taken me under his wing."

Mr. Hart is also exceptional among elderly men, for he keeps in touch with his many friends over the telephone, sometimes two to four times a day. Generally, these are lady friends who had also been friends of his deceased wife. It might be added here that Mr. Hart's role as parent and grandparent is still intact. He will make regular monthly trips to stay with his daughter and her family who live out of the state. Often he will spend a week or two with his granddaughter.

This subject's capacities for social intercourse are most remarkable in the light of one of the major cultural problems of American aging: how to replace collateral relationships, which are bound to atrophy through illness and death, with lineal ones. In other words, as the ranks of one's peers are decimated, how are substitutions to be recruited from younger generations? In societies more traditional than our own, it is less of a problem, for the cultural system of such groups (and the folkways of Old Japan and Old China are good examples here) does not generally force the generations to march lock-step through life with little exchange of wisdom and experience between them. We are all too familiar with the artifacts produced by this pattern of American culture: the isolation of the young in the six-to-ten generation (our so-called "latency period," which is by no means universal); the present-day "cult of the teenager" which seals off young people of this generation into coteries of taste, cliquishness, and rebellion; the recent proliferation of "young-married" clubs with their swapping of recipes and child-rearing techniques; and, of course, the old who are expected to move to retirement communities or attend "Golden Age" clubs. In contrast, traditional cultures will often reserve for the elderly crucial roles as patriarch, village elder, counselor, storyteller, sage, and friend. In this way, the old still participate in the power structure of the society and maintain lineal relationships. The only possibility for American aged to maintain such relationships lies in whatever individual strength and talent an older person might have to forge these links across the generations. Mr. Hart clearly has this talent.

There is an additional liability resulting from this age-segregation. The aged who sink into what we have called "pockets of anonymity" essentially lose contact with available lines of communication to the younger members of society who are in gatekeeper or aid-dispenser positions—or to those individuals who receive and transmit messages about needs for help or problems requiring external aid to appropriate social agencies. Quite a number of the subjects we talked to in these secluded situations treated the interviewers as though they were the long-sought saviors at last arrived to help them get medical aid or increase their welfare payments. For people such as these, any contact with the younger generation becomes a possible pipeline to those who are instrumentally involved in welfare functions.[5]

5A recently published collection of papers edited by Shanas and Streib (1965) contains several discussions of interest to the problem of dependency of the aged on children or welfare agencies. Margaret Blenkner, the author of one of these papers, "Social Work and Family Relationships in Later Life with Some Thoughts on Filial Maturity," comments on: ". . . the unease, ambivalence, and plain ineptitude with which the average professional worker, in agencies not devoted specifically to serving the aging, meets the problem of alienation, or worse still, may compound or exacerbate it under the mistaken notion that his sole responsibility is to free the child from the parental tie, in line with his theory of personality development and nuclear family orientation . . . . The number of case records in which one reads of the worker 'relieving his client's (the child's) guilt' or 'alleviating separa-

To return for a moment to the disengagement theory, we suspect that the psychological benefits that Cumming and Henry found accruing to the elderly by social withdrawal were due to three factors: (1) The group of older people in their sample did not need help—either physical, psychiatric, or financial—and were thus in a better position to pursue the cultural goal of individual autonomy. (2) In American society, age-grading has been extended to age-segregation; the young have little to hear from or say to the old. A predictable reaction to this situation on the part of the elderly might be summed up in the words of one of our subjects: "If they don't want me, I sure don't want them. Why should I stick my neck out?" (3) These first two factors (a drive for independence and age-segregation), compounded by the attrition of social relationships through death or illness of peers, might well lead to a decrease in social involvement—and this might be dubbed disengagement.

In addition, it may be that, by their term "disengagement," Cumming and Henry were, in part, thinking of what (in Chapter VI) we have called "relaxation" or substitution of terminal for instrumental values. As we conceive them, however, they are very different things. In the case of "relaxation," the constraints of social sanction are loosened a bit for the elderly and they take advantage of their exemptions. They are permitted to be more themselves, to conform a bit less, to cultivate their individuality—even to the point of eccentricity; but, at least in our sample, such people are not withdrawn from social life. Those in our sample who do hide themselves away from the young, those who pay ritual service to modern society's decree that the elderly should be neither seen nor heard, those who gather themselves up into a fragile shell of righteous self-reliance—these are not the happy and fulfilled elderly men and women we have met in San Francisco. They are those who, when sickness, poverty, and need at last threaten their defended little worlds, often succumb to madness.

---

tion-anxiety' is depressing as is the number of times the worker is supported in this by the agency's psychiatric consultant . . . . Most older persons under seventy-five are quite capable of taking care of themselves and their affairs. They neither want nor need to be 'dependent,' but they do want and need someone they can *depend on* should illness or other crises arise. There is a vast difference in these two conceptions which is sometimes overlooked" (Blenkner, 1965, pp. 50 and 55).

CONCLUSION

The single most critical problem of the aged we have studied in San Francisco is not the issue of disengagement *versus* engagement. We have already seen how, for some, social isolation has been a functional lifelong pattern unrelated to aging *per se*—and how, for others, it is a late-life defensive maneuver serving to hide one's needs or aberrations from public appraisal. Nor is the issue of continued instrumentality in later life the central problem, although we have found *preoccupation* with instrumental values to be maladaptive for many older people.

For our sample as a whole, there are two basic goals—survival and self-esteem. The elderly—like people of all ages—must try to survive as long as life holds more rewards than pain. And the elderly—like people of all ages—must somehow preserve self-respect in order to avoid the emotional torment that can end only in death or derangement. For most of this generation of older Americans, self-esteem is indelibly linked with the personal and cultural value of independence—autonomy and self-reliance. Yet, old age in reality is often a time when one must have help and support in order to survive. This is the fundamental dilemma. In our sample, the tragic contradiction that American culture generates for the elderly between these two basic goals is the major problem in adaptation to aging.

These elderly people, products of the "Protestant ethic" (or immigrants into it), *must* be independent in order to maintain their self-esteem. To many, even death is preferable to "becoming a burden." They do not mind receiving financial aid—and are often glad to have it—as long as they can maintain some semblance of autonomy: a room of their own, freedom of movement and choice, and avoidance of the stigma of "being paupers on charity." However, in times of real need—illness, impoverishment, emotional distress, failing sight or strength—survival may rest on the assistance and support of others. But our society finds it inefficient to make special provisions for special cases; this is expensive, time-consuming, and wasteful of trained personnel. We centralize these functions, efficiently, in large institutions—state hospitals and homes for the aged. And there even the illusion of self-determination melts away.

Some of the aged in our sample feel that, if help can be obtained only at the expense of institutionalization, if the small sphere of respectable autonomy that constitutes the aged person's shrunken life-space can be punctured like a child's balloon—then it may be best to gamble on one's own with survival. Such people will draw their curtains to avoid critical appraisals of their helplessness; they will not get enough to eat; they will stay away from the doctor and forego even vital drugs; they will shiver with the cold; they will live in filth and squalor—but pride they will relinquish only as a last resort. Many of these aged ended in our hospital sample.

But there are other elderly people who seem better able to adapt to the inevitable, however distasteful that may be. If they must have help in order to survive, they opt for survival. They may have to surrender self-determination in the end, but they find compensations in staying alive. When we last saw Miss Wimsatt, she was hospitalized for a broken hip which was not mending properly. Yet, she said, "Even if I have to stay here, I'd like to be a part of life long enough to see how some of it turns out."

Chapter IX

THE PROCESS OF AGING ADAPTATION IN AMERICAN CULTURE

> *[T]he crucial people in the aging problem are not the old,*
> *but the younger age groups, for it is the rest of us who*
> *determine the status and position of the old person in the*
> *social order. What is at stake for the future is not only*
> *the alienation of the old from the young, but the aliena-*
> *tion of the young from each other and of man from man.*
> *There is no way out of this dilemma, for young or old,*
> *without a basic re-ordering of our national aspirations and*
> *values of which the aging problem is but a token. Any-*
> *thing less than this will see us concentrating on super-*
> *ficial symptoms, especially tangible ones like housing the*
> *aged, and nibbling at the tattered edges of our problems*
> *without penetrating to their heart.*
>
> —IRVING ROSOW,
> *"Old Age: One Moral Dilemma of*
> *an Affluent Society"*
> (1962), p. 191

INTRODUCTION

GUIDELINES FOR BEHAVIOR through the transitional phases of life are ordinarily set down by the culture in the form of definitions of the new status into which the developing individual is progressing. However, where that status is poorly or un-defined or only newly perceived as a significant life phase (Chapter I), behavioral cues for the one in passage may be ambiguous, implicit, and often contradictory. People entering old age in our own culture face such adaptational problems, and it is the purpose of this chapter to make explicit what these guidelines seem to be for elderly Americans in such urban centers as San Francisco. These guidelines we are here calling "the adaptive tasks of aging in American culture," making, at the same time, no claim that these particular tasks have any cross-cultural validity or universal meaning. Before we can turn to adumbrating these tasks, however, two distinctions must be made: first, what differences exist between our use of the term, "adaptive tasks" and what such writers as

Havighurst, Erikson, and Bühler mean by "developmental tasks";[1] and, second, the differences between "adaptation" and "adjustment."

Adaptive tasks, as used in the present context, depend upon the value system of the prevailing culture and are essentially answers to the basic question: "How can I grow old and still function, adjudging myself and perceiving others to judge me as a 'good' American?" Viewed in another way, they are a set of culturally-derived "demands" placed upon modern aging Americans. In contrast, *developmental tasks* are those faced by everyone, everywhere, in the course of growth and maturation, and they include learning impulse control, managing sexuality in accordance with cultural norms, defining oneself in relation to the society's authorities, effecting independence from the nurturance of one's parents, developing the necessary social skills, internalizing the taboos, etc. These developmental tasks are not entirely culture-free, that is, societies throughout the world radically condition the perceptions and resolutions of these tasks; but they can be called "pan-cultural" insofar as people around the world must come to terms with them in one form or another. Thus, we can see that developmental tasks must take cognizance of the cultural matrix in order for them to have any meaning beyond the purely physical or "instinctual." However, adaptive tasks bring culture into the foreground where it is no longer merely a catalyst or ground, but one of the active principles or forces in a psychocultural process. In

[1]Havighurst (1952) was among the first to develop a typology of these life tasks. His principal concern was to provide an antidote to the "freedom" theory of education, that is, "the child will develop best if left as free as possible" (p. v). Accordingly, his model primarily emphasizes the necessity of learning new roles (and unlearning old ones) appropriate to the various stages of life. Each developmental task is based on biological, psychological, and cultural necessities. The models of Erikson (1959, 1960) and Bühler (1959, 1962), on the other hand, employ more the conceptualizations of ego psychology. For instance, Erikson uses such dichotomies as intimacy *vs.* isolation and integrity *vs.* disgust or despair as developmental tasks. Although Bühler does not speak of developmental tasks *per se,* her "basic tendencies" (need-satisfaction, self-limiting adaptation, creative expansion, etc.) and "end-goals" (well-being, survival, self-realization, etc.) and other constructs can be viewed as facets of developmental tasks. The specified tasks in the succeeding paragraph are thus not specifically Havighurst's, Erikson's, or Bühler's, but are prototypic of the tasks found in these developmental models.

brief, development is learning to live with oneself as one changes, while adaptation is learning to live in a particular way according to a particular set of values as one changes or as one's culture changes.

As regards the second distinction to be made, that between adaptation and adjustment, it must be noted first that the criteria for adjustment are essentially *external* to the personal system. Adjustment calls for behavior which will not arouse sanctions from the environment. In this sense, a senile lady in a state hospital can be quite adjusted to the role of psychiatric patient if she uses the toilet properly, picks up her clothes, gets to meals on time, and stays put where she "should" be. In the same way, a "pillar" of a fundamentalist church in a small American town can be considered as adjusted if he or she espouses Victorian morality and avoids any overt manifestations of vice. Also, a driving, energetic businessman may be adjusted to the demands of a highly competitive economic system, if he makes money, buys a better automobile each year, moves into a bigger house, and belongs to the "right" clubs and churches. Of course, in doing so, he may well develop an ulcer or die at forty of a coronary occlusion, but as long as he acts in harmony with the values of the milieu he occupies, he is indeed "adjusted." The criteria of adaptation, on the other hand, are the *internal and external* accommodations individuals must make to the social order in which they live. Thus, it is possible to be well-adapted without epitomizing the core-values as long as the individual does not flagrantly defy them in ways so as to bring down sanctions upon himself. In brief, the adapted person has worked out a compromise which satisfies both his society and his own personality. In this way, our "adjusted" businessman shows that he is "maladapted" when he develops his psychosomatic symptoms; he has neglected personal requirements in his wild pursuit of conforming to the ideals of success entertained by the set in which he travels.[2]

According to these definitions, then, all the members of our hospital sample were "maladjusted" at the time of their commit-

---

[2]Readers interested in further definitions of "adjustment" and "adaptation" are referred to Gould and Kolb (1964, pp. 8-10).

ment (that is, external sanctions were exerted upon them). By the time of the intensive interviews two to three years later, some of these people were "readjusted" (that is, had been returned to the community), but, of these only a few can meet the criteria of adaptation (that is, getting along well enough with society *and* oneself to preserve intact the personal functions). Similarly in the community sample, nearly all seem to be "adjusted" (no social sanctions have yet been brought to bear upon any of them). A majority were "adapted" as well, but many were not (some were found to be depressed, to have negative self-views, or were very precariously balanced with their social worlds). Many of these maladapted people seem to be avoiding an open conflict with society by remaining isolated from it. As such, we can call them "adjusted" but hardly "adapted," and, as a group, they are so similar to many of the discharged that we have difficulties in differentiating between men like Mr. Ebenhauser (CS) and Mr. Spenser (HS) or those like Mr. Butler (CS) and Mr. Ritter (HS). Had Mr. Ebenhauser a wife who would report him to the health authorities or disapprove of his eccentricities, he might well have shared the destiny of Mr. Spenser. Both Mr. Butler and Mr. Ritter espouse grandiose self-views and both suffer bouts of depression and suspicion, but Mr. Ritter acted out his castration fears and, thus, added maladjustment to his poor adaptation. In sum, the standards for adaptation are more comprehensive, for not only must the criteria of one's own society be satisfied—as with adjustment—but internal accommodations must also be made with one's own system of needs and satisfactions.

It must also be added that what are here described as "adaptive tasks" are only those problems which have commonly arisen for the aged in our sample. In other words, we have been able to perceive and define them as "tasks" only as they have become problematic for this set of people. For example, we have not defined as a major adaptive task the development of an adequate philosophy toward death, because a lack of such a philosophy does not seem to be problematic for this aging San Francisco sample, which—as we have pointed out in Chapter VII—is an amazingly secularized group of people. A handful of the elderly in this sample have presented us with clues that they have come to terms with their own imminent demise. Mr. Hart, for one, expressed to us his belief in a modified form of reincarnation, reporting that he believed his "essence" might be preserved in a new-born baby. A few others seem quite content with a vague transcendental agnosticism, such as the "sunset" afterlife dreamed of in Miss Barton's philosophy, but coming to grips with one's own hereafter does not seem to be crucial for these people. On the contrary, in Old China, one's status after death was of very real concern, if one were to join the ranks of the ancestors. The corpse had to be treated in special ways and had to be laid to rest in the ancestral burying-grounds of the family village. Because of these very important injunctions, we have reason to believe that thoughts of one's own death may be very anxiety-provoking for the elderly Chinese of San Francisco. Given the policies of present-day Communist China, it is very likely that they might entertain serious doubts about their status in the afterlife. Thus, in this subculture, coming to terms with one's own death (becoming an ancestor) might well be an adaptive task. By contrast, in other societies such as the Japanese, old age may pose few adaptive tasks, because the meaning and purpose of this period of life is spelled out in sets of expected behaviors, prerogatives, and goals. In America, however, where the major definitions of the lifespan are still congruent with the ideals of an agrarian democracy, where one perceives a productive adult life terminating in death ("a good old farmer works until he dies"), an extended, "useless" period of life can readily pose many problems in adaptation.

As we have seen in Chapter II, the phenomenological approach of this volume has yielded for us a perception of the major, most frequent problems expressed by our subjects, and the adaptive tasks outlined here have been derived from those statements essentially saying: "I'm having trouble and I cannot see a solution." When Mr. Ned Bates says, "Why look ahead? What's in it for us old people?" he is articulating a problem and implicit in his question is our perception of the task facing him—to explain what it *is* in later life that will make it worth the living. And when he gains his answer, will it be one satisfying to himself *and* his society?

The problems became evident in the two spheres of personal

and social function. In the first instance, we turned to those who had expressed a negative self-view or complained of low morale, indicating some maladaptation which could be referred to a given task. In the second instance, if a diagnosable symptomatology had developed (that is, if a consensus of others had been reached that "that guy's crazy"), the maladjustment (and maladaptation) was scrutinized to derive the task. Mr. Spenser, again, can illustrate this for us. This man's personal system was intact and his morale was high, just prior to his commitment. However, the defensive maneuvers he had undertaken to preserve his personal system created conflicts with social norms. His problem, therefore, was really one of adjustment, which (as we have seen) is, in part, but not entirely congruent with adaptation.

In addition to the criterion of commitment as an indication of social maladaptation, individuals who were involved in serious conflict with their social world were also rated. Such conflicts were regarded as maladaptive if they were threatening to the subject's well-being and to the reasonable satisfaction of his basic needs.

Five principal tasks of adaptation were precipitated from this analysis. The two authors then undertook a reliability study, rating all the intensive-sample cases (79) individually as to whether each subject was adapted in all or maladapted in any of the five tasks. Adjudication procedures were employed in cases of disagreement, and only those cases on which we could get complete agreement were regarded as reflecting or not reflecting particular adaptive problems.

By this procedure, it was determined that two-fifths of the intensive sample (excluding the 15 classified as deteriorated) were adapted, that is, showed no problems in any of the five tasks. The remainder, however, manifested problems in one or more of these areas. In cases of two or more problems, it appeared that one was primary while the other (s) were either evident or imminent.

Some of these tasks appear to be more easily accomplished than others. Most of the subjects do resolve them without being forever blocked in the area. Others pose more serious difficulties for a much larger number of people. It is in relation to these areas that we must ask if our culture's expectations for the elderly are reasonably achievable for more than just the exceptional few.

THE ADAPTIVE TASKS

As we noted in Chapter I, the purpose of this report is to show how perceptions of the self and of society are related to mental health in old age. In Chapter VIII we demonstrated that good personal function in later life rests on a social base—and that the vulnerability of older people to hospitalization for psychiatric reasons is aggravated by a dearth of social supports and interactions. At this juncture, we turn our attention away from the notion of mental health *versus* mental illness to the broader concept of adaptation of the elderly. The latter, to be sure, is related to the former; but, for our purposes here, the concept of adaptation has a wider applicability.

Our study sample purposefully contains a far greater proportion of mentally-disturbed people than is found in the population at large. Most epidemiological studies made in recent years indicate that only a small minority of people in the later years of life ever find their way to a psychiatric facility.[3] By contrast, half of our intensive-study sample (those whose protocols were used for defining these adaptive tasks) are people who have had serious emotional problems late in life, resulting in a period of hospitalization for psychiatric reasons. Fortunately, the remaining half are

[3] Ancillary research on this project has surveyed epidemiological reports of mental illness among the aged and, by correcting for differences in diagnostic nomenclatures and other variations in sampling, we have been able to compare the prevalence of mental illness in our own community sample (the group of 600 interviewed at baseline) with the prevalences found in eight other communities in the United States and abroad. According to this analysis, 15 per cent of our baseline community sample can be identified as manifesting severe or moderate impairment. This compares with adjusted prevalences ranging from the 14 per cent reported in Nielsen (1962) to the 25 per cent found by Leighton *et al.* (1963) in the Maritime Provinces. The other six comparable studies are: Sheldon (1948), 16 per cent; Bremer (1951), 24 per cent; Essen-Möller *et al.* (1956), 19 per cent; Mental Health Research Unit [Syracuse] (1961), 5 per cent severely disabled and moderate impairment unknown; Primrose (1962), 17 per cent; and Kay, Beamish, and Roth (1964), 17 per cent. Readers should bear in mind, however, that these figures are based on estimates of *prevalence* of psychiatric disability. *Incidence* rates would, of course, be lower and those hospitalized even fewer. Out of a population of 134,960 elderly people, sixty or older, residing in San Francisco during 1959, the baseline year of our hospital sample study, those admitted for psychiatric reasons to any psychiatric facility in the Bay Area represent 0.65 per cent.

like most elderly people in San Francisco—they have not experienced such disruptions. Most of these community subjects are "getting along." As Mr. VanDamm says, "Most old people rather enjoy life," and Mrs. Burbank claims that she has fewer worries now than ever before: "That's the reward of being sixty-six." Mrs. Valente agrees with this: "The best years of my life are the way I am now. I did my suffering when I was young; now I think I enjoy life as much as young people." Mr. Janisch tells us that he feels the position of older people in the United States to be improved: "Now it is better than it ever was. Before, I've seen old people work until they died on the job. Now they have many benefits and can live their older years in some comfort."

What we have seen, however, in our examination of these intensively-studied subjects is that some of the difficulties in adaptation that take some older people into the psychiatric wards have, as underlying sources, the contradictions and discontinuities of American culture—and these underlying factors are also often a source of serious concern and unrest among elderly people who never reach the point of psychiatric commitment. As an example, one of these is the value placed on productive employment—a value in conflict with existing social pressures for early retirement. A sincere belief that people should do an honest day's work seems an innocuous enough conviction, but it is proving to be a source of great difficulty for many of our subjects, among whom is Miss Louise Potter (HS).[4]

At seventy-four, Miss Potter is acutely aware that she is growing old, but she is evading any acceptance of that fact. "I hate to talk about myself. I never liked old people in my life, and now that I'm old, I hate myself." For Miss Potter, aging threatens the very foundations of a value system welded to the meaningfulness of work for personal and social identity. "I've always had my work and that was my life."

---

[4]In previous chapters of this report, we have introduced all the people whose cases are presented here, including some of their comments or some of the events of their lives. In this discussion, however, we want to give as full a picture of each subject as is required, in order to dramatize the overall personal pattern that has created barriers to resolution of some adaptive task. Thus, the case presentations may sound a bit repetitious, because of the many earlier glimpses we have had of these people.

Since the age of twenty, when Miss Potter escaped from a strict Methodist family through work away from home, she has focused her energies on a career first in teaching, and, later, exclusively in office work. She never married and does not regret it. She feels marriage would have kept her from the active, mobile life she loves. Her friendships have been largely limited to circles of co-workers, and so she has had no enduring relationships. She says she has never been able to feel close to people.

Miss Potter states that she has lived her life from day to day, traveling about the country, stopping off for several months or several years to do clerical work in various cities. She is articulate about her superior work abilities and appears to be well qualified. She loves change. The only responsibilities she has ever accepted have been those connected with her performance on the job. Before her fifties, she always felt secure in the knowledge that she could move to another area and find another position whenever she wished.

However, difficulties in finding employment brought on her first emotional depression in 1951, while she was in her early fifties. By this time, she had settled down in San Francisco. She muses now that her wanderlust had appeared to stop at that time. In 1952, she voluntarily sought help at San Francisco General Hospital's psychiatric ward from where she was transferred to spend three months at Agnews State Hospital. She left Agnews much improved. In 1953, she got a job with the Pioneer Insurance Company and worked there for four and a half years. This job temporarily restored her self-confidence. What she regards as the most traumatic experience in her life, however, occurred in 1959 when she had to leave that job. Aware that her age was well beyond the prescribed limitations, she resigned to avoid the humiliating experience of showing her birth certificate revealing her true age as seventy (Miss Potter has been in the habit since her thirties of subtracting about ten years from her age). In 1959, she was again in San Francisco General Hospital's psychiatric ward, at which time we first saw her. After two months there, she was discharged when her depressive symptoms abated. Since then, she has been able to keep herself busy and employed by finding part-time and temporary work through an employment agency. Thus far, her relationships with this agency have been satisfactory for they regard her as one of their fastest keypunch operators. Any protracted delay between jobs, however, causes her much anxiety.

Miss Potter has always felt sorry for old people and expresses dislike for them, their deterioration, and their helplessness. She has always been deeply concerned about preserving her appearance and often treats herself to facials and steam baths. At the age of sixty-five, she enrolled in the Princess School of Charm, not only to learn about beauty care and grooming, but also to improve her social manners, a newly developing concern. When first seen at the age of seventy, she could have easily passed for a woman of fifty to fifty-five, in the judgment of the interviewer. Today, she associates with people in their forties and fifties and despises Senior Citizens' groups. She hates herself for being old; it is humiliating to have to lie continuously about one's age; and it is disturbing to live in fear of exposure. Old age signifies to her enormous pressures to change her roles in life, to end her employment, and to institute new alignments in her interpersonal relationships.

It is painful for her to consider life without work. She knows she would be restless, lonely, and bored to death, and she is appalled by the prospect of a significantly lowered income. Excursions, books, or concerts could never fill the void. What she likes best is to "go and go and go," but, lately, "I can't seem to get enough money." She cannot accept the instrumental limitations imposed on the aged. Her morale rises only when she can convince herself that she is still able to pursue her former pattern of life. When her mood is good, she toys with the idea of working her way across the country again, as she used to, perhaps settling in the South. She might take up golf again. But for an injury sustained in an automobile accident, Miss Potter has never been incapacitated in her life. She studiously avoids the subject of sickness. While she shows a new willingness to explore different interests—such as her desires to improve her interpersonal relationships (an area in which she has always considered herself deficient)—she feels it unthinkable to seriously consider any re-exam-

ination of her lifelong orientation to work and instrumental
worth. She continues to resist social pressures to relinquish the
work-role as well as the activities of her earlier life. To all intents
and purposes, she has never effectively coped with her own aging.
She shares with most other Americans a belief in the value of productivity, with work assuming an almost sacred character to her.
This dominant emphasis in American life influences not only the
status of the aged, but their attitudes toward themselves; we certainly see this is Miss Potter's case. In short, we have called her
maladapted, partially through her personal default and partially
by social definition.

The following cases have been chosen to illustrate failure in
each of the five adaptive tasks of aging, and each of these has both
a personal and a social component. In some cases, the aged person
finds himself barred from completing a task in adaptation by the
rigid demands of his society or the simple lack of social supports
and sanctions for satisfactory alternatives to failing courses of
action. In other instances, the barriers lie primarily within the
aged person himself. He may simply lack the emotional or cognitive resources to initiate a change in his behavior. A departure
from habitual modes of action, even when these become physically
impractical, may generate so much fear and anxiety that even the
partial failure of old patterns is preferable to the risk of new and
untried ways. Miss Potter is an example of failure in the first of
these adaptive tasks:

(1) Perception of Aging and Definition of
Instrumental Limitations

This task of adaptation to aging requires an awareness and
an acceptance of changes in one's own individual physical and/or
mental capabilities, with acknowledgement that certain activities
can no longer be pursued as successfully as they were in one's earlier life. We have seen in Chapter VI that better-adapted subjects
conserve their health and energies, while the maladapted, denying
any need for caution, tend to be more profligate. In the social
sense, this task involves an individual's coming to terms with society's limitations on the exercise of his instrumentality. There
must be an awareness of social pressures to relinquish the roles

and activities of middle-life and a realistic assessment of what those pressures mean in terms of available supports.

Of course, not all individuals are subject to the same personal changes or social limitations. We have explored some of those variations in previous chapters. The important point in this task is that, although an individual need not *like* his own personal or social circumstances as he grows old, he must not deny the reality of certain limitations, if they exist for him. Once having admitted to these restraints, he may, if he chooses, attempt to alter his personal circumstances and their accompanying social restrictions. Without such a conscious admission, however, he is not motivated to approach the task.

In our sample, we find two kinds of people who deny that changes accompany old age. First, there are people like Miss Potter, who does everything that she can to look younger—she dyes her hair, spends a great deal of time on her wardrobe, is almost compulsive in her use of cosmetics and creams, and is conscientious in her attendance at charm school. There is a second group of elderly people, however, who do not deny the fact of physical change, but attribute these changes to sickness rather than to aging. For example, Mr. Hopland (HS), at the age of sixty-nine, says, "I still believe I have the ability to do things. I want to think I still have strength to do a lot of things I'm not doing." He is secure in the knowledge of his own worth. He sees himself as a capable, worthwhile human being, cut off from a promising future by the invasion of sickness and disability. But the physical evidence of his aging does not please Mr. Hopland. When he comes face to face with intrusive reminders of its many guises, he finds it easier to think he is more of a *sick* person than he is an old man. The incapacitation of sickness is dreadful, but it frees him from all reflections about what kind of job he has done in growing old. With Mr. Hopland, there is not a denial of change, but rather an unwillingness to consider those changes apart from the context of sickness.

Unfortunately, Mr. Hopland is poor. If his adjustment to the disability of advancing years depends upon his transmuting old age into disease, then he must have some social validation of his status as an invalid. His inability to rally such social support—due largely to his financial incapacity to purchase more than emergency medical care without further impoverishing himself and his wife—has resulted in conflicts with his familiars. Because of his poverty, Mr. Hopland's wife and sons do not feel that he is justified in spending money on "nonessentials" like expensive drugs, private physicians, or sick-room supplies. "Hell," said the younger Mr. Hopland, "he's not sick—he's just *old!*"

Mrs. Reinhardt, on the other hand, is wealthy. Although she spends her days in a wheel chair, she feels young for her age and regards herself "in perfect health, except for this condition." It is not that *she* is changing, but only her "condition." She has been able to bear invalidism with good grace and fortitude; her economic circumstances have permitted complete leisure and the best of nursing care. With dependence on nurses and servants one need not become a crippled old woman—a burden to family and friends; one can simply be a chronic invalid. "It's such a pity!" Mrs. Reinhardt's daughter told us, "Mother is so young to have such a terrible illness."

(2) Redefinition of Physical and Social Life Space

Another adaptive task involves redefining the boundaries of one's life space. The aging individual must reorganize his territoriality in order to preserve a continued optimum level of control over the personal milieu. As changes come with age, the individual may not be able to command as large a segment or the same segment of the environment as he did when he was younger. In social terms, this means that certain roles and activities must be relinquished, and there must follow a reconstitution of one's network of social relationships. For example, an aging businessman may find that he does not have the physical stamina to continue the personal daily contact with large numbers of employees and colleagues which he had had during middle-age. He may, therefore, delegate more responsibility to others and limit his personal interaction to dealings with deputies, thereby preserving his level of power and authority in the company. An aging housewife may find herself unable to perform personally all the tasks necessary to keep a house in order; she may, then (if she has ample economic resources), hire a cleaning woman to assist her and thus maintain her former standards of order and cleanliness; or she may enlist the help of her husband in these tasks; or she and her husband may close off a room or two of the house, or even move to a small apartment. These changes in territoriality sometimes, but not always, involve a constriction in social relationships. Retirement, widowhood, and other major role changes, as we have already seen, involve a more drastic change in life space than those described in these two hypothetical cases.

Mr. Edwin Butler (CS) is a public school teacher who has always wanted to be a big businessman. Mr. Butler is able to accept the fact that he is changing with age. Thus, he has successfully completed one adaptive task. He describes himself as ". . . past middle-age. I know I'm going through a sexual change and in many ways I'm out of the stream of things. I guess age is a factor here for, in many ways, I don't feel physically able to do as much as I did before. I know that there are things I want to do, but I can't, because of my age." Although Mr. Butler does not deny the fact he is growing older and is undergoing certain changes, he is having problems in adaptation, centered around his inability to redefine his life space.

From early childhood, Mr. Butler has been preoccupied with "influencing people." One of his boyhood dreams was to be a great actor. Another, one that has always been a major goal in his value system, has been: "I wanted to be a millionaire; I wanted to be a big spender." Most of his regrets center around "financial deals" that failed to materialize.

At sixty-six, Mr. Butler can best be described as a man with a very diffuse life. He is simultaneously headed in several major directions; first, he is trying to finish his term of teaching in order to receive his full pension. His goal in teaching has been to become an administrator: "The reason why I wanted to be an administrator—well, they make much more money. And it gives you the importance and responsibility you seek." Now, with only two years of teaching remaining before his retirement, Mr. Butler is compelled to face the fact that he will never achieve this goal. Now he is finding it difficult even to manage his classes. He speaks of difficulties in maintaining discipline in his classroom, in handling "behavior problems," and recently he received a reprimand from his school principal for losing his temper with a student and giving the boy a severe shaking. He admits that, with age, he has become more irritable and less able to cope with the demands of public school teaching. In spite of this fact, however, Mr. Butler is still trying simultaneously to fill his teaching position, study for a state license as a real estate salesman, arrange for the purchase and management of a large apartment building, plan business and stock investments, stabilize a precarious relationship with his wife, support a daughter in Switzerland, and maintain active contacts with a wide circle of friends.

Mr. Butler insists on keeping many irons in the fire. Yet, with the loss of energy due to advancing age, he is finding it increasingly difficult to be successful in this. He admits to making several serious errors of judgment in business within recent years; we have already pointed to his irritability and impatience with the students; also he admits to some chronic marital difficulties, in part because he is drinking so much more now than he used to (he admits that drinking has become a problem for him); and he is even concerned about maintaining friendships because he fears being "found out a phony."

Interestingly enough, Mr. Butler gave us the following formula for successful aging: "Well, keep your expectations within limits so that you can achieve your goals." Certainly, he himself has not been able to accomplish this, and his control over his environment is being eroded day after day. His horizons, once so fair and wide, now seem to be receding beyond his failing grasp. Mr. Butler is a very unhappy man.

The barriers in his completion of this adaptive task, however, are largely of his own making. His own personal values, drives, and self-expectations prevent him from trimming his world down a bit, to more manageable proportions. Mr. Helmut Kreisler (HS), at the time of the baseline interview, was having difficulties in the same task, but his barriers were socially-imposed ones. In his sixty-third year, it became increasingly difficult for him to perform efficiently his duties as a janitor and apartment-house manager. However, his employer continued to give him ever more demanding work to do until, finally, he began to do everything badly. Depressed by his failures, he took to drinking heavily and his emotional control became very shaky. Shortly after this, an outburst of violence led to his being brought to the psychiatric ward. This was an adaptive failure with its origins in the social system, but the results were a breakdown of personal function as well.

(3) Substitution of Alternative Sources of Need-satisfaction

A third adaptive task requires that aging individuals effect the substitution of feasible interests, activities, and relationships for those they can no longer pursue successfully, thus providing for themselves alternative sources of need-satisfaction. Adaptation here, in the personal system, requires a willingness and an ability to identify and engage in new, feasible pursuits, and, socially, the individual must have access to possible alternatives within his environment. For example, upon retirement, a working man loses income from wages. If he has been working for a company that has a pension plan, he may substitute these payments and Social Security benefits for the lost earned income. If, however, he refuses to think of himself as retired, but merely as "temporarily unemployed," he may thereby not avail himself of compensatory funds and consequently may suffer unnecessary economic hardships, just to prove his continuing worker status. This is a failure of adaptation within the personal system. A corresponding failure within the social system might be found in the case of a retired migrant agricultural worker, who would be happy to have substitute income, but finds that he is ineligible for Social Security benefits, has no pension due him, and has not established legal residence in the state where he lives and so is unqualified for Old Age Assistance. This failure, too, results in unnecessary economic hardships, quite beyond the control of the aged individual himself.

Mrs. Lois Willoughby (CS) is a woman having difficulty in adaptation at this stage. At sixty-five, Mrs. Willoughby is concerned about growing old: "I don't sleep nights. I lay there and worry over my health and limitations—and then you have to figure my age." She is suffering from hypertension: "When I went out to the clinic last year, they found out I have high blood pressure. I can't go up the hill, and I have a habit of rushing up the hill and that irritates me. What am I rushing *for?*"

Mrs. Willoughby is having problems adjusting to widowhood and compensating for restrictions in her social, as well as physical, life space after three decades of marriage and joint employment with her husband. Together, they managed an apartment building. She has no children. Today, her most regular contacts are with a younger sister, but there is little comfort in the relationship, for this woman is condescending toward Mrs. Willoughby and her abilities. Mrs. Willoughby feels she thinks too much about herself: "I just think about sitting here and vegetating. I didn't used to have time to think of myself before. I had my husband and we were busy taking care of the apartment house we managed." With the loss of her husband, Mrs. Willoughby's financial situation as well as her health began to deteriorate. She could not continue to manage the apartment building without her husband and so is now living on her savings and some Social Security benefits. She would like to work and try to find companionship, perhaps a man friend, but her sister has persuaded her she could probably not succeed at either endeavor. She does have misgivings about her sister's wisdom in these things but not enough self-confidence to act on her own initiative, for she is used to depending on the judgments of others: "I had to do everything my husband said because he was the boss, although I did resent it deeply." In near desperation, she seems to feel there *must* be a way for her to get some of the most pressing needs met; that somewhere, close at hand, there must be a new way of life—if only she could discover it. She would like to make a grasp at it: "I want to do something, but I don't know just what it is or how to go about it." She constantly chides herself for minutes spent in late-morning sleep when she could be doing other things, but she admits frankly she does not know what those things might be.

She is lonely and afraid she cannot much longer get around to do the things she wants to do. Perhaps she does need a boy friend: "I would even get married again, if someone would take me with all these sicknesses." She is not a social recluse. She has several friends, but she rarely sees them, because in her poor financial situation, she cannot comfortably hold up her end of a friendship. She is reluctant to invite guests over for fear she will exhaust her dwindling resources on entertainment.

Sometimes Mrs. Willoughby is fearful that her situation will only worsen: "Here I am getting older, but I'm not going anywhere. I'm not doing anything. That's a terrible way to be. I think I could be like these elderly people who shut themselves in and never see anybody." For the most part, her image of herself is quite negative and depressed. Her greatest fear is that her health and few remaining financial resources will fail her simultaneously, and that she will then succumb to a deprived, empty, meaningless old age. She seems to sense herself losing ground irretrievably in a little-understood but consuming struggle with her needs, her limitations, and the shrinking boundaries of her life.

Mrs. Willoughby has accomplished two of the tasks in adaptation to aging: she freely admits her physical limitations and attributes them correctly to old age. She performed the second task successfully—redefining her life space—when she admitted that she alone could no longer manage a large apartment building after her husband's death. In the third task, however, she is failing.

Mrs. Willoughby's emotional distress is painful to her, but fortunately so far, it has not led her to a hospitalization for psychiatric reasons. Mr. Alioto, on the other hand, developed such severe emotional problems resulting from failures in adaptation that he was admitted to the psychiatric screening ward. His case we have already presented in Chapter VII, where we saw that, for this man, retirement wrote an end to his identity as a functioning member of the social system. Retirement brought a collapse to a tightly structured personal system deficient in alternative roles. He is still unable to discover a substitute for work. It does not occur to him to look for one. For him, life *is* work. It is not the aloneness of old age that has reached out and touched Mr. Alioto; it is the uselessness. Retirement, for him, is not only an end to productivity, but, by extension, the end of life. Mr. Alioto has had woefully little practice in alternative resolutions. At present, the only one that suggests itself to him reflects his mounting despondency: "Saint Peter," he cries, "come and get me!"

(4) Reassessment of Criteria for Evaluation of the Self

A fourth adaptive task requires that the individual modify his basis for self-judgment. It is not adaptative for the older person to continue judging himself according to his excellence in the performance of productive roles. Within the social system, too, there must be developed new criteria for assessing the worth of retired people. A personal or social view of aging as attrition, loss, or inadequacy in performance of the roles of middle life is incompatible with successful survival. In order to preserve ego-strength, the aged must establish their identity on bases other than those of worker, builder, manager, or leader.

Mr. Ned Bates (CS), now sixty-nine years old, is very proud of his former self, but the man he is today pales hopelessly in comparison with the man he used to be. His past is only a memory now, of peaks of accomplishment. He lingers over the war years, ". . . when I had a hundred men under me, waiting for me to tell them what to do." In those good days, he could display his superabundance of personal strength, and revel in the warm social life of which he was the center. The present can only stand to remind him of the loss of that prominence, irretrievably gone. Age is the interloper who has robbed him of his greatness. "Ask anyone—I was at the top of the pile! Why, they even kept me on *two* more years until I was sixty-*seven!*"

Mr. Bates is not yet seventy and is still in good health for his years. However, when we asked him about his life today, he replied, "Now? Now, I don't care. You have to be realistic about this. I feel I have lived my life. There is none of me left."

It is apparent that this negative self-view is age-linked. Mr. Bates does not even hope for the preservation of any *status quo*, let alone any improvement. He feels that his life will only get worse: "What am I good for? I just keep on living. Oh, I'm not a morose man—it isn't a question of that. I have enough money to live decently. My wife is alive and the children come from time to time. I find things to do around the house to keep me busy. But it's not enough. Somehow, it's just not enough. I keep wishing I could so some good—be useful. But I know the answer: it's the end of the road."

For Mr. Bates, being of value means a great deal more than simply finding some kind of work. For more than thirty years, he was foreman in a precision-parts factory. So, even if he could get some work, he would not be content with just any job: "I don't need work, not the kind *I* could find. I may not have been a mental giant, but the kicks were in knowing that what you did made a *difference*, that you were in there, a part of things." He is unlike Mr. Alioto, who simply can find nothing at all to do now that he is unemployable. Mr. Bates has hobbies, social activities, and a still-active family life. What he lacks is a sense that what he is doing has any importance. He is a man for whom instrumentality has been a lifelong value, and one that he cannot easily forfeit. From this erstwhile instrumentality, all things radiated: "You had something to talk about to your friends. Home was a place to come back to. It's not the same thing when there's no place else to go." Even the yearly cycle of his life now still hinges upon the old rhythms of performance and rest: "In the summers, my wife and I would get away from the city. Quiet was something we looked forward to. We'd come back to the house and have the gang over and everybody talked about the summer, where they'd been, and what was going on at the plant. God, now we've got quiet coming out of our ears!"

This man still has the desire to do things, but he cannot assign any importance to what he has left yet to do. He feels that the activities open to elderly people are lacking in substance, even a little silly: "I wouldn't be caught dead in a senior center. What do I want with a lot more guys like myself?" Increasingly, his life takes on a quality of insularity. He feels less vigorous and he is painfully sensitive to the physical changes of age: "What the hell—I'm getting older, bald headed, wrinkled."

Mr. Bates has accomplished several adaptive tasks: first, he admits to being old—he knows he can no longer get and hold more than a menial job; second, he has been able to maintain his control over his environment—he is not trying to "spread himself too thin"; third, he has found substitute activities in hobbies, family life, and home improvement, and is well compensated for lost income through savings, Social Security, and a pension. But these accommodations do not suffice—he lacks self-*approval*, and he has been unable to change his criteria for self-judgment. As he says, he is not morose—he just feels "utterly useless."

(5) Reintegration of Values and Life Goals

An additional adaptive task requires that the aged person revise his individual life goals and values in order to give coherence, integration, and social meaning to his new style of life. In personal adaptation to aging, it is not enough that the elderly individual re-evaluate himself to preserve self-esteem; he must also find a new place for himself in the larger scheme of things, in order that his life may continue to have meaning and purpose. In the social system, there must be an acceptance of the place of the elderly person in society and a positive social sanction for an individual's new life goals.

Mrs. Clara Bruzinsky (CS) is a seventy-nine-year-old widow who lives with her only son and his family. Mrs. Bruzinsky was born in Vienna and had a most joyous and happy childhood and adolescence. She grew up as a member of a large, closely knit, and loving family, where it was understood that parents do anything for the children, and children do everything to please their parents. The greatest pleasures are those that arise *en famille*. Such close affective bonds with her family did not diminish upon Mrs. Bruzinsky's marriage. This union, too, left little to be desired, as she recalls it; she retained her romantic love for her husband until she was widowed at the age of fifty, and she sought to spend as much time in his company as she possibly could. She enjoyed parties, dancing, going to the theater, skiing, and traveling. She was gay and vivacious. However, the real pleasure she received from participating in these activities derived from her always being in the company of someone she loved—that is, her husband, siblings, or close friends. Harmonious human relationships have always been of supreme importance to her; friction and arguments are most disturbing.

Mrs. Bruzinsky has successfully completed the other four tasks of adaptation to aging, as outlined above. First, she is well aware of the fact that she is almost eighty, but she keeps her grey hair beautifully styled and is always tasteful and fashionable in her dress. Although her physical life space is not greatly altered (she spends time working in her son's store, attends bridge parties, and takes trips to museums) she has made some compromises in this area by curtailing her evening activities. At the age of fifty, Mrs. Bruzinsky experienced a sharp break in the pattern of her life: with her husband's death, she was never again to be a member of a close-knit family. She is not, however, lacking in substitute activities and relationships. She has a wide circle of friends, with whom she has frequent contact. She enjoys her association with customers in her son's store. She works hard, goes to the theater and movies, and delights in parties. Her style of living has not changed drastically, and she has retained all her earlier interests. Thus, she has skillfully and cleverly found new means to satisfy her needs. Her self-respect has not diminished—in fact, has never been in question. Mrs. Bruzinsky has always taken pride in being charming, gay, chic, a devoted member of her family, a hard worker, and a "cultured" lady. She feels certain she has preserved all these characteristics in her old age. The task of finding reasonable criteria for self-judgment, then, has been an easy one for her to complete.

Mrs. Bruzinsky, however, is increasingly depressed. For her, the only real meaning to life is being responsible to the people she loves. She needs to be of use to someone. Misfortunes do not get her down—she does not lose hope but only works harder. She is an enterprising, courageous, and optimistic person. However, she greatly misses the closeness of intimate family life. Her son, whose affection, warmly expressed, would mean the most to her, has "failed" her. She consoles herself that he "really loves" her but cannot show it because of "his duties" to his wife. She feels herself a stranger in his household. Carrying around a sense of being unwanted in her own son's home is most distressing to her and is becoming increasingly so. Within the last year, she has repeatedly expressed the wish to die and "have peace." She has even had to admit to herself finally that she is now afraid to live alone, so no change is "possible" for her.

Mrs. Bruzinsky experienced a number of sharp discontinuities in her earlier life. These included flights from country to country during the Second World War with loss of home, property, and income, separations from family and friends, the horror of having a son confined to a concentration camp for a number of years, and, finally, the death of her beloved husband. Throughout it all, she has shown remarkable energy, morale and efficiency in her ever-ready capacity to start anew and to tolerate such upheavals and ruptures. What made it possible was that, though separated from her family, all her activities were always directed toward survival and reunion with her remaining kin. She was flexible in all respects except her needs to sustain always an iron link with members of her family. As long as there could be an anticipation of a happy reunion, she could go on with courage. None of her adjustments to stresses in her former years involved existing without family. This is the awful confrontation she must face in her old age, and it is the one adjustment she cannot make.

In spite of all of this, Mrs. Bruzinsky fights her depressions and has charmed every interviewer with her vivacity. She carries on, does not complain, but tries to be agreeable and kind and is determined to end like a lady.

It should be made clear that Mrs. Bruzinsky has never had difficulty in relinquishing social roles and adjusting to their loss. The death of her parents, the loss of siblings, her bereavement when her husband died of tuberculosis after the family's exile from their native Austria, all of these she was able to face with equanimity. But the development of a life goal which does not center around family and kinship ties has so far eluded her. Whether or not she will eventually be able to develop such a philosophy remains to be seen.[5]

[5]Actually, in a later contact with this subject, she had, indeed, made further progress. She took courage, moved into her own apartment, and is now centering her life around her own home and friends.

A Case of Successful Aging

To complete this discussion, we will describe one additional case, that of Mr. Ed Hart (CS), a man who has skillfully adapted —both personally and socially—to all five tasks. We first saw Mr. Hart when he was ninety years old. He was born in 1870, and was the only child of middle-aged parents. He started working and contributing significantly to the household budget at a very early age; while still in his teens, he turned over his considerable savings to his parents, enabling them to purchase a home. Still in his youth, he assumed a "parental" role toward his parents, being obliged to do so because much of his father's time was spent in taking care of the then invalid mother. Mr. Hart attended school, learned cabinet-making from his father, and devoted himself to the care of his parents.

Mr. Hart idolized his father throughout his life. Cabinet work was always dear to him because it had been taught him by his father. He regarded his father's guidance as invaluable: it was he who kept his son away from the alcohol which he dearly loved, and it was also from his father that he acquired a sincere love for people. The relationship was a very harmonious one, each gladly accommodating himself to the wishes of the other. Although Mr. Hart married at the age of twenty-four, he and his wife continued to live with his parents until their death in 1912. Mr. Hart was closely attached to his wife, but his father has always remained the most important figure in his life.

He was content with cabinet work until the age of thirty-five, at which time he bought a ranch, deciding to become a financial success for the sake of his children. He describes himself during this period as overly ambitious and given to excessive chronic worry. His preoccupation in making a fortune from this ranching endeavor led to a "nervous breakdown" and confinement in a sanitarium for two months. This experience, when he was about forty, proved to be the turning point of his life. He emerged with a highly integrated personality and a satisfying personal philosophy. He had formerly been a zealous member of the Methodist Church, but following this hospitalization, he eschewed all organized religions, feeling he needed no one to dictate to him how he should serve God. Nonetheless, Mr. Hart expresses a profound belief in divinity, a love of his fellow man, a full acceptance of everything life has to offer, and an adamant refusal to be unhappy.

Following his hospitalization, Mr. Hart sold his ranch and took a position as vocational teacher for the following six years. Again, he found deep satisfaction in his work and was loved by students and fellow teachers alike. He showed great understanding and evidently displayed remarkable skill in nurturing the talents of his students, adapting his teaching to the individual child's potential. His dislike for the regimentation practiced in the school led him to resign and to return to his former vocation of cabinet-making, work he pursued up to the age of fifty-five. An injury to his arm, however, finally made him give up this successful occupation (some of his work had been exhibited at the 1939 San Francisco International Exposition). For the next twenty years, he was employed in the hotel business, work that he found congenial because of his interest in people. Retirement did not find him idle. Up to the age of ninety, he did cabinet-work as a hobby, manufacturing various items to present to his numerous friends.

Mr. Hart refers to sixty-four years of harmonious and contented married life. His first wife died suddenly after twenty-five years of marriage when he was forty-nine years old. After living alone with his children for two years, he remarried at the age of fifty-one. Thirty years later, he lost his second wife, and it was upon her "last request" that he again remarried. His third wife had been a widowed friend they had both known for almost thirty years. This final marriage lasted for nine years. During the last two years of her life, the third wife was severely ill and Mr. Hart nursed her through to the end. She died in 1960. Even during his last wife's terminal illness, Mr. Hart showed the same serenity and the same positive acceptance of life he expressed in all of our interviews with him. He does not differentiate among his wives: he describes them all as "dear, loyal women."

Mr. Hart finds it somewhat "humiliating" that he has outlived three wives and both of his sons. He took pains to raise his children as best he could and was anxious to let them develop their own individual ways. Rather than as a provider of an estate, a role he had once thought so important, he finally perceived his parental duties as the provider of good examples and wise guidance. His close relationship with his sons changed when they married, and Mr. Hart believes that it is only right that this should be so: "With marriage the offspring form independent units of their own, and parents should release their hold upon them." Mr. Hart was never possessive in his life. The persons closest to him at present are his daughter and step-daughter, who are equally dear. He mentions with pride that both have invited him to come and live with them, but he will not take this step until it is absolutely necessary. He does not wish to inconvenience them, but unlike many others of our subjects, he does not harp on the prospect of "becoming a burden" to somebody else.

From his middle years onward, Mr. Hart suffered a number of major illnesses: in 1926 he was operated on for bilateral hernia; and in 1949, for a perforated ulcer; finally, a prostatectomy and colostomy in 1953 (he was eighty-three years old at the time) resulted in complete loss of control over his bladder, requiring him to wear a urinal twenty-four hours a day. When he was ninety, his physical condition no longer permitted him to indulge in his hobby of wood-working, and, at ninety-three, his failing eyesight ruled out television and limited his reading to one hour a day. Yet he takes his declining physical function in stride, not finding it irksome to make the necessary adjustments. His mental faculties have remained remarkably intact. He is keenly aware that few men his age are as mentally alert as he is, or have aged as gracefully. He is proud of this fact and attributes it to the philosophical orientation he has worked out for himself and incorporated into his life.

Although Mr. Hart has been obliged to curtail many of his social activities, he still corresponds with numerous friends and receives almost daily visits from solicitous neighbors. He is an individual who gives much of himself and is warmly appreciated by others; he appears to be a person who brings the best out of others, which may be one of the reasons he claims he has never been disappointed by a friend. Mr. Hart has led a full, creative, and serene existence. It is, perhaps, because his life has been one of fulfillment that he is ready to surrender it at any moment; he still finds life quite enjoyable, but he is as willing to die as he is to continue living.

This man made a profound impression on all our interviewers. They found him alert, intelligent, serene, and wise. His self-acceptance is complete. He found it difficult to answer our self-image questions or to describe himself in terms of the list of various personality traits we submitted to him; he simply stated, more appropriately, "I'm Ed Hart and I don't want to be anyone else—I will be the same ten years from now, if I'm alive."

According to American middle-class standards, Mr. Hart has not been a particularly successful man. Looking at his life in one way, he has no particular reason not to be disappointed with his past and depressed with his present. He failed in his one great effort to become wealthy. After a nervous breakdown, he gave up on this venture altogether. He quit a second time when he dropped out of the teaching profession because he disagreed with established policy. One might expect him to be bitter about this, or terribly lonely, since he has outlived nearly all of his friends and relatives—but he is neither. Crippled with disease, forced to wear a urinal at all times, and nearly blind, Mr. Hart gave one of our interviewers his philosophy of life: "I have an original motto which I follow: 'All things respond to the call of rejoicing; all things gather where life is a song.' "

It is clear that Mr. Hart has adapted to aging. He has admitted to and accepted physical limitations, first giving up the demanding manual labor of cabinet-making, and later retiring without regret from hotel work.

Mr. Hart has no problems in controlling his life space—he does not over-extend himself: "As long as I don't strain myself, I'm okay. I take it easy. The other day I declined an invitation to go on board a ship, since I knew there would be stairs there."

All of his life, Mr. Hart has successfully practiced substitution, so this adaptation has been natural for him. He enjoyed married life and never remained a widower for long. He was capable of substituting one vocation for another, as necessity required, developing a deep interest and satisfaction in each. Even after his retirement from hotel work, his last job, he continued to be interested and active in union affairs. "That's my pork chop, so to speak," he says.

In personal philosophy, Mr. Hart has no problems at all. His standards for self-evaluation are not predicated on mutable factors such as productivity, wealth, or social status. He is first, last, and always himself: "I'm Ed Hart and I don't want to be anyone else." This is a standard not likely to totter with age.

However, his discovery of adaptive values and life-goals was hard-won: at forty, he early found himself unable to cope with the instrumental and achievement-oriented values of his society. He suffered a severe emotional upheaval at that time, was hospitalized for a period, and emerged with a warm, humanistic philosophy which has carried him not only through middle age, but through old age as well.

The Tasks as Distributed in the Sample

Mr. Hart is not unique in our sample, although he is perhaps one of the more articulate and endearing of our subjects. Many in the sample, like Mr. Hart, have completed all the tasks. Others are not having serious difficulties because they have satisfactorily resolved all the tasks that have so far arisen for them; other tasks have not yet required their attention. The pattern of aging among these subjects has simply not required them to come to grips at this time with all the adaptive tasks of later life.

Let us now redirect our attention to two issues touched upon earlier in this discussion: first, what is the extent of maladaptation in the intensive-study sample? Are the mentally-healthy aged nearly always adapted, and the mentally ill invariably maladapted? Second, which of the adaptive tasks is most likely to cause difficulties for the older people in the sample; are there some tasks that are more problematic than others?

With respect to the first question, we find that, while mental status (consensus) and adaptation (as rated) are highly correlated, the correspondence is not a perfect one, as the following figures show:

PROPORTIONS OF TWO MENTAL-STATUS GROUPS SHOWING GOOD
ADAPTATION TO AGING, INTENSIVE-STUDY SAMPLE

	Community Subjects %	Hospital Subjects %	Total Intensive Sample %
Adapted	61	12	42
Maladapted	39	88	58
Total rated (N=100%)	(38)	(24)	(62)
Not rated because of deterioration (N)	(2)	(15)	(17)

Even among the community subjects, almost two-fifths were having serious problems in adaptation to aging at the time of the intensive interviews. At the same time, among elderly people with a recent history of psychiatric hospitalization, the passage of a few years had enabled a few to work out quite satisfactory adaptive modes.

Turning to the second question, we find that there are, indeed, some differences in proportions of subjects who were having difficulties with the various adaptive tasks. When we classified the maladapted subjects according to the task that was most distressing to them, we obtained the following distribution:

	Per Cent
Acceptance of aging	11
Reorganization of life space	14
Substitute sources of need satisfaction	54
Reexamination of criteria for self-evaluation	14
Reintegration of values and life goals	7

It is clear that the major problem for these maladapted aged is finding other ways to get their physical, economic, and emotional needs met when old sources become unavailable to them. These are the subjects, like Mr. Alioto, who see the disruption of a formerly statisfying pattern of life as the end of life itself. It does not occur to them that old age may represent anything more than the irreplaceable loss of all they require to make life endurable. The other tasks are far less insoluble for our subjects as a group.

Substitution then, seems to be the crucial skill for aging adapta-tion in our society.[6]

Before we leave this discussion of adaptive tasks, we want to comment briefly on the kinds of people (in terms of various demo-graphic characteristics) who seem to have the easiest time in solv-ing these adaptation problems. We find that subjects who are seventy and older, in contrast with those in their sixties, are more likely to be adapted. Adaptation seems partly to be a mat-ter of time—of having enough years to work out the problems and come to terms with aging. In regard to sex differences, men seem to have found it somewhat easier to adapt in their old age than women. As we have seen, however, men have less demanding re-lationships with their children and are more frequently still liv-ing with a spouse. Women present the greatest problems in deal-ings with their children and coping with their widowhood; men, in finding substitutes for work. As one might guess, reasonably good economic status and physical health are positively related to adaptive aging. The maladaptive influence of physical disability is especially noteworthy in light of the association between older-age level and good adaptation, since the disabled group includes a much higher proportion of subjects over seventy. Apparently, the problems of ill health are strong enough to override the bene-ficial effects of advanced age in coping with the tasks of later life.

AMERICAN CULTURAL VALUES AND AGING ADAPTATION

The study sample of this research, incorporating as it does both mentally-healthy and mentally-ill subjects, has permitted us to view a cross-section of aged Americans with a wide spectrum of adaptive and maladaptive attitudes and behavioral styles. The hospitalized mentally ill have offered us a bench mark for the ex-tremes of maladaptation or individual variance in the very strik-

---

[6]It should be noted that this task is the one most dependent upon the social system and that, since the others are more linked to personal abilities, they do not pose the same order of difficulty. In other words, it may be easier to change one's thinking than to win others over to assist in one's adaptation. This is, of course, a problem for those of any age but especially so for the aged.

ing fact of their social ostracism. To this, the dischárged and the mentally healthy have added a wide variety of other maladaptive as well as adaptive life-styles. We now face the question: what can be derived from the testimony of this sample of aging Americans that might help us to understand the common problems that face all aging Americans today?

To begin with, has this group shown us any evidence of its being a part of a larger community of elders—a social group with a common internal structure and external goals? Some social scientists (see especially Barron, 1953) claim that the aged in American society today are indeed "emerging, quasi-minority group," and can legitimately be studied as such. But are they? How do they compare with other minority groups? Minority groups in our society are customarily built along the lines of color, religion, national origin, or the subcultures of "hyphenated Americans." Individuals classified in these subgroups usually possess lifelong memberships in them: they are born into them and die in them. Also, the goals of social action within these minority groups are usually directed to gain the recognition, rights, and prerogatives of the majority culture—in short, to be like everybody else. But the aged cannot "be like everybody else." Those in their ranks who try, we find, are maladapted. However, the aged as a group do share certain characteristics with the minorities. We have noted their segregation from the mainstream of American life, the discrimination practiced against them in certain retirement policies, the poorly-disguised belief in their inferiority, their resistance to being identified as second-class citizens, and their poverty. With all these social and political disadvantages, one might very likely expect them to be "emerging" as many minorities are doing today.

Our sample of elderly subjects, however, has given us no indication that the aged are "emerging" in the form of a minority movement. At the present writing, it is nowhere evident that they are functioning as a unified group with indigenous leadership, focused political power, and shared long-range aspirations. Unlike the minority groups, they have never agitated for the elimination of ther second-class status. In recent history, however, we have witnessed several short-lived attempts to organize the aged into a quasi-political force (see Landis [1946] for a brief history of these movements). The Townsend Plan movement during the Depression (Roosevelt, 1936) and the political support George McLain mustered during his candidacy for governor of California during the early Fifties were mostly limited to bread-and-butter issues for low-cost government housing, medical aid, and increase in pensions (Townsend agitated for an outright government dole). Opposition to these movements has often emphasized the demagoguery of the leaders, accusing them of shamefully exploiting the aged for political purposes. In general, however, such movements have been short-lived, the leaders die out, and new leaders have been hard to recruit and train. Evidently, too, the most successful leaders of these geronto-political groups have manifested a charisma or messianic fervor, suggesting that something of the qualities of a "savior" are required for their leadership, and successful saviors for old people are infrequent on the social scene.

But there are other reasons for the lack of continuity in these movements. A comparison of them with the recent civil-rights movement makes it immediately clear why they have lacked cohesive, sustained social force. Civil-rights leaders, for the most part, are born into the movement and early develop a philosophy of group identification. Again, they have a lifetime to devote to the work. In addition to this, the subculture has many social organizations built into it for the purposes of education, religion, and so on. These groups can be rallied to the movement and will provide their own structures in support of it and offer their own channels of communication for propaganda purposes. In contrast, most Americans (except politicians with an eye to "voting blocs") do not take seriously the problems involved in the social and political rights of the aged until they themselves approach sixty-five. If one of this age does become inspired to organize the old, consider the problems he would face: quite a few of his lifelong contacts with influential others will have atrophied, or these relationships will have been with organizations that are essentially geared to serving people of younger ages or such special interests as veterans, unions, or professional groups. He will find it very difficult to rally these organizations as allies to the movement.

This is not to say that several elderly subjects in our sample have not demonstrated sincere interest in political action to help solve the problems of older people. Mr. Ritter, for one, is very busy writing his congressman in support of legislation for the aged, and a few have even been willing to participate in temporary, short-range agitation for immediate goals. In San Francisco, a redevelopment plan under current discussion has stimulated many of the elderly residents of downtown hotels and rooming houses to join a neighborhood association combatting the plan, because it proposes to raze much of this cheap housing for new commercial buildings and entertainment-convention facilities. The vigor of this response indicates once again that the aged can be aroused to strong political action when there is an immediate threat to their security and a promptly realizable goal.

But we need not deplore this. Our sample has shown us that a primary orientation to the present is adaptive for the aged—at least, in our own culture. In contrast, a rich, elderly Japanese gentleman is engaging in adaptive behavior when he donates a row of ornamental cherry trees to his favorite shrine, because he has a strong identification with his lineage and knows that these trees will not be chopped down in five years to make way for a freeway. Elderly Americans, on the other hand, planning in this fashion for the distant future, are relying on traditions that are either weak or nonexistent. If they are well-adapted, they know that "the legacy of the past" lies very lightly in the hands of today's younger generations.

For these as well as many other reasons, the old have not banded into angry legions that march with banners. Their concern is with the present, and the futuristic direction of movements has no appeal for them. It is not to large, unified social groups that they turn. We have actually seen quite a bit of resistance to any association with other old people, but neither have we uncovered any widespread desire to cultivate associations with the young. They are very ambivalent about this: some feel that the young are indeed rejecting them; some feel the social distance too great to bridge; many would like to enhance the associations they already have with the young but fear that such gestures will be misinterpreted as "becoming a burden."

The clearest, most unequivocal finding to come out of our social analysis of this sample is the singularity of the subjects in it. This singularity is interpreted by these subjects in many ways: it is a proud independence; it is an autonomy prized as befitting "a good, upstanding American;" or it is a shrinking from others for fear of rejection, or an invasion into sacred privacy for purposes of manipulation or the offering of unwanted "charity." For others, this singularity is an intolerable loneliness out of which they cannot break because it would be "a disgrace" to have to admit to oneself and the world that one needs to lean that much on others. In this quandary, some have been driven to denials of their aging—dyeing their hair and pretending to be sleek, cool professionals who stand on their own feet and need no one; or they have been seduced into retreating to garret rooms where they play the lonely genius, soon to be discovered for remarkable inventions that will revolutionize the world. Some try to keep working, to keep themselves at the center of a vivacious social whirl, desperately trying to hold on still to the reins of love and power, but beneath such masquerades and denials is the smothered protest of devalued status. In America, one must simply not admit that, when one grows old, one will need to lean more and more upon others. In America, *no adult* has any *right* to this. At all costs, the major work must be done, the major values must be acted out. Those who cannot do these things are either "children" or fools, useless or obsolete. It is the central values of American culture which lay down such cruel alternatives, and those elderly, not wishing to be thought of as foolish or useless, often believe the only way out of such an either-or dilemma is to keep their peace, their social distance, their insularity, their independence, their inviolable selfhood—even at the awful cost of loneliness and isolation. And it is in corners such as these that we have seen breed the suspicions and fears and despairs that wreck a sizeable number of elderly Americans.

The data reported in Chapter VIII have demonstrated that this social withdrawal is maladaptive, despite the fact that American culture—as it is constituted today—makes it almost inevitable. We feel that to read this cultural phenomenon as a biological necessity is to obscure even further the interrelatedness with the world the aged treasure as long as they are alive. If, therefore, this alienation of the aged derives from the unique character of American society, it behooves us to ask why we do not do better in our relationships with our elders.

Upon their return to America after years in the field studying primitive and peasant societies, many anthropologists have been struck by the atomistic nature of American family life. Margaret Mead (1943) is one of these and has been led to comment:

> The American baby is born into a family which is isolated from both paternal and maternal lines of kindred. His parents typically live in a house by themselves. If they do not, they seek to create some sort of social isolation to recompense themselves for the presence of relatives. The mother dreams in secret of the day when 'John's mother won't have to live with us anymore.' And the father hopes that 'one of Mary's brothers will be able to take Mary's mother before long.' This attitude is conveyed to the baby. He learns that only his father and his mother are really relevant to his life, that grandparents should live at a distance, if at all, and are not really necessary. If they are all dead, he experiences no sense of loss, no feeling that his own place in the world is compromised or incomplete. . . . In old societies when the extended family or the clan is still an important part of the way of life, the child moves easily among many relatives, many of whom bear his name, with someone of whom he can almost certainly find a community of interests and even a common physique. But in America, with the family whittled down to father and mother, a child may often feel that he is like neither of them. . . . The day comes when both father and mother seem strange, forbidding figures, enforcing some meaningless moral code in a meaningless world (pp. 83-85) .

This typical family structure amounts to a very narrow base for American social learning and behavior. We have frequently observed in our sample that, when individuals abandon this narrow base because something is unsatisfactory about it or when death removes the one spouse or sibling upon whom the individual's entire social world is pivoted, it is very likely that social isolation will result. Given the difficulties Americans find in substituting for these lost relationships, it is small wonder that we find so many older Americans living in bewildered or angry loneliness.

But other characteristics of American life enhance the trend of American singularity. The British anthropologist Gorer (1948) has emphasized immigration as an alienating factor both within and between generations:

> To reject authority became a praiseworthy and specifically American act, and the sanctions of society were added to the individual motives for rejecting the family authority personified in the father; and the father, with his European character and upbringing, was often excessive in his demands for obedience. . . . The making of an American demanded that the father should be rejected both as a model and a source of authority. Father never knew best. And once the mutation was established, it was maintained; no matter how many generations separate an American from his immigrant ancestors, he rejects his father as an authority and exemplar, and expects his sons to reject him (p. 31).

Somewhat later he adds a comment which also has relevance to the typical American's attitude toward the aged:

> Respect and awe are the usual emotional response to personified authority, and are therefore among the most painful emotions that the Americans recognize, and are as carefully avoided by them as the feeling of shame-facedness is by the Japanese. In the face of peoples or situations which might evoke such feelings every effort is made by the use of levity, incongruousness, or elaboration to reduce them to a status where such feelings will no longer be appropriate (pp. 41-42).

There is yet another isolating factor in American life—our singular concept of freedom. We define it not as an opportunity to move about and establish newer and wider relationships with others; rather, in American terms, it amounts to a tendency in us to alienate ourselves from others through a tenacious insistence upon individual rights rather than social relatedness. In Williams' terms (1959):

> [Traditional Americans have] a tendency to think of rights rather than duties, a suspicion of established (especially personal) authority, a distrust of central government, a deep aversion to acceptance of obviously coercive restraints through visible social organizations. . . . This particular sort of freedom was premised on a sweeping faith: the confidence of the individual in his own competence and mastery (p. 418).

The value of individualism in American life, which, according to Williams, grows out of our singular concept of freedom, produces a particular definition of personal identity: "To be a person is to be independent, responsible, and self-respecting, and thereby to be worthy of concern and respect in one's own right" (*ibid.*, p. 435).

CONCLUSION: A SUGGESTION FOR CREATIVE RESOLUTIONS TO AGING PROBLEMS

In the preceding discussion and throughout this volume, we have explored some of the problems of aging in America today, sometimes pressing down on the issues so hard as to make these problems seem insoluble. We would be amiss to leave our readers with any such impression. Fortunately for the aged and for us all, cultures change. Their dictates are not at all as imperious as a close scrutiny of the primary values would suggest. Fortunately, there are secondary values, waiting—so to speak—in the wings or on the sidelines of the major activities of the culture. Often, these values are resorted to when life becomes unbearably ugly or perilous or dull. It is then that we set aside our competitiveness for the comfort of a little cooperation (or we call upon cooperation to aid us in our competitiveness). It is then when we remember the solace of meditation or the beauty experienced in the contemplation of quieter things. Unfortunately, most of us give little serious thought to such things as conservation until, on holidays from our exploiting of the environment, we reenter the woods and are reminded of the delicate balance of nature. Briefly, secondary values can both buttress the primary values and assuage us when our major pursuits are done.

In the light of these considerations, it appears to us that the alienation of the aged from American life is not wholly barred from any creative solutions. Those in our sample whom we found to be adapted in their old age have suggested the answer to this problem. These are the elderly who have successfully developed personal codes of values which have eased their resolution of the adaptive tasks of aging. We have just seen that these codes are not alien to American culture—they are the secondary values— and those who survive best in their later years are simply those who have been able to drop their pursuits of the primary values (as their culture has required them to do) and to go on to pick up, as workable substitutes, the alternative values which have been around all along: conservation instead of acquisition and exploitation; self-acceptance instead of continuous struggles for self-advancement; being rather than doing; congeniality, coopera- tion, love, and concern for others instead of control of others. These are the values the aged of this society have been forced to embrace.

Admittedly, this shift from one set of value-orientations to another has posed a serious, stress-ridden discontinuity for some. In order to learn if this kind of "traumatic aging" is specific to our culture, it would be to our advantage, as anthropologists, to ex- amine aging in societies where the values our aged are forced to adopt in later life are already the core values of the culture. Would we find comparable discontinuities where cooperation and conservation are modal for all?

Foster (1965) has observed in peasant societies what has great relevance to the point here. According to this writer, the culture of these societies is pivoted on an "Image of Limited Good."

> By "Image of Limited Good" I mean that broad areas of peasant behavior are patterned in such fashion as to suggest that peasants view their social, economic, and natural universes — their total environment — as one in which all of the desired things in life such as land, wealth, health, friendship and love, manliness and honor, respect and status, power and influence,

security and safety, *exist in finite quantity* and *are always in short supply,* as far as the peasant is concerned. Not only do these and all other "good things" exist in finite and limited quantities, but in addition *there is no way directly within peasant power to increase the available quantities* [emphasis his] (p. 296).

Foster goes on to observe that because of the static nature of the economic system in these peasant societies (his study communities are Mexican and Egyptian), such American virtues as competition, acquisition, exploitation of the environment, and socioeconomic mobility are held by everyone to be social evils, because such things are gained at the expense of others. It can be readily seen how such perceptions pose formidable "problems" to administrators of foreign aid to these societies. If, however, we were to substitute the words "American aged" for "peasants" in the quoted passage, it would be immediately clear what our adapted elderly have learned as well as what they wish to remind us of.

Likewise, a comparative study of societies marked by an acceptance of the inevitable and the patterns of aging found in them would be enlightening. Saunders (1954), studying the Spanish-speaking communities of the Southwest, notes the fatalism of these people as:

> . . . their somewhat greater readiness toward acceptance and resignation than is characteristic of the Anglo. Whereas it is the belief of the latter that man has an obligation to struggle against and if possible to master the problems and difficulties that beset him, the Spanish-speaking person is more likely to accept and resign himself to whatever destiny brings him. With his eyes on the future, the Anglo tells himself and his friends that "while there is life there's hope." . . . The Spanish-speaking person, by contrast, is likely to meet difficulties by adjusting to them rather than by attempting to overcome them. Fate is somewhat inexorable, and there is nothing much to be gained by struggling against it. If the lot of man is hard — and it frequently is — such is the will of God, incomprehensible, but just, and it is the obligation of man to accept it (pp. 128-129).

Once again, merely substituting "American aged" in the appropriate places, we can see what our elderly must so painfully *learn* in their later years—what the elderly of other cultures have known as "reality" from their earliest days.

In similar fashion, it would be useful to turn to those societies where group responsibility takes precedence over individual "rights." A close look at aging in Japan might confirm our suspicions that human aging is not universally traumatized with serious conflicts such as those between a drive for independence and need for help and assistance.

In the preceding section, we underscored our findings that the aged (at least, of San Francisco) lack any strong sense of themselves as a cohesive social group in our society today, inspiring loyalty, dedicated work, and intense identification with the group. They themselves will seldom undertake public action to ameliorate their lot. Only where goals are directly concerned with immediate difficulties will they band together for their own protection. Rather, the aged we have studied prefer to communicate with others, not through group action, but through face-to-face encounters. Within the preceding paragraphs, summarizing the dilemmas of aging adaptation our elderly face, we have identified them as members of our society who perforce deviate from cultural norms. If, therefore, the old today do not choose to assume identity as a group—either as a minority or as a political force— we believe them to be functioning, independently, within the network of American society as a deviant group. If the aged are to assume a role in our public life today—*within the terms that seem most acceptable to them*—it will amount to functioning as deviant private citizens, since we have no well-developed institutional roles for them.

Beyond whatever usefulness social deviants may possess as scapegoats for the troubles of society-at-large, those who do not conform, espouse or epitomize core values have often performed valuable services nonetheless for the culture. There is one somewhat negative social function they can fulfill: they can assume "dirty work" responsibilities (see Hughes, 1962, and Romano, 1965, for an elaboration of these concepts). But there are more positive tasks also available to them. As suggested in the first chapter, deviants of this type are not always the pariahs of a society: often they make the most money, live in the best houses,

and wear the finest clothes. Like the *patrones* of pre-Revolutionary Mexico, these persons deviate from the cultural norms in
such a way as to provide the only avenues of change for a society
which might otherwise stagnate. In a more dynamic society, they
are the planners, the diplomats, the innovators, and dreamers.

But deviant groups also perform another invaluable service—
as social critics—and here we begin to see how America's old can
make their greatest contribution to American life, despite their
retirement from its principal arenas. Even as Negroes remind us
of our basic democratic ideals and how far we have strayed from
achieving them, even as contemporary college students demonstrate for less-automated universities and a more humane public
life, even as Jews have played a major role in counteracting
much of the anti-intellectualism in America, advancing the arts
and honoring scholarly pursuits, so the aged, with their specific
set of experiences and learning, possess much of real value to
communicate with the majority culture. As an alienated, declassed
group, they hardly have access to the channels of mass communication and, heretofore, only the exceptional aged—the Einsteins, the
Bernard Baruchs, the Eisenhowers—have been able to address
society-at-large in this way, but our study has shown that most
older people continue to cherish communication with others (indeed, they are demoralized if they do not). The purpose of this
conclusion, therefore, has been to reaffirm that the members of our
aged population *want* to remain engaged and to suggest to them
what it is they can give us, *what* it is we desperately need from
them.

Raab and Selznick (1964) summarize what is at issue here:

> [T]he central psychological problem of old age would
> approach solution in the realization that there are activities
> that are of social and human value outside the realm of eco-
> nomic productivity and homemaking. In this sense, the prob-
> lem of the aged merely dramatizes a problem that exists in less
> aggravated form for the entire adult population (p. 443).

If the aged can adapt as we have observed, they come to a true
appreciation of America's secondary values. They, more than any
other group in our population, can attest to the fact that there is

more to life than making money, manipulating others, and winning in the marketplace. If love, conservation, resilience, relaxation, and a non-self-seeking curiosity have any survival value at all, they know it. If there is in this country any group that can provide us now with data on how Americans must learn to cope with the greater amounts of leisure time our automated society is every day making more and more possible for us all, it is the aged (see Kleemeier, 1961). Thus it is that our older citizens, whether they yet realize it or not, are a very important part of our national human resources, and, though devoid of the social and political power whose activities make headlines, they nevertheless can contribute in the quiet ways they love best to the enrichment, so urgently needed, of the quality of America's national life.

EPILOGUE

[OUR APPROACH IN THIS BOOK has been based on recorded phenomena—the experiences of over four hundred older Americans.
Throughout we have relied on their own words, but we have
been fortunate in finding a brief essay which beautifully articulates many of the concepts developed in this book: disengagement
and re-engagement, the aged person's need for relatedness, the invisibility of the old, the adaptive virtues of a non-self-seeking curiosity, and the freedom that comes with fewer social responsibilities. The author of this essay, Dr. Florida Scott-Maxwell, is a
native-born Jungian analyst with a wide reputation both in America and in England, where she currently makes her home. She is
the author of numerous volumes, among which *Women and
Sometimes Men* is the best known. The following is a slightly
abridged radio talk Mrs. Scott-Maxwell first delivered on the
Third Programme of the British Broadcasting Corporation. Shortly thereafter, it was printed in the pages of *The Listener (LII:*
1337, October 14, 1954, pp. 627-9). It was later reprinted in
Harper's Bazaar. The author and both publishers have kindly
given their permission for this reprinting.]

WE ARE THE SUM OF OUR DAYS [ABRIDGED]
FLORIDA SCOTT-MAXWELL

. . .[A]ge cannot spend all its long days, and often wakeful
nights, in seeing itself in the light of eternity. Old people may, at
a deep level, be facing their inner judges and doing it valiantly.
At a more ordinary level they spend much of their time being
astonished at their own unimportance. They feel so minute and
ephemeral, that they doubt that their identity will last as long as
it decently should. They are tired of themselves, and ready to
relinquish the rags and tatters of themselves that still cling
together.

They are also constantly bedevilled by a question that they cannot get rid of, and that is 'How long must we make ourselves last?' For the haunting thought is always in our heads that perhaps we know nothing of age. It may all lie ahead, and can only be faced day by day to its unseeable end. Each hour nibbles at our solidity, and we relinquish something in every little humiliation. Trying twice before one's knees get one upright. One's own knees! Not seeing what others see, not hearing what they hear, missing the point, and so—pretending one was not interested. Often it was true: one was not interested. The emphasis, noise, and clamour of life seem out of proportion to sense. Something else is true and must be admitted: dullness becomes very attractive. Sitting in a decent silence, enjoying the presence of the you that does not talk, and liking even better the absence of the one that does. One's mind open, in case there is any peace about; but turning away from the too personal, in search of the impersonal—we need a good deal of blankness for that.

Yet it is cold to be left out, and who wants to be treated like an effigy that no longer functions? So we demand with energy, 'Who should be interested if not we? Who else started these lives and events?' We have a great need to know certain things. We long to follow the logic in which we were a link, and—if we can—to catch a glimpse of the new thing that lies beyond us. We watch, all the time, to see where life fructifies, and where it lies dormant. If suffering comes to those we know well, we care above all that the suffering should be used to further life. Perhaps we have come to care more for the quality of life than we do for those who carry it; the old want to learn who among the young has the gift of learning. For the old can feel justified, or condemned, by all that they engendered.

But all that is what we long for, fruitlessly, very often. What we get is an odd experience of anonymity, as though we moved along the cracks between the lives of other people. I know one woman who was once so lovely that as she walked all eyes were on her, and if she turned round others turned to look at her. As she aged she noticed that everyone looked right through her, as though she were not there at all. It gave her a funny sense of freedom, but also a sense that she had become invisible. She felt she could go anywhere, into houses and out again. No one would stop her for no one would see her. She even wondered if she dared dance instead of just walking, but thought it more prudent not to try.

It may be this experience of being invisible that makes so many old people give up wearing their social masks. No longer greatly impressed by humanity, no longer sure that they themselves exist, feeling it hardly matters if they do, they gain a new ease in remaining as uncovered and limpid as children. If to be tempered in the fires of insight is the task of age, perhaps this childlike naturalness is its reward. Old people tend to enjoy indulging in mild eccentricity. This could be one aspect of our anonymity, combined with the fact that the old have so much life in them that cannot be lived; we dare to be natural at last, and really care little for the opinion of others. I have heard it said that the vigour and richness of character in a country is proved by the number of great eccentrics that it produces. So, let old people make their contribution here.

There is another aspect to age somewhat akin to this, that is almost embarrassing to speak of because of its extreme improbability. One wants to shield it from younger ears. Yet it is innocent, and may be forgiven us. It is this—the old feel very young. At moments, that is. Though we are aching, inadequate wrecks, there are times when, in our hearts, we are incurably, deliciously young. I have no idea whether we should be or we should not be. Who is to say? Undoubtedly the quality of this strange youthfulness matters greatly. And observation tells us that it varies greatly. All that I am sure of is that an unexpected freshness comes to one when old. I have seen it rise in the lined face of a woman in her nineties, and it suffused her with virginal lightness. And who has not been struck by the guileless purity in the eyes of many old men?

This puzzling newness is so bouyant a thing it is a problem how to deal with it discreetly. Explain it as you will, it feels like happiness: but also like release and exemption. If taken in too literal a manner it may make you want to start again, and how can this be done? For the absurd fact is that an irrational and very high spirited you is convinced that it now knows how to live.

And could: there is the danger. For two pins it would try. In fancy, and very nearly in fact, it is ready to start out at once and see the world. It knows clearly that the necessary physical strength is lacking, as well as the robust purse, and that the perfect companion, who would like exactly what you like has not been met in a lifetime of looking. Yet this unconquerable you, who might easily make a fool of you, must be honoured. It must be honoured greatly, for the leap of expectancy that rises in its heart is authentic, and I beg you to believe me when I say it is pristine in its freshness.

This gaiety in age is accompanied by, perhaps even partly caused by, the realisation that though our drama has been played, and that nothing much will now happen to us in the outside world, our battle too is over. And that fills us with a surge of triumph. It is like a great thrust of cognition, for we have lived our lives. We have been through that mystifying travail. We have worked and suffered, and sinned and loved, and known happiness. We have done harm and done good. We have seen ugliness and beauty. We have been broken, and we have come through. So that some part of us is free: free of trying, free of any need of hope. And somewhere we are clear. A little clear: as though at the core there was an infinitesimal diamond, and there the conflict of living is stilled.

If age is at all as I see it, then age is undeniably stormy. Stormy, but quiet; contradictory, in fact. Very well, that is what age can be. And how could it be anything less? If our true occupation is accounting for our lives, and relinquishing ourselves, no one can say that such a great matter could be accomplished easily. It is only after the combat that rest comes to the wrestler.

Facing our own truth, giving ourselves up—think of these a moment longer. Even a hint of truth feels like a spear in the heart. And so relinquish yourself? Who else have you? This question could be answered in two ways. Caution seemed to ask it, and caution could answer it. But so could abandon, and I feel that here abandon is the better guide. Let us say again: 'If you relinquish yourself what have you?' The answer comes with a rush of relief: 'Everything that isn't me!' And so we fall heir to a new richness, and marvel and meaning are clearer; and sometimes the candle of sentience which we each carry may burn with a new brightness.

It hardly needs saying that the old keep an eye on death, even trying to peer beyond death. We feel that we may indeed end there, as we have already diminished so much. But with equal strength we feel there is that within which cannot be put out. Those who have experienced, in the recesses of the soul, that which feels immortal, rest content. And since even the poorest of us receive so much, is it not natural, at the end, to bid adieu to life in the words that Jacob spoke to the Angel: 'I will not let thee go, except thou bless me'?

Appendices

Appendix A

CHARACTERISTICS OF THE STUDY SAMPLE

T HROUGHOUT THIS REPORT, but particularly in Chapters IV and V, we examine the differences in aging patterns that appear related to variations in mental and physical status. As we noted in Chapter III, we have defined three mental-status groups (community, discharged, and inpatient subjects) and two physical-status groups (impaired and unimpaired). However, these various subgroups were not preselected on the basis of any particular background characteristics such as age, sex, income, or education. Since we suspected that some of these characteristics—as well as health status—would influence aging patterns, it was necessary for us to compare the various health-status groups in terms of their demographic characteristics. In this way we could identify differences among the health-status groups that would have to be taken into account as possible intervening influences before we could attribute the functional differences we found to health status alone. The purpose of this appendix is to present those demographic comparisons.

We will first compare the three mental-status groups and then the two physical-status groups. In connection with the latter, we will also describe the measures we used for assessing physical impairment.

MENTAL STATUS GROUPS AND THEIR CHARACTERISTICS

Community and hospital discharged subjects in the study sample show nearly identical age distributions, but inpatient subjects form a much older group. Somewhat over half of both the first two subgroups are under the age of seventy, but only 28 per cent of the inpatients are in this younger age-range. Similarly, there are roughly twice as many inpatients who are eighty and over as there are in the other two subgroups. There is a disproportionately large number of women among the inpatients—nearly two-thirds of the group is female, compared with 52 per cent of community study-sample subjects and only 46 per cent of the discharged.

TABLE A - 1
DISTRIBUTIONS OF SELECTED BACKGROUND CHARACTERISTICS
IN THREE MENTAL-STATUS GROUPS

	Community Sample (N=264) %	Hospital Sample Discharged (N=90) %	Hospital Sample Inpatients (N=81) %
Age			
60-69	53	53	28
70+	47	47	72
Sex			
Male	49	54	36
Female	51	46	64
Socioeconomic Status			
High SES	63	23	14
Low SES	37	77	86
Index of Social Position			
High	54	25	21
Low	46	75	79
Ethnicity			
Native-born	67	65	59
Foreign-born	33	35	41
Education			
College	21	5	3
9-12 grades	39	27	25
0-8 grades	40	68	72
Main Gainful Occupation			
White Collar	44	27	22
Blue Colalr	30	49	46
Housewife	26	24	32
Religious Affiliation			
Roman Catholic	28	33	47
Protestant	38	48	34
Other	26	15	11
None	8	4	8
Marital Status			
Single	16	19	29
Married	37	24	11
Separated/divorced	10	23	24
Widowed	37	33	36

There are striking differences among the three mental-status groups in terms of socioeconomic status: 37 per cent of community subjects have the highest score on our scale, whereas only 8 per cent of the discharged and not a single one of the inpatients are in that affluent segment. Similarly, over half of both patient subgroups are in the poorest group, while only one out of five of the community residents are so financially deprived. Furthermore, there may have been differences in social status among members of the three groups earlier in life as well. By way of evidence, information on educational level, blue-collar *versus* white-collar occupation, and a combined index of these two factors in the form of an Index of Social Position in adult life shows consistently lower social status through the subgroups with ever-increasing mental disability. For example, 21 per cent of the community members of the study sample have attended college, while only 5 per cent of the discharged and 3 per cent of the inpatients have done so. These findings are consistent with those growing out of a number of studies on the relationship of poverty and social class to mental disorder among populations sampling all age groups.[1]

The inpatient subgroup has a slightly higher proportion of foreign-born subjects than either of the other groups. About one-third of both community and discharged subjects are foreign-born, compared with 41 per cent of the institutionalized patients. Although these generational differences are slight, we have found that more specific ethnic differences are important in the phenomenology of aging.

Another subgroup influence related to mental disability is that of religious affiliation. Roman Catholics are found among a little over one-fourth of the community residents, one-third of the dischargees, and nearly one-half of the inpatients. In part, this trend may be a reflection of differences in socioeconomic status, since the Catholic population of San Francisco is largely Irish and Italian in derivation—national groups which have been described as less well-off financially than groups of Anglo-American descent.[2] Persons of Jewish faith are found among 11 per cent of the community members, but only 5 and 3 per cent, respectively, of the dischargees and the inpatients. Protestants are about equally represented among the community and inpatient subjects, but a substantially larger proportion of the dischargees are Protestants.

1See, particularly, Hollingshead and Redlich (1958); Langner and Michael (1963); and Riessman, Cohen, and Pearl (1964).

2See Austin (1944).

Persons of various other religious affiliations (Christian Scientists, Vedantists, Buddhists, for example) and people with no religious affiliation are about equally represented in all three mental-status subgroups.

The presence or absence of family members to provide supports to the aged may be a factor in hospitalization. In order to examine this relationship, we have looked at our three subgroups in terms of marital status and presence or absence of children living in the San Francisco Bay Area. Looking first at marital status, we do indeed find that proportions of persons who are married decreased with each mental-status group. Among the community subjects, over one-third are currently married, but only a fourth of the discharged and a tenth of the inpatients have living spouses. Similarly, the more disabled the group, the larger the proportion of subjects who are single, separated, or divorced. Surprisingly— considering age differences among the three groups—there are no differences in proportions of *widowed* subjects; the widowed comprise approximately one-third of each of these mental-status groups.[3] A similar pattern is seen in the proportion of subjects who have children living in the Bay Area. These differences reflect the proportion in each subgroup subjects who ever married. Relationships between social supports on the one hand and various assessments of function on the other, are discussed throughout the main text.

PHYSICAL DISABILITY GROUPS AND THEIR CHARACTERISTICS

In order to examine the influence of physical illness on aging adjustment, apart from factors of mental health or illness, we have additionally divided our total sample—whether mentally ill or mentally well—into those who are physically disabled or not. In examining the background characteristics of these two major groupings of physically well and ill, we find the following trends. The physically well (N=255) are and always have been wealthier and better educated than the physically sick. More of them had

---

[3]This finding is more than likely an artifact of sample selection: half the original community subjects lived alone at baseline and were, therefore, more likely to be widowed.

white-collar employment as their main gainful occupation, as compared with the sick (N=180) who were more often in blue-collar jobs.

The physically well are younger than the sick. Over half the physically well are under seventy; about one-third of the sick are this young. Of the eighty-or-over subjects, more than twice as many of our sample are sick as are well.

Women predominate among the physically sick; however, the sexes are almost equally represented in the well group. There are a few more foreign-born among the sick than is the case among

TABLE A - 2
DISTRIBUTIONS OF SELECTED BACKGROUND CHARACTERISTICS
IN TWO PHYSICAL-DISABILITY GROUPS

	Physically Well (N=255) %	Physically Sick (N=180) %
Age		
60-69	58	35
70+	42	65
Sex		
Male	51	42
Female	49	58
Socioeconomic Status		
High SES	57	32
Low SES	43	68
Index of Social Position		
High	50	30
Low	50	70
Ethnicity		
Native-born	68	60
Foreign-bern	32	40
Education		
College	20	8
9-12 grades	38	30
0-8 grades	42	62
Main Gainful Occupation		
White Collar	43	27
Blue Collar	34	40
Housewife	23	33
Religious Affiliation		
Roman Catholic	32	33
Protestant	38	42
Other	22	18
None	8	7
Marital Status		
Single	18	20
Married	35	21
Separated/divorced	13	19
Widowed	34	40

the physically well, but these differences are not impressive. The sick and the well differ even less in religious affiliation. On the contrary, the distribution in both samples is strikingly similar.

The married subjects of our sample are more heavily represented among the physically well than is the case with the single, divorced, separated or widowed. The presence or absence of children in the Bay Area does not discriminate between the two groups. Approximately 40 per cent of both the well and the sick report having children in the Bay Area, and an almost equal percentage of both groups report having none at all in the vicinity. The remaining 18 to 20 per cent of both samples never married.

From these tabulations we can see that the mental and physical status groups are not matched in terms of certain important demographic variables. We have summarized these differences here, and throughout the text, we will examine the data for possible intervening effects.

MEASURES OF PHYSICAL STATUS FOR THE STUDY SAMPLE

After setting up the three mental-status subgroups of the study sample, we faced the next task of adding the dimension of physical status to this grouping. To insure groups of adequate size for statistical work, we planned simply to dichotomize each of the mental-status groups into a "well," or a physically-unimpaired group, and a "sick," or physically-impaired group, giving a total of six groups.

However, finding an appropriate measure of physical status for this purpose presented certain difficulties. The only second follow-up measure available for *all* subjects in the study sample was the social interviewer's rating of physical status, a five-point scale ranging from "robust physical health" to "severe physical impairment." Initially, we had doubts about the accuracy of this layman's rating; further, the fact that the ratings had been made by a number of different interviewers with no firm criteria for assigning scores raised questions about the reliability of the measure. However, a portion of the study sample received other physical ratings as well. All inpatient subjects, and thirty-six of the discharged subjects had been seen and examined by a project physician at the time of the second follow-up interview. On the basis of the direct physical examinations, the doctors rated each subject they saw on the same five-point scale that had been used by social interviewers for the entire sample. It seemed likely that this M.D.'s rating was the most *accurate* indicator of physical status available to us, but it was available only for the 117 subjects who had been seen by a project physician. The distribution of these subjects on the five-point scale was as follows:

ALL INPATIENTS AND 36 DISCHARGEES OF STUDY SAMPLE

M. D.'s Ratings of Physical Status	N	%
1 Robust physical health	1	0.9
2 No gross impairment	16	13.7
3 Mildly impaired	54	46.1
4 Moderately impaired	33	28.2
5 Severely impaired	13	11.1
Total	117	100.0

Fortunately, however, we found a high agreement between the physician's rating and the social interviewer's rating (90 per cent agreement within one-step variation) for the subsample of 117 for whom both ratings had been made. For this reason, we felt justified in using the social interviewer's rating for our measure of physical status. It seemed the best measure for our purposes for several reasons: (1) it was available at second follow-up for all subjects; (2) it could easily be dichotomized between "unimpaired" (ratings 1-2) and "impaired" (ratings 3-4); (3) the high agreement with the physician's rating on a subsample suggested that it was a relatively reliable measure of physical status; and (4) a rating by a social interviewer, who spends several hours with an individual talking about a wide variety of subjects, probably reflects the extent to which physical condition affects the subject's activities and way of life fairly accurately and thus serves at least as a measure of *functional* level—perhaps a more useful measure than even a better-informed clinical judgment. Dichotomizing each of our three mental-status groups on this measure, therefore, we arrived at the following six mental/physical status groups:

Physical Status	Community Sample			Hospital Sample Discharged			Hospital Sample Inpatients		
	N	%	Group #	N	%	Group #	N	%	Group #
Unimpaired	194	73	I	42	47	III	19	24	V
Impaired	70	27	II	48	53	IV	62	76	VI
Total	264	100		90	100		81	100	

The distributions of the lowest and highest psychological status groups on physical status are skewed in the expected directions, while the middle group splits almost in half. The small number of subjects in Group V creates difficulties, though it is certainly not surprising; it is doubtful whether any accurate measure of physical status would have given us more subjects in that group. These six groups are examined in this study on a variety of social and attitudinal items.

Appendix B

THE MEASUREMENT OF MORALE

IN ATTEMPTING TO UNDERSTAND the personal world of the mentally-ill aged, we felt a need for a measurement of an effective dimension of experience which would be somewhat independent of self-evaluation.

We had obtained, during the first two rounds of interviewing of our larger samples, some gross ratings of affect and mood tone, as inferred and assessed by project staff members who had examined the subjects. What we did not have, however, was a detailed view of the subject's *own* opinion of his morale which we could express in terms of a numerical score which would enable us to draw statistical comparisons among subgroups within the larger sample, or to compare our results with those of other studies.

At the time of the second-year follow-up study, therefore, we introduced a number of questions relating to affect, optimism, interest in life, and the like. In all, there were 45 such questions asked. We subjected these responses to cluster analysis (Tryon, 1959); this procedure yielded eight oblique clusters. The first of these, defined in part by three items used by Thompson, Streib, and Kosa (1960) as a measurement of what they called "satisfaction," appears to be a bi-polar dimension composed of items indicating *depression* at one pole and *satisfaction* at the other. It is this cluster, which we called the Depression/Satisfaction score, that we have used in this volume as our measure of morale. The cluster contains the following items:

1. How satisfied are you with your life today?
2. How much happiness would you say you find in life today?
3. How have your spirits been lately?
4. How often do you get the feeling that your life today is not very useful?
5. Do you often feel moody and blue?
6. Have you felt lately that life is not worth living?

7. Are you less interested in things like your personal appearance and table manners and things like that?
8. How much do you plan ahead the things you will be doing next week or the week after?

The other seven dimensions derived from our cluster analysis would be of interest to colleagues who are working on similar problems; however a complete discussion of them (as well as the methodological problems we encountered) is beyond the scope of this report. We have, however, prepared a separate paper on this topic. See Clark, Pierce, and Camacho (publication pending).

REFERENCES

Achenbach, Thomas, and Zigler, Edward: Social competence and self-image disparity in psychiatric and nonpsychiatric patients, *Journal of Abnormal and Social Psychology, 67*:197-205, 1963.

Albrecht, Ruth E.: *Aging in a Changing Society.* Gainesville, University of Florida, 1962.

Anderson, Barbara G.: Stress and psychopathology among aged Americans: an inquiry into the perception of stress, *Southwestern Journal of Anthropology, 20*:190-217, 1964.

Anderson, Barbara G.: Bereavement as a subject of cross-cultural inquiry: an American sample, *Anthropological Quarterly, 38*:181-200, 1965.

Arensberg, Conrad M. *The Irish Countryman: An Anthropological Study.* New York, Macmillan Company, 1937.

Aubert, V., and Messinger, S. L.: The criminal and the sick, *Inquiry, 1*:137-160, 1958.

Austin, Leonard: *Around the World in San Francisco: A Guide to the Racial and Ethnic Minorities of the San Francisco-Oakland District.* San Francisco, The Abbey Press, 1944.

Axelrod, Morris: Urbane structure and social participation, *American Sociological Review, 21*:13-18, 1956.

Barrabee, Paul, and von Mering, Otto: Ethnic variations in mental stress in families with psychotic children, *Social Problems, 1*:48-53, 1953.

Barron, Milton L.: Minority group characteristics of the aged in American society, *Journal of Gerontology, 8*:477-482, 1953.

Bartek, John F., and Pardue, Austin: *Life Out There: A Story of Faith and Courage.* New York, Charles Scribner's Sons, 1943.

Becker, Ernest: *The Birth and Death of Meaning: A Perspective of Psychiatry and Anthropolgy.* New York, The Free Press of Glencoe, 1962.

Becker, Howard S. (ed.): *The Other Side: Perspective on Deviance.* New York, The Free Press of Glencoe, 1964.

Benedict, Ruth F.: *Patterns of Culture.* Boston, Houghton Mifflin Company, 1934.

Benedict, Ruth F.: Anthropology and the abnormal. In Haring, Doug-

451

las G. (ed.), *Personal Character and Cultural Milieu*. Syracuse, New York, Syracuse University Press, 1948, pp. 176-194.

Benedict, Ruth F.: Continuities and discontinuities in cultural conditioning. In Kluckhohn, Clyde, and Murray, Henry A. (eds.), *Personality in Nature, Society, and Culture*. New York, Alfred A. Knopf, 1953, pp. 522-531.

Bernicot, Louis: *The Voyage of the Anahita*. London, Rupert-Hart-Davis, 1953.

Blau, Zena S.: Structural constraints on friendships in old age, *American Sociological Review*, 26:429-439, 1961.

Blenkner, Margaret: Social work and family relationships in later life with some thoughts on filial maturity. In Shanas, Ethel, and Streib, G. F. (eds.), *Social Structure and the Family: Generational Relations*, Englewood Cliffs, New Jersey, Prentice-Hall, 1965, pp. 46-59.

Bloom, Kenneth L.: Age and the self-concept, *American Journal of Psychiatry, 118*:534-538, 1961.

Bogue, Donald J.: *Skid Row in American Cities*. Chicago, Community and Family Study Center, 1963.

Bremer, Johan: A social psychiatric investigation of a small community in northern Norway, *Acta Psychiatrica et Neurologica Scandinavica Supplementum 62*, Copenhagen, Ejnar Munksgaard, 1951.

Buhl, Hermann: *Lonely Challenge* [Hugh Merrick, trans.]. New York, E. P. Dutton and Company, 1956.

Bühler, Charlotte: *Der Menschliche Lebenslauf als Psychologisches Problem*. Göttingen, Hogrefe, 1959.

Bühler, Charlotte: *Values in Psychotherapy*. New York, The Free Press of Glencoe, 1962.

Burnell, George M., and Thurnher, Majda: Ego function of time experience: with specific reference to aging, Geriatrics Research Program Staff Paper Number 1.50 (publication pending).

Burney, Christopher: *Solitary Confinement*. New York, Clerke and Cockeran, 1952.

Butler, Robert N.: The life review: an interpretation of reminiscence in the aged, *Psychiatry, 26*:65-76, 1963.

Caro Baroja, Julio: *The World of Witches* [Nigel Glendinning, trans.]. The Nature of Human Society Series, Julian Pitt-Rivers and Ernest Gellner (eds.), London, Weidenfelt and Nicolson, 1964.

Charny, Israel W.: Regression and reorganization in the 'isolation treatment' of children: a clinical contribution to sensory deprivation research, *Journal of Child Psychology and Psychiatry, 4:*47-60, 1963.

Christ, Adolph E.: Patterns of geriatric mental illness: attitudes toward death among a group of acute geriatric psychiatric patients, *Journal of Gerontology, 16:*56-59, 1961.

Clark, Margaret, Pierce, Robert C., and Camacho, Terry: Problems in the measurement of morale among the aged (publication pending).

Cohen, Yehudi A.: *Social Structure and Personality: A Casebook.* New York, Holt, Rinehart, and Winston, 1961.

Cumming, Elaine, and Henry, William E.: *Growing Old: The Process of Disengagement.* New York, Basic Books, 1961.

Cumming, M. Elaine: New thoughts on the theory of disengagement. In Kastenbaum, Robert (ed.) *New Thoughts on Old Age.* New York, Springer Publishing Company, 1964, pp. 3-18.

Czaplicka, Mary A.: *Aboriginal Siberia: A Study in Social Anthropology.* Oxford, Clarendon Press, 1914.

Dotson, Floyd: Patterns of voluntary association among urban working-class families, *American Sociological Review, 16:*687-693, 1951.

Eiseley, Loren: *The Immense Journey.* New York, Random House, 1957.

Ellam, Patrick, and Mudie, Colin: *Sopranino.* New York, W. W. Norton and Company, 1953.

Erikson, Erik H.: Identity and the life cycle, *Psychological Issues, 1:*1-171, 1959.

Erikson, Erik H.: The problem of ego identity. In Stein, Maurice R., Vidich, Arthur J., and White, David Manning (eds.), *Identity and Anxiety,* New York, The Free Press of Glencoe, 1960, pp. 37-87.

Essen-Möller, Erik, Larsson, Hans, Uddenberg, Carl-Erik, and White, Gayler: Individual traits and morbidity in a Swedish rural population, *Acta Psychiatrica et Neurologica Scandinavica, Supplementum100,* Copenhagen, Ejnar Munksgaard, 1956.

Feifel, Herman: Attitudes of mentally-ill patients toward death, *Journal of Nervous and Mental Disease, 122:*375-380, 1955.

Feifel, Herman: Older persons look at death, *Geriatrics, 11:127-130,* 1956.

Feifel, Herman: Attitudes toward death, paper presented at the 34th Annual Meeting of the American Orthopsychiatric Association, 1958.

Feifel, Herman: *The Meaning of Death.* New York, McGraw-Hill Book Company, 1959.

Fenichel, Otto: *The Psychoanalytic Theory of Neurosis.* New York, W. W. Norton and Company, 1945.

Fortune, Reo F.: *Sorcerers of Dobu.* New York, Dutton, 1932.

Foster, George M.: Peasant society and the image of limited good, *American Anthropologist, 67:*293-315, 1965.

Frank, Lawrence K.: Cultural control and physiological autonomy. In Kluckhohn, Clyde and Murray, Henry A. (eds.), *Personality in Nature, Society, and Culture,* New York, Alfred A. Knopf, 1948, pp. 113-116.

Friedmann, Eugene A.: The impact of aging on the social structure. In Tibbitts, Clark (ed.), *Handbook of Social Gerontology,* Chicago, University of Chicago Press, 1960, pp. 120-144.

Fromm-Reichmann, Frieda: Loneliness, *Psychiatry, 22:*1-16, 1959.

Gesell, Arnold: *Wolf Child and Human Child: The Life History of Kamala, the Wolf Girl.* London, Methuen and Company, 1941.

Gorer, Geoffrey: *The American People: A Study in National Character.* New York, W. W. Norton and Company, 1948.

Gould, Julius, and Kolb, William L.: *A Dictionary of the Social Sciences.* New York, The Free Press of Glencoe, 1964.

Hall, Edward T.: *The Silent Language.* Garden City, New York, Doubleday and Company, 1959.

Hallowell, A. Irving: *Culture and Experience.* Philadelphia, University of Pennsylvania Press, 1955.

Harrington, Michael: *The Other America.* New York, Macmillan Company, 1963.

Haven, Clayton: Social interaction, Geriatrics Research Program Staff Memorandum Number 3B.37, (November 26) 1963.

Havighurst, Robert J.: *Developmental Tasks and Education.* New York, Longmans, Green and Company, 1952.

Havighurst, Robert J.: Employment, retirement, and education in the mature years. In Webber, Irving L. (ed.), *Aging and Retirement,* Gainesville, University of Florida Press, 1955, pp. 57-62.

Havighurst, Robert J., and Albrecht, Ruth: *Older People.* New York, Longmans, Green and Company, 1953.

Havighurst, Robert J.; Goldhamer, H.; Burgess, E. W., and Cavan, Ruth S.: *Personal Adjustment in Old Age.* Chicago, Science Research Associates, Inc., 1949.

Havighurst, Robert J.; Neugarten, Bernice L., and Tobin, Sheldon S., Disengagement and patterns of aging, paper presented at the International Social Science Research Seminar, Markaryd, Sweden (August 6-9), 1963.

Henry, William E.: The theory of intrinsic disengagement, paper presented at the International Social Science Research Seminar, Markaryd, Sweden (August 6-9), 1963.

Herskovits, Melville J.: *Man and His Works.* New York, Alfred A. Knopf, 1948.

Holliday, J. S.: The lonely sheepherder, *The American West, 1:*37-45, 1964.

Hollingshead, August B.: *Two-Factor Index of Social Position,* New Haven, Connecticut: unpublished mimeographed paper, 1957.

Hollingshead, August B., and Redlich, Fredrick C.: *Social Class and Mental Illness.* New York, John Wiley and Sons, 1958.

Honigmann, John J.: *Culture and Personality.* New York, Harper and Brothers, 1954.

Honigmann, John J.: *The World of Man.* New York and Evanston, Harper and Row, 1959.

Hooton, Earnest A.: *Up from the Ape.* New York, Macmillan Company, 1946.

Howells, William W.: *Mankind So Far.* New York, Doubleday, Doran, 1944.

Hsu, Francis L. K.: *Clan, Caste, and Club.* Chicago, D. Von Nostrand, 1963.

Hughes, Everett C.: Good people and dirty work, *Social Problems, 10:*3-11, 1962.

Itard, Jean-Marc-Gaspard: *The Wild Boy of Aveyron* [George and Muriel Humphrey, trans.]. New York, Appleton-Century-Crofts, 1962.

Jaco, E. Gartly: Mental health of the Spanish-American in Texas. In Opler, Marvin K. (ed.), *Culture and Mental Health,* New York, Macmillan Company, 1959, pp. 467-485.

Kardiner, Abram: *The Individual and His Society.* New York, Columbia University Press, 1939.

Kardiner, Abram, and Ovesey, L.: *The Mark of Oppression.* New York, W. W. Norton and Company, 1951.

Kay, D. W. K., Beamish, P., and Roth, Martin: Old age mental disorders in Newcastle-upon-Tyne, Part I: a study of prevalence, *British Journal of Psychiatry, 110:*146-158, 1964.

Keene, Donald: *Living Japan.* Garden City, New York, Doubleday and Company, 1959.

Kennedy, Donald A.: Key issues in the cross-cultural study of mental disorders. In Kaplan, Bert (ed.), *Studying Personality Cross-Cul-*

turally, Evanston, Illinois, Row, Peterson and Company, 1961, pp. 405-425.

Kinsey, Alfred C., Pomeroy, Wardell B., and Martin, Clyde E.: *Sexual Behavior in the Human Male*. Philadelphia, W. B. Saunders Company, 1948.

Kinsey, Alfred C., Pomeroy, Wardell B., Martin, Clyde E., and Gebhard, Paul H., *Sexual Behavior in the Human Female*. Philadelphia, W. B. Saunders Company, 1953.

Kleemeier, Robert W. (ed.) : *Aging and Leisure*. New York, Oxford University Press, 1961.

Kluckhohn, Clyde: *Mirror for Man*. New York, Whittlesey House, 1949.

Kluckhohn, Florence Rockwood, and Strodtbeck, Fred L.: *Variations in Value Orientations*. Evanston, Illinois, Row, Peterson and Company, 1961.

Kooy, Gerrit A.: Social system and the problem of aging. In Williams, Richard H., Tibbitts, Clark and Donahue, Wilma (eds.) , *Processes of Aging*, New York, Atherton Press, 1963, Vol. II, pp. 43-60.

Kroeber, Alfred L.: *The Nature of Culture*. Chicago, University of Chicago Press, 1952.

Kutner, Bernard, Fanshel, David, Togo, Alice M., and Langner, Thomas S.: *Five Hundred Over Sixty*. New York, Russell Sage Foundation, 1956.

La Barre, Weston: *The Human Animal*. Chicago, University of Chicago Press, 1954.

Landis, J. T.: Old age movements in the United States. In Havighurst, Robert J. (Chairman) : *Social Adjustment in Old Age*, New York, Social Science Research Council, 1946, pp. 64-66.

Langner, Thomas S., and Michael, Stanley T.: *Life Stress and Mental Health: The Midtown Manhattan Study*. New York, The Free Press of Glencoe, 1963, Vol II.

Leighton, Dorothea C., Harding, John S., Macklin, David B., Macmillan, Allister M., and Leighton, Alexander H.: *The Character of Danger: Psychiatric Symptoms in Selected Communities*, Stirling County Study of Psychiatric Disorder and Sociocultural Environment. New York, Basic Books, 1963, Vol. III.

Lewis, Oscar: *The Children of Sanchez*. New York, Random House, 1961.

Lilly, John C.: Mental effects of reduction of ordinary levels of physical stimuli on intact, healthy persons, *Psychiatric Research Reports, No. 5*, American Psychiatric Association, June 1956.

Linton, Ralph: *The Cultural Background of Personality*. New York, Appleton-Century-Crofts, Inc., 1945.

Lowenthal, Marjorie F.: Some social dimensions of psychiatric disorders in old age. In Williams, Richard H., Tibbitts, Clark, and Donahue, Wilma (eds.), *Processes of Aging*. New York, Atherton Press, 1963, Vol. II, pp. 224-246.

Lowenthal, Marjorie F.: *Lives in Distress*. New York, Basic Books, 1964a.

Lowenthal, Marjorie F.: Social isolation and mental illness in old age, *American Sociological Review, 29*:54-70, 1964b.

Lowenthal, Marjorie F., and Boler, Deetje: Voluntary vs. involuntary social withdrawal, *Journal of Gerontology, 20*:363-371, 1965.

Lowenthal, Marjorie F.: Antecedents of isolation and mental illness in old age, *Archives of General Psychiatry, 12*:245-254, 1965.

Lowenthal, Marjorie F.; Berkman, Paul L., and Associates: *Aging, and Mental Disorder in San Francisco* [working title]. San Francisco, Jossey-Bass Inc. (in press).

Lowenthal, Marjorie F., and Trier, Mella K.: The elderly ex-mental patient, *International Journal of Social Psychiatry* (in press).

Lowie, Robert H.: *Social Organization*. New York, Rinehart and Company, 1948.

Lowie, Robert H.: *Toward Understanding Germany*. Chicago, University of Chicago Press, 1954.

Maddox, George L.: Disengagement theory: a critical evaluation, *The Gerontologist, 4*:80-82, 1964.

Many, Karen R.: Index of physical disability, community sample, Geriatrics Research Program Staff Memorandum Number 3B.16 (June 9) 1961.

Mason, Evelyn P.: Some correlates of self-judgments of the aged, *Journal of Gerontology, 9*:324-337, 1954.

Maves, Paul B.: Aging, religion, and the church. In Tibbitts, Clark (ed.), *Handbook of Social Gerontology*, Chicago, University of Chicago Press, 1960, pp. 698-749.

May, Rollo: *The Meaning of Anxiety*. New York, Ronald Press, 1950.

Mead, George H.: *Mind, Self, and Society*. Chicago, University of Chicago Press, 1934.

Mead, Margaret: *And Keep Your Powder Dry*. New York, William Morrow and Company, 1943.

Mead, Margaret: *Male and Female*. New York, William Morrow and Company, 1949.

Mental Health Research Unit, New York State Department of Mental Hygiene: *A Mental Health Survey of Older People.* Utica, New York, State Hospitals Press, 1960, 1961.

Merton, Robert K.: *Social Theory and Social Structure.* Glencoe, Illinois, The Free Press, 1957.

Moustakas, Clark E.: *Loneliness.* New York, Spectrum Books (Prentic-Hall), 1961.

Murphy, H. B. M.: Culture and mental disorder in Singapore. In Opler, Marvin K. (ed.), *Culture and Mental Health,* New York, Macmillan Company, 1959, pp. 291-316.

Neugarten, Bernice L., Havighurst, Robert J., and Tobin, Sheldon S.: The measurement of life satisfaction, *Journal of Gerontology, 16:*134-143, 1961.

Neugarten, Bernice L., and Gutmann, David L.: Age-sex roles and personality in middle age: a thematic apperception study, *Psychological Monographs,* p. 470, 1958.

Neugarten, Bernice L., and Associates: *Personality in Middle and Late Life.* New York, Atherton Press, 1964.

Nielsen, Johannes: Geronto-psychiatric period-prevalence investigation in a geographically delimited population, *Acta Psychiatrica et Neurologica Scandinavica, 38:*307-330, 1962.

Opler, Morris E.: *An Apache Life-Way.* Chicago, University of Chicago Press, 1941.

Osgood, C.: *The Koreans and Their Culture.* New York, Ronald Press, 1951.

Owen, Robert: *A New View of Society or, Essays on the Formation of the Human Character* [Facsimile reproduction of the third edition printed in London in 1817]. Glencoe, Illinois, The Free Press, n.d.

Parsons, Talcott, and Shils, Edward A. (eds.) : *Toward a General Theory of Action.* Cambridge, Harvard University Press, 1952.

Pitt-Rivers, Julian A.: *The People of the Sierra.* London, Weidenfeld and Nicolson, 1955.

Primrose, E. J. R.: *Psychological Illness: A Community Study.* Springfield, Illinois, Charles C Thomas, 1962.

Raab, Earl, and Selznick, Gertrude Jaeger: *Major Social Problems,* Second Edition, New York, Harper and Row, 1964.

Reichard, Suzanne, Livson, Florine, and Petersen, Paul G.: *Aging and Personality: A Study of Eighty-Seven Older Men.* New York, John Wiley and Sons, 1962.

Riesman, David: *Individualism Reconsidered.* Glencoe, Illinois, The Free Press, 1954.

Riessman, Frank, Cohen, Jerome, and Pearl, Arthur (eds.) : *Mental Health of the Poor.* New York, The Free Press of Glencoe, 1964.

Rivers, William H. R.: *The Todas.* London, Macmillan Company, 1906.

Rivers, William H. R.: The disappearance of useful arts. In Krober, Alfred L., and Waterman, T. T. (eds.), *Source Book in Anthropology,* New York, Harcourt, Brace and Company, 1931, pp. 524-535.

Romano-V, Octavio I.: The warehousing of people in complex society, paper presented at the 64th Annual Meeting of the American Anthropological Association, Denver, Colorado (November 18-21), 1965.

Roosevelt, Nicholas: *The Townsend Plan: Taxing for Sixty.* Garden City, New York, Doubleday, Doran, 1936.

Rose, Arnold M.: The impact of aging on voluntary associations. In Tibbitts, Clark (ed.), *Handbook of Social Gerontology,* Chicago, University of Chicago Press, 1960, pp. 666-697.

Rosow, Irving: Old age: one moral dilemma of an affluent society, *The Gerontologist, 2:*182-191, 1962.

Rosow, Irving: *Housing and Social Integration of the Aged,* Final Report of a Study submitted to the Cleveland Welfare Federation and the Ford Foundation. Cleveland, Western Reserve University, 1964.

Rubin, Isadore: *Sexual Life After Sixty.* New York, Basic Books, 1965.

Saunders, Lyle: *Cultural Difference and Medical Care: The Case of the Spanish-Speaking People of the Southwest.* New York, Russell Sage Foundation, 1954.

Shanas, Ethel, and Streib, Gordon F. (eds.) : *Social Structure and the Family: Generational Relations.* Englewood Cliffs, New Jersey, Prentice-Hall, 1965.

Sheldon, J. H.: *The Social Medicine of Old Age: Report of an Inquiry in Wolverhampton.* London, Oxford University Press, 1948.

Sheldon, Henry D.: The changing demographic profile. In Tibbitts, Clark (ed.), *Handbook of Social Gerontology,* Chicago, University of Chicago Press, 1960, pp. 27-61.

Simmons, Leo W.: *The Role of the Aged in Primitive Society.* New Haven, Yale University Press, 1945.

Simmons, Leo W.: Aging in preindustrial societies. In Tibbitts, Clark (ed.), *Handbook of Social Gerontology*, Chicago, University of Chicago Press, 1960, pp. 62-91.

Simon, Alexander, Lowenthal, Marjorie F., and Epstein, Leon: *Crisis and Intervention: The Elderly Mental Patient* (working title, publication pending).

Simon, Alexander, and Neal, Miron W.: Patterns of geriatric mental illness. In Williams, Richard H., Tibbitts, Clark, and Donahue, Wilma (eds.), *Processes of Aging*, New York, Atherton Press, 1963, Vol. I, pp. 449-471.

Spence, Donald L.: Adjustment and the recall of difficult and pleasant events, paper presented at the Annual Meeting, Pacific Sociological Association, Vancouver, B.C. (April 7-9), 1966.

Sullivan, Harry Stack: Interpersonal relations. In Mullahy, Patrick (ed.), *A Study of Interpersonal Relations*. New York, Hermitage Press, 1949, pp. 98-121.

Thompson, Wayne E., Streib, Gordon F., and Kosa, John: The effect of retirement on personal adjustment: a panel analysis, *Journal of Gerontology, 15:*165-169, 1960.

Tobin, Sheldon S., and Neugarten, Bernice L.: Life satisfaction and social interaction in the aging, *Journal of Gerontology, 16:*344-346, 1961.

Trillin, Calvin: Wake up and live, *The New Yorker* (April 4), 1964, pp. 120 ff.

Tryon, Robert C.: *Identification of Social Areas by Cluster Analysis*. Berkeley, University of California Press, 1955.

Tryon, Robert C.: Domain sampling formulation of cluster and factor analysis, *Psychometrika, 24:*113-135, 1959.

United States Senate, A Report of the Special Committee on Aging: *Developments in Aging: 1959 to 1963*, Report Number 8, Washington, D.C., U.S. Government Printing Office, 1963.

van Gennep, A.: *Les Rites de Passage*. Paris, Nourry, 1909.

Wallace, Anthony F. C.: *Culture and Personality*. New York, Random House, 1961.

Washburn, S. L., and Wolffson, Davida (eds.): *The Anthropological Papers of Franz Weidenreich*. New York, Viking Fund, Inc., 1949.

White, Leslie A.: Anthropology 1964: retrospect and prospect, *American Anthropologist, 67:*629-637, 1965.

Wilensky, Harold L.: Life cycle, work situation, and participation in formal associations. In Kleemeier, Robert W. (ed.), *Aging and Leisure*. New York, Oxford University Press, 1961, pp. 213-242.

Williams, Richard L., and Wirths, Claudine G.: *Lives Through the Years*. New York, Atherton Press, 1965.

Williams, Robin M.: *American Society: A Socoiological Interpretation*. New York, Alfred A. Knopf, 1959.

Wood, Margaret M.: *Paths of Loneliness*. New York, Columbia University Press, 1953.

Wylie, Ruth C.: Some relationships between defensiveness and self-concept discrepancies, *Journal of Personality, 25*:600-616, 1957.

Wylie, Ruth C.: *The Self-Concept: A Critical Survey of Pertinent Research Literature*. Lincoln, Nebraska, University of Nebraska Press, 1961.

Zilboorg, Gregory: Loneliness, *The Atlantic Monthly* (January) 1938.

Zinberg, Norman E.: The relationship of regressive phenomena to the aging process. In Zinberg, Norman E., and Kaufman, Irving (eds.), *Normal Psychology of the Aging Process*. New York, International Universities Press, 1963, pp. 143-159.

Ziskind, Eugene, and Augsburg, Theodore: Hallucinations in sensory deprivation: method or madness? *Science, 137*:992-993, 1962.

NAME INDEX

RESPONDENT INDEX

SUBJECT INDEX

A

"Abnormal" behavior (See Mental disorder)

Acculturation, 110-111, 114, 302-303 (See also Ethnicity; Immigrancy)

Acquisitiveness, as a value, 185-186, 207

Activity, 97-98, 149-168, 195, 227, 231-232, 379-380 (See also Social interaction level)

Adaptation to aging, 17-18, 30, 79, 80, 234, 255-256, 355, 360, 392-433
  compared with "adjustment," 394-395
  and social disengagement, 350-351, 357-358, 383-385
  and value-orientations, 206-208, 390-391

Adaptive tasks, 392-421
  compared with developmental tasks, 393-394
  defined, 393

Adjustment, 394-395

Adolescence, 6, 78

Adult status, cultural definitions of (See Status)

African cultures, 9n, 24, 31

Age differences within the sample, 70, 441-442, 445
  effect of, on social interaction, 162-163
  effect of, on status index, 140-141
  in morale, 122-124
  in self-evaluation, 83-84, 89
  and time orientation, 192

Age-segregation (See Segregation of aged)

Age status (See Status)

Aged (See Elders; Status)

Aging problems (See Adaptation to aging)

Alcoholism, 139, 239-240, 281, 376, 406, 407

Alienation of aged, 362-372, 375, 387-388, 392, 425-428 (See also Anomie; Intergenerational conflict)

American values (See Values)

Anomie (of elderly), 140
  cultural factors in, 10-18
  Srole scale of, 116n

Apache (Western), 6

Aspiration level, 197-199, 405-406

Attitudes, 75, 79 (See also Adaptation; Values)
  of old toward young, 364, 366-370
  toward position of aged in U.S., 364-367

Autonomic functions, 31

Autonomy (See Independence)

Avocation, hobbies, 174, 183, 219, 411

B

Behavioral environment, 36-38 (See also Phenomenology)

Bemba (African tribe), 31, 31n

Bereavement, 224-226, 231, 249-256, 300, 323, 382 (See also Death; Widowhood)

Biological aging (See Longevity)

Blindness (See Sensory loss)

Blue Collar Workers, 132 (See also Occupation; Socioeconomic status)

C

Catholics, Roman (See Religion)

Children, relationships of aged to (See Parenthood)

China, ancient, 11, 311, 387, 396

Chinese in San Francisco, 396

Church attendance (See Religion)

Cluster analysis, 449-450

Cognitive change (See Intellectual function)

Community subjects, 72-73, 85-86, 89, 90, 117-119, 120-121, 123, 126, 137-140, 142, 145, 148, 153-160, 167-168, 353-355 (See also Mental status; Respondent index; and Samples)
  adaptive problems of, 419-421
  attitudes of, toward age status, 365-367

471

GROWING OLD

An Arno Press Collection

Birren, James E., et al., editors. **Human Aging**. 1963

Birren, James E., editor. **Relations of Development and Aging**. 1964

Breckinridge, Elizabeth L. **Effective Use of Older Workers**. 1953

Brennan, Michael J., Philip Taft, and Mark Schupack. **The Economics of Age**. 1967

Cabot, Natalie H. **You Can't Count On Dying**. 1961

Clark, F. Le Gros. **Growing Old in a Mechanized World**. 1960

Clark, Margaret and Barbara G. Anderson. **Culture and Aging**. 1967

Crook, G[uy] H[amilton] and Martin Heinstein. **The Older Worker in Industry**. 1958

Derber, Milton, editor. **Aged and Society**. 1950

Donahue, Wilma, et al., editors. **Free Time**. 1958

Donahue, Wilma and Clark Tibbitts, editors. **New Frontiers of Aging**. 1957

Havighurst, Robert J. and Ruth Albrecht. **Older People**. 1953

International Association of Gerontology. **Old Age in the Modern World**. 1955

Kaplan, Oscar J., editor. **Mental Disorders in Later Life**. 1956

Kutner, Bernard, et al. **Five Hundred Over Sixty**. 1956

Lowenthal, Marjorie F. **Lives in Distress**. 1964

Munnichs, J.M.A. **Old Age and Finitude**. 1966

Nassau, Mabel L. **Old Age Poverty in Greenwich Village**. 1915

National Association of Social Workers. **Social Group Work with Older People**. 1963

Neugarten, Bernice L., et al. **Personality in Middle and Late Life**. 1964

Orton, Job. **Discourses to the Aged**. 1801

Pinner, Frank A., Paul Jacobs, and Philip Selznick. **Old Age and Political Behavior**. 1959

Reichard, Suzanne, Florine Livson and Paul G. Peterson. **Aging and Personality**. 1962

Rowntree, B. Seebohm. **Old People**. 1947

Rubinow, I[saac] M[ax]., editor. **Care of the Aged**. 1931

Shanas, Ethel. **The Health of Older People**. 1962

Shanas, Ethel, et al. **Old People in Three Industrial Societies**. 1968

Sheldon, J[oseph] H. **The Social Medicine of Old Age**. 1948

Shock, N[athan] W., editor. **Perspectives in Experimental Gerontology**. 1966

Tibbitts, Clark, editor. **Social Contribution by the Aging**. 1952

Tibbitts, Clark and Wilma Donahue, editors. **Social and Psychological Aspects of Aging**. 1962

U.S. Dept. of Health, Education, and Welfare. **Working With Older People**. 1970

Vischer, A[dolf] L[ucas]. **Old Age**. 1947

Welford, A[lan] T[raviss], and James E. Birren, editors. **Decision Making and Age**. 1969

Williams, Richard H., Clark Tibbitts, and Wilma Donahue, editors. **Processes of Aging**. 1963